THE SIGN

La rose scientifique , 1962   by Ladislav Novák

THE SIGN

SEMIOTICS AROUND THE WORLD

R.W. Bailey, L.Matejka and P.Steiner, editors

Ann Arbor

MICHIGAN SLAVIC PUBLICATIONS

This book was set in IBM Composer Press Roman
by Daphne Swabey

P
99
S48

Michigan Slavic Contributions, No. 9.

79-132-26

CONTENTS

PREFACE

"The forward movement of our epoch in art," wrote Sergei Eisenstein in 1929, "must be to blow up the Chinese Wall that stands between the primary antithesis of the 'language of logic' and the 'language of images.'" Profoundly as Eisenstein's practice affected the cinema, the full implications of his theoretical preoccupation—the cultural problem of the creation and transmission of sign systems—is only becoming fully articulated in our own time. Yet almost at the same moment that Eisenstein wrote, the paradigm that forms the basis of contemporary semiotics was being shaped: Jakobson and Tynjanov denouncing the use of static models to represent human languages, Ogden and Richards reviving discussion of Peirce's "dynamical interpretant," and Bogatyrev arguing for a recognition of the polysemy of signs in ethnography. Today, scholars round the world follow such pioneers in exploring the syncretism that arises from descriptive practice and theoretical speculation. In order to do so, many are looking anew at the history of our understanding of the sign. This volume is a contribution to that history.

Semiotics derives its energy and power from the study of semiosis, the process by which things and events come to be recognized as signs by a sentient organism. Semiosis is involved in the mutual "recognition" and matching of a pair of strands of DNA, of an antibody and a particular bacterium, of parasite and host in a biosystem, of a pollen grain and an embryo in a flower, in the social and sexual behavior of animals. Semiotics encompasses the entire sphere of biological signs, but its primary emphasis and accomplishment lie in the idea of human beings as sign-processors. No longer is theory restricted to a conception of *homo loquens*; the task of contemporary semiotics is to explain cultural behavior from the basic assumption of *homo symbolicus*.

By their very nature, sign systems are coherent and have value. Coherence arises from the recognition by the participants in the sign-exchange that a given token represents a type. Boundaries of both tokens and types may be sharp and "logical" or fuzzy and "imagistic," but in either case the participants assign them to a place in a system which itself may be open or closed. Simultaneously, their placement attaches a value to the token, calls forth an evaluation of the type to which the token is assigned, and places the system of which both are a part in relation to adjacent systems.

A simple example of semiosis can be drawn from ordinary life. Suppose that a woman walking through a park observes the surrounding trees, grass, shrubs, and sky as a simultaneous image of colors and shadows—scenery in which all is familiar but nothing "stands out" for particular notice. All at once, she sees a round, flat' object lying on the ground, distinct from other impressions in the scene. Her recognition of this object as a penny calls forth both a sequence of logical operations and one or more impressions of imagery. This token, the particular coin, represents a type, and the type in turn belongs to a system or several systems at the same time. She may regard it, for instance, as the least valued coin in an inflated currency, hardly worth picking up. She may treat it as "found money" and consequently lucky or as a "bad penny" returning to bring her misfortune. She may see it as having a place in the monetary system that will allow her to convert it to a different type in a related system, a piece of candy or a chance to weigh herself on a public scale. She may also give an aesthetic value to the penny, either within its bounds (a bright, shiny one) or as a part of the context (blending in with the pebbles on the path). The semiosis that has taken place influences the woman's mental processes and the actions that she will take as a result of her recognition of the sign, its placement and value in her personal system of signs, and the consequences of her role as a recipient and contributor to the cultural and social sign systems of which she is a part.

Even such a simple example as this one opens issues of great complexity: the process of forming a coherent sensory impression, the recognition of an external object, the invocation of tacit knowledge to fill in the parts not directly perceived (here the side of the penny on the ground that cannot be seen by the woman), the translation of sensory impression into mental data, the role of subjective and personal knowledge, the social and public systems that bear on the event, the articulation of an appropriate response. All such issues bear on the process of semiosis. None of them are simply explained or easily understood, but all have been the subject of intense reflection and have given rise to accumulated knowledge. If we are to begin to break down the Great Walls that separate us from understanding, we need to know as much as possible about these issues, seeking always the assistance of those who have devoted their energies to studying them.

Essays in this volume deal in various ways with the process of semiosis. For St. Augustine, the cardinal issue was in the divinity of sacred texts; for Locke, the philosophical consequences of the semiotic; for Freud, the assignment of tokens to sign systems in psychosis; for Eisenstein, the problem of composition uniting distinct systems in the cinema; for more recent theoreticians—Mukařovský, Greimas, Lotman, and Kristeva—the nature of semiotics itself.

Though by no means exhausting the subject, the contributions published here do reveal the common concerns of past and present. Toward an
understanding of the nature of present-day semiotics, the contributors trace
parallel themes in the work of earlier scholars and identify the distinctive
ideas of those at work in centers of semiotic study around the world. Originally, this collection was intended for distribution to participants at the
International Conference on the Semiotics of Art held at the University of
Michigan in May 1978,[1] but the delay in publication has enabled us to
publish more finished versions of the papers submitted for that occasion and
to include papers that would not otherwise have been available. All but one
of them were written especially for this volume; none of them has appeared
in English elsewhere.

September 1978

---

[1] The conference was made possible through a grant from the National Endow-
ment for the Humanities.

THE BIRTH OF OCCIDENTAL SEMIOTICS

Tzvetan Todorov

> *Different traditions:* Semantics. Logic. Rhetoric. Hermeneutics. *The Augustinian synthesis*: Definition and description of the sign. Classification of signs 1. according to the mode of transmission, 2. according to origin and usage, 3. according to social status, 4. according to the nature of the symbolic relation, 5. according to the nature of that which is designated, sign or thing: a) letters, b) metalinguistic usage. *Some conclusions.*

The ambitious title above requires that I begin with a restriction. From my initially sketchy notion of what semiotics is, I shall extract two essential criteria: we are treating semiotics as a discourse whose objective is knowledge (rather than poetic beauty or pure speculation), and whose subject matter is the whole variety of sign phenomena (not only for example words). These two conditions were fulfilled for the first time, it seems to me, in the work of St. Augustine, although he did not invent semiotics. One might say, on the contrary, that he hardly invented anything; he merely combined ideas and notions from different spheres. As a result, I have had to go back to his "sources"—those found in grammatical and rhetorical theory, in logic, and so on. However, I have not attempted a complete historical survey of each of these disciplines up to the time of Augustine even if they were able to inspire new developments in semiotics at other times. The tradition prior to Augustine is thus treated here only in so far as it found its way into his work, hence the (incorrect) impression which these pages might convey that the whole of Antiquity leads to Augustine. This is obviously not the case; thus, to cite just one example, if the Epicurean philosophy of language is not treated here, it is simply because its relation to the semiotics of Augustine is not significant.

*This article is the first chapter of Tzvetan Todorov's *Théories du Symbole* (Paris:Editions de Seuil, 1977); the English translation of *Théories* will be published by Cornell University Press. Seuil and Cornell have kindly permitted the publication of this text, which was translated by Daphne Swabey and Judith Mullen.

These considerations explain the plan adopted for this essay: one part is devoted to Augustine's predecessors, regrouped under headings that correspond more to an understanding of discourse than to truly isolated traditions; the other, to the study of Augustinian semiotics per se.

DIFFERENT TRADITIONS

SEMANTICS

I trust I will be forgiven for beginning my survey with Aristotle; he will reappear elsewhere under several different headings. For the moment, I shall concentrate on his theory of language, such as it appears, in particular, in the first chapters of his treatise *On Interpretation*. The key passage is as follows:

> Sounds emitted by the voice are symbols of states of soul, and written words, the symbols of words emitted by the voice. And just as writing is not the same for all men, spoken words are not the same either, even though the states of soul for which these expressions are the immediate signs are identical among all, as are the things for which these states are the images (16a).

In this brief paragraph, if we compare it to other parallel developments, we can distinguish several claims.

1. Aristotle talks about *symbols*, of which words are a special case. We should hold onto this term. The term "sign" is used in the second sentence as a synonym; it is important however that it does not appear in the initial definition; as we shall see in a moment, "sign" for Aristotle has another technical sense.

2. The type of symbol used immediately as an example is composed of words. These are defined as a relation of three terms: sounds, states of soul, and things. The second term serves as an intermediary between the first and the third, which do not communicate directly. Hence this term supports two relations whose natures are different, as are the terms themselves. Things are identical to themselves, always and everywhere; states of soul are too. They are independent of individuals. They are thus united by a motivated relation in which, as Aristotle says, one is the *image* of the other. On the contrary sounds are not the same in different countries. Their relation with states of mind is unmotivated: one signifies the other without being its image.

This leads us to the ancient controversy over the cognitive power of names, and correspondingly, the origin of language, natural or conventional, the most famous discussion of which is Plato's *Cratylus*. This debate emphasizes problems of knowledge or origin which we shall not consider here, and which is concerned only with words, rather than with all kinds of signs. However we should retain the distinction it makes since we can (and do) say that signs are either natural or conventional. This was already the case in Aristotle who adhered in this debate to the conventionalist hypothesis. This assertion often occurs in his work; it permits him notably to distinguish between language and the cries of animals, which are also vocal and interpretable. "We have already said," he writes, "that a name signifies this or that *by convention*. No sound is by nature a name. It becomes one, becoming a symbol. Inarticulate noises mean something—for instance, those made by beasts. But no noises of that kind are names" (ibid). Symbols then can be either "names" (conventional) or "signs" (natural). In the *Poetics*, 1456b, Aristotle provides another basis for the distinction human sounds/animal sounds: the latter cannot be combined into significant and larger units; but this suggestion seems not to have had any consequences on the thought of the Ancients, (on the other hand it is headed in the same direction as the theory of double articulation).

Let us add that, advocating the unmotivated relation between sounds and sense, Aristotle is sensitive to the problems of polysemy and synonymy which illustrate it. He talks about it on several occasions, for example in *Sophist Refutations* (165a), or in *Rhetoric III* (1405b). These discussions make evident the non-coincidence between sense and referent: "It is not exact, as Bryson claimed, that there are no obscene words, since to say one thing in place of another always signifies the same thing; there is an error there, since a word can be more precise, more similar, or more suitable for putting the thing before one's eyes" (1405b; cf. another example in *Physics*, 263b). More generally, though also in a more complex way, the term *logos* designates, in certain texts, what the word signifies, as opposed to the things themselves; cf. for example, *Metaphysics*, 1012a: "the notion, signified by the name, is the definition itself of the thing."

3. Although considered at once as a privileged example of a symbol, words are not alone in this case (it is precisely here that Aristotle's text goes beyond the framework of a strictly linguistic semantics); letters are cited as a second example. We shall not insist here on the secondary role assigned letters relative to sounds; it has become a familiar notion since the work of J. Derrida. Let us mention rather that it is difficult to imagine how the tripartite subdivision of the symbol (sounds—states of soul—things) could be applied to these special symbols that are letters.We are only

talking here about two elements, written words and spoken words.

4. One further remark on the central concept of this description: the states of soul. First, this is a psychic entity, something which is not in the word but in the mind of the users of the language. Secondly, although a psychic fact, this state of soul is not at all individual: it is identical for everyone. This entity thus derives from a social or even universal "psychology" rather than from an individual one.

One problem remains that we shall merely formulate here without being able to study it: the relation between "states of soul" and significance, such as it appears, for example, in the text of the *Poetics* where the name is defined as a "composite of signifying sounds" (1457a). It would seem (but I refrain from any categorical assertion) that one can speak of two states of language: in the *in posse*, as it is envisaged in the *Poetics*, where all psychological perspective is absent; and in action, as in the text *On Interpretation*, where sense becomes a lived sense. Be that as it may, the existence of significance limits the psychic nature of sense in general.

Such are the preliminary results of our inquiry. We can hardly speak of a semiotic conception: the symbol is clearly defined as something larger than the word, but it does not seem that Aristotle seriously considered the question of non-linguistic symbols, nor that he tried to describe the variety of linguistic symbols.

There is a second incidence of reflection on the sign in Stoic thought. We know that access to this thought is extremely difficult since we only have fragments of it derived moreover from authors who were in the main opposed to the Stoics. We shall have to be satisfied, therefore, with a few brief indications. The most important fragment is in Sextus Empiricus, *Against the Professors, VIII*, 11-12:

> The Stoics say that three things are linked [together]: the signified, the signifier, and the object. Of these things, the signifier is the sound, for example "Dion"; the signified is the thing itself which is revealed and which we grasp as subsisting in dependence on our thought, but which the barbarians do not understand, even though they are capable of hearing the word pronounced; and the object is that [thing] which exists outside of us: for example, Dion in person. Two of these things are corporeal: the sound and the object; while one is incorporeal, which is the entity which is signified, the expressible [dicible] (*lekton*), which is true or false.

Let us notice once again several important points.

1. One will remark that the terms "signifier" and "signified" make their appearance here (with a meaning that Saussure, we note, will not give them), but not that of sign. This absence, as we shall soon see, is no accident. The example given is a word, or more exactly, a proper name, and nothing indicates that the existence of other kinds of symbols was envisaged.

2. Here, as in Aristotle, three categories are simultaneously given. Notice that in both texts the object, although exterior to language, is necessary for the definition. No significant difference distinguishes, in these two the first and third elements, sound and object.

3. If there is a difference it is in the *spoken*, [dicible] spoken or signified. A great deal has been written, in modern literature, about the nature of this entity. Since controversy on the matter continues, we have decided to keep the Greek term. We must remember first of all that its status as "incorporeal" sets it apart in the resolutely materialistic philosophy of the Stoics. This means that it is impossible to conceive of it as an impression in the mind, even though it be conventional: such impressions (or "states of soul") are for the Stoics, incorporeal. "Objects" on the other hand do not necessarily have to belong to the world observable through the senses. They can be psychic as well as physical. The *lekton* is not located in the mind of the speaker but in language itself. The reference to barbarians is revealing. They hear the sound and see the man, but do not understand the *lekton*, that is to say the fact that this sound evokes this object. The *lekton* is the capacity of the first element to signify to the third. In this sense, the fact of having, for instance, a proper name is highly significant, since the proper name, unlike other words, has no sense, but like other words, has a designatory capacity. The *lekton* depends on thought but does not confuse itself with it. It is not a concept; it is not even, as was once thought possible to say, a Platonic idea. It is rather that upon which thought operates. In the same way the inner expression of these three terms is not the same as it was in Aristotle. There are no longer two radically distinct relations (of signification and image). The *lekton* is that which allows sounds to relate to things.

4. The final remark of Sextus, according to which the *lekton* can be true or false, prompts us to give it the dimension of a proposition. The example cited however, which is an isolated word, has a different meaning. Here, other fragments, from Sextus or Diogenes Laertius will allow us to understand more clearly.

First, the *lekton* can be either complete (a proposition) or incomplete (a word). Here is the text from Diogenes: "The Stoics distinguish between complete and incomplete *lekta*. The incomplete are those whose expression is incomplete, for example "writes". We ask: Who? The complete *lekta* are those that have a complete sense:"'Socrates writes'." (*Life*, VII, 63). This distinction had already been made by Aristotle, and leads to the grammatical theory of parts of speech which does not concern us here.

Secondly, propositions are not necessarily true or false: truth or falsity is a property only of assertions, and there are, moreover, imperatives, interrogatives, oaths, imprecations, hypotheses, vocatives, etc. (ibid.,65). And here again we find a commonplace of the era. We can no more talk about an explicit theory of semiotics here than in Aristotle. What is at stake for the time being is the linguistic sign, and it alone.

LOGIC

It is somewhat arbitrary to set up different headings such as "semantics" or "logic" when the Ancients did not do so. But in this way we can see more clearly the autonomy of texts which, from a later standpoint, treat related problems. We shall review the same authors as before.

In Aristotle the theory of the sign in logic is presented in the *Prior Analytics* and *Rhetoric*. Here is the definition: "The thing of which the existence or the production entails the existence or the production of another thing, either prior or posterior to it, is a sign of the production or the existence of the other thing." (Pr.An. 70a). The example that illustrates this notion, and which is destined to have a long career, is: the fact that this woman has milk is a sign that she has given birth.

One must first situate this notion of the sign in its context. For Aristotle, the sign is a truncated syllogism, one whose conclusion is missing. One of the premises (the other can equally be absent as we shall see) serves as the sign: the designated is the (absent) conclusion. And here we must insert a first correction: for Aristotle, the syllogism illustrated by the above example does not differ in any way from the common syllogism (of the type "If all men are mortal...."). Today we know that it does not work that way. The traditional syllogism describes the relation of the predicates within the proposition (or that of predicates appearing in related propositions), while the example cited is based on propositional not predicative logic. The relations between predicates are no longer pertinent; only inter-propositional relations count. This is what ancient logic hid under the word, intended to describe cases such as this as "hypothetical syllogism."

It is essential to go from one proposition ("this woman has milk") to another ("this woman has given birth"), and not from one predicate to another ("mortals" to "men"), for we pass at the same time from substance to event, and this greatly facilitates one taking into consideration non-linguistic symbolism. We have seen elsewhere that Aristotle's definition spoke about things and not propositions (the opposite is found in other texts). We are not surprised, consequently, to ascertain that Aristotle now envisages explicitly non-linguistic signs, or more precisely, visual signs (70b); the example envisaged is: large limbs can be the sign of courage in lions. Aristotle's perspective here is more epistemological than semiotic. He wonders whether it is possible to acquire knowledge from such signs. From this point of view, he will distinguish the necessary sign (*tekmerion*) from the sign that is only probable. We shall not concern ourselves with this direction of thought.

Another classification envisages the content of predicates in each proposition. "Among signs, one defines the relation of the individual to the universal, the other of the universal to the particular" (*Rhetoric, I*, 1357b). The example of the woman who has given birth illustrates the latter case. An example of the first type is: "A sign that the wise are just, is that Socrates was wise and just." Here again, we see the damaging results of the confusion between the logic of predicates and the logic of propositions. If Socrates (learned, just) is the individual vis-a-vis the universal, so too, the proposition that this woman had milk and that she had given birth are two facts on the same logical level. They are two "particulars" in relation to the general law "if a woman has milk, she has given birth."

As far as language is concerned, signs are implied propositions, but not every implied proposition, Aristotle warns us, is evoked by a "sign." There are, in fact, implicit propositions which come either from the collective memory, or the logic of the lexicon; in other words, synthetic propositions and analytical propositions ("for example, when one says that X is a man, one has also said that X is an animal, that he is animated, that he is a biped and is capable of reason and knowledge," *Topics*, 112a). In order for there to be a sign, there must be something more than this implicit sense, but Aristotle does not say what this is.

At no moment is the theory of the logical sign joined to that of the linguistic symbol (nor, as we shall see later, to that of the rhetorical trope). The technical terms themselves are different, here sign, there symbol.

We find the same idea in the Stoics. Here is one of the passages from Sextus Empiricus:

The Stoics, wanting to define the notion of sign, say that it is a proposition which is the antecedent in the major premise and which reveals the consequent. (...) They call antecedent the first proposition in a major premise that begins with the true and ends with the true. It serves to reveal the consequent because the proposition "a woman has milk" seems to be indicative of "she has conceived" in this major premise: if a woman has milk she has conceived (*Outlines, II,* XI).

Here we find many elements of the Aristotelian analysis, including his key example. The theory of the sign is related to the theory of demonstration, and once again what interests these authors is the nature of the knowledge one derives from it. The only difference—but it is important—is that the Stoics, who practised propositional logic and not the logic of classification are aware of the logical properties of this kind of reasoning. The consequences of the preferential attention paid to the proposition are surprising. As we already remarked in Aristotle's case, it is because of the proposition that one begins to pay such sustained attention to what we would call non-linguistic signs. The logic of Aristotle's classification "suits a philosophy of substance and essence" (Blanchet); while propositional logic seizes facts in the act of becoming events. Now, it so happens that it is precisely events (and not substances) that one can treat as signs. The change in the object of knowledge, (classifications to propositions) therefore brings about a widening of the level of matter under contemplation (the non-linguistic is added to the linguistic).

The absence of connection between this theory and the preceding one (that of language) is still more flagrant here because of the closeness of the terms used. We have noted that in their theory of semantics the Stoics did not talk about the sign but only about the signifier and the signified. Nevertheless the relationship is striking, and the skeptic Sextus was quick to point it out. It is in his criticism, which explains the necessity of relating the diverse theories of the sign, that lies a significant new step towards the constitution of semiotics. Sextus pretends to believe that the "sign" in question is one and the same in both cases. However in comparing the pair signifier—signified with that of antecedent—consequent, he observes several differences and this induces him to formulate the following objections:

1. The signifier and the signified are simultaneous, while the antecedent and the consequent are successive. How can one call the two relations by the same name?

The antecedent can not serve to reveal the consequent, since the latter is, relative to the sign, the thing signified, and is therefore apprehended along with it. (...) If the sign is not apprehended before the thing signified, it cannot reveal what is apprehended along with it and not after it... (*Outlines, II, XI,* 117-118).

2. The signifier is "corporeal" while the antecedent, being a proposition, is "incorporeal."

Signifiers are distinct from signifieds. Sounds signify but the *lekta* are signified, including in propositions. And since propositions are signifieds and not signifiers, the sign can not be a proposition *Against the Professors*, 264).

3. The passing from the antecedent to the consequent is a logical operation. However anyone can interpret the facts that he observes, even animals.

For if the sign is an (act of) reasoning, and the antecedent in a valid major premise, those who have no idea of reasoning and who have never studied logical technicalities ought to be totally incapable of interpreting signs. But this is not the case; for often illiterate sailors and farmers unskilled in logical theorems interpret signs excellently: the former those of the sea, foretelling squalls and calms, storms and fair weather; the latter those of the farm, predicting good and bad harvests, droughts and rain. Yet why speak of men, when certain of the Stoics have attributed even to irrational animals an understanding of signs? For, in fact, the dog, when he follows a beast by its tracks , is interpreting signs; but he does not draw this form of judgment: "if there is a track, there is a beast." In the same way, at the prod of a spur or the crack of a whip, the horse leaps forward and begins to run; but he does not form a logical argument from the premise, such as "if someone has cracked the whip I must run." Thus, the sign is not a reasoning in which the antecedent would be the true major premise (*ibid.*, 269-271).

It must be admitted that if often the criticisms of Sextus are purely quibblings about form, in this case they are substantive. The assimilation of two species of signs really creates problems. Let us imagine that Sextus sought not the inconsistency within Stoic doctrine but the connection between the two theories. His objections then become so many constructive criticisms, which may be reformulated thus:

1. Simultaneity and successivity are the consequence of a more fundamental difference: that is, in the case of the linguistic sign (word or proposition) the signifier directly evokes its signified; in that of the logical sign, the antecedent, as a linguistic segment, has its own sense, which will be upheld. It is only as a secondary consideration that it evokes something else as well, namely the consequent. The difference is that between direct and indirect signs, or, in a terminology opposed to that of Aristotle, between signs and symbols.

2. Direct signs are composed of heterogenous elements: sounds, incorporeal *lekton*, object. Indirect symbols are composed of entities whose nature is similar: one *lekton* for instance evokes another.

3. These indirect symbols can be linguistic as well as non-linguistic. In the first case, they take the form of two propositions. In the second, of two events. In this latter form, they are accessible not only to logicians but also to the uninitiated and even to animals. The substance of the symbol does not prejudge its structure. On the other hand, one should not confuse a capacity (the inference) with the possibility of talking about it (the logician's discourse).

If we reconsider the classification of the *lekta* in terms of completes and incompletes, we see that it is possible to reconstitute a chart with one empty box:

	WORD	PROPOSITION
direct	incomplete lekton	complete lekton
indirect	?	sign

This absence is all the more strange (but perhaps this fault is due simply to the fragmentary state of the Stoic writing which has come down to us) since the Stoics were the founders of a hermeneutic tradition that is based on the indirect sense of *words*—on *allegory*. This however takes us into the framework of another discipline.

Before leaving the Stoic theory of logic we should mention another problem. Sextus reports that they divide signs into two classes: commemorative and revealing. This subdivision results from a previous categorisation of things, according to which things are either evident or obscure, and in this latter case, obscure once and for all, either by chance or by nature. The first two classes that result from this, things which are evident or things which are obscure for ever, do not make the sign intervene. It is the latter two that do this, thus providing the basis of two species of signs:

> Those which are obscure for a moment and those which are uncertain by nature are graspable by signs, not by the same signs, but the first by commemorative signs (or by recall), the second by revealing signs (or indicative). We call a commemorative sign a sign which—having been manifestly observed at the same time as the thing signified, as soon as it falls upon our senses, no matter how obscure the thing—pushes us to remember what has been observed along with it, even if it does not fall manifestly upon our senses, as it is the case with smoke and fire. The revealing sign, according to what they say, is the one which has not been manifestly observed at the same time as the thing, but which of its own nature and constitution indicates whatever it is a sign of, as the movements of the body are the sign of the soul (*Outlines, II, X*, 99-101).

Other examples for this kind of sign: commemorative—the scar for the wound, puncture of the heart for death; revealing—sweating for the pores of the skin. This distinction does not appear to call into questions the properly semiotic structure of signs and only poses an epistemological problem. However, in his criticism of the distinction, Sextus brings the debate back to more familiar grounds. For he does not believe in the existence of revealing signs. He modifies therefore, first the relation between these two classes, by elevating the one—commemorative signs—to the rank of genre, and relegating the other—revealing signs—to that of kind, in whose existence however he does not believe (*Against the Professors*, 143). From that point, his discussion casts doubt upon two other oppositions: polysemic and monosemic signs, natural and conventional signs. The debate can be summarized thus: Sextus contests the existence of revealing signs by asserting that these do not allow for certain knowledge to be extracted, since a thing can symbolize, potentially, an infinite number of other things. It is therefore not a sign. To which the Stoics retort: but commemorative signs (whose existence Sextus acknowledges) can equally well be polysemic and evoke several things at once. Sextus admits this fact, but shows that he stands on a different footing: commemorative signs can only be polysemic by force of a convention. Now revealing signs are natural by their own definition (they exist as things before being interpreted). Commemorative signs are either natural (thus, smoke for a fire), in which case they are monosemic, or they are conventional and as such they can be either monosemic (such as words) or polysemic (such as the lighted torch which on one occasion can announce the arrival of friends, on another the arrival of enemies). Here in any event is the text from Sextus:

> In answer to those who draw conclusions from the commem-
> orative sign and quote the case of the torch or that of the
> sounds of the bell (which can be announcing the opening of
> the meat market or the necessity of watering the roads), we must
> declare that it is not paradoxical for such signs to be capable of
> announcing several things at the same time. For these signs are
> established by lawgivers, and it is in our power to make them
> reveal one thing or several. But since the revealing sign is above
> all supposed to suggest the signified thing, it must necessarily
> only indicate one single thing. (*Against the Professors*, 200-201).

This criticism by Sextus is not only interesting in that it attests to the idea that the perfect sign must only have one sense, and Sextus' preference for conventional signs, but as well, as we have seen, the natural-conventional opposition was applied up to this point to the origin of words, and that it was necessary to opt for one *or* the other solution (or a compromise between the two). Sextus himself applies it to signs in general (words are only one special case), and, as well, he conceives of the simultaneous existence of one *and* the other kind of sign, natural and conventional. The difference is of capital importance. In this way his vision is properly semiotic. Was it just coincidence that this vision required a certain eclectism in order to develop (that of Sextus in this case)?

RHETORIC

We have seen that if the "sign", in the Aristotelian sense, was treated by him within a rhetorical framework, his analysis properly belongs to logic. For now, we shall study not the "sign" but indirect meanings, or *tropes*.

Once again, we must start with Aristotle, for it is with him that the opposition, literal–transposed, originates, which will interest us first of all. But in its beginnings, the opposition was not what it became later. Not only is there an absence of all semiotic perspective in the description given by Aristotle, but the opposition does not have the preponderant role that we are accustomed to seeing it have. The transposition, or metaphor (a term that for Aristotle designates tropes altogether), is not a symbolic structure that would possess, among other things, a linguistic manifestation, but a kind of word: a kind where the signified is other than the usual signified. It appears at the heart of a list of lexical classifications, which, at first glance anyway, comprises eight terms. It is a complimentary species of the neologism, or innovation in the signifier. To be sure, the existing definitions are slightly more ambiguous. One reads in the *Poetics*: "Metaphor [transposition] is the bringing forward of a displaced name " (1457b); and a parallel passage from *Topics*, but one in which the term metaphor [transposition] does not appear: "Those who call things by displaced names (calling, for example, the plane tree, *man*), thus transgressing current usage" (109a). In discussing how tropes operate *Rhetoric* talks about "that which one does not name, even while naming" (1405a). It is clear that Aristotle is hesitating between two definitions of metaphor, or else he defines it by this very duplicity. It is either the non-literal sense of a word (a carrying-over, a transgression of current usage) or the non-literal expression used to evoke a sense (a displaced name, a naming that avoids proper naming). Whatever the case, metaphor remains a purely linguistic category. Even more, it is a sub-class of words. Choosing metaphor rather than a non-metaphorical term stems from the same tendancy that makes us choose this synonym rather than that one. One always seeks what is appropriate and proper. Here is a passage which illustrates this idea.

> If we wish to magnify our object, we must borrow the metaphor from what is more elevated in the same genus; if to depreciate it, from what is of less value; I want to say, for example, since the opposites are of the same genus, that to affirm in one case that he who begs prays, and in another that he who prays begs (these two actions being one and the other kinds of asking), is to do what we have just said (*Rhetoric*, III, 1405a).

Transposition is one stylistic means among others (even if it is Aristotle's preference) and not a way of being of meaning that one would need to articulate with direct signification. In turn, what is literal is not the direct but the appropriate. One can understand that under these conditions, it is not possible to find an opening toward a typology of signs in the theory of transposition.

Things do not stop there. Beginning with Aristotle's disciples, Theophrastes for example, figures of rhetoric will play an increasingly more important role. We know that this movement will not end until the death of rhetoric which will reach it when it is transformed into a "figuratic." Even the multiplication of terms is significant. Along with "transposition", always used in its generic sense, *trope* and *allegory*, irony and figure appear. Their definitions are not far removed from Aristotle's. For example, pseudo-

Heraclites writes: "The figure of style that says one thing but signifies another, different from the thing said, is called by its proper name 'allegory'." And Tryphone: "The trope is a way of talking diverted from literal meaning." The trope and its synonyms are defined here as the appearance of a second sense—not as the substitution of one signifier for another. But it is the position and the overall function of tropes which slowly change; they tend more and more to become one of two possible poles of signification (the other being direct expression); the opposition is for example much stronger in Cicero than in Aristotle.

Let us rapidly examine the last link in the rhetorical chain of the ancient world, by looking at the man who made a synthesis of the tradition—Quintilian. We shall not find here, any more than in Aristotle, a semiotic examination of tropes. Thanks to the comprehensiveness of his treatise, Quintilian ends up by accepting into his treatment several suggestions abounding in this sense. His lack of rigor however prevents him from formulating the problems explicitly . While indirect expression was classified by Aristotle among numerous other lexical means, Quintilian tends to present it as one of two possible modes of language: "We prefer to make things be understood rather than to say them openly." (*On the Education of the Orator, VIII, AP*, 24). But his attempt to theorize the opposition between "say" and "make understandable", which relies on the categories of literal and transposed comes to naught. In the end, tropes are literal as well: "Exact metaphors are also called literal" (VIII,2,10).

The presence of onomatopoeia in tropes constitutes a curious fact. It is difficult to understand this property if one restricts oneself to the definition of trope by change in sense (or by the choice of an improper signifier, for we find both conceptions in Quintilian). The only possible explanation resides precisely in a semiotic conception of trope, namely, that it is a motivated sign. This is the only trait common to metaphor and onomatopoeia. But this idea is not formulated by Quintilian. We have to wait until the 18th century before this idea is set forth by Lessing.

Quintilian devotes pages to allegory, but this quantitative importance has no theoretical counterpart. Allegory is defined, as it was in Cicero, as a series of metaphors, as a strung-out metaphor. This sometimes creates problems that one comes across in the definition of example. Example, unlike metaphor, maintains the sense of the initial assertion which contains it, and yet Quintilian connects it to allegory. But this problem (subdivisions at the heart of indirect signs) goes unnoticed, in the same way as the dividing line between tropes and figures of thought remains blurred.

The domain of rhetoric itself does not contain theories of semiotics. However, it does prepare them and does so because of the attention paid to the phenomena of indirect sense. Thanks to rhetoric, the literal-transposed opposition becomes familiar to the ancient world (even if there are uncertainties about its content).

HERMENEUTICS

The hermeneutic tradition is particularly difficult to grasp, abundant and multifaceted as it is. The very acknowledgment of its object seems to have been acquired from earliest Antiquity, if only in the form of an opposition between two regimes of language, direct and indirect, clear and obscure, *logos* and *muthos*, and, consequently between two modes of reception—comprehension for the one, interpretation for the other. In describing the word of the oracle at Delphi, the famous fragment of Heraclites testifies to this: "The master, whose oracle is at Delphi, says nothing, hides nothing, but signifies." The teaching of Pythagorus is evoked in similar terms: "When he conversed with his friends, he exorted them, either by developing his thought, or by using symbols" (Porphyry). This opposition is maintained in later writings, with no attempt at justification however. Here is an example from Dionysius of Halicarnassus: "Certain men dare to claim that the figured form is not permitted in discourse. According to them, one should speak or not speak, but always simply, and by renouncing hereafter the use of speaking by implication" (*Art of Rhetoric*, IX).

Within this extremely general conceptual framework numerous exegetical practices come to be inscribed which we might divide into two parts, both of which greatly differ from each other: the *commentary* on texts (especially those on Homer and the Bible) and *divination*, in all its most varied forms (mantic).

One might be surprised to see divination appear among hermeneutic practises. However, we are dealing here with the discovery of a meaning for objects that did not have one, or of a secondary sense, for the others. First of all let us establish, as a primary step towards a semiotic conception, the variety of substances that become the starting point of an interpretation: from water to fire, from the flight of birds to the entrails of animals, everything seems capable of becoming sign and thus giving rise to interpretation. One can assert moreover that this type of interpretation is related to that which indirect modes of language constrain us, that is to say, allegory. Two authors can testify here to an extremely heterogeneous tradition.

First of all, Plutarch, when he seeks to characterize the language of oracles, inevitably brings it closer to indirect expression, thus:

Concerning the clarity of oracles, an evolution parallel to other changes in accepted opinion took place. Formerly the strange and peculiar style of oracles, ambiguous and periphrastic, was grounds for the crowd to believe in its divine character, and to be filled with admiration and religious respect. But later they wanted to understand each thing clearly and easily without exaggeration or recourse to fictions, and they accused the poetry which surrounded the oracles of opposing knowledge of the truth by surrounding the revelations of the gods with obscurity and shadow. They were even suspicious of metaphors, enigmas, equivocal phrases, as being a way out or a refuge for divination, and used to allow the priest to retire and hide in case of error. (*On the Pythian Oracles, 25*, 406 F-407 B).

Here oracular language is equated with the transposed and obscure language of poets.

Second witness: Artemidorus of Ephesus, author of the famous *Key to Dreams*, who summarizes and systematizes an already rich tradition. First of all, the interpretation of dreams is constantly put into relation with that of words, sometimes by resemblance;

In the same way that masters of grammar, once they have taught children the value of letters also show them how to use them all together, so I will add some final and brief indications to be followed, so that even a beginner can easily find instruction in my book (*III, Conclusion*).

and sometimes by contiguity;

It is also necessary, when dreams are mutilated and do not offer a hold so to speak, that the interpreter of dreams adds something by himself from his experience, and especially to those dreams where one sees either letters that do not present the complete sense, or a word that has no relation with the thing; the interpreter of dreams must then use either metathesis, changes, or additions of letters of syllables (I, 11).

In addition, Artemidorus opens his book with a distinction between two kinds of dreams, and this distinction clearly indicates its origin: "Among dreams, some are *theorematic*, some are *allegorical*. They are theorematic whose fulfillment resembles that which they have made apparent. . . . Allegorical by contrast are those dreams that signify certain things by means of other things" (I, 2). This opposition is probably copied from that of literal and transposed, two rhetorical categories, but it applies here to non-linguistic matter. We find moreover a connection, unintended perhaps, between dream images and rhetorical tropes even in Aristotle, who, on one hand asserts that "to make metaphors well is to perceive resemblances well" (*Poetics*, 1459a), and, on the other hand, that "the most skilful interpreter of dreams is he who can observe resemblances" *(On Prophesying by Dreams*, 2); Artemidorus also writes that, "the interpretation of dreams is nothing more than the connection between likeness and likeness" (II, 25).

Let us now return to the principal hermeneutic activity: textual exegesis. In the beginning it is a practise that implies no particular theory of the sign, but rather what we might call a strategy of interpretation, varying from one school to another. We have to wait until Clement of Alexandria to find an effort in the direction of semiotics at the heart of the hermeneutic tradition. First of all, Clement very explicitly enunciates the unity of the symbolic domain—marked, by the way, by the systematic use of the word "symbol". Here is an example of the enumeration of the varieties of the symbolic:

> The formalities that took place with the Romans for testaments, such as the presence of scales and small change to evoke justice; manumission to represent the division of goods, and the touching of ears for an invitation to serve the mediator (*Stromates*, V,55,4).

All these procedures are symbolic, as is also indirect language:

> Aeteas, king of the Scythians, to the people of Byzance: "Do not interfere with the collection of contributions or my horses will drink water from your rivers." By means of this symbolic language, the Barbarian was announcing the war that he would wage against them. (V, 31, 3).

If the assimilation between non-linguistic symbolism and linguistic symbolism takes place here, nevertheless a clear distinction is maintained between symbolic and non-symbolic language (indirect and direct). Scripture contains passages written in both languages, but different specialists will initiate us into their reading, the Didaskalia on one hand, the Pedagogue on the other.

Clement is also the author of some reflection on the writings of the Egyptians, who profoundly influenced the interpretation of writing during the following centuries. Clement's reflections are a revealing example of his tendency to treat different substances in the same terms, and more particularly of applying rhetorical terminology to other kinds of symbolism (visual in this case). Clement asserts the existence of several kinds of writing that the Egyptians used. One of them is the hieroglyphic method. Here is the description:

> The hieroglyphic genus expresses in part things in themselves (chirologically) by means of primary letters, and in part it is symbolic. In the symbolic method, a species expresses things through imitation, another kind written so to speak in a tropic method, while a third kind is clearly allegorical by means of certain enigmas. Thus, the Egyptians, if they wanted to write the word "sun" drew a circle, and for the word "moon" they drew the figure of a crescent; this being the cyriological genus. They wrote in the tropic manner, diverting meaning and transposing signs in view of a certain relation. In part they substituted them with other signs, and in part they modified them in different ways. So that, in wanting to transmit the praises of kings through religious myths, they inscribed them on bas-reliefs. And here is an example of the third kind of writing, that which uses enigmas: they represent other plants as serpents because of their sinuous course; the sun on the other hand they drew as a scarab because the scarab forms a ball of dung that he rolls in front of him (V, 4, 20-21).

In this well-known text, several points are worth noting: first of all the possibility of finding the same structures through different substances: language (metaphors and enigmas), writing (hieroglyphic), painting (imitation). This type of unification already marks one step towards the constitution of a theory of semiotics. On the other hand, Clement proposes a typology of the entire domain of signs; the brevity of his proposition makes it necessary for us to make certain hypothetical reconstructions. One might summarize the classification thus:

Hieroglyphic Writing	{	chirologic (literal)	
		symbolic	{ by imitation (chirology)
			tropic
			by allegory and enigma

Two points evidently cause a problem in this distribution: the fact that the literal method (chirological) appears in two distinct places on the sketch, and that allegory, considered in rhetoric as a trope, in this instance forms a class by itself. In order to try and maintain the coherence of the text, we might propose the following explanation based on the examples cited. First the chirological kind and the symbolic chirological kind have at the same time common and divergent traits. They share in common the fact that this relation is *direct*. The letter designates the sound, as the circle does the sun, without any detour. They possess no other significance, prior to this one. They can also be distinguished however. The relation between letter and sound is *unmotivated* while that of the sun and the circle is *motivated*. This difference in turn can arise from other causes passed over in silence here. Thus the opposition between chirological and symbolic kinds is that of the unmotivated for the motivated; whereas the opposition at the heart of symbolic writing between the chirologic kind and other kinds is that of the direct or the indirect (transposed).

On the other hand, the deciphering of tropic writing implies two steps: the pictogram designates an object (by direct imitation). This in turn evokes another, through resemblance, or participation, or contraries, etc. What Clement calls enigma or allegory, implies in turn three relations: between the pictogram and the scarab—direct imitation; between the scarab and the ball of dung—contiguity (metonymic); finally between the ball of dung and the sun—resemblance (metaphoric). The difference between tropes and allegory is thus in the length of the chain: one diversion only in the first case, two in the second. Rhetoric had already defined allegory as a prolonged metaphor; but for Clement, this prolongation does not follow the surface of the text. It operates in some way without moving, in depth.

If one accepts that the difference between tropic writing and allegorical writing is that between two *or* three relations, the place of symbolic chirological writing becomes clear. It comes before the others because it demands the constitution of a single relation, that between the circle and the sun, the image and its meaning (there is no detour). Such an interpretation would explain the classification proposed by Clement and would show at the same time the underlying theory of signs.

Even apart from this essential (but hypothetical) theoretical contribution Clement remains a most important figure for he paves the way for Saint Augustine regarding two essential points: 1) the material variety of symbolism—which can be perceived by any of the senses and which can be linguistic or non-linguistic—does not diminish its structural unity; 2) the symbol joins itself to the sign as does the transposed sense to the literal sense, thus rhetorical concepts can be applied to non-verbal signs.

THE AUGUSTINIAN SYNTHESIS

DEFINITION AND DESCRIPTION OF THE SIGN

St. Augustine is not trying to be a semiotician; his work is organized around an objective of a completely different nature (religious); it is only along the way, and in the interest of this other objective, that he formulates his theory of the sign. However, the interest that he brings to semiotic problematics seems to be greater than he admits or even than he thinks: in effect, throughout his life he will continue to come back to these same questions. His thoughts about these questions do not stay constant, and it will be necessary to observe them in their evolution. The most important texts, from our point of view, are: a treatise from his youth, considered sometimes as inauthentic, *Principles of Dialectic* or *On Dialectic*, written in 387; *On Christian Doctrine*, the central text in all respects, written—at least the part in which we are interested—in 397; and *On The Trinity* which dates from 415. Numerous other texts, however, contain important indications.

In *On Dialectic*, we read the following definition: "A sign is that which shows itself to the senses, and which, outside of itself, shows something more to the spirit. To speak is to give a sign with the aid of articulated sound" (V). We shall retain many of the characteristics of this definition. First, it is here that a property of the sign makes its appearance which will subsequently play a significant role in what is to follow : that of a certain non-identity of the sign to itself, which rests on the fact that the sign is originally double: sensible *and* intelligible (nothing similar is to be found in Aristotle's description of the symbol). On the other hand, even more strongly than in the past, it is asserted that words are only one kind of sign; this assertion is only the more accentuated in the later writings of Augustine. Now, it is this assertion which is fundamental to the semiotic perspective.

The second important sentence is the following (the opening of Chapter V of *On Dialectic*): "The word is the sign of a thing, able to be understood by the listener when proferred by the speaker." This is again a definition, but a double definition, because it brings out two distinct relations: the first between the sign and the thing (this is the framework of designation and signification); the second between the speaker and the hearer (this is the framework of communication). Augustine links the two at the interior of one single sentence, as if this co-existence did not present any problems. The insistence on the communicative dimension is original: it was absent in the Stoics, who developed a pure theory of signification, and it is much less evident in Aristotle, who spoke, it is true, of "states of soul"; thus of speakers, but who left this context of communication entirely in the dark. We have here a first indication of the two principle tendencies in Augustinian semiotics: its eclecticism and its tendency towards psychologizing.

The very ambiguity that produced the juxtaposition of several perspectives is repeated in the analysis of the sign when it is broken into its constitutive elements (in a particularly obscure page of the treatise). "There are these four things to be distinguished; the word, the expressable (*dicible*), the expression (*dictio*), and the thing." Of the explanation that follows (made difficult by the fact that Augustine takes as his example of a thing the *word*), I shall retain only what will enable us to understand the difference between *dicible* and *dictio*. Here are two exerpts:

> In a word, all that is perceived, not by the ear but by the spirit, and that the spirit keeps in itself, is named *dicible*, expressable. When the word exits from the mouth, not in its own name, but to signify some other thing, it is named *dictio*, expression.

And:

> Suppose then that a pupil has been asked by a grammarian in this way: to what part of speech does the word *arma*, arms, belong? The word *arma* is enunciated here with regard to itself; that is, it is a word enunciated with regard to the word itself. That which follows: "to which part of speech does this word belong?" is added, not for itself, but with respect to the word *arma*; the word is understood by the spirit or enunciated by the voice: if it is understood and seized by the spirit before it is enunciated, it is thus the *dicible*, the expressable, and, for the reasons that I have given, if it is made manifest outside by the voice, it becomes *dictio*, expression. *Arma*, here only a word, was, when it was pronounced by Virgil, an expression. It was in effect not pronounced with regard to itself, but in order to signify either the wars in which Aeneas fought, or the shield and other armor which Vulcan made for Aeneas.

On the lexical level, this series of four terms apparently comes from an amalgam. As J. Pépin has shown, *dictio* translates *lexis*; *dicible* is the exact equivalent of *lekton*; and *res* could be there for *tughanon*; which would give in Latin an exact copy of the Stoic tripartition of signifier, signified, and thing. On the other hand, the opposition between things [res] and words [verba] is familiar; we shall see it later in the rhetoric of

Cicero and Quintilian. The telescoping of the two techniques creates a problem, because we then have at our disposal two terms which designate a signifier, namely *dictio* and *verbum*.

Augustine seems to resolve this terminological imbroglio by reconciling it with another ambiguity which is already familiar to us: that of meaning belonging at the same time to the processes of both communication and designation. Thus on the one hand, we have one term too many; on the other, a double concept: simultaneously *dicibile* will be reserved for the experienced meaning [*sens vécu*] (here in opposition to Stoic terminology), *dictio* being attracted towards the referent meaning [*sens référant*]. *Dicibile* will be experienced either by the one who speaks ("understood and grasped by the spirit before the enunciation") or by the one who hears it ("that which is perceived by the spirit"). *Dictio*, in turn, has a meaning which, (like the *lekton*), plays between the sound and the thing, not between the interlocuters; it is what the word signifies independent of its users. *Dicibile* participates simultaneously in the stages of the following succession: first the speaker conceives the meaning, then he enunciates the sounds, finally the one spoken to perceives, first the sounds, then the meaning. *Dictio* operates in the simultaneity: the referent meaning is realized at the same time as the enunciation of the sounds: the word only becomes *dictio* if (and when) "it is manifested outside by the voice." Finally, *dicibile* is proper to propositions envisaged in the abstract, whereas *dictio* belongs to each individual enunciation of one proposition (the reference is realised in the *token*, and not the *type*, propositions, in the terminology of modern logic.)

At the same time, *dictio* is not simply of the senses; it is the enunciated word (the signifier), provided with its denotative capacity. *Dictio* is "the word which exits from the mouth," that which is "shown outside by the voice." Reciprocally, *verbum* is not the simple sound, as one would be tempted to imagine, but the designation of the word as word, the metalinguistic use of language. It is the word which "refers to itself; that is, in a question or discussion about the word itself . . . . That which I call *verbum* is a word and signifies a word."

In a text written some years later, *On Order*, the compromise will be formulated in a different fashion: designation becomes an instrument of communication:

> Man not being able to have a solid society with man without the aid of speech by which he transmits his soul and thoughts to another, reason understands that it was necessary to give names to things, that is, certain sounds provided with signification, so that, because they cannot perceive the spirit by means

of the senses, men will make use of the senses as so many interpreters in order to unite their minds (II, XII, 35).

In Chapter VII of *On Dialectic*, Augustine gives another example of his synthesizing spirit. He introduces there a discussion on what he calls the force (*vis*) of a word. Force is that which is responsible for the quality of an expression as such, and which determines its perception by the listener. "The force is relative to the impression which words produce on whoever is listening." Sometimes force and meaning are considered as two kinds of signification: "Our examination results in the word having two significations, one for revealing the truth, the other for watching over its propriety." One suspects that what is going on here is an integration of the rhetorical opposition between clarity and beauty with a theory of signification (an integration which is, however, problematic, because the significance of a word is not to be confused with its figurality, or perceptibility). The kinds of this "force" recall equally the rhetorical context: force is shown by sound, by meaning, or by the agreement of the two.

One can see a development of the same theme in *On the Teacher*, written in 389. Here the two "significations" seem to become the property of either the signifier or the signified: the function of the first is to act on the senses; that of the second, to assure the interpretation. "All that which is emitted as a voiced sound articulated with signification. . . strikes the ear in order to be perceived, and is entrusted to the memory in order to be known" (V, 12). This relationship will be explained with the help of a pseudo-etymological reasoning. "What if, of these two things, the word takes its appellation from the first, and the name, from the second? for "word" can be derived from "strike" (*verberare-verbum*), and "name" from "to know" (*noscere-nomen*), so that the first term would thus be called a function of the ear, and the second a function of the soul" (*ibid*). In this double process, perception is submitted to intellection, because from the instant we understand, the signifier becomes transparent for us. "Such is the law, bestowed naturally with a very great force: when signs are heard, attention is directed towards the signified things" (VIII, 24). This second formulation, proper to the treatise *On the Teacher*, seems to be a step backwards with respect to what we found in *On Dialectic*, because Augustine no longer conceives here that the signified can also have a perceptible form (a "force") which strikes the attention.

Let us now pass on to the central treatise, *On Christian Doctrine*. Given its importance in our context, a brief glance at its whole plan will be justified. We have here a work devoted to the theory of interpretation—and, to a lesser degree, to the expression—of Christian texts. The unfolding of the exposé is built around several oppositions: signs-things, interpretation-expression, difficulties arising from ambiguity-obscurity. We can present its plan in the form of a schema, where the numbers designate the four parts of the treatise (the end of the third and fourth parts not having been written until 427, thirty years after the first three):

$$
\left\{
\begin{array}{l}
\text{(things (1)} \\[2ex]
\text{(signs}
\end{array}
\right.
\left\{
\begin{array}{l}
\text{interpretation} \\[2ex]
\text{expression (4)}
\end{array}
\right.
\left\{
\begin{array}{l}
\text{obscurities (2)} \\[2ex]
\text{ambiguities (3)}
\end{array}
\right.
$$

We shall not stop here on the apparent meaning of Augustine's ideas with respect to the manner of understanding and enunciating discourse (H.I. Marrou has already shown the originality of this). What will be retained above all is the synthesizing procedure, already present in the plan. Augustine's project is, in the beginning, hermeneutic; but he adds on to it a productive part (the fourth book), which is the first Christian rhetoric. In addition, he encases the whole within a general theory of the sign, where a properly semiotic procedure unites with what we distinguished above under the headings "Logic" and "Semantics." This book, more than any other, must be considered as the first properly semiotic work.

Let us now take up the theory of the sign which is formulated in it. If we compare this theory to the one in *On Dialectic*, we see that there no longer exists any sort of meaning other than experienced meaning. Thus the incoherence of the schema diminishes. What is even more surprising is the disappearance of the thing, or referent. In effect, Augustine indeed speaks about things and signs in this treatise (and in that he is faithful to the rhetorical tradition, as it was maintained since Cicero), but he does not envisage the first [things] as the referents of the second [signs]. The world is divided into signs and things, according to whether or not the object of perception has a transitive value or not. The thing participates in the sign as signifier, not as referent. Let us note before going on that this overall affirmation is moderated by another assertion, which however remains more an abstract principle than a characteristic proper to the sign: "things are learned by signs" (I, II, 2).

The articulation of signs and things extends to two essential functions, using and enjoying. In fact, this second distinction is located within things; but things to be used are transitive like signs, and things which can be enjoyed are intransitive (now here we have the category which allows the opposition of things to signs).

To enjoy, in effect, is to attach ourselves to a thing by love of the thing itself. To use, on the contrary, is to restore the object which we use to the object which we love, if however it is worthy of being loved. (I, IV, 4).

This distinction has an important theological extension: in the last analysis, no thing except God is worthy of being enjoyed or cherished in itself. Augustine develops this idea in speaking of the love which man can have for his fellow man:

> It is to be asked whether man is to be loved by man for his own sake or for the sake of something else. If for his own sake, we enjoy him; if for the sake of something else, we use him. But I think that man is to be loved for the sake of something else. For happiness is to be found in the Being who is to be loved for Himself. Even though we do not have this happiness in its reality, the hope of possessing it consoles us. But "cursed be the man that trusteth in man" (Jer.17.5). But no one ought to enjoy himself either, if you observe the matter closely, because he should not love himself on account of himself but on account of Him who is to be enjoyed (I, XXII, 20-21).

It follows that the only thing which is absolutely not a sign (because it is the object to be enjoyed par excellence) is God; which, in our culture, reciprocally colors with divinity every final signified (that which is signified without signifying in turn).

The relation between signs and things having been thus articulated, we are now given the definition of the sign. "The sign is a thing which causes us to think of something beyond the impression the thing itself makes upon the sense" (II, I, 1). We are not far from the definition given in *On Dialectic*, only "thought" has replaced "spirit". Another formulation is more explicit: "Our only reason for signifying, that is, for making signs, is to bring forth and transfer to another mind the action of the mind in the person who makes the sign" (II, II, 3). It is no longer a question of defining the sign, but of a description of the reasons for the activity of signifying. It is not any the less revealing to see that there is no question here of the relation of designation, but only of communication. That which signs present to the mind, is the experienced meaning, that which the enunciator carries in his spirit. To signify is to exteriorize.

The schema of communication will be specified and developed in some later texts. Thus in the *Beginner's Catechism* (dating from 405), Augustine begins with the problem of the slowness of language in relation to thought. He states his frequent dissatisfaction with the enunciation of a thought and explains it thus:

> The reason for it is above all that this intuitive conception floods my soul like a rapid flash of lightning, while my speech is long, slow, and quite different from it [my intuitive conceptions]. In addition, even while it is unfolding itself, this conception is already hidden in its retreat. It leaves however in the memory, in a marvelous manner, a certain number of imprints, which subsist during the course of the brief expression of syllables and which allow us to fashion the phonetic signs known as language. This language is Latin, or Greek, or Hebrew, etc., whether the signs are thought by the spirit or expressed by the voice. But the imprints are neither Latin, Greek, or Hebrew, nor do they belong as such to any nation (II, 3).

Augustine envisages thus a state of meaning where meaning does not yet belong to any given language (it is not at all clear whether there exists or not a Latin or Greek signified outside of the universal meaning; it would seem not, because language is described only in its phonetic dimension). The situation is not very different from that which Aristotle described: there, as here, the states of soul are universal, and languages, particular. But Aristotle explained this identity of psychic states by the identification to itself of the referent-object; now here, in Augustine's text, it is not a question of the object. We shall notice as well the instantaneous nature of the "conception" and the duration necessary to discourse (linear); more generally, the necessity of thinking of the linguistic activity as provided with a temporal dimension (marked by the role of imprints). Here again there are many of the characteristics of the process of communication (the whole page is witness, moreover, to a very nuanced psychological analysis).

The theory of the sign present in *On the Trinity* is yet another development of that of the *Catechism* (like that which figures in Book XI of the *Confessions*). The schema here remains purely communicative.

> Are we speaking to another? The word [*verbe*] remaining immanent, we make use of a spoken word [*parole*] or some sensible sign in order to call forth in the soul of our listener, by this sensible evocation, a word [*verbe*] similar to the one which remains in our soul while we are speaking. (IX, VII, 12).

This description comes very close to that of the act of signifying, present in *On Christian Doctrine*. On the other hand, Augustine distinguishes even more clearly here between what he calls the *word* which is the ante-cedent to the division into language, and the linguistic *signs* which allow us to know it.

One thing is the meaning of the *word*, this word whose syll-ables—whether they are pronounced or thought—occupy a certain space of time; another different one is the meaning of the *word* which is imprinted on the soul with all that is known (IX, X, 15). This [latter] word in fact belongs to no tongue, to none of those which are called the tongues of nations, of which our Latin tongue is one. . . . For the thought that is formed by the thing which we know already is the word which we speak in the heart: which word is neither Greek nor Latin, which belongs to no language. But when it is needful to convey this to the knowledge of those to whom we speak, then some sign is assumed whereby to make it understood. (XV, X, 19).

Words do not directly designate things; they only make them ex-pressed. What they express is not always the individuality of the speaker, but an interior, prelinguistic word. This, in turn, is determined by other factors—two, it would seem. These are, on the one hand, the imprints left in the soul by objects of knowledge; on the other hand, immanent knowledge whose source can only be God.

It is necessary for us to go on as far as that word of man. . . which is neither pronounced in sound nor thought in the manner of sound, which is necessarily implied in all language, but which precedes all the signs by which it is translated, and is born of the immanent knowledge of the soul, when this knowledge expresses itself in an interior word, whatever that really is (XV, XI, 20).

This human process of expression and signification, taken in its entir-ety, forms an analogy with the Word of God, whose exterior sign is not a word, but the world. The two sources of knowledge, in the end, amount to only one, to the extent that the world is the divine language.

The word [*verbe*] that sounds outwardly is thus the sign of the word that shines inwardly, and which, before all others, merits the name of word. That which we utter with the mouth is only the vocal expression of the word: and if we call this

expression a word, it is because the word assumes it in order
to translate it outwardly. Our word becomes thus in some way
a material voice, assuming this voice in order to manifest itself
to men in a sensible fashion. as the Word of God was made
flesh, assuming this flesh in order that itself also might be manifested to man's senses (XV, XI, 20).

We see being formulated here the doctrine of universal symbolism,
which will dominate the medieval tradition.

To summarize, one could establish the following sequence (which is
repeated, symmetrically inverted, either with the speaker or the listener):

divine power	immanent knowledge objects of knowledge	interior word	exterior thought word	exterior spoken word

In particular, we see how the relationship word-thing is· found to be
charged with successive mediations.

Concerning semiotic theory, it remains that the materialist doctrine
of the Stoics, which rested on the analysis of designation, is found, in
Augustine, progressively but firmly ousted by a doctrine of communication.

CLASSIFICATION OF SIGNS

It is especially in *On Christian Doctrine* that Augustine devotes himself
to classifying signs and thus to nuancing the very notion of sign. The other
writings permit a refinement of the details. What immediately strikes us in
the Augustinian classifications is precisely their high number (even by
effecting certain regroupings, we still have at least five oppositions), as well
as the absence of real coordination among them. Here as elsewhere, Augustine gives evidence of his theoretical ecumenism, in juxtaposing things which
could be linked together. We shall thus examine these classifications, and the
oppositions which underlie them, one by one.

1. According to the mode of transmission

This classification, destined to become canonical, is already an example
of the synthesizing spirit of Augustine; since the signifier must be sentient,
one can divide all signifiers according to the sense by which they are perceived. Aristotle's psychological theory thus joins the semiotic description.

Two facts merit attention here. First, there is the limited role of signs being perceived by senses other than vision and hearing: Augustine envisages their existence for obvious theoretical reasons, but he immediately de-emphasizes their interest. "Among the signs by means of which men express their meanings to one another, some pertain to the sense of sight, more to the sense of hearing, and very few to the other senses" (II, III, 4). A single example will suffice to illustrate the other channels of transmission:

> Our Lord gave a sign with the odor of the perfume spread on his feet (John 12.3-7). He signified his will, by the sacrament of his Body and his Blood, by tasting it first. He also gave a signification to the gesture of the woman, who, by touching the hem of her garment, was healed (Luke 22.19-20).*(ibid)*.

These examples serve to mark the exceptional character of the signs which reside in the senses of smell, taste or touch.

In *On the Trinity*, by contrast, it is a question of only two modes of transmission of signs: sight and hearing. Augustine likes to emphasize their similarity.

> This sign, most of the time is a sound, sometimes a gesture: the first is directed to the ears, the second to the eyes, so that corporeal signs transmit to senses equally corporeal that which we have in our mind. Making a sign by gesture, is this in fact anything except speaking in a visible way? (XV, X, 19).

The opposition of sight and hearing permits us to situate, in a first approximation, words among signs (and it is the second point which interests us here). In effect, for Augustine, language is by its nature auditory (we shall return to the description of writing). Thus, the immense majority of signs are auditory—because the immense majority of signs are words. "The innumerable multitude of signs by means of which men discover their thoughts is made up of words" (*On Christian Doctrine, II, III, 4*). The privilege of words is apparently only quantitative.

2. According to origin and usage

A new distinction produces two pairs of kinds of signs; but it is possible to unite them, as Augustine himself does, into one unique category. This distinction is prepared for in the first book of *On Christian Doctrine*; this part of the work begins with a division between signs and things. As soon as it is made, however, the distinction is abolished, for signs, far from being opposed to things, are themselves things—"thing" being taken in the largest sense of all that is. "Every sign is also a thing, otherwise it would be nothing at all" (I, II, 2). The opposition can only be constituted on another level—a functional, and not a substantial one. In effect, a sign can be envisaged from two points of view: a thing as such and a sign as such (this is the order which the exposé of Augustine follows):

> Writing on things, I first of all warned that one should only consider them for what they are, and not for what they signify beyond themselves. Now in treating signs, I am warning that one not pay attention to what the things are, but on the contrary to the signs that they represent, that is, to what [the things] signify (II, I, 1).

The opposition is not between things and signs, but between pure things and sign-things. Nevertheless, there exist things which owe their existence solely to the fact of their being used as signs; these evidently most closely approach pure signs (without being able to reach the limit). It is this possibility of signs to put in parenthesis their nature as things which allows the new categorisation introduced by Augustine.

He will oppose, in effect, natural signs and intentional signs (*data*). This opposition has often been badly understood, being seen as the more common opposition of natural-conventional in Ancient thought; a study by Engels cleared up this point in a most useful way. Augustine writes: "Among signs, some are natural and others are intentional. Those are natural which, without any desire or intention of signifying, make us aware of something beyond themselves" (II, I, 2). The examples of natural signs are: smoke for fire, the tracks of an animal, the face of a man. "Intentional signs are those which living creatures show to one another for the purpose of showing, insofar as they are able, the motion of their souls, that is, all that they are sensing and all that they are thinking" (II, II, 3). The examples of intentional signs are above all human (words), but also linked up here are animals' cries, announcing the presence of food or simply the presence of the emitter of the sounds.

We see how the opposition between natural and intentional signs is linked to that between things and signs. Intentional signs are things which have been produced in view of their use as signs (origin) and are only used towards this end (usage). To put it in another way, they are things whose function as thing has been reduced to a minimum. Intentional signs are thus those which come closest to being pure signs (non-existent). These intentional signs are not necessarily human, and there is no obligatory correlation between the natural or intentional character and their mode of transmission (the classification of these modes comes up with respect to intentional signs; however, it is not clear why). Let us note also that words are intentional signs, which after their auditory nature, constitute their second characteristic.

We can also see in this opposition the echo of the one found in a passage in Aristotle and commented on above (*On Interpretation, 16a*). However, the example of the cries of animals, which appears both here and there but in opposite classifications, will permit us to situate better the position of Augustine. For Aristotle, the fact that these cries had no need of any institution sufficed for them to be considered as "natural." For Augustine, on the contrary, the intention of signifying, attested to, permits him to include them among intentional signs: intentional here is not the same as conventional. We shall suppose that this distinction belongs to Augustine: based on the idea of intention, it agrees completely with its general project which, as we have seen, is psychological and oriented towards communication. This distinction also permits him to overcome the objection which Sextus addressed to the Stoics: namely that the existence of signs does not necessarily imply a logical engendering structure: certain signs are given in nature. We also perceive that the integration of two kinds of signs is produced here; these two kinds of signs had remained completely isolated in all of Augustine's predecessors:the sign in Aristotle and the Stoics becomes "natural sign," the symbol in Aristotle and the combination of signifier and signified in the Stoics becomes "intentional signs" (however, the examples are always the same). The term "natural" is a little misleading: it would perhaps be clearer to oppose signs which *already exist* as things with signs which are *created purposely* with an end toward signification.

3. According to social status

Such a terminological precaution would be all the more desirable in that Augustine introduces, elsewhere in his text, the subdivision—much more familiar as we have seen—of signs into natural (and universal), and institutional (or conventional). The first kind are understandable in an immediate and spontaneous manner; the second kind require a learning process. In fact, in *On Christian Doctrine*, Augustine only envisages the case of signs by institution, and this with regard to an example which apparently goes in the opposite direction.

> The signs that the actors make, in dancing, would not have any meaning if they got it from nature and not from the institution and consent of men. Otherwise the public crier in early times would not have had to explain to the Carthaginian populace what the dancer wished to express during the pantomime. Many old

men still remember this detail, as we have heard them say. Now, we must believe them, for even today if anyone unacquainted with such trifles goes to the theatre and no one else explains to him what these motions signify, he watches the perform- ance in vain (II, XXV, 38).

Even the pantomime, at first glance a natural sign, needs a convention, and thus a learning process. Thus, Augustine takes up again, within his typology, the opposition applied habitually to the origin of language (as Sextus had already done before him).

This opposition is not—any more than the preceding ones—explicitly articulated to the others. We can assume that if Augustine does not give any examples here of natural signs (in the sense that we have just seen it), it is because his treatise is explicitly devoted to intentional signs. Now, natural signs would only be found among signs which were already existing; the sign intentionally created· implied a learning process and thus institution. But is every sign which already exists natural, that is to say apprehensible outside of every convention? Augustine does not say so, and counter-examples come easily to mind. Nevertheless, in the *Beginner's Catechism* he describes as natural a sign which in *On Christian Doctrine* figured among non-intentional signs.

Impressions are a production of the mind, just as the face is an expression of the body. Thus, anger, *ira*, is designated one way in Latin, another way in Greek, in yet another way every- where else, due to the diversity of tongues. But the expression on the face of an angry man is neither Latin nor Greek. Thus, someone who is angry says, "*Iratus sum*"; no one except the Latins will understand him. But if the passion of his soul, in- flamed, shows up on his face, transforming the expression, all observers will be able to judge: "Here is an angry man" (II, 3).

Same assertion in the *Confessions*:

Gestures are like the natural language of all peoples, made up of facial expressions, winks of the eye, and movements of the limbs, and also of the tone of voice which betrays the senti- ment of the soul in pursuit, possession, rejection, or flight from things (I, VIII, 13).

Natural signs (the example is however debatable for us) share here in the universality of impressions on the soul, whose properties we have already seen. Augustine, approaching Aristotle in this, sees the relation between words and thoughts as arbitrary (conventional), and that between thoughts and things as universal, and therefore natural.

This insistence on the necessarily conventional nature of language allows us to guess how little hope Augustine puts in motivation: to his eyes, motivation cannot be substituted for knowledge of conventions.

> Everybody looks for a certain resemblance in the fashion of signifying, so that signs themselves reproduce, as much as possible, the signified thing. But since one thing can resemble another in many ways, such signs cannot have, among men, a determined meaning unless men agree unanimously to it. (*On Christian Doctrine*, II, XXV, 38).

Motivation does not do away with convention; the above argument, summed up in one sentence, is developed at length in *On The Teacher*, where Augustine shows that one can never be certain of the meaning of a gesture without the aid of a linguistic commentary, and thus of the institution which language is. By this very fact Augustine refuses all decisive importance to the natural-conventional (or arbitrary) opposition; the attempts of the eighteenth century, taken up by Hegel and Saussure, to found thereon the opposition between signs (arbitrary) and symbols (natural), find themselves already surpassed.

This "arbitrariness of the sign" leads naturally to polysemy.

> Since things are similar under multiple aspects, let us be careful not to take as a rule that a thing always signifies what, by analogy, it signifies in one place. For the Lord used the word "leaven" in the sense of a reproach when he said, "Beware of the leaven of the Pharisees (Matt.16.11), and in the sense of a praise when he said "The kingdom of heaven is like a woman who put leaven in three measures of flour in order to make all the dough rise" [Luke 13.20-21] (*On Christian Doctrine*, III, XXV, 35).

4. According to the nature of the symbolic relationship.

After the classifications into intentional-non-intentional, and conventional-natural, Augustine envisages a third time the same facts and arrives at yet another different articulation: that of *literal* signs with *transposed* signs (*translata*). The rhetorical origin of this opposition is evident, but Augustine—like Clement before him but in a more precise manner—generalises in terms of signs what rhetoric said of the meaning of words.

Here is how the opposition is introduced:

For signs are either literal or transposed. They are called literal when they are used to designate objects on account of which they were created. For example, we say "an ox" when we are thinking of an animal which all men using the Latin language call by that name just as we do. Signs are transposed when the very objects which we designate by their literal signs are used to designate another object. For example, we say "an ox" and by that syllable understand the animal which is ordinarily called by that word. But again, that animal makes us think of the evangelist, that the Scripture, according to the interpretation of the Apostle, designated by these words: "Thou shalt not muzzle the ox that treadeth out the corn" (I Cor.9.9) (*On Christian Doctrine*, II, X, 15).

Literal signs are defined in the same way as intentional signs: they have been created with respect to their usage as signs. But the definition of the transposed sign is not exactly symmetrical: these are not "natural" signs, in other words those which have an existence before being used as signs. They are defined, more generally, by their secondarity: a sign is transposed when its signified becomes, in turn, a signifier. In other words, the literal sign is based on one single relationship; the transposed sign, on two successive operations (we have already seen that this idea appeared in Clement.

In fact, we are immediately situated within intentional signs (since Augustine is preoccupied exclusively with them), and it is within them that we reiterate the operation which served to isolate them: literal signs are simultaneously created purposely with respect to a use as signifier, and at the same time used according to this initial intention. Transposed signs are equally intentional signs (the only examples given are words), but instead of being used according to their initial destination, they are diverted for a secondary use: just as things were when they were turned into signs.

This structural analogy—which is not an identity—explains the affinity between transposed signs (linguistic, however), and non-intentional signs ("natural" and non-linguistic). It is not an accident if the examples are joined together: the bull does not owe his existence to semiotic finality, but he *can* signify; he is at the same time a natural sign and (a possible ingredient of) a transposed sign. This third approach to the same phenomenon is, from a formal point of view, the most satisfying: it is no longer an empirical contingency which serves to distinguish between signs (already existing or created on purpose, immediately comprehensible or through the use of a convention), but a difference of structure: the symbolic relationship, simple or double. At one stroke, language no longer forms a class apart within signs: one part of linguistic signs (indirect expressions) is now to be found on the same side as non-linguistic signs. The formulation of this opposition, based on an analysis of form and not of substance, represents the most important theoretical acquisition of Augustinian semiotics. Let us notice at the same time that this very articulation contributes to the partial erasing of the difference between the two phenomena, which had been more or less separate in Aristotle (symbol vs. sign), in the Stoics (signifier-signified vs. sign), or in Clement (direct language vs. symbolism).

The origin of the literal-transposed opposition is rhetorical; but the difference between Augustine and the rhetorical tradition is not only in the extension which leads us from the word to the sign; it is the very definition of the "transposed" which is new: it is no longer a word which changes meaning, but a word which designates an object which, in turn, conveys a meaning. This description can in effect be applied to the example cited above (like the bull, the Evangelist, etc.) which does not resemble a rhetorical trope. On the following page, however, Augustine gives another example of a transposed sign, which conforms perfectly to the rhetorical definition. Rather than a confusion between two kinds of indirect meaning, what is in question is probably an attempt on Augustine's part to enlarge the category of transposed meaning in order to permit him to include Christian allegory. In talking about the difficulties which arise during interpretation, he envisages two kinds of difficulties, which indeed correspond to these two forms of indirect meaning. The opposition will be better formulated in *On the Trinity*, where Augustine conceives two kinds of allegory (in other words, transposed signs), according to words or according to things. The origin of this distinction is perhaps in one of the sentences of Clement, who believes however that it is a question of two alternative definitions of one and the same notion.

Another attempt at subdivision within transposed meaning will lead later on to the celebrated doctrine of the fourfold meaning of the Scriptures. The question remains controversial, to know whether, yes or no, Augustine founded this doctrine. We have at our disposal several series of texts. In one, represented by *De utilitate crecendi*, 3, 5, and by a completely parallel but shorter passage in *De Gen. ad lit. lib. imperf.*, 2, we can distinguish in a very precise way four terms: history, etiology, analogy, and allegory. But it is not certain that these are meanings, properly speaking. Rather, it is probably a question of different operations to which one would submit the text to be interpreted. In particular, analogy is the process which, in order to explain a text, consists in having recourse to another text. Etiology has a problematic status; it consists of looking for the cause of the event or fact evoked by the text. It is an explanation, thus a meaning, but it is not certain if the meaning belongs properly to the text analysed; the meaning rather is supplied by the commentator. Thus there remain only two meanings: historical (literal) and allegorical. The examples which Augustine gives of the latter indicate, however, that he is not distinguishing among kinds of allegorical meanings in the way that the tradition after him will do. These examples include: Jonas in the whale for Christ in the tomb (typology in later tradition); the punishments of the Jews during the Exodus as stimulus not to sin (tropology); the two women, symbols of the two Churches (anagogy). It must be added here that Augustine does not distinguish either between spiritual meaning and transposed meaning (he gives the same definition to both). If we compare him with later tradition, codified by St. Thomas, we find the following redistribution:

	Literal meaning	Transposed meaning	Spiritual meaning
Augustine	literal meaning	transposed meaning	
Thomas	historical meaning		spiritual meaning

To summarize: there is only one essential dichotomy for Augustine (literal-transposed): the rest is of little importance.

There is one more text, however, which should be examined here. It is found in *De Gen. ad lit.*, I, 1; Augustine is talking here about the contents of the various books of the Bible: there are those, he says, which evoke eternity, others which report facts, others which announce the future, others which give rules for behaviour. This is not the same as asserting a fourfold-meaning in the same passage; nevertheless, the theory is here in embryonic form.

In his effort to specify the status of transposed signs, Augustine compares them with two connected semantic facts: ambiguity and falsehood. Ambiguity holds his attention at length: beginning with *On Dialectic*, where difficulties in communication are divided up according to whether they are due to obscurity or to ambiguities (this subdivision can already be found in Aristotle). The latter allow, as one of their subdivisions, ambiguities due to transposed meaning. The same hierarchical articulation reappears in *On Christian Doctrine*: "The ambiguity of Scripture arises either from terms taken in the literal meaning, or terms taken in the transposed meaning" (III, I, 1). By ambiguity due to the literal meaning, we mean an ambiguity where semantics has no role; this kind of ambiguity is thus auditory, graphic, or syntaxic. Semantic ambiguities simply coincide with those which are due to the presence of a transposed meaning. The possibility of semantic ambiguities based on lexical polysemy is not envisaged.

Transposed signs, which are a species of the genus "ambiguity," must be, by contrast, clearly distinguished from falsehoods, even though neither of the two really say what is true, if they are taken literally.

> God keeps us from attributing to them [the parables and figures in the Bible] a false character. Otherwise it would be necessary to inflict with the same epithet the long series of figures of rhetoric, and particularly to metaphor, thus named because it carries a word from the thing which it properly designates to another thing which it improperly designates. When we say, for example, the waving corn fields, pearled vines, the flower of youth, snowy hair, there are certainly not in the things named either waves, pearls, flowers, or snow; thus it is necessary to term as falsehood the transposition which brings about these terms? (*Against Falsehood*, X, 24).

The explanation of this difference is given shortly after: it resides precisely in the existence of a transposed meaning, absent in falsehoods, which allows the restitution of truth to tropes. "These words and these actions. . . are made in order to give us the intelligence of the things to which they are referred" (*ibid*). Or again: "Nothing of that which is made or said in a figured sense is a falsehood. Every word must be related to what it designates, for those who are in a position to understand its signification" (*Against Falsehood*, V, 7). Lies are not true in a literal sense, but they do not have a transposed meaning, either.

5. According to the nature of the designated, sign or thing.

Transposed signs are characterised by the fact that their "signifier" is already a completely separate sign; we can now envisage the complementary case, where it is no longer the signifier but the signified which is in turn a complete sign. We shall in fact unite under this heading two cases which remain isolated in Augustine: that of letters, the signs of sounds, and that of the metalinguistic use of language. In each of these cases, the sign is designated, but in the first case what is in question is the signifier, in the second case, the sound signified.

a) letters

Concerning letters, Augustine always keeps to the Aristotelian saying: letters are the signs of sounds. Thus, in *On Dialectic*

> When it is written, it is not a word, but the sign of a word, which, presenting its letters to the eyes of the reader, shows to his spirit that which he must verbally emit. What, in fact, do letters do, if not present themselves to the eyes and, in addition, present words to the spirit? (V).

The same in *On The Teacher*:

> Written words... must be understood as signs of words (IV,8).

Or in *On Christian Doctrine*:

> Words are shown to the eyes not by themselves but by the signs which properly belong to them (II, IV, 5).

And in *On the Trinity*:

> Letters are the signs of sounds just as sounds in conversation are signs of thought (XV, X, 19).

We find, however, brought up by Augustine, several supplementary characteristics of letters. The first, in *On Dialectic*, forms a paradox: letters are the signs of sounds, but not just any sounds—only articulated sounds. Now, articulated sounds are those which let themselves be designated by a letter. "I call an articulated sound that which can be represented by letters" (V). Letters, one could say, repose on an implicit phonological analysis, because they represent the only invariables. Taken in a larger meaning, "writing" appears equally indispensable for language: this is the case with these "impressions" of which the *Catechism* talked about and of which words are only the translation.

In *On Christian Doctrine*, Augustine insists on the durational nature of letters, in opposition to the punctual nature of sounds: "Because, as soon as sounds have struck the air, they pass away immediately and remain no longer than they sound, we have fixed their signs by means of letters" (II, IV, 5). Thus, letters permit one to escape from the constraint of the "now" which weighs on every spoken word. In *On The Trinity*, Augustine goes even further in the same direction: writing permits the envisaging not only of "another time", but also of "another place." These corporeal signs and others of this kind presuppose the presence of those who see us, listen to us and to whom we speak; writing, by contrast has been invented to permit us to converse also with the absent" (XV, X, 19). Writing is defined by its complicity with absence.

b) metalinguistic usage

At no time does Augustine take into consideration the fact that letters are special in that they designate other signs (sounds). And yet, it is a situation familiar to him, because he is always interested in the problem of the metalinguistic usage of words. In *On Dialectic*, Augustine notes that words can be utilised either as signs of things or as names of words. The distinction is utilised throughout the *Teacher*, where Augustine warns against the confusions which could result from these two completely distinct uses of language.

Again in *On Dialectic*, Augustine notes in passing; "We cannot speak about words without recourse to words" (V). This remark will be generalized in *On Christian Doctrine*: "All these signs, whose kinds I have briefly sketched here—it is with words that I have been able to express them; but words I could not have by any means expressed by these signs" (II, III, 4). Thus not only can words be used in a metalinguistic fashion, but they are also the only ones susceptible to being used in a metasemiotic fashion. This statement is of capital importance, for it permits us to focus on the specificity of words among signs. Unfortunately, it remains isolated and non-theorized by Augustine; nowhere does he try to link it up with the other classifications which he outlines. One might wonder, for example, if all verbal signs (literal and transposed), possess this capacity to the same degree, or what is the property of words which enables them to assume this role. Here again, Augustine is content to observe and to juxtapose, without attaining a theoretical articulation.

SOME CONCLUSIONS

Let us attempt to draw some conclusions concerning the double object of this first chapter: Saint Augustine and semiotics.

First, we have seen what is the proper position of Augustine. Throughout his semiotic work, he is moved by a tendency which consists of inscribing the semiotic problem within the framework of a psychological theory of communication. This movement is all the more striking in that it contrasts with his point of departure, that is, the Stoic theory of the sign. That is not to say that he is entirely original: the psychological perspective

was already Aristotle's. It remains that Augustine develops this tendency
more than any of his predecessors; one can explain this development by
the theological and exegetical usage to which he wanted to put the theory
of the sign.

But if the originality of detail in Augustine is limited, his synthetic
"originality"—or rather, his ecumenical capacity—is enormous. It results
in the first construction which, in the history of Western thought, merits
the name of semiotics. Let us review the major articulations of this ecumenism: a rhetorician by profession, Augustine first submits his knowledge
to the interpretation of a particular text (the Bible). Hermeneutics thus
absorbs rhetoric; in addition, to it will be annexed the logical theory of
the sign—at the expense, it is true, of a shift from structure to substance,
since instead of the "symbol" and the "sign" of Aristotle, we discover intentional and natural signs. These two conglomerations come together again
in *On Christian Doctrine* to give birth to a general theory of signs, or semiotics, in which "signs" coming from the rhetorical tradition become in the
meantime hermeneutic, which is to say "transposed signs," find their place.

This extraordinary ability for synthesis (which is not diminished by
the fact that Augustine has precursors in the way of eclecticism) indeed
corresponds to the historical place of Augustine, the meeting-place through
which the traditions of Antiquity will be transmitted to the Middle Ages.
This power is detectable in numerous other domains, which sometimes touch
upon ours: thus, in particular, several passages in the treatise *On Dialectic*,
where historical changes in meaning (in the etymological part of the treatise),
are described in terms of rhetorical tropes. History now appears only to be a
projection of typology in time. Again: for the first time the Aristotelian
classification of associations, which are found in Chapter II of *On Memory*
(by means of resemblance, proximity, contrast) will be utilized to describe
the variety of these relations of meaning, synchronic or diachronic.

It is precisely here that it becomes necessary to turn from Augustine's
personal destiny and ask ourselves what price knowledge had to pay in order
to engender semiotics. Since language exists, the first question in any semiotic, empirically if not ontologically, becomes: what is the place of linguistic signs among signs in general? As long as one questions oneself only on
verbal language, one remains within a science (or a philosophy) of language.
Only the breaking up of the linguistic framework justifies the founding of
semiotics. And it is precisely this which constitutes Augustine's inaugural
gesture: what was said about words, in the framework of a rhetoric or of a
semantic, he will carry to the level of sign, where words only occupy a place
among others. But which one?

One can wonder, in looking for an answer to this question, if the price
paid for the birth of semiotics was not too high. On the level of general

enunciations, Augustine does not situate words (the linguistic signs) except within two classifications. Words depend, on the one hand, on the auditory; on the other, the intentional. The intersection of these two categories gives linguistic signs. In doing this, Augustine does not perceive that he does not provide himself with any means for distinguishing them from any other "intentional auditory signs", unless it is by their frequency of use. His text could not be any more revealing in this respect: "Those signs which pertain to hearing are, as I have said, the more numerous, especially in language. But the trumpet, the flute, and the zither emit most frequently a sound, are not only pleasing but also significant. However, all these signs, compared with words, are very few" (*Doctrine*, II, III, 4). Between the trumpet which announces attack (to take an example where the intentionality is certain), and words, would not the only difference be in the larger frequency of the latter? This is all that we are explicitly offered by the semiotics of Augustine. We see, among other things, how much phonetic prejudice is responsible for the blindness before the problem of the nature of language. The necessity of attaching words to a "meaning" conceals their specificity (a purely "visual" conception of language, identifying it with writing, would suffer the same reproach). Augustine's synthesizing gift turns against him here: it is perhaps not by accident that the Stoics, no more than Aristotle, did not want to give the same name to the "natural" sign (assimilated in their writings into an inference) and to the word. Synthesis is fruitful only if it does not obliterate differences.

In fact, we have also noted that Augustine brings up certain properties of language which do not let themselves be explained by their intentional-auditory character, and above all their metasemiotic capacity. But he does not ask himself the question: what is the property of language which assures it this capacity? Now, only an answer to this fundamental question could permit one to settle another problem, which proceeds from it, namely that of the "price" of the semiotic foundation: is it useful to unify within one single notion—the sign—that which possess this metasemiotic property and that which does not possess it (it is to be remarked that this new question contains, circularly, the term "semiotic" in itself)? Usefulness that one can not measure before knowing what is at stake in the opposition between linguistic and non-linguistic signs. It is thus from ignorance, if not from the repression—of the difference between words and other signs, that the semiotics of Augustine is born—and Saussure's, fifteen centuries later. Which makes problematic indeed the very existence of semiotics.

Augustine had nevertheless caught a glimpse of a possibility of escaping from this impasse (even though he remained, probably, unconscious of the possibility of this impasse in itself). This possibility consisted in the extension to the domain of signs of the rhetorical category of literal-transposed. This category transcends the substantial opposition of linguistic-non-linguistic (since the category applies in the two domains). It equally transcends the intentional-natural or conventional-universal oppositions, which are pragmatic and contingent, and this category allows the articulation of two large modes of designation, for which one would be tempted today to employ two distinct terms: signification and symbolization. From there, one will ask oneself about the difference which founds them—and which indirectly explains the presence or the absence of a metasemiotic capacity. In other words, semiotics does not merit existence unless semantics and symbolics were already linked in the same gesture which founded them. This is what allows us to appreciate, sometimes in spite of itself, the founding work of Augustine.

BIBLIOGRAPHIC NOTICE

Complementary references to this expose will be found in the histories of the different disciplines which I have used, as follows: R.H. Robbins, *A Short History of Linguistics,* London, 1969 (French translation, Paris, 1976); W. and M. Kneale, *Development of Logic,* Oxford, 1962; R. Blanché, *La Logique et son histoire,* Paris, 1970; C.S. Baldwin, *Ancient Rhetoric and Poetic,* Gloucester, 1924; G. Kennedy, *The Art of Persuasion in Greece,* Princeton, 1963; G. Kennedy, *The Art of Rhetoric in the Roman World,* Princeton, 1972; J. Cousin, *Études sur Quintilian,* Paris, 1935; J. Pépin, *Mythe et Allégorie,* Paris, 1958.

The texts are quoted from the bilingual Budé or Garnier editions, except for the *Organon* and the *Metaphysics* of Aristotle, quoted from the Tricot translation.

The most complete study of Augustinian semiotics is that of B. Darrell Jackson, "The Theory of Signs in Saint Augustine's *De Doctrina Christiana,*" *Revue des études augustiniennes,* 15 (1969), 9-49; reprinted in R. A. Markus (ed.), *Augustine,* Garden City, N.Y., 1972, 92-147; one will also find there references to earlier studies, among which can be added J. Pépin, *Saint Augustine et la Dialectique,* Villanova, 1976. On the other hand, R. Simone's "Sémiologie Augustinienne," *Semiotica,* 6 (1972), 1-31, can be left aside. I was not able to consult C.P. Mayer, *Die Zeichen in der geistigen Entwicklung und in der Theologie des jungen Augustinus,* Würzburg, 1969. I have quoted the texts of Augustine in the translations of the Bibliothèque Augustinienne.

SEMIOTIC PHILOSOPHY?

Elmar Holenstein

ABSTRACT

The philosophical interest in semiotics arose out of its chief aim, the elucidation of the foundations and forms of knowledge. Since Locke and Leibniz it has been recognized that signs not only serve to present and communicate knowledge already given, but also open up certain domains of knowledge that would otherwise be inaccessible.

Since the use of sign systems presupposes insight into the rule-governed construction of these systems, it is more appropriate to speak of a semiotic complementation than of a "semiotic transformation of philosophy" (Apel). With the exception of elementary forms of knowledge , which are, however, fundamental, all knowledge rests on an interdependence of intuitive and semiotically mediated cognitions.

In the contemporary philosophy of science a *planificatory function* joins the *cognitive function* of signs. Signs serve to plan and steer actions and operations. The cybernetic sciences as a semiotic discipline have succeeded, for the first time since the breakthrough of modern science, in reversing the relation between the natural and the human sciences. A model from the human sciences has successfully been superposed upon natural sciences and technical disciplines.

I. *The cognitive function of signs*

In his writings on the philosophy of language, Karl-Otto Apel (1973: 271, 353) repeatedly advances a "linguistically oriented" or, in more general and pertinent terms, a "semiotic transformation" of transcendental philosophy. There are no doubt clever outsiders who will assume that philosophy has now joined the ranks of the many younger as well as older sciences already sucked into the wake of the all-pervasive and influential disciplines of linguistics and semiotics. Philosophy, in contrast to most other sciences, can counter this charge on historical grounds. Semiotics, the name included (Locke, 1690: §4.21.4), was child and ward of philosophy up to Peirce and Saussure. However, philosophy is no more subject to history than it is to fashion—apart from the fact that history consists largely of a succession of fashions. An orthodox philosopher is concerned only with the *Sachen selbst*. The basic subject matter of philosophy is the *cognoscibile*, the questions, 'What can we know?' and 'How do we acquire knowledge?'.

It was this paramount philosophical theme that spurred on the development of semiotics in the works of modern philosophers from Locke (1632-1704) via Leibniz (1646-1716), Wolff ((1679-1754), Lambert (1728-1777), Condillac (1715-1780), and Bolzano (1781-1848) to Peirce (1839-1914) and Husserl (1859-1938).[1] The most interesting and exhaustive discussions do not, as might be expected, deal with the long dominant psychological aspect of signs, their emotive function, the expression of inner data, feelings and ideas, nor with the currently prevailing sociological aspect, their communicative function, but rather with what can be called the cognitive function of signs and sign systems. Thus it comes as no surprise that the above-mentioned philosophers explore semiotics largely in connection with mathematics and logic.

An important function of signs, the finding of philosophical semiotics, consists in making possible and extending consciousness, knowledge and understanding.[2] Locke paved the way in his *Essay Concerning Human Understanding* (1690), not in the third book, 'Of Words,' but rather in the second 'Of Ideas,' in the sixteenth chapter on numbers. He suggests that we would be unable to produce or clearly distinguish more complex numbers if we had no names for the sums arrived at by the successive addition of units. In support of his thesis, he cites American Indians who, having no words for higher numbers, e.g. 1000, depend on vague figurative means such as pointing to the hair on their heads to indicate a larger sum.

> By the repeating. . .the idea of an unit, and joining it to another unit, we make thereof one collective idea, marked by the name two. And whosoever can do this, and proceed on, still adding one more to the last collective idea which he had of any number,

[1]For a survey, see Coseriu 1968 ff.; Jakobson 1975. For an older, diversified, systematic and also historical presentation of semiotic problems, see Vol. II of Gomperz' *'Weltanschauungslehre'*, entitled *Noologie* (1908). Gomperz began a correspondence with Husserl upon sending him Vol. I (1905). Vol. II is sometimes (Jakobson 1965:345) considered a possible link between Saussure and older philosophical semiotics.

[2]"The third branch of science may be called *sēmeïotikè̀*, or the *doctrine of signs*. . . the business whereof is to consider the nature of signs, the mind makes use of *for the understanding of things*, or conveying its knowledge to others" (Locke 1690:§4.21.4). (The final italics are the author's).

and gave a name to it, may count, or have ideas, for several collections of units, distinguished one from another, as far as he hath a series of names for following numbers, and a memory to retain that series, with their several names... For, without such names or marks, we can hardly well make use of numbers in reckoning, especially where the combination is made up of any great multitude of units; which put together, without a name or mark to distinguish that precise collection, will hardly be kept from being a heap in confusion" (Locke 1690:§2.16.5).

In Book III, Locke attributes to words in general the function of improving knowledge. A predominant function of language[3] is to classify. On the one hand, words guarantee the lasting fusion of different modes and relations in one complex idea. Without the word *triumphus*, we would probably have descriptions but no unified and lasting idea of all that belongs to the essence of this ceremony (*ibid*. 3.5.10). On the other hand, words provide generalizations of both simple and complex ideas; names can be transferred to similar data (*ibid*. 3.3). Locke's theory of language is almost exclusively restricted to the lexical stratum and within this stratum to the class of substantives, i.e. to that part of language whose structure is the least homogeneous, thus yielding abundant support for his atomistic approach. Arbitrarily selected relations of similarity and contiguity between ideas act as the principles of linguistic classification.

Condillac (1746: §1.4.2.27) radicalizes and generalizes Locke's discovery of the necessity of signs. Of all the modes of consciousness only sensation and perception can be generated entirely without recourse to signs. Higher modes of consciousness such as awareness and imagination depend for their perfection and autonomy upon signs, upon artificially created signs (*signes d'institution*). Artificial signs free the human mind from its dependence upon real events, to which accidental and natural signs are bound. Memory and operations of the mind such as reflection, judgment and conclusion are utterly impossible without signs (*ibid*. 1.2. 4 f.; 1.4.1 f.). Condillac's concluding attack on the Cartesian thesis of innate ideas is rather timely. In his opinion, this thesis is not only a bias refuted by Locke's discovery of the necessity of signs for the imagination of numbers, which had served as the model illustration of innate ideas since

---

[3]Locke usually places communication second (§3.3.20; 4.21.1 and 4). An exception is §3.5.7, where communication is called "the chief end of language."

Augustine; it has also obstructed scientific progress: "Comment soupçonner la nécessité des signes, lorsqu'on pense, avec Descartes, que les idées sont inées. . . ?" (*ibid*. 1.4.2.27)

Leibniz and Lambert, building upon Locke's reflections, move in another direction. Leibniz (1765: § 2.16.5) observes that a mere accumulation of names has only a limited usefulness in the constitution of the natural numerical series. "A certain order and a certain replication"[4] are necessary to prevent our memory from being burdened with too many new names. Leibniz advances beyond Locke by surmounting his atomistic approach. Attention is no longer focused on relations of similarity and contiguity among individual ideas but rather, to use Lambert's terminology, on the figurative or metaphorical, or, to use Peirce's terminology, on the iconic or diagrammatical interpretation and evaluation of systematic relations among ideas.

Signs can be called scientific "when they not only present concepts or things, but also reveal relations such that the theory of the thing and the theory of its signs can be interchanged" (Lambert, 1774:§2.23).

One of the most instructive examples of such figurative sign systems is Lambert's graphic presentation of the modes of propositions and conclusions in *Dianoiologie oder Lehre von den Gesetzen des Denkens*, the first book of his *Neues Organon (ibid*. 1.196 ff.). It can be viewed as a precursor of the Euler Circles, which have survived in logic and set theory as the superior illustration. For the different propositions, Lambert uses lines of varying length, placed under or next to each other depending on the mode of the proposition. Today, relations between statements and classes are represented by concentric, intersected and adjacent circles. With Lambert's method, the two propositions 'All *M* are *P*' and 'All *S* are *M*' yield figure 1 below. The more figurative Euler Circles yield figure 2.

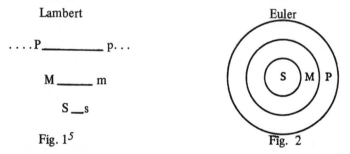

Fig. 1[5]   Fig. 2

[4] "La mémoire seroit trop chargée, s'il falloit retenir un nom tout à fait nouveau pour chaque addition d'une nouvelle unité. C'est pourquoy il faut un certain ordre et une certaine replication dans ces noms, en recommencant suivant une certaine progression."

[5] See 1.201 and 209 ff. The dotted line indicates that the extension is undefined.

The interpretation of the diagrams reads: "The extension of M is greater than that of S; and that of P greater than that of M. Further, all S are M, and all M are P." The cognitive value of the drawing lies in its representing six propositions at once, namely, in addition to the two illustrated, the following four: 1) Some M are S. 2) Some P are M. 3) Some P are S. 4) All S are P. In fact, even more. Impossible conclusions are revealed as well (e.g. "All P are S," *ibid*. 1.201 f.; 3.29). A figurative-iconic presentation is fruitful since it not only encompasses the cognitions that led to its construction but discloses others as well. It has, in Peirce's terms, a "capacity of revealing unexpected truth."

> For a great distinguishing property of the icon is that by the direct observation of it other truths concerning its object can be discovered than those which suffice to determine its construction. . . . Given a conventional or other general sign of an object, to deduce any other truth than that which it explicitly signifies, it is necessary, in all cases, to replace that sign by an icon." (Peirce 1931:§2.279).

Lambert (*ibid*. 3.34) considered arithmetic number systems more perfect as figurative signs than symbols, emblems, and even Egyptian hieroglyphics, but it was Husserl (1891: 250ff.)[6] who offered the most profound discussion of the semiotic structure of numerical systems as developed by Lambert along the lines of Leibniz stimulated by Locke. The naming of numbers is more than a question of mere nomenclature. There is also more involved than the extension and increase of knowledge, than the extension of the natural numerical series through signs beyond directly and intuitively grasped sums and the disclosure of systematic relations between individual numbers and groups of numbers. Husserl, as Lambert before him, pursued practical interests in addition to the psychological and theoretical cognitive ideal. The calculating methods yielded or at least simplified by

---

[6]Husserl's most interesting contribution to semiotics is not to be found in his 1890 manuscript "On the Logic of Signs (Semiotics)", first published in 1970, but rather in the last three chapters of the *Philosophy of Arithmetic* (1891). In his manuscript headed "Semiotics", Husserl develops a classification of signs based on a similar classification undertaken by Bolzano. In his *Wissenschaftslehre* (1837), Bolzano, on the other hand, does not present his classification in the chapter entitled "Semiotics" in the table of contents and "Theory of Signs" in the body of the text (§ 4.637 ff.). Here he deals broadly with questions of applied semiotics such as what new signs introduced by logic should be like. His classification of signs appears in a paragraph (*ibid*. 3.285) devoted to the "Designation of our Ideas".

arithmetic sign systems are of prime concern in their evaluation. This pragmatic approach explains why Roman numerals gave way to the Indian system of position in which the numerical series is based upon a basic unit (10) with each decimal assigned a certain position (columns, in written form). Thus, in the Indian system the arithmetic operations of addition, subtraction etc. for complex numbers can be separated into single, easily grasped stages in which the operations in question are carried out successively for each column.

> Every numerical system grounds mechanisms of calculation appertinent to it, and the best system is surely the one that allows the shortest and easiest ones. From this point of view, those systems are especially advantageous whose base number is divisible by as many other numbers as possible and whose addition and multiplication tables are not all too taxing on our memories. For this reason, mathematicians consider the duodecimal system superior to the now established decimal system. (Husserl, 1891: 267 f.).[7]

From Leibniz to Peirce, algebra is considered "the most perfect illustration of the [figurative] *characteristica*" (Lambert, 1764: § 3.35). The algebraic equation is an icon; it uncovers a multitude of relations among the quantities represented by signs. Geometric and physical phenomena are captured by a system of signs "through whose skilful connection all possible truths may be brought to light" (Wolff, 1719: § 324). The choice of algebra again combines cognitive and practical interests. To determine the path of a body in free fall, we can measure each unit of interest to us and set up a table of results. We proceed as if the results were not related to each other. Quite another picture emerges when we focus on the relation between each of the measurements. The relation no longer rests on a simple rule of association, a relation of similarity or contiguity, but instead takes the form of an algebraic equation. This distance covered by a falling object in t seconds is $\frac{g}{2}t^2$. The lengthy table with data on each second can be replaced by this short, handy formula.[8]

---

[7]Not all sign systems are equally practical for both human and mechanical calculators. Thus, the dyadic number system is obviously less suited to the human mind and memory than to the electronic computer.

[8]This example stems from G. Miller and is taken from a paper by Jerome S. Brumer (1964: 59) significantly entitled, "Going beyond the information given."

Modern science owes much of its progress to the development of ever new mathematical theories for which a representation or interpretation is subsequently found in nature. Mathematical theories are the most striking illustration for the cognitive or—in the nomenclature normally used in this context—heuristic value of semiotic systems.[9]

For Lambert (1764: §3.58) and Peirce (1931: §2.279), only figurative or iconic signs are so structured as to further cognition.[10] Comprehension of arbitrary signs necessitates a "theory derived not from a picture but directly from the thing itself" (Lambert, 1764: §3.58). However, figurative or iconic signs also depend upon ordinary language interpretations for their exact determination (ibid. 3.33 and 3.58 f.). Verbal determination of a sign replaces or reinforces contextual determination. We can usually tell from the context whether, for instance, the stylized front view of an automobile refers only to the front view or to the whole car. This drawing in a spare parts' catalogue would probably call for the former interpretation, while on a traffic sign restricting through-traffic, it calls for the latter interpretation. Adequate legal certainty, however, can be obtained only by the verbal commentary of the author. Yet even this linguistically mediated certainty does not satisfy a radical philosopher. The meaning of words and sentences in ordinary language is influenced by experience, perceptions and actions which are themselves not less undefined than the iconic signs whose determinations is being sought.

To what extent is language itself an iconic sign system and consequently one that furthers cognition? Among the older philosophers, the most positive reply to this question comes from Leibniz (1765: §3.7.6), their most linguistic and structuralistic representative: "Je croye veritablement, que les langues sont le meilleur miroir de l'esprit humain, et qu'une analyse exacte

---

[9]According to Locke (1690: §3.3.11), ideas are signs no less than words. The crux of the matter would be grossly neglected if this were taken to indicate a naive mentalism. Expressions such as representation, imagination, perception, thought, etc. all have a subjective and an objective sense, a distinction strictly and consistently maintained in philosophy only since Husserl's critique of psychologism. Subjectively, these expressions mean the act of representation, imagination, perception, thought etc.: objectively, they mean the intentional object of these acts, the represented, the imagined, the perceived, the thought, etc. as such, i.e. the state of affairs which is represented, imagined, or thought. Such a state of affairs can also be a mathematical theory. What may be considered untenable in Locke is not so much his mentalism as his 'imaginativism', his pictorial view of abstract ideas, which gives rise to Berkeley's inquiry about measuring the angles of the abstract idea, triangle.

[10]Wolff (1729: §952; cf. 1733: §97) also discusses the cognitive value of the natural signs that Peirce was to classify as indices. "In specie Signum demonstrativum dicitur, cujus signatum praesens: Signum prognosticum, cujus signatum futurum est: Signum denique rememorativum, vel Memoriale cujus signatum praeteritum est." The terminology suggests that an older tradition is involved in this classification.

de la signification des mots feroit mieux connoistre que toute autre chose les operations de l'entendement." This statement concludes a passage in which Leibniz uncovers a general meaning underlying the uses of the English term 'but', for which Locke claims as many different meanings as there are uses. For Leibniz the uses of 'but' ('but to say no more,' 'I saw but two planets,' etc.) all mark a *non plus ultra*. According to Peirce (1931: § 2.280), the iconic mode of designation on the lexical level has all but disappeared. Logical icons on the other hand are to be found in the syntax of every language (cf. Jakobson, 1965d: 350 ff.).

Today, the interpretation of language as a wellspring of logical and ontological cognitions with which the human mind is equipped prior to all philosophical reflection is advanced above all by ordinary language philosophy and generative semantics. Every child reveals with his language competence that he has unconsciously mastered insights, that have often escaped generations of professional philosophers.

This can be illustrated by the terms 'belief' and 'knowledge.'[11] Both are modes of consciousness distinguished by an intuition so vague that philosophers have been known to attempt a definition of knowledge as belief. The vagueness of our intuition stands in contrast to the conspicuously divergent use of 'belief' and 'knowledge' in ordinary language, thus defeating every attempt to reduce the one term to the other (cf. Tillman, 1967: 38 f.; Ryle, 1974: 7 f.).

Knowledge is forgotten; a belief is lost. It is possible to speak of a loss of knowledge, but this refers not to a known fact but to a potential, or a faculty of knowledge such as a library destroyed by fire or those centers of the brain in which our knowledge is actually founded. Belief is a capacity or an attitude. As such it can only be lost but not forgotten.

We can of course both stop knowing and stop believing something because we have learned better. But when I stop believing that Descartes was a linguist, I can still state retrospectively: "Until the day before yesterday, I believed that Descartes was a linguist." In the case of knowledge, however, I cannot say: "Until the day before yesterday, I knew that Descartes was a linguist." The change of knowledge modifies the judgment of my former state of consciousness; the change of belief entails no such consequences. Semioticians are often accused of knowing nothing about pre-Lockian history. There is in fact a wealth of semiotic literature from both Antiquity and the Middle Ages, not to mention non-European, Indian contributions. My thesis is, nevertheless, that Locke represents a caesura. From a structural point of view, ancient and medieval studies may well surpass

---

[11]These two terms will be useful in elucidating Augustine's view of the function of signs. See fn. 3.

much found in modern and contemporary studies. From a functional point of view, however, Locke clearly ushers in a new epoch.[12]

In Antiquity, from Pythagoras (Proclus, 1908: §16) to Augustine (see 1952: §36), *cognito rei* preceded *cognitio verbi*.[13] Medieval Schoolmen set up a *sequitur* hierarchy beginning with modes of being of an object, followed by modes of cognition, to which modes of designating and signifying were applied and adapted.[14] The words *orthotēs onomátōn* and *congruitas* sum

[12]The opposite thesis is maintained by—among others—Coseriu (1968 ff., Part I, p. 136): "Thus it can also happen that, at the end of the seventeenth century, John Locke seems to be declaring something entirely new when he speaks of the necessity of semiotics. In reality, he hardly says anything novel by pointing out the necessity of semiotics—as if it had never existed before and was yet to be established." With my thesis, I do not wish to exclude completely the possibility of isolated steps taken in Antiquity and the Middle Ages in the same direction as Locke's interpretation of signs. With a bit of historical diligence, forerunners can be found for any idea. But the question remains: What value is assigned to such an idea; is its effect on the author himself or on his followers heuristic and systematizing, paradigmatic in the sense of Thomas S. Kuhn's conception of the history of science, or does it fall by the wayside, unexploited?

[13] "Cum enim mihi signum datur, si nescientem me invenit cujus rei signum sit, docere me nihil potest: si vero scientem, quid disco per signum?. . . Itaque magis signum re cognita, quam signo dato ipsa res discitur" (*ibid.* 33).–Augustine's argumentation rests on a thoroughly atomistic doctrine of signs. The fact that compound signs (complex numbers) and combinations of signs (premises, conclusions) can yield new cognitions is either overlooked due to the fixation on the correspondence between thing and sign or repressed by interpreting what is gleaned from statements of others as mere belief and not knowledge. Thus, according to Augustine (*ibid.* 37), the story of the three youths in the oven does not add to my knowledge. It only provides me with something to believe. What happens, however, when I hear another version of the deliverance of the three youths, which for reasons internal or external seems more convincing, or when I learn from a biblical scholar that the story is not historical fact but didactic legend? I lose my belief in the factuality of the events in the story. The state of affairs constituted by the story still remains a datum of knowledge as a state of affairs in itself. In Augustine, the relation between knowledge (*scire*), evidence (*intellegere*), and belief (*credere*) is not satisfactorily elucidated. Every belief implies an affair-complex and knowledge that can be true or false in reference to a particular real or possible world. The question is whether the human mind would be capable, without the support of signs, of comprehending and remembering a complex story like that of the three youths in the oven (quite apart from the linguistic semiosis which the story itself contains in the form of *reported speech*) as a coherent whole.

[14]"Modi essendi seu proprietates rerum seu entium praecedunt modum intelligendi, sicut causa effectum. . . Modum autem intelligendi sequitur modus seu ratio signandi, quia prius intelligitur res et etiam concipitur antequam per vocem signetur quia voces sunt signa passionum. . . Modum autem signandi sequitur modus significandi sicut rem sequitur modus rei" (Sigerus de Cortraco [Siger von Kortrijk], see 1913: 93 f.).

up the treatment of the epistemological problem in ancient and medieval semiotics. The question reads: Does the sign match the thing? Negative findings were attributed to the inadequacy of language or classified as linguistic fictions (nominalism).[15]

Since Locke and Leibniz, the relationship between *modi intelligendi* and *modi signandi/significandi* has been reversed. First Locke drew attention to the role played by signs in the cognitive grasp of objects, whereupon Leibniz proposed that it was not designations as such but rather an ordered systematic mode of designation that paves the way for cognition. In medieval terminology, *modi significandi* act as *modi intelligendi*.

The reversal of the relation of foundedness between designating and knowing led to a revaluation of verbal and semiotic fictions. Fictions not directly matched by a perceivable reality or an intuitively accessible ideality were no longer shunned; on the contrary, they were thrust into the foreground as constructions furthering cognition. A theoretical grasp of relations between perceivable and concrete data is in many cases possible only with such constructions..

The mathematician Lambert was the first to succeed in proving the consistency of non-Euclidean geometry. As a semiotician, he was no longer concerned with the immediate evidence of his theses. He was content with a sign system built upon "secure rules". Society now systematically exploits or reveals this insight into the dependence of consciousness on the so-called external designation. The language of advertising and politics provide the most striking illustrations. In West Germany, not only those who were actually driven out by Soviet occupation but refugees who fled in anticipation of possible banishment are officially registered as expellees. Thus, they profit from the moral justification of compulsory displacement and from the social status and economic privileges of genuine expellees. East Germany, on the other hand, seeks to suppress the negative experiences of the past by underscoring the current status of this group with the designation "new settlers" or "new citizens."[16]

This point is well illustrated by the Jew in Max Frisch's *Andorra* (1961). A foundling is thought by the people of Andorra to be a Jew. As the play progresses, the connotations typically associated with this designation in anti-semitic circles are projected onto him, until he finally begins to behave accordingly, displaying a sharp intellect, lack of warmth and trust,

---

[15]Locke retains this orientation in Book III of his *Essay*. The direction semiotics has taken in modern times, however, does not spring from Book III but rather from the chapter on the idea of numbers in Book II.

[16]This example is taken from Lübbe, 1975: 141 ff.

obsession with money, broken relationship with native country, etc. After
he has been murdered, the people of Andorra learn that he was not a Jew
after all. The image one has of a person itself creates what it claims only to
reproduce.

Science treats its linguistic constructions as such and usually considers
their existence justified exclusively by the instrumental value of indirectly
mediated cognition. Language coiners in the political and business worlds,
on the other hand, adhere *bona sive male fide* to pre-contemporary semiotics
according to which signs merely provide names for that which by its nature
is accessible through preverbal channels as well.

2.   *The semiotic transformation of philosophy*

In view of the pragmatic evaluations of semiotics, the philosopher is
confronted with two questions: 1) Is all cognition mediated semiotically
or are there regions directly accessible to us, such as perception? 2) What
about signs themselves? Are systems and means of designation given to us
as a neurological-physiological mechanism, as a habitus—in Ryle's nomenclature a *knowing how* or in Husserl's nomenclature an *anonymously
functioning intentionality*—in any case, as something of which we have no
direct, objective knowledge (knowing that)? The extent of the proposed
semiotic transformation of philosophy depends on the reply to the first
question; its radicality on the reply to the second.

The development of Husserlian philosophy may serve as a guide in
answering these questions. Husserl's *Philosophy of Arithmetic* (1891) is
perhaps the most comprehensive study on the semiotic conception of the
idea of number as launched by Locke and Leibniz. Ten years afterward in
his *Logical Investigations* (1901), Husserl astonished his teacher, Brentano
(and probably still astonishes anyone aware of the significance of sign
systems for cognition), by advancing a theory of cognition with Platonic
undertones focused exclusively on immediate insight into the essence of
things and "state of affairs" *(Sachverhalte)*. Toward the end of his life,
he wrote a highly stimulating essay entitled—upon posthumous publication
in 1939—"On the Origins of Geometry". Therein he takes up ideas first
advanced by Locke (cf. 1690: § 4.1.8.) and Leibniz on the inevitability of
complementing intuitive knowledge by symbolic knowledge in the progress
of science: advances in knowledge, made by such highly developed sciences
as mathematics, are intrinsically bound up with a successive semiotization
and thus with the sedimentation of antecedent intuitive cognitive steps
removed from direct evidence.

This position in this essay is a development and extension of his original position, but neither here nor in his *Philosophy of Arithmetic* does he
subscribe to an absolute semioticism. The mode of numerical cognition can
be divided into three stages. The smallest whole numbers (a maximum of

twelve, according to 1891:250) are accessible to us by direct intuition. The genesis of this direct intuition of numbers, however, rests on the sensory perception of objects. In other words, cognition is possible without the mediation of signs but not without a sensory base as a point of departure. Thus, the thesis of a direct intuition of ideal objects such as numbers is relative although neither the inner structure nor the spatial-temporal order of the sensory substratum plays a constitutive role. Once number concepts have been abstracted, the sensory substratum can be dispensed with. The constitution of higher numbers, as we have said, requires systematic semiotic mediation.

Between the intuitive and the semiotic grasp of numbers, there lies an intermediate mode of cognition which rests on a figurative moment or, in the more familiar terminology of Gestalt psychology, on a Gestalt quality. A specific Gestalt quality enables us to grasp a multiplicity of concrete objetcs without actually counting them, such as a lane of trees, a row of columns, or a flock of birds; likewise, we can estimate a set of numbers on the basis of figural moment. However, according to Husserl, we cannot make accurate judgments beyond a set of five elements. Other authors increase this limit to an average of twenty and, in special cases, e.g. with dice or dominoes, experienced people are said to grasp up to forty units at a glance. Figural moments belong to the psychological aspect of numerical ideas while semiotic apprehension is based on their logical aspect (Husserl, 1891: 244 f., 287 ff.).

Husserl's rejection of his seemingly modern operationalist conception of mathematical cognition, according to which mathematical entities and operations are founded in an appropriate mode of designation, was apparently motivated by the insight that the mode of designation itself must be systematic and rule-governed, i.e. that it rests on a cognition whose fundament is a direct act of evidence, an intuitive datum.[17] Furthermore, the application of Husserl's analyses of consciousness from mathematics and logic to all fields of cognition reveals that perception, i.e. the fundamental form of consciousness, can be taken neither as a (mere) consciousness of

[17]This line of thought is clearly expressed in a critical letter from Brentano to Husserl (9.1.1905): "Is not the discovery of differential calculus also and especially the discovery of a methodological procedure, so that even the positive determination of a certain mode of designation by Leibniz, superior to that of Newton, proved a great step forward? Even the invention of the computers could be included.–True, one does not simply learn to add, one also learns individual laws of the equation of several addends with one sum, e.g. $2 + 5 = 7 . . .$ " Husserl's transcendence of Brentano's semiotic operationalism could be compared with Carnap's later transcendence of Bridgman's metric operationalism. The designation and measurement of data are preceded by a "theoretical" conception of data which yields the framework for possible operationalizations.

signs or pictures nor as an objective interpreting of several data.

In a picture, appearance and that which appears are not the same. The red paint on the canvas is not a property, a part of the rose depicted there. When I look at the real rose, however, the color in which it appears to me is a part of it without which it would not be what it is (and not merely a sign for a property not perceived directly. A thing is given (although never completely) in the perception of its appearance and not signified as something that is "in itself" independent of its appearances (Husserl, 1931: 99).

The naive mephenomenological concept of perception as an objective interpretation of sense data, i.e. as a semiotic act, is based on the contradictory notion of amorphous sense data. Form is intrinsic to the most primitive sensory data, even if it is only the formal relation of difference between figure and background. It is not the result of an interpretive act. The data of a field of perception refer to each other intentionally through the associative relations of similarity, contiguity, and contrast. On the basis of this network of references, they form manifold phenomenal entities. Associative references are not semiotic relations; they only constitute the basis for potential semiotic relations. A house refers to the village in which it appears, but this does not mean that it functions *ipso facto* as sign for the village. Nor do disconnected straight lines placed more or less at angles of 45° become a triangle because of an innate idea which enables the percipient to interpret the straight lines as sides of a triangle. Lines refer beyond themselves. The tendency to extend beyond their ends is intrinsic to their perception. Similarly, the Gestalt tendency to become a closed figure is intrinsic to open figures such as loosely disconnected lines. The shaping of perception is never primarily a matter of intellectual interpretation (Holenstein, 1972a: 146, 294).

Husserl's reasons for maintaining a cautious attitude toward semiotics are supplemented today by a third reason for approaching a semiotic transformation with reserve, a reason deriving, surprisingly enough, from the philosophy of language. Speech-act theory cleared new territory for semantics by questioning the classical conception of meaning. Besides the designative functions of naming and describing, verbal utterances can also order, ask, promise, greet, etc. There are verbal utterances whose primary function consists of constituting a social situation. Nevertheless, even when the foremost intention of a performative utterance such as "I promise to come" is a social commitment, it still involves a designation, albeit an unusual one, namely an auto-reference. The performative utterance designates at the same time that which it constitutes. In this respect, it is similar to numerical designations through which higher numbers acquire an intersubjectively accessible existence.

In his later work, Husserl increasingly reflected upon the gaps in the evidence with which theoretical states of affairs are given to us. He returned to Locke's insight (although he does not expressly mention him) that a highly developed science such as geometry would be impossible if at every stage of research we wanted to reactivate in full evidence all the preceding stages. Since a higher-leveled problematic not only succeeds earlier phases but is also founded in them, it necessarily shares their deficiencies in evidence (Husserl, 1939: 373).

The entwinement of directly intuitive and semiotically transmitted cognition applies, in my opinion, not only to highly developed sciences but also to perception and motor action, upon which the opponents of a wholly linguistic conception of human consciousness and correspondingly a semiotic-linguistic transformation of philosophy base their arguments. Illustrations of a partial precedence and independence of perception and action over language are not hard to find. The obvious asymmetry between polar terms such as "up/down," "front/back," and "right/left" corresponds to an equally obvious asymmetry in the fields of perception and action. Something that is up is generally more visible and more mobile. What lies down below the surface of the earth is out of sight. In terms of visibility and availability, what is in front also has precedence over what is in back. And finally, most people seem more comfortable using the right hand than the left. In a metaphorical context, the spatial terms "up", "front", and "right" rather than "down", "back", or "left" are used in positive statements. A participant in a contest who chooses the right direction may come out in front and on top (up). A person with two "left feet" falls back(wards) and down.

The dependence of mathematical insights on action or rather acts of coordinated behavior is strikingly illustrated by Piaget's (1970) example of a mathematician's childhood discovery. The child had lined up a number of pebbles and was astonished to find that there were always ten pebbles whether he counted them from right to left or from left to right. Thereupon he arranged them in a circle and again counted the pebbles in both directions. There were still ten. The number remained constant no matter how he arranged the stones. Thus, through a series of actions, the young mathematician had discovered the law of commutativity, namely that the sum is independent of the order of its elements.

This process is imbued with semiotics. 1. Probably even a trained intuition can grasp a number of only ten units without a numerical sign, under optimal conditions. The optimal conditions are not likely to be fulfilled when a comparison of several counts is involved rather than the mere grasp of one isolated numerical set. 2. Instead of counting arrangements of pebbles appearing in the perceptual field simultaneously, successive arrangements of pebbles were compared with each other. A directly given arrangement is confronted with others given indirectly in memory or in planificatory anticipation, i.e. semiotically, as a (mental) scheme (perhaps even more abstractly but nonetheless semiotically, in the form of a rule of spatial arrangement). 3. The conclusion is generalized. The various arrangements are taken to represent x possible arrangements.

Without a project or semiotic anticipation, we are capable of only the simplest actions, namely those triggered by the objects of perception through reflexes or association. In their study of children with speech impediments, Luria and Yudovich (1968) demonstrate that children cannot handle behavioral sequences of any length unless they are—in this particular case—linguistically able to formulate a strategy. Action becomes a graduated unfolding of a plan. The individual objects are no longer subjected to random treatment depending on the momentary situation in which they enter the child's field of vision. Rather, the objects preserve a constant meaning throughout the duration of the action. Their meaning does not depend on the immediate phase of action but rather on the entire project. (Blocks, for example, are not put away because the act of throwing them is in itself pleasurable, but in order to make room to set up a train). The progress of the action is constantly checked and evaluated in terms of the project. ("Is the tunnel dark inside?" "No, it isn't dark enough," etc.)

It is more difficult to determine to what extent perceptions are mediated semiotically. The difference in describing a picture—the linguistically underdeveloped child merely names some of the objects in it, while his more skilled counterpart describes the states of affairs that he perceives (*ibid.*)—does not necessairily indicate progress in perception. It testifies above all to progress in the mastery of descriptive means.

The benefit of verbal predication as well as of the algebraic equation lies not so much in a faithful record of perception as it does in enabling us to depart from perception by transforming its structure and varying its elements. Instead of saying "Saint Christopher carries the child," I can say "The child is carried by Saint Christopher"; instead of "across the river", I can say "across the street". Semiotic formulation affects perception, as may be assumed, by passively yielding greater receptiveness to unexpected variations and actively stimulating imaginary modifications of the field of perception.

If we wish to adhere to the insightfulness of our own use of signs, then a transcendental, i.e. cognitive, phenomenological transformation of semiotics is quite as urgent as postulating a semiotic transformation of transcendental philosophy. On the other hand, investigations such as those by Luria and Yudovich demonstrate the need for caution in proclaiming the existence of domains that are "non-verbal", as Husserl did of perception, Piaget of behavior, and hermeneutics (Ricoeur, 1974: 21) of art and play. The borderline in all these fields between a purely intuitive and a semiotic-linguistically mediated performance of constitution still remains to be found. There is much that indicates not only a fluid borderline but also one that is drawn very early.

3.   The planificatory function of signs

I started out with signs whose primary function lies in constituting cognitive entities such as numbers. In the course of the reflections, brief mention was made of signs such as promises and declarations, whose primary function lies in instituting social relations. Finally, a third function of signs was discussed, the planning of actions. This leads us to the current philosophical tendency to focus less on the theoretical questions posed at the beginning of this paper, "What can we know?" and "How do we acquire knowledge?" and more on the pragmatic interests and consequences of knowledge. Linguistic theory is exploring the implications of the speech act for the addresser and its effects on the addressee of the message. The elucidation of the semiotic implications of praxis seems to me, however, still more fruitful than the elucidation of the pragmatic implications of semiotics. The way for such research has been paved by Soviet Russian psycholinguistics and the cybernetic sciences from automata theory to biology.

A productive approach to this topic is supplied by a phenomenon neglected by current theories of praxis, namely apraxia. The studies on aphasia, that have proved to be so illuminating for a general theory of language should stimulate increased investigation of apraxia. In motor apraxia, as opposed to paralysis, physical mobility remains intact. Unlike agnostically disturbed behavior, in which the projective representation of the action to be performed is impaired, we can find cases of apraxia in the narrow sense of the word which manifest a perfectly intact "ideational preparation of action." One of the apraxia specialist H. Liepmann's (1905) patients was able to execute an action with his left hand that he could not perform with his right. He was also able to formulate and communicate his representation of the action ("the formula of movement"). Liepmann explains this disability as a deficiency of automatic movements normally triggered by intermediate imaginations of a goal. This explanation leads Merleau-Ponty (1945: 161) to criticize classical theories of action for their intellectualism. Not every anticipation of an action need take the shape of a representation before it becomes automatic. According to Merleau-Ponty, Liepmann's patients suffer from an impaired motor intentionality which he describes as "being in the world". In the interests of clarity, one should, in my opinion, dispense with the terminology of existential philosophy. Liepmann's patient suffers from a deficiency of associative references. Every sense datum points beyond itself to its environment and thus motivates our vision or our motor organs to attend to this environment (Holenstein, 1972: 116). In fact every movement points beyond itself to a potential continuation.

The analysis of this case of apraxia and Merleau-Ponty's charge of intellectualism reveal a distinction vital to semiotics. I would call intellectualistic a semiotics that interprets all associative references as a relation between a signum and a signatum (and empiricist a semiotics that reduces all relations to a merely associative relation). Black refers to white by association, without, however, functioning as a sign for white. Associative references found and motivate sign relations, but not every reference is *ipso facto* a sign as well. A sign relation consists of the intentional representation of one entity by another.[18]

Premack's (1971: 817) now famous chimpanzee Sarah matches up both the plastic chip that she has learned means apple and the apple itself with the pieces of plastic for red (vs. green) and round (vs. square), although the plastic chip for apple is neither round nor red; it is a blue triangle. She has grasped that something with the physical properties of other things is not to be taken as a thing with these properties, but rather as a representation of something else, i.e. as (word)-sign. She seems to have learned that there are categorial distinctions based not on the physical properties of things but on their use—in this case, their highly abstract use as signs.

The criterion for determining that something is acting as a sign is not individual introspection but an intersubjectively observable substitution. What is to guarantee, however, that Premack's chimpanzee has not simply been conditioned to produce the same response to the sign for apple as to the apple itself, just as Pavlov's dog learned to react to a light signal in the same way as to food? Unequivocal proof of genuine understanding rather than mere associative transferral can only be supplied by the use of compound signs, which can be exchanged for other, differently structured signs according to certain laws of transformation. The structure of signs is not significant in the substitution of one simple sign for another ("autumn"—"fall"). For compound signs, however, structure is the decisive factor in determining the admissibility of a substitution. A child cannot grasp that a cube measuring 2 x 4 x 6 cm has the same volume as one measuring 2 x 3 x 8 cm, until he has mastered and comprehended the rules governing the relations between the properties of the cube—its length, width, height—and that the shortening of one dimension is compensated by the lengthening of another. Similarly, he demonstrates his understanding of a sentence by ad-

[18]"A l'intention d'une Psyché s'est substituée la traduction d'un message" (Jacob, 1970: 10).

mitting only those modifications that preserve its meaning ("a is larger than b"–"b is smaller than a"-"a surpasses b in size," etc.). The modification of one element implies rule-governed modifications of other elements. Compound signs are understood when the rules governing their translation into each other are mastered and when the relations governing the individual elements of a sign system are grasped.

Understanding must not be misconstrued as a static grasp of relations. A relation is not grasped in isolation but only as part of a more comprehensive relation, as congruent with an identical relation, or in contrast to a different relation. Thus even the introduction of simple signs involves acts of translation. The referent is usually entwined with something else that could be intended with the same pointing of one's finger or the same iconic representation. Indeterminacy can be reduced by positive and negative definitions and circumscriptions: "That is red. 'Red' does not designate a spatial extension. 'Red' is a color."–"The photograph in the hairdresser's window depicts the hairdo in fashion and not the person modelling it."

Intralingual transformations are as well as interlingual translations usually involve a slight shift in meaning. Correspondingly, the mere mastery of all possible transformations does not suffice for the complete understanding of a sentence. Total understanding is demonstrated by the ability to comment upon the extent of the semantic shift in such transformations or by the situationally appropriate use of transformations.

By substituting "translatable" as the determination of the *signatum* for the classical determination "intelligible", as suggested by Jakobson (1965d: 345) following Peirce (1931: §4. 127), a semiotic conception of understanding replaces the mentalist conception, which has been explicated psychologically as empathy and biologically as assimilation. Understanding thus becomes an intersubjectively accessible operation.

Significantly, not only the transcendental-hermeneutic concept of understanding is explicated as translation but another fundamental concept as well, the concept of life,[19] neglected by philosophy since Bergson and Driesch.

Molecular biology has extricated two processes basic to all life. According to the one process, a nucleotide sequence which specifies a gene is replicated when two strands of the sequence along which the nucleotides are arranged in a rigorously complementary order split, whereupon the unit complementary to each nucleotide is reconstituted. This replication, a tautological repetition, underlies the stability of the species, which often

---

[19]For some additional aspects of a semiotic restructuration of philosophy, see Holenstein (1976: 134 ff.).

spans millions of years. According to the other process, genetic information consisting of the arrangement of nucleotides in groups (words) of three units each (letters) is translated into a sequence of amino acids, the building blocks of proteins, by pairing each triplet (word) of the nucleic sequence with a specific protein unit. These so-called codons, consisting of three nucleotide bases, obey "syntactic" laws of distribution in forming more complex units, cistrons and operons, whose start and end are marked by three special codons with no corresponding amino acid, comparable to the delimitative devices well known in phonology since Trubetzkoy (Monod, 1970: 119 f.; Jakobson, 1974: 51).

The build-up of the organism as a whole is ultimately regulated by the genetic information contained in the composition of the amino acid sequences in proteins. In contrast to a machine whose design depends upon the planning of an independent mind and the action of external forces, a living being is created by an autonomous, self-regulating morphogenesis.

In addition to regulation through protein structure, upon which all is founded, there are constantly new self-regulating homeostatic processes on the macroscopic levels of biology such as physiological homeostasis in the maintenance of a constant body temperature or, on a still higher level, ecological homeostasis in the oscillation of the population of predatory animals and their victims. These homeostatic processes can be devided into two subprocesses, i.e. into two distinct effects. The primary process results in the production of something, warmth for instance. The secondary process, seen in isolation, can also be described as production. In a homeostatically regulated heating element for example, it can be described as the thermodynamic expansion of a chemical substance, which at a certain point of expansion triggers a mechanical process that in turn influences the main process by stopping or accelerating it. Instead of describing this performance as thermodynamic and mechanical production, it can from a holistic and teleonomic point of view be described as "control", as a process that regulates the main process according to a functionally more or less meaningful program.

In contrast to conscious behavior, biological processes of a homeostatic nature make no distinction between the signs in which the information for executing a process is constituted and the process itself. The information is already translated in the arrangement itself, i.e. in the course of a process, as in a paternal slap in which communication of what the son deserves and the execution of the punishment coincide. The son can deduce the "message" transmitted by his father only after the fact from the act itself. Likewise, in the case of physiological homeostasis, science can derive the "information" transmitted to the heating agent by the biological process that functions as a "thermostat" only after the fact from the effect of the thermostat on the heat source.

Processes of understanding and life processes can both be explicated as translation. The differences, however, must not be obscured.

Understanding is an intentional process. The translation, as which it can be defined, is reversible, unlimited and non-arbitrary. "A is larger than b" can be translated into "b is smaller than a" and conversely. There is no limit to the possible circumscriptions of these sentences. On the other hand, translation is not random; it is bound to the semantic content of the sentence and its components.

The process defined as translation in molecular biology is purely mechanical. On the whole, biologists hold that translation is irreversible, finite and arbitrary. There is no process in which a certain arrangement of proteins can ever act in reverse upon the arrangement of nucleic units. Corresponding to each nucleic unit there is only one single protein unit and not a chain of possible alternative translations. There is no chemical reason in the form of a steric affinity for pairing a nucleic unit with one particular protein unit and no other. Thus, phonological theories of word formation and word assignment are a more suitable model for the process of translation in molecular biology than the processes explicated on the linguistic level as translation and transformation. The formation and assignment of words is basically arbitrary. The fact that an oak tree is called an oak and not a maple is not based on any affinity between the designated tree and the phonemic elements that constitute the word "oak".

Homeostatic processes of feedback are also mechanical processes that are finite inasmuch as closed, merely repetitive operations are involved, and arbitrary (according to prevalent opinion) inasmuch as they owe their genesis to chance and merely their continued existence to the functional advantage they have to offer.

* * *

Modern philosophy was motivated to explore semiotics by the discovery of the cognitive function of signs, their ability to promote, extend, and pinpoint knowledge. In current scientific theory, a different function of signs has come to dominate: the planning and control of actions.

In modern times, the natural sciences have prevailed in the philosophy of science imposing their models on the humanities.

With the planning and control function of signs, a semiotic discipline has become the first of the humanities to reverse this relation of foundedness and to supply a humanist model as the base for several natural sciences and technical disciplines. This radical change in turn had a liberating effect on the humanities themselves. The computer sciences had no small influence on the supersession of behaviorism by cognitive psychology (Neisser, 1967: 8 f.). Their highly differentiated, non-mechanical notion of the machine proved a fruitful model for the operation of the human mind, of which it was originally a rough copy. Computers are physical systems whose operation leads not only to processes which, being physical achievements, can be described in physical language, but they also lead to processes which can be described in humanist language as elaborations of information and as control of behavior. As in phonology with its distinction between *phonetics*, which investigates the physical and physiological properties of sounds, and *phonemics*, whose target is their linguistic function, the computer sciences can distinguish between an *etic* discipline aimed at the physico-mechanical aspects of the computer and an *emic* discipline aimed at its computing performance.

We must not forget that the transmission of information in self-regulating systems is achieved by totally mechanical means. Viewed in isolation, the informational process is mechano-causal; only the holistic, teleonomic concept of its function is revolutionary. Furthermore, as already mentioned, current biological theory holds that teleonomic processes, inasmuch as they can be found in nature and do not have their source in human production, like automatic machines, are of completely and utterly fortuitous origin. Nevertheless, the humanist who believes in the primacy of Gestalt (form) and meaning (function) over mechanical causality may be consoled—and encouraged—by the fact that apparently even in the realm of nature, "creations" distinguished by perfection of form and high sensefulness are superior to other formations which make no contribution to increased order in the cosmos. The criterion for selection in a fortuitously initiated evolution is functionality.

Appendix

What still remains to be clarified is the role of the communicative function. The communicative function appears as an independent function when signs are posited for no other purpose than to establish or prolong contact between addresser and addressee (Malinowski's phatic function). However, it can also be of service to other functions. Semiotic communication offers considerable advantages on both the cognitive and planificatory-cybernetic planes.

On the cognitive plane, it has been shown that higher-level cognitions require the semiotic presentiation of the cognitions upon which they are founded. Through intersubjective written and oral communication, scientists have access to semiotic versions of sciences, upon which they can build directly without having to find and follow the long path of scientific development themselves. When a scholar wishes to check the path already cleared by science, the semiotically transmitted tradition provides him with one clue after the other on how to "bundle" the infinite multiplicities encountered in perception and thought to the best advantage.

On the planificatory-cybernetic plane, a more primal form of communication, sexuality; can demonstrate the role of semiotic-verbal communication. Before sexuality appears in evolution, every genetic program is a faithful copy of one single program, from which it has split off and according to which it regenerates itself. The possibility of variation is restricted to mutations determined by the accumulation of quanta-like disturbances. With obligatory sexual reproduction, variation becomes integrated into programming. Every new program springs from the combination of two older programs. With each new generation, new combinations are not only possible, but compulsory (Jacob, 1970: 330 f.). Similarly, linguistic communication can yield a wealth of new programs, which would be unthinkable without it. In contrast to sexual communication, its realisation is voluntary; and not every realisation represents a gain. In contrast to nature, the mind recoils from disastrous realisations.

For the philosopher, the subordination of the communicative function to the cognitive and planificatory-cybernetic functions cannot be the final word. The ultimate aim of all human activity is the human subject or rather the communicating society of human beings. This hierarchy explains the repugnance towards realizable but disastrous programs of action. With the subordination of the other two functions, communication becomes *meaningful* and is no longer mere contact for the sake of contact as in the exclusively phatic function of language.

On the genetic plane, the communicative function also holds first plane. The primary motive for learning language is its suitability as a means of contact and communication. But very early, already in the so-called egocentric language of the child, the cognitive and planificatory function becomes evident as an increasingly independent aspect of language. It has been demonstrated that the child uses language more and more for the cognitive and planificatory mastery of a task when difficulties emerge demanding conscious insight and deliberation. Egocentric language is still closely connected with communicative language, of which it is an offshoot. It resembles communicative language as far as vocalization and grammatical structure are concerned and usually occurs only in the presence of other people who, it is assumed, understand the utterances. Egocentric language is then gradually internalized and ultimately replaced by inner language at about the age of seven. Compared with external language, inner language displays an extremely elliptical structure on the phonological and grammatical levels (Vygotsky, 1934).

REFERENCES

Apel, Karl-Otto. 1973. *Transformation der Philosophie* II, Frankfurt/Main: Suhrkamp.

Augustinus. 1952. *De Magistro: Oeuvres de Saint Augustin*, vol. VI, ed. F.J. Thonnard, Paris: Desclée De Brouwer, 14-121.

Bolzano, Bernhard, 1837, *Wissenschaftslehre*, 4 Bände, Sulzbach: Seidel.

Brentano, Franz. 1905. Letter to Edmund Husserl, in *Wahrheit und Evidenz*. Leipzig: Meiner, 1930. 153-159.

Bruner, Jerome S. 1964. "Going beyond the information given," *Contemporary Approaches to Cognition*, Cambridge, Mass.: Harvard University Press, 41-69.

Carnap, Rudolf. 1928. *Der logische Aufbau der Welt*, Hamburg: Meiner, 1962, 2. Auflage.

Condillac, Etienne Bonnot de. 1746. *Essai sur l'origine des connaissances humaines: Oeuvres philosophiques*, ed. G. Le Roy, Paris: PUF, 1947, vol. I, 1-118.

Coseriu, Eugenio. 1968. *Die Geschichte der Sprachphilosophie von der Antike bis zur Gegenwart*, Tübingen: Tübinger Beiträge zur Linguistik.

Frisch, Max. 1961. *Andorra*, Frankfurt/Main: Suhrkamp.

Gomperz, Heinrich. 1908. *Weltanschauungslehre* II, *Noologie*, Jena.

Holenstein, Elmar. 1972. *Phänomenologie der Assoziation*, Den Haag: Nijhoff.

_____ . 1974. "A new essay concerning the basic relations of language," *Semiotica* 12, 97-127.

_____ . 1976. *Linguistik, Semiotik, Hermeneutik*, Frankfurt: Suhrkamp.

Husserl, Edmund. 1890. "Zur Logik der Zeichen (Semiotik)," *Husserliana*, Band XII, Den Haag: Nijhoff, 1970, 340-373.

_____ . 1891. *Philosophie der Arithmetik: Husserliana* XII, Den Haag: Nijhoff, 1970.

_____ . 1901. *Logische Untersuchungen*, Teil II, Halle: Niemeyer, 1. Auflage.

_____ . 1913. *Ideen zu einer reinen Phänomenologie und phänomenologischen Philosophie* I: Husserliana *III, Den Haag: Nijhoff, 1950.*

_____ . 1939. "Vom Ursprung der Geometrie,"*Husserliana* VI, Den Haag: Nijhoff, 1954, 365-386.

Jacob, François. 1970. *La Logique du vivant*, Paris: Gallimard.

Jakobson, Roman. 1965. "Quest for the essence of language," *Selected Writings* II, The Hague: Mouton, 345-359.

_____ . 1974. *Main Trends in the Science of Language*, New York: Harper & Row.

_____ . 1975. Coup d'oeil sur le développement de la sémiotique, (Rapport à l'ouverture du Premier Congrès de l'Association Internationale de Semiotique, Milan, 2 juin 1974), Bloomington, Ind.: Indiana University.

Lambert, Johann Heinrich. 1764. *Neues Organon: Philosophische Schriften* I-II, Hildesheim: Olms, 1965, (Reprint of Leipzig edition, 1764).

Leibniz, Gottfried W. 1765. *Nouveaux essais sur l'entendement humain: Die philosophische Schriften* V, hg. von C.J. Gebhardt, Berlin: Weidmann, 1882.

Liepmann, H. 1905. *Ueber Störungen des Handelns bei Gehirnkranken*, Berlin: Karger.

Locke, John. 1690. *An Essay Concerning Human Understanding*, ed. Alexander Campell Fraser, New York: Dover, 1959.

Lubbe, Hermann. 1975. "Sein und Heissen," *Fortschritt als Orientierungsproblem*, Freiburg/Breisgau: Rombach, 134-153.

Luria, Alexandr R., and F. La Yudovich. 1968. *Speech and the development of mental processes in the child*, London: Staples Press.

Merleau-Ponty, Maurice. 1945. *Phénoménologie de la perception*, Paris: Gallimard.

Monod, Jacques. 1970. *Le hasard et la nécessité*, Paris: Seuil.

Neisser, Ulrich. 1967. *Cognitive Psychology*. New York: Appelton.

Peirce, Charles Sanders. 1931 ff., *Collected Papers*, Cambridge, Mass.: Harvard University Press.

Piaget, Jean. 1970. *Genetic Epistemology*, New York. Columbia University Press.

Premack, David. 1971. "Language in chimpanzee?" *Science* 172, 808-822.

Proclus. 1908. *Procli Diadochi in Platonis Cartylum Commentaria*, ed. Georgius Pasquali, Leipzig: Teubner.

Ricoeur, Paul. 1975. "Phénoménologie et herméneutique," (Paper read at the International Phenomenological Study Days in Berlin).

Ryle, Gilbert. 1974. "Mogli in Babel," *Philosophy* 49, 5-11.

Sigerus de Cortraco. 1913. *Summa Modorum Significandi: Les oeuvres de Siger de Coutrai*, éd. G. Wallerand, Louvain: Institut Supérieur de Philosophie de l'Université, 93-125.

Tillman, Frank. 1967. "Transcendental phenomenology and analytic philosophy," *International Philosophical Quarterly* 7, 31-40.

Vygotsky, Lev S. 1934. *Thought and Language,* Cambridge, Mass.: MIT Press, 1962.

Wolff, Christian. 1719. *Vernunfftige Gedancken von Gott, der Welt und der Seele des Menschen,* Frankfurt und Leipzig.

_____ . 1729. , *Philosophia prima sive Ontologia,* Frankfurt und Leipzig.

_____ . 1733. *Der vernünfftigen Gedancken von Gott, der Welt und der Seele des Menschen und auch allen Dingen überhaupt Anderer Theil,* Frankfurt am Mayn, 3. Auflage.

WILLIAM DWIGHT WHITNEY AND THE ORIGINS OF SEMIOTICS

Richard W. Bailey

New disciplines, or even new approaches to old intellectual problems, may appeal for their sanction to revolution or to reverence for earlier scholars unjustly neglected. In either case, proponents of the new tend to re-write their history, scourging the acknowledged masters (exemplified in Chomsky's treatment of Bloomfield or in Culler's of Jakobson) or identifying respectable but heretofore unacknowledged antecedents who lend sanction to the new formulation (exemplified in Robin Lakoff's rediscovery of Sanctius or in E.F.K. Koerner's revival of Saussure). Whichever the strategy, the result is likely to be the same: the historical context is distorted as the passion of advocacy submerges concern for historicity.

Semiotics, for instance, is neither as revolutionary nor as continuous with earlier work as various ones of its proponents sometimes argue. Its analytic methods find their roots in pragmatic philosophy and general linguistics, and its theoretical preoccupations in the nominalist-realist controversy of scholasticism. As a discipline, it emerges in a time when the politics of university appointments and of research grants is especially sympathetic to supposedly interdisciplinary teaching and study. By incorporating the social context of sign-making, semiotics acknowledges belief without requiring commitment to a particular ideology; by recognizing the similarity of such disparate phenomena as the genetic code, folk art, and social behavior, it appeals to persons discontented with the traditional paradigms of the intellectual life. Perhaps as a natural consequence, semiotics today is characterized by theoretical reflexivity and a preoccupation with arguments over principles rather than a dedication to empirical application, and its advocates too often postpone investigation of sign systems in favor of immediate refinement of semiotics itself.

In such circumstances, the achievement of William Dwight Whitney (1827-1894) is worthy of attention. Not only was Whitney among the first to establish the modern foundations of linguistic theory, but he also provides an instructive example for working out the consequences of theoretical principles in concrete analysis. Until very recently, however, his contributions have been neglected or viewed only as they appear to anticipate current trends. McCawley, for instance, has found intimations of the concept of the cyclic application of phonological rules in Whitney's *Sanskrit Grammar* (McCawley 1967) and in his work on English grammar has discovered an "implicit conception of syntax" involving base rules and transformations (McCawley 1973:566).[1] On the other hand, a monograph-length treatment of American structuralism includes only parenthetical mention of Whitney's work, despite his justifiably revered reputation abroad among the founders of that approach to language (Hymes and Fought 1975). Within the framework of semiotics, in which human language is but a special case of a sign system, Whitney's contributions are both interesting as history and instructive as a guide to further research.

Born in Northhampton, Massachusetts, Whitney came from a particularly American intellectual community, the home in earlier generations of Jonathan Edwards and the first Timothy Dwight. With his brothers and sister, he became one of the ornaments of nineteenth-century academic life. His siblings occupied posts at Harvard, the Boston Public Library, and Beloit and Smith Colleges; from 1849 until his death, Whitney himself was associated with Yale University. Thanks to a collection of books brought from Germany by his older brother, Whitney began his study of comparative philology and Sanskrit as a youth at home in private reading, and he carried Bopp's grammar with him on a geological expedition into the wilds of Lake Superior shore. From 1850 to 1853, he studied with Weber, Bopp, and Lepsius in Berlin and with von Roth in Tübingen (with the latter he was to edit and publish the *Atharva-Veda*). A first-hand recollection of Whitney's days as a student in Germany gives an amusing and insightful view of the mixture of American virtues and German scholarship that formed the basis of his intellectual career:

> Fraulein Schaal [daughter of Whitney's landlady during his studies at Tübingen] spoke of the delight her mother and herself had felt at the messages sent them by the professor who had become so celebrated, but who had not forgotten them, and showed the visitor Professor Whitney's room, all unchanged, a typical *Studentenzimmer*; in the middle, a long plain table, and by it an uncushioned armchair. That, said she, was Professor Whitney's chair, and in it he used to sit for hours at that table, almost without moving. When he moved the chair more than a little, I knew that it was time for me to take him his mug of beer, and perchance a bit of bread. As a very small girl then, I wondered at the table, which was covered with little

---

[1] Although I have not been able to obtain the articles by Popa-Tomescu (1970, 1971), she appears to be another who views Whitney selectively as a pre-modernist.

bits of paper, which he had arranged in a certain order, and was very particular that no one should disturb. The only adornment which he had in the room was an American flag draped over the mirror; and on the Fourth of July he said he would work an hour less than usual, as it was the anniversary of American independence (Lanman 1987:437).

The traits epitomized in this anecdote—hard work, patience, attention to detail, and patriotism—characterized Whitney's life as a scholar, and they were attributes he passed on to his students. Yet they are also incidental since his influence was characteristic of neither the speculative nor the empirical traditions of America and Germany; instead, he was the first American to be engaged fully as an international in linguistic debate, and he was able to persuade others to accept the principles which, having become almost universally accepted in general linguistics, promise now to extend their influence to semiotics. As Ferdinand de Saussure wrote in a manuscript essay composed as a memorial to Whitney: "What Whitney first did in 1867, as it is universally recognized, has not been rendered void in 1894. That is a fact more instructive than much commentary, one to serve as a touchstone in the appraisal of a thinker" (quoted by Jakobson 1971:xxxii).

Whitney's scholarship continues to have influence today—directly through his *Sanskrit Grammar* (1879) and through the *Century Dictionary* (1889-91), and less directly through the professional societies in which he was active: the American Philological Society, the American Oriental Society, the Modern Language Association, and the American Dialect Society. In his lifetime, he was known to the educated public through his English, German, and French grammars, and, especially, through a continuing and combative series of essays published in magazines of general circulation that were, among other subjects, devoted to correcting the linguistic speculations of Sir Frederich Max Müller of Oxford. Of all of these efforts, however, it was his two books devoted to principles of general linguistics that established his reputation among the theoreticians of language: *Language and the Study of Language* (1867; henceforward *LSL*) and *The Life and Growth of Language* (1875; *LGL*). The former consists of a series of lectures given first at the Smithsonian Institution and then at the Lowell Institution in Boston; the latter was conceived as a book for the general public—one that Whitney hoped would also serve as an introductory book for university students. Both went through many editions. *Language and the Study of Language* was published in New York and London and, as each edition was sold, repeatedly reprinted; it was almost immediately translated into German and Dutch. *The Life and Growth of Language*, likewise popular in English, was translated into German, French, Italian, Dutch, and Swedish (Seymour 1894:418). These two works had a profound impact on the international community of scholarship and were particularly revered by Saussure. In particular, as Roman Jakobson has pointed out, Whitney's influence reached the other influential founders of structuralism as well, particularly Jan Baudoin de Courtenay, F.F. Fortunatov, and T.G. Masaryk. Curiously, as Jakobson also notes, "in his native country, the immediate impact of Whitney's contribution to the general science of language was far weaker" (Jakobson 1971: xliii).

In the mid-nineteenth century, Whitney had to contend not only with Biblical theories of the origin of diverse languages (illustrated by Noah Webster's etymologizing), but also with other doctrinaire views of the role of language in nature. "Words are signs of natural facts," Emerson wrote. "The use of natural history is to give us aid in supernatural history. The use of outer creation is to give us language for the beings and changes of inward creation" (Emerson 1836:1050). To such views, Whitney opposed a positivistic perspective: the question of the relation of language to some transcendent reality "will be readily settled (so far as it is capable of being settled at all) when the grand principles of linguistic philosophy are placed upon a firm basis, when it is no longer the case that even scholars of the highest rank are disagreed as to such points as the nature of language and its relations to the mind and to thought. . . and the relation of human expression to that of the lower animals" (Whitney 1870:280). Such a "firm basis," Whitney believed, would eventually be provided by empirical study of languages on scientific principles derived from language itself and from a thorough study of language in its social context.

Like his disciple, Saussure, Whitney saw the study of language as part of a larger investigation of a "sign-making faculty" (LSL, 103) typical of human beings. "In a wider and freer sense," he wrote in his second—and for Saussure, at least, his more influential—book, "everything that bodies forth thought and makes it apprehensible, in whatever way, is called language" (LGL, 1). And just as Saussure postponed the study of the "science that studies the life of signs within society" or "semiology" (Saussure 1915: 16), so too did Whitney restrict himself to the investigation of human languages. While he occasionally draws examples from a wider semiotic perspective—for instance, by citing the architecture of medieval cathedrals as a sign system—his use of such illustrations is only to remind his readers of parallels between language and other social systems of signs.

In his two books, as in many of his essays for general readers, Whitney again and again defines *language*, most commonly as "the means of expression of human thought" (LGL, 1), but often in more detail: language "is not a faculty, a capacity; it is not an immediate exertion of the thinking power; it is a mediate product and an instrumentality" (LGL, 278). By rejecting the definition of language as a psychological capacity, Whitney established principles to be elaborated in behaviorist and "mechanist" structuralism in the twentieth century. Yet what he hoped to do was to discriminate mental processes (which could be independent of language) from the specifically semiotic process of articulation. "Thought," in other words, is not the same thing as the "means of expression" of that thought. Though he gave language primary attention, he fully recognized that several types of "expression" are available to human beings: "gesture and grimace, pictorial or written signs, and uttered or spoken signs" (LGL, 2).

To regard the connection between thought and language as a "natural" one (as Müller did) would be for Whitney to violate the essential character of language, its arbitrary and conventional nature as a sign system. Yet he was also fully aware of the psychological dialectic between "conception" and "sign," and he regarded the process of fixing thought in language as central to the creative principle of human sign systems. Unlike the instinctive signs of animals, human semiotic processes involve individual creativity mediated by the social requirements of acceptable communication; "every item of knowledge and of self command that [the mind] conquers it fixes in assured position by means of language; and it is always reaching out for more knowledge, and gaining additional control of its powers, and fixing them in the same way" (LGL, 140).

In defining language as a "mediate product and instrumentality" of the mind, Whitney was careful to allow for individual creativity in sign-making and for the changes in sign systems typical of all human communities. At the same time, he was opposed to the notion of a sign-making capacity distinct from other mental processes:

> Nor is there any peculiar faculty of the mind, any linguistic instinct, or language-sense, or whatever else it may be called, involved in the process [of innovation]; this is simply the exercise in a particular direction of that great and composite faculty, than which no other is more characteristic of human reason, the faculty of adapting means to ends, of apprehending a desirable purpose and attaining to it (LGL, 145).

By detaching language from other human mental processes, scholars in Whitney's time found it difficult to describe the characteristics of the "language sense" they had isolated, and since experimental psychology had not yet emerged as a discipline, this sense could only be described through some set of principles of logic or reason that themselves had no basis in observed fact.

Whitney's solution to this dilemma was an empirical and even positivist one.[2] If language is the means by which "our inner consciousness is externized, turned up to the light for ourselves and others to see and study" (LGL, 304), then the focal task of linguistics must be the study of the data that can be observed. Unlike some of his structuralist successors, Whitney did not wish to postpone indefinitely the study of the underlying nature of the "sign-making faculty," but he expected to arrive at conclusions about its nature through the study of observed language behavior.

Even more important for the future of semiotics than his perception of language as an "instrumentality" was Whitney's notion of structure. In his view, the root comparisons compiled by his contemporaries in comparative philology were "worthless" (LGL, 268). Furthermore, "merely to classify, arrange, and set forth in order the phenomena of a spoken tongue, its significant material, usages and modes of expression, is grammar and lexicography, not linguistic science. The former state and prescribe only; the latter seeks to explain" (LSL, 25). Though as Terracini (1949:100) points out, Whitney's notion of structure was indeterminate and vague (particularly when viewed in light of Saussure's subsequent refinement of the idea), the principle of structure itself is clearly stated in his works. In overlooking this fundamental tenet of Whitney's thought, Chomsky arrives at a mistaken formulation of his contribution to the rise of modern linguistic theory. In *Language and Mind*, Chomsky provides the following summary and criticism:

> According to Whitney, Humboldtian linguistic theory, which in many ways extended the Cartesian views that I have been discussing, was fundamentally in error. Rather, a language is simply "made up of a vast number of items, each of which has its own time, occasion, and effect." He maintained that "language in the concrete sense... is... the sum of words and phrases by which any man expresses his thought"; the task of the linguist, then, is to list these linguistic forms and to study their individual histories. In contrast to philosophical grammar, Whitney argued that there is nothing universal about the form of language and that one can learn nothing about the general properties of human intelligence from the study of the arbitrary agglomeration of forms that constitutes a human language (Chomsky 1968:17-18; his ellipsis).

[2]Terracini (1949) traces parallels in Whitney's views in the work of Herbert Spencer and John Stuart Mill.

This account (also stated earlier in Chomsky 1966:90) gives an entirely misleading impression of Whitney's views. It is true tht Whitney regarded the
varieties of semiotic products as "infinite," and claimed that "there are no
limits to the diversity which may arise by discordant growth between languages originally one" (LGL, 269). Yet he also insists, as does Chomsky himself, on a unifying set of principles rooted in the sign-making faculty that
allows infants in every human culture to acquire language along with other
conventional signifying behavior. "The unity of human nature," Whitney
asserted, "makes human speech alike in the character of its beginnings and
in the general features of its after-history" (1885:421).

As must already be apparent, Whitney did *not* see language as only "the
sum of words and phrases by which any man expresses his thought,"[3] nor
does he regard its concrete manifestation as merely "an arbitrary agglom-
eration of forms." In the first of his two theoretical books, Whitney stated
forcefully that "a language... is no mere aggregate of similar particles; it
is a complex of related and mutually helpful parts" (LSL, 19):

> A language is, in very truth, a grand system of highly com-
> plicated and symmetrical structure; it is fitly comparable with
> an organized body; but this is not because any human mind has
> planned such a structure and skillfully worked it out. Each single
> part is conscious and intentional; the whole is instinctive and
> natural (LSL, 23).

In his second book, he continued to elaborate this view, urging not only that
the principal object of linguistics should be that grand system, but also that
linguists must recognize that all human languages are elaborate structures.
His illustrative examples make clear that he distinguished writing from
speech, perceived that English selects from "theoretically infinite" articulations "about forty-four distinctly characterized sounds" (LGL, 67), and
understood linguistic *value* in terms of systematic contrasts (LGL, 214;
see Koerner 1793:98-99 for amplification of Whitney's notion of *value* and
its influence on Saussure). Far from restricting the linguist to the compilation
of lists, Whitney argued that "no fact in human expression is fully estimated
until it is seen in the light of related facts all through the domain of universal
expression" (LGL, 191).

Just as he was careful to distinguish sign from mental image, so too
Whitney perceived the structure of sign-making as independent of its manifestation. "It is a blunder of our educated habit to regard the voice as the

---

[3]Chomsky has slightly altered the passage he quotes to enhance this impression
(see Whitney 1873:372).

specific instrument of expression; it is only one of several instruments" (LGL, 289). On this point, Saussure dissented:

> Whitney, to whom language is one of several social institutions, thinks that we use the vocal apparatus as the instrument of language purely through luck, for the sake of convenience: men might just as well have chosen gestures and used visual symbols instead of acoustical symbols. ... Whitney goes too far in saying that our choice happened to fall on the vocal organs; the choice was more or less imposed by nature (Saussure 1915:10).

Though Saussure's view has prevailed in mainstream linguistics for half a century, the separation of structure and expression remained a vital idea for Hjelmslev and for his successors. While the material of sign systems surely penetrates and revises the latent structure (as, for instance, in the projection of sound repetition into the patterning of verse), Whitney nontheless invites consideration of structure as primary. In this way, his view anticipates that of the semioticians of the Moscow-Tartu school in which the organization of events in music, architecture, poetry, the visual arts, and cultural behavior is understood to derive, by means of a secondary modeling system, from the underlying structure of natural languages. For Whitney, the sign-making faculty takes precedence over the particular expression of that faculty in its several "mediate products and instrumentalities." Such a perspective applies equally to the origin of language and social behavior in prehistory as it does to the task of the infant in learning the conventional sign systems of culture. Whitney found "no plausibility in the suggestion that [man] should have begun social life with a naturally implanted capital of the means of social communication—and any more in the form of words than in that of gestures" (LGL, 289). Instead, he regards human beings as possessing a capacity for sign-making that is actualized through interaction with the community'

As Koerner has shown (1973:74-100), Whitney's most immediately influential views concerned the nature of language as a social institution. In place of the psychological tradition carried on by Steinthal and Müller, Whitney emphasized the role of the social group in the regulation of language: "the community's share in the work [of language-making] is dependent on and conditioned by the simple fact that language is not an individual possession, but a social" (LGL, 149). Without normal social life, the infant cannot actualize the sign-making faculty and will never gain speech or the other codes that radiate from it.

When changes occur in semiotic systems, they do not move in haphazard fashion but respond to latent tendencies governed by both universal principles and particular features of a given system:

> The real effective reason of a given phonetic change is that a
> community, which might have chosen otherwise, willed it to be
> thus; showing thereby the predominance of this or that one
> among the motives which a careful induction from the facts of
> universal language proves to govern men in this department of
> their action (LGL, 74).

Such views of the immanence of change and the regulatory role of the community directly influenced Saussure, who seems, as Koerner shows (1973:85-
87), to have drawn these ideas from Whitney rather than from Durkheim or
Tarde as some historians have claimed. In the dialectic between particular
facts of a given language system and the principles of "universal language,"
Whitney regarded analogy and economy as the proximate sources of change,
but he also recognized a more general tendency for sign systems to be self-
regulating in characteristically human ways. This tendency is not distinct
from other regulating influences on human behavior. "The varieties of linguistic growth," Whitney wrote, "will always be of the same character as
other varieties of historical development: incorporations of the varieties of
human character and capacity, working themselves out under the direction
of the varieties of circumstance; to be traced out with more or less thorough
comprehension, but not to be determined à priori" (Whitney 1878:259;
also 1885:424). Thus Whitney was among the first to distinguish clearly
between the internal and external history of languages and anticipated the
articulation of formal and functionalist descriptions in the work of the
Prague School.

In treating the role of language within the community, Whitney recognized that sign systems, though designed primarily for communication, also
serve other ends (LGL, 285). Among other roles, he mentions the use of
language for pure expression (parallel to Jakobson's "emotive function"),
for enlarging our store of perceptions through name-giving, and for influ-
encing the behavior and beliefs of others. Language, he believed, in part
controls perception and understanding: "the mind which was capable of
doing otherwise has been led to view things in this particular way, to group
them in a certain manner, to contemplate them consciously in these and
these relations" (LGL, 22). Yet this system also contains within itself the
potential for new learning and new discoveries. Whitney's views of the
functions of sign systems immensely complicates the task of the semiotician
but does so properly by acknowledging their richness and diversity. As
Saussure prepared his review of Whitney's achievement, he reflected on his
predecessor's theory of:

the very complex nature of the particular semiology called language. Language is nothing more than a *special case* of the Theory
of Signs. But precisely by this fact alone it is absolutely impossible that it be a simple thing (or a thing directly perceivable by
our minds in its mode of being).

   The chief effect of the study of language on the theory of
signs, the forever new horizon it will have opened up, will be to
have taught and revealed *a whole new aspect of the sign*; namely,
that the latter begins to be really understood only when it is seen
to be a thing which is not only transmittable but by its nature
destined to be transmitted [and] modifiable. But for anyone who
wants to work on the theory of language this is a hundredfold
complication (quoted by Jakobson 1971:xxv-xxxvi).

Out of this recognition, Saussure elaborated his concept of linguistic *value*
(a term apparently derived from the use of *valeur* in the French translation
of Whitney's *Life and Growth of Language*). Linguistic value, for Whitney
as for Saussure, emerges not from any intrinsic property of the sign but
from the relative position of the sign within the system—both from the
perspective of syntagmatic and associative axes—and as it is used in particular utterances by the community of speakers. Whitney thus helped to
shift the emphasis of the science of signs from an ontological preoccupation
with race characteristics and naive Darwinism to a teleological emphasis
implied by a focus on the nature of the sign as "destined to be transmitted."

   For Whitney as for his contemporaries, linguistics and the study of
sign systems generally was one of the historical sciences, and he made no
sharp distinction between synchronic and diachronic studies. Yet he recognized that mere observation and classification could not succeed without a
firm body of accepted and scientific principles deriving from a broad knowledge of the life of signs within society. "Comparative philology and linguistic science," he wrote,

   are two sides of the same study: the former deals primarily with
   the individual facts of a certain body of languages, classifying
   them, tracing out their relations, and arriving at the conclusions
   they suggest; the latter makes the laws and general principles of
   speech its main subject, and uses particular facts as illustrations
   (LGL, 315).

Thanks to Whitney's example, the principles of "linguistic science" emerged
as a field of study co-equal with the tradition of philological study, and this

consequence has perhaps obscured Whitney's distinctive contribution. Yet Saussure gave primary emphasis to Whitney as a founder of general linguistics:

> You give me great honor in asking me to appraise Whitney *as a comparative philologist*. But Whitney never was a *comparative philologist*. He has left us not a single page allowing us to appraise him as a comparative philologist. He has left us only works which deduce from the results of comparative grammar a higher and general view of language: that being exactly his great originality since 1867 (quoted by Jakobson 1971:xxxi).

Whitney's "higher and more general view of language" contributed important insights, not only for Saussure and other European founders of structuralism, but for such American linguists of the next generation as Boas and Sapir (see Davis 1975:1655). His assertions about the systematic nature of sign systems parallel those of C.S. Peirce, and, though Peirce does not acknowledge any influence from Whitney's theoretical writings, he must have been thoroughly familiar with them.[4] For the general public, however, his two books were regarded for fifty years as "perhaps the most widely read of all English books on the subject [; they] have merited their popularity through the soundness of the views which they present and the lucidity of their style" (Smith 1911:28:612).

For Whitney, the personal implication of his theoretical principles was to engage in the study of particular human languages and to assist others in doing so. According to Landar (1975:1338), he encouraged and assisted James C. Pilling of the Bureau of Ethnology in adapting a phonetic alphabet to the study of Amerindian languages and helped him to devise a questionnaire for field work in the American west. In addition to the school grammars of English, French and German (which grew out of his teaching at Yale and at the Sheffield Scientific School in New Haven), he accepted the "superintendence" of the *Century Dictionary* and, using his great influence, was able to persuade the publisher to undertake the most extensive and scholarly English dictionary of any published in America to this day. In his grammars and scholarly works on Sanskrit, he provided linguistics with a variety of apparatus (including a syntactic notation system

---

[4]Peirce was a collaborator of Whitney's in the editing of the *Century Dictionary* and wrote definitions for terms in mathematics, astronomy, weights and measures, philosophy, and psychology among other fields. He doubtless wrote the entry for *semiotics* (in the modern sense) that appears there for the first time in any dictionary.

and a contribution to the development of the phonetic alphabet). By valuing all languages equally, he encouraged the study of dialects and persuaded others that an established literary culture is not a cultural prerequisite for attention by the linguist and ethnographer.

Whitney's contribution to the rise of semiotics is mainly indirect, but he was a pioneer in treating signs as arbitrary and conventional and in seeing that no semiotic fact can be described outside the system of which it is a part. By grasping the idea that structural properties of signs must be viewed as they function in the social life of a community, Whitney recognized the inherent complexity of the task facing the semiotician, and thus he provided for the study of sign systems a set of basic principles that continue to have vital interest today.

REFERENCES

Chomsky, Noam. *Cartesian Linguistics: A Chapter in the History of Rationalist Thought.* New York: Harper and Row, 1966.

_____ . *Language and Mind.* New York: Harcourt, Brace and World, 1968.

Davis, A. Morpurgo. "Language Classification in the Nineteenth Century," in *Current Trends in Linguistics: Historiography of Linguistics* (vol. 13), ed. Thomas A. Sebeok. The Hague: Mouton, 1975. Pp. 607-716.

Emerson, Ralph Waldo. "Nature," in *The American Tradition in Literature,* eds. Sculley Bradley *et al.* New York: Grosset & Dunlap, 1974. Vol. 1, pp. 1040-75.

Hymes, Dell, and John Fought. "American Structuralism," in *Current Trends in Linguistics: Historiography of Linguistics* (vol. 13), ed. Thomas A. Sebeok, The Hague: Mouton, 1975. Pp. 903-1176.

Jakobson, Roman. "The World Response to Whitney's Principles of Linguistic Science," in *Whitney on Language,* ed. Michael Silverstein. Cambridge, Mass.: The MIT Press, 1971. Pp. xxv-xlv.

Koerner, E.F.K. *Ferdinand de Saussure: Origin and Development of His Linguistic Thought in Western Studies of Language.* Braunschweig: Vieweg.

Landar, Herbert. "Native North America," in *Current Trends in Linguistics: Historiography of Linguistics* (vol. 13), ed. Thomas A. Sebeok. The Hague: Mouton, 1975. Pp. 1331-57.

Lanman, Charles Rockwell. "Memorial Address" (1897), in *Portraits of Linguists: A Biographical Source Book for the History of Western Linguistics, 1746-1963*, ed. Thomas A. Sebeok. Bloomington and London: Indiana University Press, 1966. Vol. I, pp. 426-39.

McCawley, James D. "The Phonological Theory behind Whitney's *Sanskrit Grammar*," in *Languages and Areas: Studies Presented to George V. Bobrinskoy*. Chicago: Humanities Division of the University of Chicago, 1967. Pp. 77-85.

_____ . "William Dwight Whitney as a Syntactician," in *Issues in Linguistics: Papers in HOnor of Henry and Renee Kahane*, eds. Braj. B. Kachru *et al*. Urbana: University of Illinois Press, 1973. Pp. 554-68.

Popa-Tomescu, Teodora. "Un stralucit precursor al lingvisticii moderne: William Dwight Whitney." *Limba Romana 19 (1970):189-202.*

_____ . "William Dwight Whitney: elemente ale lingvisticii moderne in opera lui," *Studii si Cercetari Lingvistice* 22 (1971):205-13.

Seymour, Thomas Day. "William Dwight Whitney" (1894), in *Portraits of Linguistis: A Biographical Source Book for the History of Western Linguistics, 1746-1963*, ed. Thomas A. Sebeok. Bloomington and London: Indiana University Press, 1966. Vol. I, pp. 399-426.

Smith, Benjamin Eli. "William Dwight Whitney," *Encyclopedia Britannica* (11th edition), vol.28, pp. 611-12.

Terracini, Benvenuto. "Le origini della linguistica generale: Whitney," in his *Guida allo studio della linguistica storica: I Profilo storico-critico*. Roma: Edizioni dell' Ateneo, 1949, Pp. 73-121.

Whitney, William Dwight. *Language and the Study of Language*. (1867), abridged in *Whitney on Language*, ed. Michael Silverstein. Cambridge, Mass.: The MIT Press, 1971. Pp. 7-110.

_____ . "On the Present State of the Question as to the Origin of Language" (1870), in his *Oriental and Linguistic Studies*. New York: Scribner Armstrong, and Co., 1973. Pp. 279-91.

_____ . "Steinthal and the Psychological Theory of Language" (1872), in his *Oriental and Linguistic Studies*. New York: Scribner, Armstrong, and Co., 1873. Pp. 332-75.

_____ . *The Life and Growth of Language: An Outline of Linguistic Science. [1875]*. New York: D. Appleton and Company, 1890.

_____ . "On the Principle of Economy as a Phonetic Force" (1878), in *Whitney on Language* (as above). Pp. 249-60.

_____ . "Philology" (1885), *Encyclopedia Britannica* (9th edition), vol. 21, pp. 414-30.

PEIRCE AND JAKOBSON ON THE NATURE OF THE SIGN

Elizabeth W. Bruss

Roman Jakobson is our great intellectual cosmopolitan, and it therefore comes as no surprise that his work in semiotics, like his work in poetics and in linguistics proper, should transcend the boundaries of nationality and history. As a theorist, he has never been afraid to synthesize, and over time, his assimilations have a tendency to become a chief source of information about obscure or "alien" traditions, preserving and transmitting crucial concepts that might otherwise have been lost. Thus despite chronology, it is no paradox to speak of "Peirce's debt to Jakobson," for the citations and generous allusions to Peirce that figure in his "follower's" essays have contributed to the "forebearer's" reputation as a pioneering semiotician, helping to establish a sense of Jakobson's indebtedness (as it were) *a posteriori*. Indeed the reverse formulation -- "Peirce's influence on Jakobson" -- may be rather misleading. The borrowings from Peirce occur in the midst of Jakobson's career, too late for Bloomian "anxiety." Most of Jakobson's attitudes have already matured by the time he draws upon Peirce; he has already formulated much of the basic framework for his semiotics. Thus he is a selective reader, using Peirce to supply additional support for his own positions, deploying him polemically as the exemplar of an alternative to the Saussurian tradition. His readings of Peirce never seems to demand any serious revisions of his own categories.

In this respect, Jakobson is no different than most contemporary students of Peirce, who find the American philosopher full of useful fragments but dauntingly idiosyncratic in terms of his full program. According to John Lyons, the contemporary uses of such key Peircian distinctions as "syntactics, semantics, and pragmatics," or "icon, index, and symbol," have little in common with Peirce's original conceptions. "Much of Peirce's influence has, in any case, been indirect."[1]

The Peirce that Jakobson presents is therefore Jakobson's Peirce, and it is just as interesting and perhaps more revealing to consider what has been left out in Jakobson's account and to ponder the source of this interference as it is to consider the borrowings themselves. For what Jakobson assimilates

[1]Lyons, *Semantics*, 1 (Cambridge Univ. Press, 1977), pp. 99 and 119.

and what he resists, what he treats as essential to Peirce's thought and what he regards as accidental, provides a direct and graphic illustration of his own fundamentally different purposes and assumptions. In the following pages I shall speak broadly of Peirce's semiotic inquiries and note how emphases are altered in Jakobson's discussion of them. The affinity between these two thinkers may be less profound than their differences, differences that spring ultimately from how each views semeiosis itself, what each takes as the paradigmatic semiotic situation, the basic unit of meaning, and the goal of semiotic analysis. We shall see each man more clearly, I hope, in the light of their divergence.

i.

Few writers have expended more time or intellectual effort in pursuit of the "meaning of meaning" than C.S. Peirce—indeed, according to Justus Buchler, Peirce's is "the first deliberate *theory* of meaning in modern times."[2] The effort is all the more extraordinary because Peirce did not limit himself to verbal meaning alone (as the medieval logicians he cites as his predecessors had done), but sought to extend the concept of meaning to other domains as well. The comprehensiveness of his study provoked and continues to provoke doubt:

> Smoke means fire and the word *combustion* means fire, but not in the same sense of *means*. The word *mean* is ambiguous. To say smoke means fire is to say that smoke is a symptom, sign, indication, or evidence of fire. To say that the word *combustion* means fire is to say that people use the word to mean fire. Furthermore, there is no ordinary sense of the word *mean* in which a picture of a man means a man or means that man. This suggests tht Peirce's theory of signs would comprise at least three rather different subjects: a theory of intended meaning, a theory of evidence, and a theory of pictoral depiction. There is no reason to think that these theories must contain common principles[3]

Gilbert Harman's scepticism is important not only for our reading of Peirce but for our interest in semiotics itself. If Peirce is misguided, deluded by an ambiguity, then semiotic research as a whole is, as Harman later argues,

---

[2]Buchler, ed., *Philosophical Writings of Peirce* (New York: Dover, 1955), p. xi.

[3]Gilbert Harman, "Semiotics and the Cinema," *Quarterly Review of Film Studies*, Winter (February, 1977), p. 23.

"really a collection of three or four disparate subjects." [4] It is crucial, then, to ask why Peirce believed there was a single subject matter and a common principle, why he even sought such a unified theory at all.

Although too simple by far, it is not unfair to say that Peirce actually began by trying to relate the meaning of verbal statements more closely to observable evidence and ended by making evidence one of the modes of meaning. The impulse behind Peirce's unified study of signs is part of his overall effort to reconcile philosophic speculation with the methods and aims of the empirical sciences, to provide better grounds for belief and disbelief and to instruct us on "how to make our ideas clear" enough to measure our commitment to them. Although Peirce's ultimate theory of meaning was never so crude as the positivist demand for "verifiable" propositions only, he did anticipate them in his own insistence that for a statement to have meaning, it must have empirical consequences—some set of observations it leads us to expect or some program of action it leads us to undertake.

> Now the problem of what the "meaning" of an intellectual concept is can only be solved by the study of the interpretants, or proper significate effects of signs . . . The first proper significate effect of a sign is a feeling produced by it . . . . This *"emotional interpretant,"* as I call it, may amount to much more than the feeling of recognition; in some cases it is the only proper significate effect that the sign produces. Thus the performance of a piece of concert music is a sign. It conveys, and is intended to convey, the composer's musical ideas; but these usually consist merely in a series of feelings. . . further effect will always involve an effort. I call it the *energetic interpretant.* The effort may be a muscular one, as it is in the case of the command to ground arms; but it is much more usually an exertion upon the Inner World, a mental effort. . . It [such an effort] can never be the meaning of an intellectual concept, since it is a single act, [and] such a concept is of a general nature. But what further kind of effect can there be?. . . I will call it the *logical interpretant,* without as yet determining whether this term shall extend to anything beside the meaning

---

[4] See Justus Buchler, "What is the Pragmaticist Theory of Meaning?," in *Studies in the Philosophy of Charles Sanders Peirce*, ed. Philip P. Wiener and Frederic H. Young (Cambridge, Mass.: Harvard Univ. Press, 1952), pp. 28-30.

of a general concept. . .[5]

Peirce's impatience with idealist canons of meaning—an impatience which reminds one of Wittgenstein's similar impatience with philosophical quibbles that arise when the actual use of a term is ignored—led him to seek for meaning in "the significate effect the sign produces." His recognition that interpretation may, in fact, take several forms—from primitive recognition to gestures to acts of association (which may include mental images or tentative synonyms)—already takes Peirce beyond verbal language. Ultimately, according to Peirce, there is no end to interpretation; the meaning of a proposition unfolds continuously, "develops," as we come to see more and more of its implications. The final significate effect, or "logical interpretant," is a product of Peirce's later speculations.[6] But even here the apparent resting place in an endless chain of translation is not a rest at all; the meaning of a concept must be general, it cannot be exhausted on any single occasion of use but must extend to ever new instances. Peirce's logical interpretant is therefore a rule (a "law" or "habit" as he later called it) of interpretation which includes all possible uses and all possible users. As John J. Fitzgerald remarks, citing Peirce's own words:

> The final interpretant is that "which *would finally* be decided to be the true interpretation if consideration of the matter were carried so far that an ultimate opinion were reached. . . the effect the sign *would* produce upon any mind upon which circumstances should permit it to work out its full effect." Here we are concerned, not with what does in fact happen as a result of the sign, but with the sign as a law. . .[7]

Not every kind of sign, however, is capable of producing this level of interpretation. Music, for example, is limited to conveying no more than a series of untranslatable feelings, unless some mental effort is exerted to provide a substitute interpretant for what one hears—a more "conceptual" and therefore more general response which is capable of further translations and developmental refinements.

[5]Peirce, *the Collected Papers of C. S. Peirce,*, ed. Charles Hartshorne and Paul Weiss, V (Cambridge, Mass.: Harvard Univ. Press, 1931-35), p.475.

[6]See George Gentry, "Habit and the Logical Interpretant," in Wiener and Young ed., pp. 75-90.

[7]*Peirce's Theory of Signs as Foundation for Pragmatism* (The Hague: Mouton and Co., 1966), pp. 79-80.

As a scientist, Peirce was interested in the relationship between laws—predictive and general propositions—and individual occurrences. He was early to recognize the impossibility of deriving universals from particulars; theories were achieved by "abduction" rather than "induction" and hypotheses were then deduced to see if individual observations would bear out what the theory predicted. Peirce's sensitivity to the nature of scientific laws, and particularly their logical status, is inextricably linked to his theory of signs. The effort to express the distinctive power of such laws led Peirce to construct an entire system of justificatory categories, one portion of which we now know as his semiotics. "Just as the logicians were seeking [in the last part of the Nineteenth Century and the present century] logical principles from which to derive mathematics, so too Peirce was seeking principles in his formal logic from which he could derive his pragmatic principle."[8] Understanding Peirce's ultimate goals in constructing his logic helps one to appreciate his characteristic "triadic" analysis, his insistence on a system of logical classes based on "firstness," "secondness," and "thirdness."

The triad originates in Peirce's phenomenology—that branch of his philosophy which treats appearances and experiences without regard for their ontological status. Drawing upon his readings of Kant and Mill, Peirce proposes three *a priori* categories of experience—a simple element, "complete in itself;" a dyadic relation, "elements which are what they are relatively to a second;" and a triadic relation, in which a mediating element connects two other elements. Each of these three categories is irreducible, each provides us with some basic aspects of awareness. "Firstness," for example, is at work in our perception of qualities, while we could not recognize individual existents without some notion of dyadic relations—the ability to discriminate between "same" and "different." "Thirdness" as a category reflects Peirce's thoughts on the nature of universals and laws—something that transcends the "hic et nunc" of individual manifestations, yet can not be said to exist without them. These categories exhaust our basic repertoire of experience, although more complex experiences can be built up from them.[9]

Since Peirce himself remarked that the whole of his philosophic program could be reduced to "the study of methods of inquiry"[10]—that is, inquiry into the status of appearances   and experience—it is not

[8]Fitzgerald, p. 11.

[9]See Fitzgerald, Chap. 11, *passim* and Isabel S. Stearns, "Firstness, Secondness, and Thirdness," in Wiener and Young, pp. 195-208.

[10]Buchler, ed., p. 1.

surprising to find that this basic repertory of phenomenological categories reappear throughout his work. As the *sine qua non* of observation itself, which science and philosophy simply make more systematic, "firstness," "secondness," and "thirdness" serve as a natural heuristic framework for organizing any other study, including the study of signs. Moreover the sign itself—in Peirce's view—is a premier example of "thirdness," one of the paradigmatic irreducible triadic relations.

> A sign. . . is something which stands to somebody for something in some respect or capacity. It addresses somebody, that is, creates in the mind of that person an equivalent sign, or perhaps a more developed sign. That sign which it creates I call the *interpretant* of the first sign. That sign stands for something, its *object*. It stands for that object, not in all respects, but in reference to a sort of idea, which I have sometimes called the *ground*. . . [11]

For anything to be a sign, it must have all three elements: "representamen" (or vehicle), "object," and "interpretant." The representamen must mediate between interpretant and object, be a necessary stimulus of a response to something other than itself. For Peirce, this is the crucial distinction between semiotic processes and simpler processes such as sequence or causation; a "genuine significate effect" (or interpretant) must not be conflated with simpler, unmediated effects. It is, then, this mediation, this triadic relation that serves as the "common principle" in Peirce's semiotic theory, the grounds which allow him to treat evidence, pictoral depiction, and language as in some important way the same. Whether it is a picture, a puff of smoke, or the proverbial shout in a crowded theater, the significate effect is equally mediated—although the mode of mediation changes.

Despite the fact that the sign is an irreducible triad, it is still possible to decompose it, in the abstract, into simpler dyadic and monadic elements.

> Signs are divisible by three trichotomies; first, according as the sign in itself is a mere quality, is an actual existent, or is a general law; secondly, according as the relation of the sign to its object consists in the sign's

---

[11]Peirce's writings on the sign are scattered throughout his published and unpublished work. Buchler collects several passages together under the title, "Logic as Semiotic," in Buchler, ed., pp. 98-119, from which the above is taken, p. 99.

having some existential relation to that object, or in its relation to an interpretant; thirdly; according as its Interpretant represents it as a sign of possibility or as a sign of fact or a sign of reason. [12]

Thus one can artificially isolate the sign-vehicle from its semiotic function and speak of different vehicle types; those where it is the quality (Qualisign) alone (e.g. color) which acts as the signifier; those where the whole being (Sinsign), and not just one or another of its properties, serves as the vehicle; and those where the seeming vehicle is only a token instantiating a general type (Legisign).

> Every legisign signifies through an instance of its application, which may be termed a *Replica* of it. Thus the word "the" will usually occur from fifteen to twenty-five times on a page. It is in all these occurrences one and the same word, the same legisign.[13]

While Peirce's type-token distinction has been influential, the remainder of this attempt to classify signs according to vehicle type has not.[14] Far more important for his later admirers has been his second division of signs into "icon," "index," and "symbol." In this case, it is the "secondness" of the sign—the relationship between vehicle and object or between vehicle and interpretant—that Peirce is considering. The popularity of this single dimension of his thought, the fact that it alone has survived in the work of most of his followers, suggests how difficult it is for us to assimilate Peirce's full conception of the nature of semeiosis. What he held to be essentially triadic, others take to be dyadic, a simple relationship between signifier and signified (or between stimulus and response) rather than a complex interdependency involving all three. But for Peirce there is no semiotics, no true sign, without signification *and* interpretation. "Meaning" requires translation as well as representation; signs must participate in a circle of exchange and substitution before they can count as signs.

[12]Buchler ed., p. 101.

[13]Buchler ed., p. 106.

[14]However, Nelson Goodman's *The Languages of Art* (Indianapolis: Bobbs-Merrill, 1968) presents an independent attempt to develop a comprehensive theory based on the nature of the sign-vehicle.

Without knowledge of Peirce's phenomenological system, his description of icon, index, and symbol can give rise to confusion. For example, when he says of the icon that it "denotes merely by virtue of characters of its own, and which it possesses, just the same, whether any such Object exists or not," the statement sounds contradictory.[15] If the relationship between sign-vehicle and Object is a matter of similarity, how can there be an icon of an Object which may not exist? For Peirce, however, resemblance is based on qualities inherent to the sign-vehicle itself—the "secondness," or relationship to its Object, depends on a prior "firstness." It is important to recall that Peirce is speaking here only of the *capacity* to serve as a sign. Until the qualities of the potential sign-vehicle are recognized and associated with an object by an act of interpretation, it does not yet function as a sign. When it does so function, however, Peirce insists that it will (if it is iconic) do so in virtue of properties which the sign-vehicle actually exhibits and the comparisons these properties evoke. Thus Peirce's theory of iconicity is not a sentimental appeal to "natural resemblances" and, in fact, allows for changing mimetic conventions. Icons are "motivated" signs only insofar as the grounds of interpretation are the inherent qualities of the sign-vehicle itself.

The same kind of confusion often attends Peirce's discussion of the "index."

> [An index] refers to its object not so much because of any similarity or analogy with it . . . as because it is in dynamical (including spatial) connection both with the individual object, on the one hand, and with the sense or memory of the person for whom it serves as a sign on the other.[16]

The index has no necessary "firstness;" it is a relationship rather than a quality. Hence the signifier need have no particular properties of its own, only a demonstrable connection to something else. The most important of these connections are spatial co-occurrence, temporal sequence, and cause and effect. It is the fact of such a relationship between sign-vehicle and Object or between sign-vehicle and Interpretant which makes the vehicle a potential bearer of meaning. As with icons, Peirce is basing his classification on something which must exist prior to any interpretation, something which semiotic activities may then exploit.

[15]Buchler ed., p. 102.
[16]Buchler ed., p. 107.

Hence, once again, there is ample room for changing conventions of indexicality, although as a scientist and a philosophic Realist, Peirce remained committed to the belief that indexical relations exist independently of such conventions. Indeed, his need to discriminate between icons and indicies arose from his desire to discriminate between appearances and evidence; only indicies could serve as evidence of an Object's existence, or (in the case of Interpretant response) proof that there was a stimulus.

"Symbols" have, on the whole, provoked less apparent confusion; the "arbitrariness of the sign" is well enough established in most minds to make this third category, where the grounds of relationship between signifier and Object and between signifier and Interpretant are entirely conventional, seem familiar. Yet Peirce adds to his notion of arbitrary signification one further criterion. Not only do symbols "denote by virtue of a law" (rather than by virtue of inherent qualities or existential relations) but, while capable of denoting particular individuals on any given occasion of use, their true scope is far more general. "A genuine symbol is a symbol that has a general meaning."[17] From such statements one can see that Peirce believes that the relationship between sign-vehicle and Object also includes stipulations about the nature of the Object itself. Hence his "Object" is not any given referent but the denotation of the sign, all of its possible referential values. Icons are capable of referring to qualities, indicies of referring to individuals, and symbols to whole, openended sets of individuals. Symbols are therefore hypothetical and predictive in just the same way that scientific theories are, and the move from index to symbol is the move from evidence to theory writ small.

The final phase of Peirce's complex system of classification, the categorizing of signs according to their Interpretants, is the most fragmentary and inconsistent of all his efforts, despite the fact that it was, for him, the most important area of semiotics, the "thirdness" which finally separated signs from non-signs. There are several, apparently separate proposals: a distinction between "emotional," "energetic," and "logical" Interpretants (cited above); a distinction between interpretations of "possibility," "fact," and "reason"; and a distinction that involves the function of the sign in propositions—whether it may serve as an attribution (or Rheme), a referring expression (or Dicent), or the expression of a full Argument.[18] Using the final set of categories, and combining them with his former

[17]Buchler ed., p. 112.

[18]Peirce's commentators disagree about whether he is here contradicting or revising himself, or whether these formulations represent subcategories of Interpretants; cf. Fitzgerald, p. 78.

divisions into "Qualisign"/"Sinsign"/"Legisign," and "Icon"/"Index"/
"Symbol," respectively, Peirce eventually devised what he hoped would
be an exhaustive typology of all possible signs, a "periodic table" as it were,
which might serve as the basis for a new, more synoptic logic.[19] But to the
last, his goal remained the discovery of "what *must be* the characters of all
signs used by a "scientific" intelligence, that is to say, by an intelligence
capable of learning by experience."[20] Thus semiotics is forever subordinate
to Peirce's superordinate interest in a more scientific epistemology, a more
corrigible metaphysics, a foundation for belief and action in a sceptical
modern world.

ii

> I can say, not with pride but with bitterness, that I was the
> first linguist who utilized the works of Peirce.[21]

In such a remark (from Jakobson's address to the 1975 "Charles
Sanders Peirce Symposium on Semiotics and the Arts"), the speaker is
not only claiming something for himself but also trying to establish a claim
upon himself. By officially indebting himself to Peirce, Jakobson makes
himself the heir of a lost American tradition: no longer the purveyor of
exotic Continental theories—and therefore subject to what he sardonically
calls "attacks for un-American activities"—but the proponent of native
tendencies invisible to the natives themselve. What Peirce really represents
for Jakobson, however, is less a matter of nationality than of intellectual
legitimacy, proof that some of his own most characteristic concerns—especially his concern for communication in the broadest sense—have a history,
that they are neither idiosyncratic nor peripheral to the formal study of
communicative systems.

Peirce has, of course, come to serve this function for many contemporary thinkers, although (paradoxically) he was himself distinctly an exotic
and an outcast. In his Symposium address, Jakobson provides an acute
description of another reason why Peirce is so tempting to would-be epigones:

[19]See Paul Weiss and Arthur Burks, "Peirce's Sixty-Six Signs," *Journal of the
History of Ideas*, XLII (1945), pp. 383-88.

[20]Buchler ed., p. 100.

[21]"A Few Remarks on Structuralism," *MLN*, 91 (December, 1976), p. 1536.

Peirce was the last man whose thought was static—his views changed... one cannot *read* the Collected Papers of Peirce. One can only *study* them, changing completely, so to say, the whole perspective, the whole view of his works.[22]

Out of the fragments, one can—indeed, one *must*—continuously construct and re-construct the implied philosopher; small wonder that the figure who emerges is so frequently cast in the reader's own image.

But there are ample grounds for Jakobson to find in Peirce a compatible mind. Both are drawn to the same tradition of medieval speculative grammar; both have a marked methodological bent for the construction of typologies. As Jakobson explains his own method, such "typological confrontation... reveals universal invariants;"[23] it reveals the more abstract core of any subject matter. When confronting a subject as vast as semiotics, then, each man automatically begins by seeking a finite set of recurrent categories capable of producing the appearance of random diversity by systematic combination and recombination. But this shared tendency to seize on a small number of recursive elements—"firstness," "secondness," and "thirdness," in the case of Peirce; "similarity" and "contiguity" in the case of Jakobson—seems to have led Jakobson to overstate the underlying similarity of method and assumption:

The division of signs into indexes, icons, and symbols, which was first advanced by Peirce in his famous paper of 1867 and elaborated throughout his life, is actually based on two substantial dichotomies. One of them is the difference between contiguity and similarity... In contradistinction to the factual contiguity between the car pointed at and the direction of the forefinger's pointing gesture, and to the factual resemblance between this car and an etching or diagram of it, no factual proximity is required between the noun *car* and the vehicle so named. In this sign the signans is tied to its signatum "regardless of any factual connection".... There is no question of three categorically separate types of signs but only of a different hierarchy assigned to the interacting types of relation between the signans and signatum of the given signs, and in fact, we observe such transitional varieties as symbolic icons, iconic symbols, etc.[24]

[22]pp. 1535-36.

[23]"Language in Relation to Other Communication Systems," in *Roman Jakobson: Selected Writings*, II (The Hague: Mouton, 1971), pp. 699-700.

[24]"Language in Relation to Other Communication Systems," *Selected Writings*, p. 700.

Jakobson's claim that Peirce constructs his classification of signs by "the interplay of the two dichotomies—contiguity/similarity and factual/imputed" is nowhere to be found in Peirce's original manuscripts. What we see instead are Jakobson's own familiar binary oppositions and his own insistence that it is the hierarchy of components and not the components themselves that effects distinctions. In his eagerness to name Peirce "a genuine and bold forerunner of structural linguistics," Jakobson in fact turns Peirce on his head—"Here we have from the beginning a clearly structural approach to phenomenological problems."[25] There is no indication that Peirce's analyses of semiotic structure were in fact governed by his phenomenological categories, nor does Jakobson acknowledge that Peirce's "structuralism" was strictly ancillary, a means and not an end.

It is not surprising, then, that Jakobson pays scant attention to those places where Peirce's semiotics is least "structural" and most phenomenological. For example, Peirce's attempt to classify the "firstness" of the sign—the properties or qualities it has as an appearance without relationship to anything other than itself—all but disappears in Jakobson's revisionary reading. His single allusion to the "Legisign" (and there are no allusions to "Qualisigns" or "Sinsigns") treats it as an alternative term for "symbol." When Jakobson himself embarks on a classification of signs according to their "material," he speaks not of appearances, but of perceptual channels—sight and hearing in particular:

> . . . the nature of the signans itself is of great importance for the structure of messages and their typology. All five external senses carry semiotic functions in human society. . . it is evident that the most socialized, abundant, and pertinent sign systems in human society are based on sight and hearing. An essential trait distinguishes auditory messages from visual ones. Within the systems of auditory signs never space but only time acts as a structural factor, namely, time in its two axes, sequence and simultaneity; the structuration of visual signantia necessarily involves space and can be either abstracted from time, as in immobile painting and sculpture, or superinduce the time factor as in the motion picture. The prevalence of icons among purely spatial, visual signs and the prevalence of symbols among purely temporal, auditory signs permit us to interconnect several criteria relevant in the classification of sign patterns and further their semiotic analysis and psychological interpretation. The two particularly elaborate

[25]"A Few Remarks," p. 1535. While Peirce does recommend attention to "structure" rather than "material" in classifying phenomenological experience, his "structures" are arrived at a priori, and are not subject to further decomposition or distributional analysis.

systems of purely auditory and temporal signs, spoken language and music, present a strictly discontinuous, as physicists would say, granular structure. They are composed of ultimate discrete elements, a principle alien to spatial semiotic systems. These ultimate elements and their combinations and rules of patterning are special, ad hoc shaped devices.[26]

For Jakobson, the "nature of the signans" is important only to the extent that it may have certain consequences for the "structure of messages." He is not, like Peirce, interested in the appearance or ontology of the sign-vehicle, nor does he treat these vehicles as having properties than can be defined in isolation. The crucial characteristics of auditory and visual signs emerge only by opposing them, one to the other. Indeed, it seems that Peirce's notion of "firstness" is unthinkable for Jakobson—literally inconceivable within the terms of his own most fundamental assumptions. He even praises Peirce for recognizing that "existence lies merely in opposition"[27]—something that Peirce did in fact believe. To exist something must be judged identical to itself and distinct from anything else. But in saying this, Peirce placed existence among those phenomena that display "secondness," treating identity and opposition as dyadic relations similar in kind to those other relations—cause and effect, sequence, and co-occurrence—which in fact interested him far more. Peirce therefore never challenged the possibility of a class of absolute qualities, appearances that were self-evident in themselves and capable of being defined without comparison or opposition. His insistence on the possibility of "firstness," then, reveals how little of the structuralist Peirce actually was, while, by the same token, Jakobson's need to revise or ignore him at just such points reveals how much the structuralist he actually remains. At base, Jakobson's semiotics is still more Saussurian than Peircian, committed to the diacritical nature of each aspect and every instance of the sign.

This is clear even when one turns from sign-vehicles to their meanings and interpretations. Peirce's "icon" and "index" seem to confirm Jakobson's own notions of the primacy of "similarity" and "contiguity"—and this, one suspects, must have been the source of the original attraction. Yet, "iconicity" is not quite "similarity," not a mediated likeness based on some shared function or some shared paradigm, but a likeness grounded on immediate qualities of the sign-vehicle itself. Since the "index" is a true dyad in Peirce's system, there is less distortion in assimilating it to "contiguity." Indeed Peirce's thoughts about the indexical nature of pronouns—which receive their value either from contiguous elements in the sentence itself or contiguous

[26]"Language in Relation," *Selected Writings, p. 701.*

[27]"A Few Remarks," p.1537.

elements in the extraverbal context—coincide with Jakobson's almost perfectly.[28] Thus one finds the same systematic ambiguity which appears in
Jakobson's treatment of "metonymy"—now an extra-semiotic relation, now
a contiguity within the text or artifact itself—coloring Peirce's treatment of
the "index" as well. Jakobson's reflections on the "symbol," however, show
them once again at variance. Peirce does mention that the vehicle for symbolic or "rule-governed" meanings is actually only the token of a more abstract type, but he does not explore the structure of the symbol much further than this; it is sufficient for his purposes to establish that symbols are
mediated and general in their scope of reference. It is left ot Jakobson to
explore the relationship between generality and mediation. To be a symbol,
a sign must be capable of displacement, independent of particular stimuli,
on the one hand, and particular substance of embodiment, on the other.
Under what conditions does a sign attain such independence? Only when
it undergoes analysis and its seemingly inevitable wholeness is broken down
into reuseable components.

> The uniqueness of natural language among all other semiotic sys-
> tems is manifest in its fundamentals. The properly generic mean-
> ings of verbal signs become particularized and individualized
> under the pressure of changeable contexts or of non-verbalized
> but verbalizable situations. The exceptionally rich repertoire of
> definitely coded meaningful units (morphemes and words) is
> made possible through the diaphonous system of their merely
> differential components devoid of proper meaning (distinctive
> features,, phonemes, and the rules of their combinability).
> These components are semiotic entities *sui generis*. The signature
> of such an entity is bare otherness, namely a presumable seman-
> tic difference between the meaningful units to which it pertains
> and those which *ceteris paribus* do not contain the same entity.[29]

A more succint illustration of his differences from Peirce is hardly
imaginable. For Peirce, the essence of semeiosis is the triadic nature of
the sign, its "standing" in relation to an interpretant and for an object. For
Jakobson, it is the articulation of the sign that is most important; the basis

---

[28]One of Jakobson's earliest citations of Peirce is therefore to be found in the
classic article, "Shifters, Verbal Categories, and the Russian Verb," *Selected Writings*,
pp. 131-32.

[29]"Language in Relation, " *Selected Writings*, p. 707.

of semeiosis is systematic distinctiveness and not reference. Thus in Jakobson's work, the mechanism of encoding is central, while in Peirce's there is no reflection at all, to speak of, on the system to which any individual sign belongs or on the process that produces it. Peirce therefore tends to conflate single words with entire propositions, since his interest is neither in the construction of the message nor in the larger code from which its components are drawn. Significantly, the model he constructs of the basic semiotic situation provides for "objects" and "interpretants" and "sign-vehicles"—elements that Jakobson also includes within his own—but lacks the additional poles of "sender" and "code." Here, then, is the trace of Peirce's original scientific intentions, his interest in "evidence"—which has neither a conscious producer nor a grammatical code—and his subsequent attempt to assimilate other semiotic events to the same model. For Jakobson, the situation is reversed; beginning with language, he must then find a way to avoid imposing its structure of communication on everything else.

> The need for their interpretation as something that serves to infer the existence of something else . . . makes the unwitting indexes into a variety of signs, but we must consistently take into account the decisive difference between *communication* which implies a real or alleged addresser and *information* whose source cannot be viewed as an addresser by the interpreter. . .[30]

Given these distinct initial orientations, the inquiries of Peirce and Jakobson can never entirely converge. Instead, what Jakobson frequently does is to discover the radical implications of Peirce's semiotic thought which, because of his empiricism and Realism, Peirce himself was blind to. This is particularly clear in Jakobson's recasting of the notion of "interpretant."

> . . . one of the most illuminating of Peirce's theses propounds that the meaning of a sign is the sign it can be translated into. When I read in today's newspaper: "OPA permits pork price rises," I personally don't know what OPA is, but I do know the meaning of the words *permits, price, rises,* and *pork.* How can

[30]"Languages in Relation," *Selected Writings*, p. 703.

pork be defined from a linguistic point of view? "Pork is pig meat used as food." Such an equational context is perfectly acceptable for the speech community....There are different ways of interpreting the word *pork* in other signs. We used a circumlocution, and we always may: as Peirce incisively defined the main structural principle of language, any sign is translatable itself into another sign in which it is more fully developed. Instead of an intralingual method, we may use an interlingual way of interpretation by translating the word *pork* into another language. The method would be intersemiotic if we would resort to a non-linguistic, for instance, to a pictoral sign. But in all these cases we substitute signs. Then what about the relation between sign and thing?...[such meanings] constituted by the pattern of analytic relationship of one expression to other expressions, do not presuppose presented things.[31]

Yet "presented things" was precisely what Peirce's semiotics *did*, consistently, presuppose; for him, the referent, or "object," of the sign was crucial to its meaning, something he refused to treat as just another variety of "interpretant." At the same time, as his work progressed, he was forced to acknowledge the distinction between his semiotic "Object"—what a sign is capable of picking out—and ontological or even phenomenological objects. Thus Jakobson's reformulation, which makes the "object" just another element in the series of "equational contexts" which together constitute the meaning of the sign, eliminates an inconsistency in Peirce and separates semiotic questions from metaphysical questions. The meaning of a sign is not a thing, but meaning may include a *capacity* to indicate, describe, depict, and otherwise refer to things, under appropriate conditions.

But if he must reformulate so drastically and so often, what does Jakobson gain from his borrowings from Peirce, what need has he for him? First, Peirce seems to allow Jakobson a way out of the impasse that arises from Saussure's doctrine of the "arbitrariness of the sign." It is not that Jakobson objects to the diacritical or purely relational value of signs; indeed, the effect of all of his revisions is to make Peirce's work more consistent with this view. But he does object to the "dogma" that all signs,

[31]"The Conference of Anthropologists and Linguists," *Selected Writings*, pp. 566-67.

even linguistic signs, are to be evaluated according to the same criteria.

> Peirce's concern with the different ranks of coassistance of the three functions in all three types of signs, and in particular his scrupulous attention to the indexical and iconic components of verbal symbols, is intimately linked with his thesis that "the most perfect of signs" are those in which the iconic, indexical, and symbolic characters "are blended as equally as possible." Conversely, Saussure's insistence on the conventionality of language is bound to his assertion that "the entirely arbitrary signs are the most appropriate to fulfill the optimum semiotic process"...Saussure himself attentuated his "fundamental principle of arbitrariness" by making a distinction between the "radically" and the "relatively" arbitrary elements of language...."The mind manages to introduce a principle of order and regularity in certain parts of the body of signs.". . The iconic and indexical constituents of verbal symbols have too often remained underestimated or even disregarded; on the other hand, the predominantly symbolic character of language and its consequent cardinal difference from the other, chiefly indexical or iconic, sets of signs likewise awaits due consideration in modern linguistic methodology.[32]

Peirce provides legitimacy for the investigation of iconic and indexical aspects of the linguistic code and for comparing that code to other semiotic systems. This, in turn, makes room for "paranomasia" and for other functions—such as the poetic and the expressive—in language; if iconicity and indexicality are central to language, then poetry and the rest no longer seem "epiphenomenal," trivial or alien structures that move against the grain of the system. Peirce is therefore part of the larger effort:

> ...to overcome the Saussurian model of *langue* as a static, uniform system of mandatory rules and to supplant this oversimplified and artificial construct by the dynamic view of a diversified, convertible code with regard to the different functions of language and to the time and space factors, both of which were excluded from the Saussurian conception of the linguistic system.... any degree of self-restriction and rigor-

---

[32]"Quest for the Essence of Language," *Selected Writings*, pp. 349 and 357-58.

ous specialization is perfectly legitimate. What would be, however, erroneous and pernicious is any degradation of all the other facets of language as supposedly residual, second-rate linguistic questions, and especially, any attempt to expel these topics from linguistics proper...Such have been, also, the recently revived Saussurian propensities to confine analysis merely to the code (*langue*, competence) in spite of the indissoluble, dialectic unity *langue/parole* (code/message, competence/ performance).[33]

Although these remarks are directed towards linguistic theory, it is not hard to see their relevance for semiotics as well. For any theory which treats the iconic and indexical elements in language as "residual," which is insensitive to "time and space factors" and the relationship between code and context, will necessarily be forced to treat non-verbal communicative systems as "second rate" in precisely the same way. Yet the question remains whether, as Jakobson goes on to insist, these "items ... require the same structural analysis as any other intrinsic constituent of language," or whether new theories and methods of analysis will have to be devised.

---

[33]"Linguistics in Relation to Other Sciences," *Selected Writings*, pp. 668 and 666-67.

MODERN AMERICAN SEMIOTICS
(1930-1978)

Wendy Steiner

The period of American semiotics which concerns us here starts at the publication of the first volume of Peirce's *Collected Papers* (1931) and continues to the present. During this time, isolated topics dispersed throughout philosophy, linguistics, aesthetics, and other fields coalesced into the discipline of semiotics, which in its more grandiose moments claims to be the organizing principle for the rest of knowledge. At present, semiotics is trying to make a case for itself in American universities, and events like the conference honored in this volume will determine the nature of interdisciplinary curricula throughout the country. Because of the aesthetic orientation of the Ann Arbor conference, this paper will focus mostly on trends in American semiotics relating to the humanities, an area in which the conflicting tendencies in the American approach to semiotics create profound difficulties.

A list of the figures concerned with semiotics from 1930-1945 in this country should give a fair indication of the sources of the conflict. Peirce's papers presented sign theory within the frame of pragmatic philosophy, and Charles Morris, John Dewey, and George H. Mead contributed a behaviorist orientation. With the immigration to America of Rudolf Carnap, Hans Reichenbach, and Otto Neurath, the logical empiricism of the Vienna School added its bias to the native trends. The semiotic treatment of art became an issue when the New Critics condemned it as anti-humanistic. And in the early forties, Ernst Cassirer and Suzanne Langer were propounding a neo-Kantian philosophy in which the central project was the understanding of symbolic form. This diversity makes the history of American semiotics a sequence of unresolved disputes rather than uninterrupted gains, and explains in part the late blooming of semiotics in American academia.

The first call in our period for a discipline of semiotics arose from the Unified Science Movement created by the transplanted logical empiricists. Their aim was "to form an *Einheitswissenschaft,* i.e., a unified science comprising all knowledge of reality accessible to man without dividing it into separate, unconnected special disciplines. . . . The way to attain this [was] by the use of the *logical method of analysis,* worked out by Peano, Frege, Whitehead, and Russell, which serves to eliminate metaphysical assertions and problems as meaningless as well as to clarify the meaning of concepts and sentences of empirical science by showing their immediately observable content—'das Gegebene' " (Joergensen 1951, 4). Carnap's logical investigations were an attempt to develop just such a "thing-language" which would unite the whole range of scholarship, "so that all scientific theories [could] by means of it be reduced to as few deductive systems as possible, preferably to a single one" (Joergensen 1951, 77-78). It was this desire, too, that led to a broad-based interest in semiotics, a meta-discipline under whose rubic woul fall all other disciplines concerned with signs, and the discourse of all disciplines.

The logical empiricists brought their journal, *Erkenntnis,* with them when they came to America, rechristening it the *Journal of Unified Scienc* Their efforts became focused quite soon on an encyclopaedist attempt to p_{..} into concrete form their vision of unified knowledge. In 1938, under the editorial guidance of Otto Neurath, the University of Chicago Press began publishing what was intended as the introduction to this encyclopaedia, bu⁺ which finally stood as the whole *International Encyclopedia of Unified Science.* Among these works are Kuhn's famous study *On the Structure of Scientific Revolutions,* Dewey's *Theory of Valuation,* Carnap's *Foundations of Logic and Mathematics,* Bloomfield's *Linguistic Aspects of Science,* and, most significant for our purpose, Charles W. Morris' *Foundations of the Theory of Signs* (1938b).

Morris' presentation is strongly marked by his studies of Peirce and his teacher, George H. Mead, at the University of Chicago. Mead's influence is reflected in the behaviorist basis of Morris' semiotics,[1] an orientation which became more pronounced in each of his succeeding works. In a paper presented at the 8th International Congress of Philosophy in Prague (1934),[2] called "The Concept of Meaning in Pragmatism and Logical Positivism," Morris grounds meaning in the context of social behavior as "a set of expectations aroused by the symbolic functioning of some object, while the object

---

[1] According to Thomas A. Sebeok (1971), "semiotics" as a singular term was coined by Margaret Mead in 1962 on the model of ethics, mathematics, etc. Both Peirce and Morris used "semiotic" as the noun and adjective; under the influence of French, a number of writers today speak of "semiology." In the interests of consistency, Sebeok and his associates are promoting "semiotics" which seems destined for acceptance in America and, eventually, the English-speaking world at large.

[2] Significantly, this conference was attended by members of the Prague Linguistics Circle (e.g., Jan Mukařovský, Roman Jakobson) who were directly involved in an attempt to combine semiotics and the structuralist study of art, language, and folklore. That Morris seems not to have made contact with them is disappointing, considering the important similarities between his and Mukařovský's theories (see P. Steiner forthcoming).

meant . . . is any object which satisfies the expectations" (Morris 1934, 133). Four years later, this concept of meaning had been replaced by a carefully and extensively worked out theory of signs in which signification is defined as a "mediated taking account of" what the sign designates.

This work of 1938, *Foundations*, provided definitions of key semiotic terms, a justification of semiotics within the Unified Science program, a suggestion of semiotic applications to the various disciplines, but most importantly, a definition of semiotics as the totality of semantics, pragmatics, and syntactics. That is, a study of the semiotic nature of a sign would be incomplete unless it included a consideration of what and how the sign vehicle signified, how the sign affected its interpreter, and how it related to other signs. For Morris' colleagues in the Unified Science movement, this approach was the culmination of the entire empiricist development from Locke to Carnap: "Whereas the older form of empiricism concerned itself mainly with the first [the semantic dimension of semiosis], pragmatism with the second [the pragmatic dimension], and logical positivism with the third [syntactic] of these dimensions of meaning, Morris thinks that, by considering all of them equally, a synthesis may be reached which signifies at the same time an expansion of the concept of meaning and an associated extended form of empiricism which he calls 'scientific empiricism' " (Joergensen 1951, 56).

To others, however, Morris' approach did not seem so salutary. Immediately upon the publication of *Foundations* and a companion article in the *Journal of Unified Science*, "Esthetics and the Theory of Signs" (1938a), the New Critics launched into a biting scrutiny of Morris' semiotics. The dialogue that ensued in one of the main new critical journals, *The Kenyon Review*, documents another of those mishaps which, like Peirce's falling out with academia, set back the development of American semiotics by decades. For where Morris proposed to unify the humanities with the sciences under the rubric of semiotics, the New Critics' point of departure was a belief in the fundamental incompatibility of art and science and the need to protect the arts, and poetry in particular, from the reductivism and abstraction of science (see, for example, Ransom 1938).[3]

It was the behaviorist underpinnings of Morris' work that especially offended the New Critics, who saw in Morris' reluctance to postulate a perceiving mind and a code a failure to account adequately for the aesthetic experience. Allen Tate, for example, complains that " 'Meaning' has been

---

[3]For a full discussion of the interchange between Morris and the New Critics, consult my manuscript, "The Case for Unclear Thinking: The New Critics versus Charles Morris."

replaced by a concept of 'operational validity'—that is to say, the 'true' meaning of a term is not its definition; it is the number of statements containing it which can be referred to empirically observed events. Along with meaning and definition, universals also disappear; and with universals, cognition" (Tate 1941, 26-27). Morris' successor as the leading figure in American semiotics, Roman Jakobson, deliberately ignored Morris' behaviorism, choosing instead aspects of Saussure, Husserl, and Peirce. However, the notion that a behaviorism-free semiotics was possible was not apparent to the New Critics who largely rejected sign theory.

The central concept of Morris' semiotics of art in "Esthetics and the Theory of Signs" is his definition of the aesthetic sign as an icon whose designatum is a value. Since the icon contains its own sign vehicle as one of its denotata (it is *like* what it signifies and hence it signifies itself), the work has a double referential thrust—to reality and to itself. It is also value-laden, and can give insight into the world whose values it contains. But Tate argues that treating the art work as an icon shifts its value onto what it imitates rather than onto what is essentially artistic in it (Tate 1941, 42).[4] The enormous influence of the New Critics on scholarship and university curricula in literature effectively killed any possibility for semiotics to enter, never mind encompass, the study of literature. That situation has remained virtually unchanged until the very recent past.[5]

Another approach to semiotics making its mark in America during the early 1940s was that of the German philosopher, Ernst Cassirer, who had immigrated to the United States in 1941. His works began to appear in English translation around the time of his death in 1945, but Susanne Langer, one of his translators and closest followers, had already published her popular *Philosophy in a New Key* by 1942, propagating Cassirer's position that man is essentially an *animal symbolicum*. Cassirer and Langer traced the development of man's symbol-making from his early creations of language, myth, and ritual to the emergence of art and finally science. In the modern age "the edifice of human knowledge stands before us, not as a vast collection of sense reports, but as a structure of facts *that are symbols* and *laws that are their meanings*. A philosophical theme has been set forth to a coming age: an epistemological theme, the comprehension of science. The power of symbolism is its cue as the finality of sense-data was the cue of a former epoch" (Langer 1951, 29).

[4]Under the influence of Tate's and Ransom's criticism, Morris rejected the idea that the artistic sign is necessarily iconic (Morris 1946, 276 & 296).

[5]Though Wimsatt's title, *The Verbal Icon,* appears to embrace the semiotic approach, the explanation that the epigraph offers for this term is a complete distortion of Morris' formula.

For Cassirer and Langer, the fundamental semiotic distinction is that between symbol and what Langer calls "sign" in the first edition of *Philosophy in a New Key* and later "signal" (following Morris). A sign-signal amounts to something close to Peirce's and the early Morris' index, in that it is based on an existential "association" on a one-to-one basis between sign vehicle and referent (Langer 1951, 58), and evokes "action appropriate to the presence of its object" (Langer 1951, 61). "Symbols," on the other hand, "are not proxy for their objects, but are *vehicles for the conception of objects.* . . . In talking *about* things we have conceptions of them, not the things themselves: and *it is the conceptions, not the things, that symbols directly 'mean'* " (Langer 1951, 61). Man's ability to manipulate concepts rather than merely the material reality around him is what the development of ever more complicated symbolic modes reveals, and for Langer the symbol-signal opposition marks the distinction between human and sub-human sign use. Morris' behaviorism precludes a treatment of the symbol as conceptual, and since language is made up largely of symbols the disagreement over the symbol has been a recurring dispute in American linguistically oriented semiotics.

The famous notion of art as 'significant form' and the strongly humanistic orientation of Langer's and Cassirer's writings did much to popularize the notion of man as *animal symbolicum* and the modern world as the scene of a philosophical struggle over the nature of signs. However, the imprecision of much of this discourse and the toleration of quasi-mystical notions left Langer and Cassirer out of the mainstream of American semiotics. Morris notes that "Ernst Cassirer's *Philosophie der symbolischen Formen* and *An Essay on Man* . . . show great sensitivity to a wide range of symbolic phenomena, and so act as valuable correctives to oversimplified versions of semiotic; but their failure to deal adequately with the core problem as to the nature of sign-processes makes their work at the wider circumference more suggestive than scientific" (Morris 1946, 229 note A). And by the mid-fifties, even Susanne Langer was taking the view that "the whole study of symbols and meaning seems to me to be temporarily exhausted" (Langer 1956, 55). She blamed this on the imprecision of Cassirer's definition of the symbol, which, like Freud's, had proved vacuous upon rigorous philosophical inquiry. As she puts it, "The proof of a pudding is in the eating, and I submit that Cassirer's pudding is good; but the recipe is not on the box" (Langer 1956, 56).

At the opening of the post-war period (1946), Morris produced his major treatise on semiotics, *Signs, Language, and Behavior.* Here, the homely notion of "mediated taking account of" is replaced by the preparatory stimulus as the new definition of the sign. The new formulation of sign process is as follows: "If anything, A, is a preparatory-stimulus which in the absence of stimulus-objects initiating response-sequences of a certain behavior-family causes a disposition in some organism to respond under certain conditions by response-sequences of this behavior-family, then A is a sign" (Morris 1946, 87). The enormous dependence here upon behaviorist psychology creates a sharp contrast to the earlier *Foundations,* and Morris repeatedly feels obliged to account for his position (Morris 1946; 80, 103, 339, etc.).

Despite the hostility it aroused, particularly in the arts and linguistics, Morris' behaviorism had one very important result for the future of American semiotics, and that was the explicit introduction into semiotics of sub-human sign use, what Sebeok later would call "zoosemiotics." Morris uses two key examples of semiosis throughout *Signs, Language, and Behavior:* a laboratory animal responding to lights or sounds which he has been trained to associate with food, and a person warning a driver of a blocked road ahead. The question of whether these sign situations are truly analogous Morris leaves open. But the animal figures virtually throughout the exposition, often in preference to the person, whose sign usage at times appears too complicated for the purposes of clear illustration! This fact is a symptom of Morris' desire to avoid all reference to a code, mentally located conventions, and so on.[6] He insists that language signs do not exist outside of their use, and that the sign families they belong to are the resultants of a common usage; "the implication that language has an existence apart from utterances is avoided on the basis of this formulation" (Morris 1946, 113). This aspect of Morris' semiotics has had relatively little success among most semiotically inclined linguists, who go back to Peirce's (and Saussure's) definition of the categorematic word as a symbol, i.e., a sign-vehicle linked to its reference by a socially held convention and linked to other symbols through their place in the code.

One of the major tasks Morris sets himself in *Signs, Language, and Behavior* is the classification of types of discourse. These types were to be defined as the interaction of the various uses and modes (the latter referring to the kind of thing a sign signifies). By juggling modes and uses, Morris comes up with sixteen types of discourse to which he gives conventional names such as "poetic," "religious," "scientific." He makes it clear that these terms are just a convenience, but the danger in choosing them is evident when we look at Morris' chart below. Even with his explanations, it is hard to link individual mode-use dyads to their respective discourse resultants.

---

[6] In *Foundations* (pp. 37-38), Morris speaks of conceptions lying behind symbols, but these are "rules of usage" rather than ideas, and the term drops out of his system by 1946.

EXAMPLES OF THE MAJOR TYPES OF DISCOURSE
(Morris 1946, 203)

Use / Mode	Informative	Valuative	Incitive	Systemic
Designative	Scientific	Fictive	Legal	Cosmological
Appraisive	Mythical	Poetic	Moral	Critical
Prescriptive	Technological	Political	Religious	Propagandistic
Formative	Logico-mathematical	Rhetorical	Grammatical	Metaphysical

Some of Morris' explanations of these types of discourse are as follows:

> The liberating quality of fictive discourse lies in the exploration which it permits of how life might be lived in various ways in various environments. (209)
> The general signification of mythical discourse lies in the fact that it informs the interpreter in a vivid manner of the modes of action approved and disapproved by some group. (214)
> The great significance of poetic discourse lies in the vivid and direct way that it records and sustains achieved valuations, and explores and strengthens novel valuations. In poetry the object is turned, as it were, before our eyes with symbolic fingers, and as we look at the object described and exemplified by the poet, we come in varying degrees and for a longer or shorter time to take the valuative perspective of the poem in terms of which the object signified has the apprehended significance. (216)

The subjectivity of much of this discussion and the crudeness of its pigeonholing immediately force exceptions to mind. Nevertheless, the importance of such a typology of discourse to the development of semiotics as the overarching sign system and the vehicle of the Unified Science movement is obvious. Nor does Morris' contribution stop here. For his notion of signs goes beyond language, and prefigures the eruption in the 1960s and 1970s of disciplines concerned with non-verbal sign-systems. Acknowledging the centrality of "spoken-heard signs" in man's life, Morris considers the fixation of semiotics on them "a great error, and one from which semiotic must now free itself. For not only does the spoken-heard language depend in crucial places on other signs, and itself give rise to signs which are not spoken and heard (post-language signs), but such a language is not coextensive with all signs drawn from sounds and has never supplanted its great rival—visual signs. . . . [I]nterpersonal relations are as much determined by the signs gained by the sight of other persons (manner of dress, gestures, facial movements, physical appearance) as by the sounds he utters" (Morris 1946, 271-2). The seeds of kinesics, paralinguistics, proxemics, and so much more of contemporary sign theory lie in these words.

In 1943, three years before *Signs, Language, and Behavior* appeared in print, the New York Linguistic Circle was founded by scholars of Columbia University and the Ecole Libre des Hautes Etudes. The orientation of the Circle was international and interdisciplinary. Thus, in the first number of its journal, *Word*, Claude Lévi-Strauss, advocating a structuralist anthropology based on a comparison of kinship systems and phonological systems, stated: "un revue linguistique comme WORD ne peut se limiter à l'illusion de thèses et de points de vue strictement linguistiques. Elle se doit aussi d'accueiller les psychologues, sociologues et ethnographes anxieux d'apprendre de la linguistique moderne la route qui mène à la connaissance positive des faits sociaux" (Lévi-Strauss 1945, 33). Consequently, *Word* contains the etymologies of Leo Spitzer, studies of surrogate languages such as George Herzog's "Drum Signaling in a West-African Tribe," Kurt Goldstein's report on the relevance of his psychological investigations of aphasia for linguistics, Rulon Wells's study of Saussurian structuralism, Jakobson's structuralist approach to the Russian verb, as well as work in semantics, artificial languages, literary analysis, folklore, and historical linguistics.

The interdisciplinary range and the centrality of structuralism in the articles in *Word* indicate the spiritual dependence of the New York group on the Prague Linguistic Circle that had come before it. In this group, semiotics and structuralism had been intimately related,[7] and in the second number of *Word* Cassirer explicitly sets out this connection. He claims that the conflicting positions of Mill and Husserl had presented modern linguistics with a dilemma. Mill had argued for a logic rooted in reality, with no logical relation valid that did not hold in the realm of facts. Husserl dismissed any empirical

---

[7]This approach was the seedbed of modern structuralism, although the Prague contributions are seldom cited in the West because many of them remained untranslated. See P. and W. Steiner (1976) for a survey of the various structuralist-semiotic currents in the movement.

or psychologically grounded logic, insisting on the independence of logic from fact and hence its purely formal truth. But because of the traditional dependence of linguistics (grammar) on logic and the impossibility of omitting either the factual or the formal from linguistic investigation, Cassirer finds that modern linguistics is the realm in which the distinctions between the factual and the formal is erased. This development "appears in Saussure's *Cour de linguistique générale* (2nd ed., Geneva, 1922), in the works of Trubetzkoy, of Roman Jakobson, and of other members of the 'Cercle Linguistique de Prague' " (Cassirer 1945, 104). The reason that linguistics can bring about this reconciliation of the empirical and the ideal, according to Cassirer, is that its subject-matter is semiotic in nature. "Language is a 'symbolic form.' [Though it has a material aspect] it consists of symbols, and symbols are no part of our physical world. They belong to an entirely different universe of discourse. Natural things and symbols cannot be brought to the same denominator. Linguistics is a part of semiotic, not of physics" (Cassirer 1945, 114-115). Thus, Cassirer describes the philosophical basis of structuralism as a function of its semiotic subject matter.

Word also registers the confusion of the postwar years regarding the relation between semiotics, linguistics, and semantics. Semantics at this time was suffering from lack of definition because of the diverse input of such scholars as Tarski, Korzybski, Carnap, and Wittgenstein; and the appearance of semiotics, loosely defined as the study of meaning, severely exacerbated this identity crisis. The British semanticist, Stephen de Ullman, remarks in *Word* that "if the various schools of semanticists—behaviorists, logical positivists, champions of the context theory, and other advocates of symbolic logic—claim to be independent of linguistics, they are confident that their theory of signs will annex and include the domain of language, and that such inclusion will ultimately redound to the advantage of linguistics proper" (Ullmann 1946, 114). To equate Morris' semiotics (which Ullmann explicitly mentions here) with semantics, and then state that this semiotics-semantics is to encompass linguistics is to court confusion. Such notions along with chauvinism toward academic field, are responsible for many of the charges of 'linguistic imperialism' and 'semiotic imperialism' leveled at structuralists and semioticians. Certainly Morris' position on this issue is clear. As Allen Walker Read pointed out in another article in *Word* (Read 1946, 87), semantics, along with syntax and pragmatics, is one of three dimensions of semiosis. Thus, Uriel Weinreich begins his encyclopaedia article (1968) on "Semantics and Semiotics" as follows: "Semiotics in the study of sign phenomena. Specialized research into natural human language—the semiotic sphere par excellence—constitutes linguistics; within linguistics, semantics is concerned with the conveyance of meaning by the grammatical and lexical devices of a language" (Weinreich 1968, 164-165). This hierarchy is now generally accepted by American semioticians,[8] but confusion still remains (see Kalish 1967).

The most notable semiotician of the New York Circle was Roman Jakobson. Having come to America in 1941 after helping to found the Prague Linguistic Circle and the Moscow Linguistic Circle before it, Jakobson developed a semiotic approach to linguistics, poetics, and folklore studies that reflected the work of Ferdinand de Saussure, the pragmatic philosophy of Charles S. Peirce, and—a topic only recently under investigation—the sign theory of Edmund Husserl (see Holenstein 1976).

The result of this cross-fertilization of sources places Jakobson in a special position among semioticians. He points to a fundamental split between the American and French approaches: "Peirce's concern with the different ranks of coassistance of the three functions in all three types of signs, and in particular his scrupulous attention to the indexical and iconic components of verbal symbols, is intimately linked with his thesis that 'the most perfect of signs' are those in which the iconic, indexical, and symbolic characters 'are blended as equally as possible' "; for Saussure, on the other hand, the arbitrary sign (symbol) created the most adequate semiosis (Jakobson 1965, 349). Jakobson himself follows Peirce here, revealing in intricate and original analyses the ways in which indexes and icons participate in the apparently symbol-dominated system of language.

In "Shifters, Verbal Categories, and the Russian Verb" (parts I and II, 1950; completed, 1956), Jakobson defines shifters as indexical symbols, concluding that "shifters are distinguished from all other constituents of the linguistic code solely by their compulsory reference to the given message" (Jakobson 1956, 132). And in "Zeichen und System der Sprache" (1959), he extends the indexical property of language to the *signans-signatum* relation itself, redefining Saussure's principle of arbitrariness: "Der Zusammenhang zwischen einem signans und einem *signatum,* den Saussure willkürlicherweise arbiträr nennt, ist in Wirklichkeit eine gewohnheitsmäßige, erlernte Kontiguität, die für alle Mitglieder der gegebenen Sprachgemeinschaft obligat ist" (Jakobson 1959, 272-273).

Jakobson also argues for a thoroughgoing iconicity of language. For example, in his "Quest for the Essence of Language" (1965) he claims that "the temporal order of speech events tends to mirror the order of narrated events in time or in rank [e.g., *Veni, vidi, vici*] " (349). And just as Peirce

---

[8]Jakobson (1968) adds a dimension in this hierarchy: "Semiotic, as an inquiry into the communication of all kinds of messages, is the nearest concentric circle that encompasses linguistics, whose research field is confined to the communication of verbal messages, and the next, wider concentric circle is an integrated science of communication which embraces social anthropology, sociology, and economics" (p. 698).

found algebra a sort of diagram (and hence an icon), Jakobson claims (with Peirce) that "the arrangement of the words in the sentence, for instance, must serve as *icons,* in order that the sentence may be understood" (Jakobson 1965, 350). "[T]hese and many similar facts of linguistic experience prove to be at variance with the Saussurian averment that 'in the sound structure of the signans there is nothing which would bear any resemblance to the value or meaning of the sign" (Jakobson 1965, 352).

The discovery of iconic and indexical properties in language raised the question of the relation between sign function in language and other media. For Jakobson discovered that "it is impossible to analyze exhaustively a single system of signs without constant reference to the general problems of semiotics, and in the context of this new and rapidly developing science the question of the relation between the various systems of signs is one of the fundamental and burning questions. We face the task of constructing an over-all model of sign production and sign perception and separate models for different types of signs" (Jakobson 1964, 338-339).

Thus, he outlines some of the important semiotic differences between visual and auditory signs, discovering a "manifold dichotomy of signs": "Primarily representational signs, which display a factual similarity or contiguity with their objects, prove to be mostly visual, in contradistinction to non-representational signs, which are predominantly auditory. The former deal foremost with space, the latter with time; simultaneity in the one case and successivity in the other is the principal structuring device. In contrast to the first semiotic type, the second implies a compulsorily hierarchical arrangement and discrete elementary components, conceived, selected, and organized to serve the given purpose" (Jakobson 1963, 337).

The opposition between simultaneity and successivity in the discussion of visual and auditory signs above is related to another of Jakobson's contributions to sign theory. In the early 1950s, aware of Gelb, Goldstein, and Luria's experiments with aphasic patients, Jakobson observed a correlation between the two basic kinds of aphasia and the two fundamental operations of language, selection and combination. Aphasics are either unable to associate elements of a paradigm (which exists as a simultaneity as part of *langue*) or they are unable to combine them with other elements so as to form a speech chain (which exists as a successivity). Paradigmatic association and syntagmatic combination "provide each linguistic sign with two sets of *interpretants,* to utilize the effective concept introduced by Charles Sanders Peirce: there are two referents which serve to interpret the sign—one to the code, and the other to the context, whether coded or free, and in each of these ways the sign is related to another set of linguistic signs, through an *alternation* in the former case and through an *alignment* in the latter" (Jakobson 1954, 244).

The relative importance of these two referential sets—the code and the context—gives rise to two poles in art: the metaphoric, in which the code is the most important interpretant set, and the metonymic, in which the context dominates. Jakobson argues that realism is heavily metonymic, while romanticism and symbolism are charged with metaphoric relations.

Jakobson's notion of selection (and hence of paradigm and metaphor) is a primary point of contrast with the behaviorist position in that it postulates a code which every normal speaker internalizes. This notion is consistent too with the influence of Goldstein, who claims to have proved the existence of ideation—conceptualization—in language use through the observation of aphasics who have lost it (Goldstein 1946). As a result of this position, Jakobson very carefully distinguishes between symbol and signal, intentional communication and unintentional information, human sign usage and that of machines or animals. "[W]e must consistently take into account the decisive difference between *communication* which implies a real or alleged addresser and *information* whose source cannot be viewed as an addresser by the interpreter of the indications obtained" (Jakobson 1968, 703). By 1967, Jakobson was asserting that the "transition from 'zoosemiotic' to human speech is a huge qualitative leap, in contradiction to the outdated behaviorist creed that the 'language' of animals differs from men's language in degree but not in kind" (Jakobson 1967, 673). The lines here are clearly drawn between Morris' approach to semiotics and that of Jakobson.

Corresponding to the typology of discourse which Morris had presented in *Signs, Language, and Behavior,* Jakobson developed a typology of language functions in his crucial "Closing Statement: Linguistics and Poetics" (Jakobson 1958) delivered at the 1958 Conference on Style held at Bloomington, Indiana (see Sebeok 1960). Here he reduced the elements of the communication situation to six essential components: the sender, receiver, code, message, channel, and context. To each of these he assigned a language function: the emotive, conative, metalinguistic, poetic, phatic, and referential (respectively). Interjections, for example, are dominated by the emotive function in that they primarily reflect the state of mind of the sender; imperatives are dominated by the conative function in that they primarily attempt to affect the receiver; poetry is dominated by the poetic function in that it focuses attention upon the message itself; and so on. Jakobson claims an essential polyfunctionality in all language use, although usually one function predominates in a given utterance. This approach frees him from the confusingly arbitrary divisions of discourse which Morris' table shows, since Jakobson was outlining functions and not categories of discourse. Thus, the poetic function can operate in discourse which is not poetry, and what is traditionally termed poetry can come to be dominated by other functions than the poetic. Moreover, where Morris' uses seem quite arbitrary, Jakobson has grounded his functions in the essential elements of the communication model. Instead of arguing, like Morris, that poetry is valuative in use and appraisive in mode, Jakobson's poetic function performs a purely linguistic operation on language, rearranging the normal relation between selection and combination; "The poetic function projects the principle of equivalence from the axis of selection to the axis of combination"; "in poetry the equation is used to build a sequence" (Jakobson 1958, 358). As a result, the poem is pervaded with equivalences; its iconicity is vastly increased, especially in the sense that internal elements of the poem resemble each other. Parts become icons of each other and the poem becomes overwhelmingly self-referential. Our attention is focused on the message itself and not upon any of its other functional relations.

In this discussion of Jakobson we have been jumping rather chaotically back and forth from 1950 to 1968. Had we proceeded chronologically, the growing establishment of semiotics as a discipline would have been evident. Advances in other fields made it possible for Jakobson to ground his linguistic semiotics in ever-widening spheres of knowledge—psychology, cybernetics, information theory, semantics, biology, sociology, anthropology, even genetics. Perhaps the most important reason for the growth of semiotically oriented disciplines in the social sciences and sciences was the rise of information theory and cybernetics in the 1950s. Morris' *Signs, Language, and Behavior* was a prime source for such research, as is apparent in Colin Cherry's popularization of information theory of 1966, *On Human Communication,*[9] which divides the communication process into its syntactic, semantic, and pragmatic aspects, calling Peirce and Morris the path-breakers in the field.

In 1958 the Conference on Style (mentioned above) was held in Bloomington. "This Bloomington meeting was doubtless the initial one in a series of get-togethers, nominally devoted to the verbal arts, but distinctly tinged with a trace of already perceptible semiotic coloring. In the 1960's such conferences rapidly expanded in two directions: they became international as to participants, and turned increasingly pansemiotic as to subject matter" (Sebeok 1975c, 22).

The growing pansemiotic thrust was the result of rapid developments in semiotic fields beyond linguistics.[10] For information theory and semiotics had made it apparent that human semiosis was not limited to language. Key works by H. L. Smith (1952) and Trager (1958) outlined a new study,

---

[9] W. John Smith (1974, 568-569) claims that his theory of zoosemiotics is a direct outgrowth of *Signs, Language, and Behavior* and communication theory as presented in Cherry (1966).

[10] For a handy summary of current issues in several of the major areas of semiotics, see Sebeok (1974b).

paralinguistics. The semiotic study of human gestures was initiated by Ray L. Birdwhistell's *Introduction to Kinesics* (1952) and concerns the ways that the face and body are used to convey information. The popular version of this study is the much discussed "body language" (Fast 1970). Man's use of the space around him as a semiotic medium is studied in the field of *proxemics.* The term was coined by the anthropologist Edward T. Hall in about 1955 as the study of how people structure the space around them: "the distance between men in conduct of daily transactions, the organization of space in his houses and buildings, and ultimately, the layout of his towns" (Watson 1974, 312). Erving Goffman has brought many of these issues to public attention through his widely read *Presentation of Self in Everyday Life* (1959). And much of proxemics, kinesics, and paralinguistics is covered under the general heading of non-verbal communication, which Mary Ritchie Key (1974, 267) divides into the "Sensory, Tactile, Proxemics, Silence, Sign Language Systems, and Artifacts such as clothes and hair."

This growth of semiotic disciplines also provided a frame of reference for many older studies of communicative behavior. The investigation of secondary sign systems such as writing, of surrogate speech (drum and whistle systems), of artificial languages (computer languages, logical notation, etc.) now found a home under the umbrella of semiotics. The hand language of the deaf and dumb—sign language per se—has been studied by semioticians, American Sign Language receiving its definitive treatment by William C. Stokoe (1972). And biology, long concerned with the communication of bees, ants, chimpanzees, etc., acquired a semiotic branch which Thomas A. Sebeok christened zoosemiotics.

This discipline challenges Jakobson's claim that human and nonhuman sign usage are separated by a vast gulf. And W. John Smith, for example, suggests a connection between animal communication and the rise of language: "language did not arise as a capacity of a non-communicating animal. Initially it competed with, coexisted with, zoosemiotic forms of communicating employed by the same individuals. It still does. Man's zoosemiotic systems must have had some shaping influence on the early evolutionary history of language" (W. J. Smith 1974, 614-615).

The fact that this position resembles Morris' in *Signs, Language, and Behavior* is understandable, partly because the biologist is more or less forced to adopt a behavioristic rather than mentalistic account of sign use—he can observe only the behavior of animals—and partly because the major figure in zoosemiotics, Thomas A. Sebeok, studied with Morris. But Sebeok's semiotic activity goes far beyond the realm of zoosemiotics. He has become the central figure in semiotic studies in America, founding and running the semiotic center in Bloomington, arranging conferences in semiotics, editing semiotic series and the journal *Semiotica,* researching the history of the field and contributing theoretical articles. His approach is catholic; by refusing to prejudge the distinctions between human and nonhuman sign usage, Sebeok is trying to move closer to a universal theory of semiosis.

The explosion of semiotic studies in America in the sixties and seventies, however, is more the result of the rise of structuralism in France and the growth of interdisciplinary activity in American universities than the influence of individual scholars, as Sebeok himself remarks. "Apart from Morris's own *Signs, Language, and Behavior*, neither an introductory nor an advanced synthesis has yet been produced by any single American or other Anglophone semiotician in the postwar era to date. Restraints on the semiotic floodgates began at first to be lifted, with the onset of the 1960's, both here and abroad, less by dint of the creative efforts of individual scholars than through the common academic collaborative instrumentality of a host of colloquia, conferences, seminars, and all sorts of other meetings, many of them international and interdisciplinary" (Sebeok 1975c, 15-16).

This trail of conferences culminated in the North American Semiotics Colloquium held in Tampa, Florida in 1975, co-ordinated with a semiotics program in the summer session of the State University of Florida and the Linguistic Institute of the Linguistic Society of America. At the Tampa meeting, the Semiotic Society of America was founded. It held its first annual meeting in Atlanta during October of 1976. Speakers ranged through virtually every formal discipline, the program being divided approximately evenly among zoosemiotics, Peircian philosophy, and semiotic approaches to the arts, anthropology, and sociology. The SSA publishes a quarterly bulletin entitled *Semiotic Scene*[11] under the editorship of Daniel Laferrière of Tufts University.

By the 1970s the scope of semiotic activity worldwide had become bewildering, and the already complex American scene was further complicated. French developments in semiotics and structuralism are reflected in the journals *Semiotext(e)* (Columbia University), *Diacritics* (Cornell University), and *Sub-Stance* (University of Wisconsin), in a great many theoretical books (e.g., Scholes 1974, Culler 1970, Macksey 1970), and in French departments throughout the country. Soviet Semiotics is beginning to penetrate America as a result of the emigration of such scholars as S. Šaumjan and the translations of the work of the Tartu School in *Semiotica*, the University of Michigan Slavic Publications, etc. (see *Dispositio* 3, May, 1977 for a full issue devoted to the Soviet semiotics of culture, with bibliography). The semiotic contributions of the major Czech figure in the Prague Linguistic Circle, Jan Mukařovský, are being introduced to America in a two-volume translation

---

[11] Preceding it are three issues of a similar periodical also edited by Laferrière entitled the *Bulletin of Literary Semiotics*.

of his theoretical essays published by Yale University Press (Mukařovský 1977).

Beyond these international influences on the American sphere, new disciplines are constantly entering the semiotic compass. One of the oldest fields concerned with semiotics as symptomatology—medicine—is witnessing new developments in the semiotics of psychiatry (e.g., Shands 1970, Bär 1971). Literary criticism, after a wholesale rejection of sign theory by the New 'Critics, is beginning to look kindly on this discipline (see Richards 1970).[12] Art criticism, following the impetus of Meyer Schapiro, has formed centers of semiotic study at the University of Colorado and SUNY Buffalo. Even the traditional discipline of biblical commentary is reflecting a structural-semiotic orientation in such journals as *Semeia* (see Jacobson 1977).

The growing acceptance of semiotics in American academia is visible in the fact that courses and even programs in semiotics are now beginning to appear. After the hiatus following Morris' seminars at the University of Chicago during the early 1940s, there is now a 'Concentration on Semiotics' at Brown University (begun in 1975), courses at the University of Colorado, Yale, Stanford, Berkeley, the University of Southern Florida, and the University of Michigan, and Sebeok's Pilot Program in Semiotics in the Humanities at Indiana University. This last tentative step of semiotics into the cultural life of America is perhaps the surest sign of its taking root in what one might argue is its native soil.

BIBLIOGRAPHY

For more detailed bibliographies than what follows the reader should turn to the various bibliographies in *Versus*, especially 8/9, 1974 (American semiotics) and those of Sebeok listed below.

Bailey, Richard and Seymour Chatman. 1974. Literary Semiotics in North America. *Versus* 8/9, 227-280.

Bär, Eugen. 1971. The Language of the Unconscious According to Jacques Lacan. *Semiotica* 3, 241-268.

Birdwhistell, Ray L. 1952. *Introduction to Kinesics*. Louisville, Ky.

---

[12]Nevertheless, when Richard Bailey and Seymour Chatman prepared their bibliography, "Literary Semiotics in North America" (1974), they were forced to admit that "the term 'semiotics' is still relatively strange to most American literary scholars. . . . The following list consists largely of titles whose authors have been affected in some way by developments in linguistics" (227).

Bloomfield, Leonard. 1939. *Linguistic Aspects of Science*. Chicago.

Carnap, Rudolph. 1939. *Foundations of Logic and Mathematics*. Chicago.

Cassirer, Ernst. 1944. *An Essay on Man*. New Haven, Conn.

_____ . 1945. Structuralism in Modern Linguistics. *Word* I, 2.

_____ . 1953. *The Philosophy of Symbolic Forms*. New Haven, Conn.

Cherry, Colin. 1966. *On Human Communication*. Cambridge, Mass.

Chomsky, Noam. 1957. *Syntactic Structures*. The Hague.

Dewey, John. 1939. *Theory of Valuation*. Chicago.

Fast, Julius. 1970. *Body Language*. New York.

Gardner, Beatrice T. and R. Allen Gardner. 1971. Two-Way Communication with an Infant Chimpanzee. In: *Behavior of Nonhuman Primates: Modern Research Trends*, eds. Allen M. Schrier and Fred Stollnitz, Vol. 4, 117-184. New York.

Goffman, Erving. 1959. *The Presentation of Self in Everyday Life*. New York.

Goldstein, Kurt. 1946. On Naming and Pseudonaming from Experiences in Psycho-pathology, *Word* II, I.

Greimas, Algirdas J., *et al*. 1970. *Sign, Language, Culture*. The Hague.

Hall, Edward T. 1955. The Anthropology of Manners. *Scientific American* 162 (April), 85-90.

_____ . 1959. *The Silent Language*. Greenwich, Conn.

Hjelmslev, Louis. 1953. *Prolegomena to a Theory of Language*. Baltimore.

Holenstein, Elmar. 1976. *Roman Jakobson's Approach to Language: Phenomenological Structuralism*. Bloomington, Indiana.

Jakobson, Richard. 1977. Biblical Semiotics. *Semiotic Scene* I, 1, 5-26.

Jakobson, Roman. 1954. Two Aspects of Language and Two Types of Aphasic Disturbances. In: Jakobson 1971b, 239-260.

_____ . 1956. Shifters, Verbal Categories, and the Russian Verb. In: Jakobson 1971b, 130-148.

_____ . 1958. Closing Statement: Linguistics and Poetics. In: Sebeok 1960.

_____ . 1959. Zeichen und System der Sprache. In: Jakobson 1971b, 272-280.

_____ . 1963. Visual and Auditory Signs. In: Jakobson 1971b, 334-338.

_____ . 1964. On the Relation between Visual and Auditory Signs. In: Jakobson 1971b, 338-345.

_____ . 1965. Quest for the Essence of Language. In: Jakobson 1971b, 345-360.

_____ . 1967. Linguistics in Relation to Other Sciences. In: Jakobson 1971b.

_____ . 1968. Language in Relation to Other Communication Systems. In: Jakobson 1971b, 697-711.

_____ . 1971b. *Selected Writings II: Word and Language.* The Hague.

Joergensen, Joergen. 1951. *The Development of Logical Empiricism.* Chicago.

Kalish, Donald. 1967. Semantics. *Encyclopedia of Philosophy* 7, 348-358.

Key, Mary Ritchie. 1974. U.S.A.-Nonverbal Communication. *Versus* 8/9, 248-280.

Kuhn, Thomas S. 1970. *The Structure of Scientific Revolutions.* Chicago.

Laferrière, Daniel. 1976. Bibliographies and Surveys of Literary Semiotics. *Bulletin of Literary Semiotics* 1,2,3.

Lamb, Sydney M. 1966. *An Outline of Stratificational Grammar.* Washington, D.C.

Langer, Susanne. 1951^2 [1042^1]. *Philosophy in a New Key.* New York.

_____ . 1956. On a New Definition of "Symbol." *Philosophical Sketches.* Baltimore, 1962.

Lévi-Strauss, Claude. 1945. L'analyse structurale en linguistique et en anthropologie. *Word* I, 1.

Macksey, Richard and Eugenio Donato. 1970. *The Structuralist Controversy: The Languages of Criticism and the Sciences of Man.* Baltimore.

Matejka, L. and I.R. Titunik, eds. 1976. *The Semiotics of Art.* Cambridge, Mass.

Morris, Charles W. 1934. The Concept of Meaning in Pragmatism and Logical Positivism. *Actes du huitième congrès international de philosophie à Prague, 2-7, sept., 1934.* Prague, 1936.

_____ . 1938. Esthetics and the Theory of Signs. In: Morris 1971, 415-434.

_____ . 1938b. *Foundations of the Theory of Signs.* In: Morris 1971, 17-75.

_____ . 1946. *Signs, Language, and Behavior.* In: Morris 1971, 75-401.

_____ . 1971. *Writings on the General Theory of Signs.* Approaches to Semiotics 16. The Hague.

Mukařovský, Jan . *On Poetic Language*. Lisse.

_____ . 1977a. *The Word and Verbal Art*. New Haven, Conn.

_____ . 1977b. *Structure, Sign, and Function*. New Haven, Conn.

Peirce, Charles S. 1931-58. *Collected Papers of Charles Sanders Peirce*. Cambridge, Mass.

Ransom, John Crowe. 1938. *The World's Body*. New York.

Read, Allen Walker. 1948. An Account of the Word "Semantics." *Word* IV, 2.

Richards, I.A. 1970. Jakobson's Shakespeare. *Times Literary Supplement,* May 28, 1970.

Šaumjan, S.K. 1970. Semiotics and the Theory of Generative Grammars. In: Greimas, 1970, 244-56.

Saussure, Ferdinand de. 1972. *Cours de linguistique generale*. Paris.

Schapiro, Meyer. 1969. On Some Problems in the Semiotics of Visual Art: Field and Vehicle in Image-Signs. *Semiotica* 1, 223-242.

_____ . 1973. *Words and Pictures: On the Literal and the Symbolic in the Illustration of a Text*. Approaches to Semiotics 11. The Hague.

Sebeok, Thomas A., ed. 1960. *Style in Language*. Cambridge, Mass.

_____ , ed. with Hayes and Bateson. 1964. *Approaches to Semiotics*. The Hague.

_____ . 1971. Foreword to Morris 1971.

_____ . 1974a. Semiotics: A Survey of the State of the Art. In: Sebeok 1974b, 211-264.

_____ , ed. 1974b. *Current Trends in Linguistics,* Vol. 12, *Linguistics and Adjacent Arts and Sciences*. The Hague.

_____ , ed. 1975a. *The Tell-Tale Sign: A Survey of Semiotics*. Lisse.

_____ . 1975b. Six Species of Signs. *Semiotica* 12, 233-260.

_____ . 1975c. The Semiotic Web: A Chronicle of Prejudices. *Bulletin of Literary Semiotics* 2, 1-65;3, 25-29 (index).

Shands, Harley C. 1970. *Semiotic Approaches to Psychiatry*. Approaches to Semiotics 12. The Hague.

Smith, H.L. 1952. *The Communication Situations*. Washington, D.C.

Smith, W. John. 1974. Zoosemiotics: Ethology and the Theory of Signs. In: Sebeok 1974b, 561-629.

Steiner, Peter. To appear. Jan Mukařovský and Charles W. Morris: Two Pioneers of the Semiotics of Art. *Semiotica.*

_____ and Wendy Steiner. 1976. The Relational Axes of Poetic Language. Foreword to: Mukařovský 1976.

Steiner, Wendy. To appear. The Semiotics of Portraiture. *Semiotica.*

_____ . "The Case for Unclear Thinking: The New Critics versus Charles Morris." Unpublished manuscript.

Stokoe, William C., Jr. 1972. *Semiotics and Human Sign Languages.* Approaches to Semiotics 21. The Hague.

Tate, Allen. 1941. Literature as Knowledge. *Reason in Madness.* New York.

Trager. 1958. Paralanguage: A First Approximation. *Studies in Linguistics* 13, 1-12.

Ullmann, Stephen de. 1946. Language and Meaning. *Word* II, 2.

_____ . 1974. Proxemics. In: Sebeok 1974b, 311-345.

Weinreich, Uriel. 1968. Semantics and Semiotics. In: *International Encyclopedia of Social Sciences 14, 164-169. New York.*

THE BIRTH OF PSYCHOANALYSIS IN SEMIOTICS, OR OF SEMIOTICS IN PSYCHOANALYSIS

Neal Bruss

The first two indications that Sigmund Freud (1856-1939) would shortly articulate any semiotic theory, let alone one very similar to that which would follow from Saussure, are Freud's enthusiastic observations at thirty of the use of hypnotism in research and treatment of hysteria by the French physician Jean-Martin Charcot and his brief concluding remark in *On Aphasia* five years later that the linguistic disorders of aphasics could be found in the speech of healthy persons under stress.[1] What makes these small events so important for semiotics is that Freud, like Charcot, was at that time a conventional neurologist, grounded in anatomy and physiology—in strictly physical sciences. Except for the concluding remark (and use of an intriguing but conventional associationalist model of language production), *On Aphasia* deals with brain function and structure. For his part, Charcot never extended his research to reach the semiotic crux of Freud's psychoanalysis, that physical symptoms could arise as expressions of meanings rather than from physical causes, and until the end of this period, Freud had not either.

But in 1895, at 39, Freud fully stated this defining principle of psychoanalysis in the *Studies on Hysteria.* Taking hypnosis beyond Charcot, Freud found that hysterics were able to state ideas in speech under hypnosis which corresponded to symptoms suffered under ordinary consciousness. Freud's case studies were a *tour de force,* with the symptoms of several of his patients resolving themselves into puns on German cliches (which preserve their meanings in English). For example, the case of Frau Cäcilie M.:

> A particular series of experiences of hers were accompanied by a
> stabbing sensation in the region of the heart (meaning 'it stabbed
> me to the heart'). The pain that occurs in hysteria of nails being
> driven in the head was without any doubt to be explained in her

---

[1] See Freud's essay, "Charcot," trans. James Strachey, in *The Standard Edition of the Complete Psychological Works of Sigmund Freud,* gen. ed. James Strachey, 24 vols. (London, Hogarth Press, 1953-1974, hereafter referred to as *Standard Edition*), [1893] III: 9-23. *On Aphasia,* trans. E. Stengel (New York, International Universities Press, 1953), p. 153.

case as a pain related to thinking. ('Something's come into my
head.') Pains of this kind were always cleared up as soon as the
problems involved were cleared up. Running parallel to the sensation of a hysterical 'aura' . . . in the throat, when that feeling appeared after an insult, was the thought, 'I shall have to swallow
this.'[2]

Freud added in a public lecture that violent pains in the patient's right heel
were connected with fears of being unable to " 'find herself on a right footing' " with friends of her husband.[3] Although psychoanalysis is ordinarily
thought to emerge with *the Interpretation of Dreams,* in which Freud provided a method for analyzing symptoms, including the substitution of the
free association method for hypnosis, the essence and direction of psycho-
analysis is evident in the *Studies.* Freud's semiotics and psychoanalysis are
virtually the same thing, differing only in the slightest shade of emphasis: the
implication of the *Studies* for psychoanalysis was that an extensive range of
disease symptoms incurable by physical medicine were shown to be treatable
by decoding; the implication of the work for semiotics was that a vast range
of "involuntary" behavior was revealed to be a type of language. Indeed,
Freud's self-conscious attempt to hold the credulity of the readers of the
Studies in the face of the dazzling simplicity with which the meaning of
symptoms was revealed addresses both the emergence of a new therapy and a
new study of language:

> I have not always been a psychotherapist. Like other neuro-
> pathologists, I was trained to employ local diagnosis and electro-
> prognosis, and it still strikes me myself as strange that the case
> histories I write should read like short stories and that, as one
> might say, they lack the serious stamp of science. I must console
> myself with the reflection that the nature of the subject is evi-
> dently responsible for this, rather than any preference of my
> own.[4]

---

[2] Sigmund Freud and Josef Breuer, *Studies on Hysteria,* trans. James Strachey and
Alix Strachey, II: 180-81. Freud's authorized biographer Ernest Jones, in *The Life and
Works of Sigmund Freud* (New York, Basic Books, 1953), pp. 250-56, provides evidence
that Freud's contribution overshadowed Breuer's in the *Studies.* All references and quo-
tations from the *Studies* are taken from sections explicitly attributed by the *Standard
Edition* to Freud rather than Breuer.
    [3] "The Mechanism of Hysterical Phenomena," lecture to the Vienna Medical
Society, 11 January 1893, trans. James Strachey, *Standard Edition* III: 34.
    [4] P. 160.

The most obvious indication of the importance of semiotic concerns to Freud is the frequency and priority of passages on language in his work. Language figures throughout the Freudian corpus, with the most linguistically-insightful passages occurring in works like the *Interpretation* which are of first importance for psychologists, but there are also short papers which focus on language rather than other psychological issues, papers like "The Antithetical Meaning of Primal Words," in which Freud compares the purported representation in ancient languages of opposite concepts by single words to the equivalence of opposites in dreams.[5] There are frequent passages in Freud's work in which he explicitly describes the domain of psychoanalytic symptoms as a language or a family of languages, as in "The Claims of Psychoanalysis to Scientific Interest":

> . . . the unconscious speaks more than one dialect. According to the differing psychological conditions governing and distinguishing the various forms of neurosis, we find regular modifications in the way in which unconscious mental impulses are expressed. While the gesture-language of hysteria agrees on the whole with the picture-language of dreams and visions, etc., the thought-language of obsessional neurosis and of the paraphrenias (dementia praecox and paranoia) exhibits special idiomatic peculiarities which, in a number of instances, we have been able to understand and inter-relate. For instance, what a hysteric expresses by vomiting an obsessional will express by painstaking protective measures against infection, while a paraphrenic will be led to complaints or suspicions that he is being poisoned. These are all of them different representations of the patient's wish to become pregnant which have been repressed into the unconscious, or of his defensive reaction against that wish.[6]

To base Freud's stature as a semiotician on the frequency or explicitness of such passages may not be convincing in that there is no way to show that these uses were not merely metaphorical. Although language seems to be an important concern in Freud's psychological writing, it never occurs for example in his correspondence with his psychological colleagues. A second way of assessing its importance, then, would be to chart how closely his linguistic thought parallels that of a theoretician like Saussure. A close correspondence with Saussure would be especially favorable to structuralist semiotics, for Freud apparently never knew of Saussure, and such a

[5] Trans. Alan Tyson, in *Standard Edition* [1910] XI: 153-161.
[6] Trans. James Strachey, in *Standard Edition* [1913] XIII: 177-78.

convergence would validate those principles which two thinkers reached through separate routes.

A reading of Freud's work shows such a body of concepts which corresponds directly with the principles of the *Course in General Linguistics.* Most important, and as Roman Jakobson noted, the two formative principles of dream formation and the keys to all psychoanalytic phenomena, "condensation" and "displacement" in the *Interpretation of Dreams,* are equivalent to the functions of Saussure's syntagmatic and paradigmatic axes of language.[7] Saussure's "langue" and "parole" can be seen in terms of the individual patient by Freud and reflected in his crucial distinction in the *Interpretation* between "manifest dream content" and its heavily modified instantiation in latent dream thought."[8] The double-articulation of the sign into material and conceptual aspects is presupposed in the manifest-latent distinction but charted in detail in the study of jokes, slips of the tongue and other "psychopathologies of everyday life," in which the urgency of the meaning of one sign for a speaker forces its sound onto the sound of another sign, or in the phenomena of dreams or hysteric symptoms, in which similarities of sound as in rhyming or identity of meaning as in punning allow the meaning of one sign to be expressed in the sound of another.[9] The principle of the arbitrariness of the sign is manifest in Freud's insistence that the psychoanalyst could not guess the underlying meaning of a symptom or dream symbol from its superficial appearance or from its past meaning but must rely on the patient's own free association to establish meaning by tracing the phenomenon through the condensations and displacements which formed it.[10] The negativity of the sign, which stated that sound- and meaning-elements of particular signs derive their particular form only in opposition to those of all the other signs in the language, is reflected in Freud's refusal to take an interpretation of a given dream or symptom from a partial analysis of its parts, and in particular, by his discovery and constant recognition of over-determination, the representation of multiple meanings by single

[7] *The Interpretation of Dreams,* trans. James Strachey, IV and V of *Standard Edition* [1900], esp. pp. 239, 195-300 and 460-78. "Two Aspects of Language and Two Types of Aphasic Disturbance," pt. 2 of Roman Jakobson and Morris Halle, *Fundamentals of Language,* Janua Linguarum ser. min. 1 (The Hague, Mouton, 1957), pp. 910-36. Ferdinand de Saussure, *Course in General Linguistics,* ed. Charles Bally and Albert Sechehaye, trans. Wade Baskin (New York, McGraw Hill, 1966), esp. pp. 122-134.

[8] Saussure, esp. pp. 17-20. *Interpretation,* pp. 277-78.

[9] Saussure, pp. 65-67. *The Psychopathology of Everyday Life: Forgetting, Slips of the Tongue, Bungled Actions, Superstitions and Errors,* trans. Alan Tyson, vol. VI of *Standard Edition* [1901], pp. 80-81, 112-13.

[10] Saussure, pp. 67-70. *Five Lectures on Psycho-Analysis,* trans. James Strachey, in *Standard Edition* [1910] XI: 35.

elements in dreams or symptoms.[11] Saussure's model of the construction of a diachronic perspective out of successive synchronic analyses is manifest in therapeutic terms by Freud's creation of a clinical model consisting of weekly or even daily analytic hours frequently continuing for several years and in terms of psychological literature, by his creation of the genre of the case study, and of memorable case studies like those of Dora, the Wolf Man and the Rat Man, in which the reader could watch meaning and psychological disorder reveal themselves, change and dissipate through the analytic method and the therapist's presence.[12]

This convergence of key psychoanalytic and Saussurean concepts would provide a stronger proof of the semiotic nature of Freud's work if the Saussurean principles were not so highly focused on the sign rather than the larger communication situation. A comparison with another semiotic schema, one broader in scope but more precise and still central to semiotics, might constitute a third index of Freud's stature as a semiotician. Roman Jakobson's model of the "constitutive factors in any speech event, in any act of verbal communication" is one which has passed into semiotics as a paradigm for all communication, and it is a further development of Saussure's own model of communication. Jakobson stated: —

> THE ADDRESSER sends a MESSAGE to the ADDRESSEE. To be operative the message requires a CONTEXT referred to ("referent" in another, somewhat ambiguous, nomenclature), seizable by the addressee, and either verbal or capable of being verbalized; a CODE fully, or at least partially, common to the addresser and addressee (or in other words, to the encoder and decoder of the message); and finally, a CONTACT, a physical channel and psychological connection between the addresser and the addressee, enabling both of them to enter and stay in communication. All these factors inalienably involved in verbal communication may be schematized as follows:

CONTEXT

MESSAGE

ADDRESSER _ _ _ _ _ _ _ _ _ _ _ _ ADDRESSEE

CONTACT

CODE[13]

[11] Saussure, pp. 71-78; "Fragment of an Analysis of a Case of Hysteria," trans. Alix Strachey and James Strachey, in *Standard Edition* [1901] VII: 47.

[12] Saussure, pp. 79-100. "The Psychogenesis of a Case of Hysteria in a Woman," trans. Barbara Low and R. Gabler, in *Standard Edition* [1920] XVIII: 145-172; "From the History of an Infantile Neurosis," trans. Alix Strachey and James Strachey, in *Standard Edition* [1918] XVII: 3-122; and "Notes on an Obsessional Neurosis," trans. by Alix Strachey and James Strachey, in *Standard Edition* [1909] X: 152-319.

[13] "Closing Statement: Linguistics and Poetics," in *Style in Language,* ed. Thomas A. Sebeok (Cambridge, Mass., MIT Press, 1960), p. 353.

To prove by this third standard that Freud's work amounts to a structural semiotics, it is necessary to show that Freudian psychology's principal categories coincide with those of Jakobson.

ADDRESSER: The Freudian "addresser" is defined by his or her resistance or repression intervening between emotions and thoughts and their outward expression. Victims of the psychopathologies, typified by the classic figures in the case studies such as Little Hans (neurosis) and Dr. Schreber (schizophrenia) are those for whom the resistance is most intense and enduring, but all persons who dream, laugh at or tell jokes, make slips of the tongue or experience any of the other "psychopathologies of everyday life" undergo resistance and for that moment enter the Freudian domain.[14] It is perhaps significant that in one of its standard formulations, the resistance itself was explained in a semiotic personification as the "censor," which edited and distorted underlying material in ways Freud charted in dreams and other psychoanalytic symptoms. [15]

MESSAGE: Virtually any mode of behavior, including the absence of behavior, was for Freud capable of expressing repressed material, and throughout his career Freud added to the catalogue of types. If the catalogue began in 1895 with the physical symptoms of hysterics discussed in the *Studies,* it was supplemented within ten years by phenomena discussed in three major works: dreams, in the *Interpretation* (1900); slips of the tongue, customs and gestures, and cases of forgetting, in *The Psychopathology of Everyday Life* (1901); and jokes, in *Jokes and Their Relation to the Unconscious* [1905].[16] Clinical practice, including Freud's own self-analysis, would provide an increasingly delicate range of symptoms, such as phobias like Little Hans' fear of horses; "accidents" such as a woman's spilling red ink on a tablecloth to express shame over an unconsummated marriage; "ordinary" behavior such as a young woman's walking with her lover in clear view of her father but out of sight of her mother; and a quotational use of speech following a failure of toilet training which expressed empathy of a child for his mother.[17]

[14]"Analysis of a Phobia in a Five-Year-Old Boy," trans. Alix Strachey and James Strachey, in *Standard Edition* [1909] X: 5-152. "Psycho-Analytic Notes upon an Autobiographical Account of a Case of Paranoia (Dementia Paranoides)," trans. by Alix Strachey and James Strachey, in *Standard Edition* [1911] XIII: 1-82.
[15]"Analysis Terminable and Interminable," trans. Joan Riviere, in *Standard Edition* [1937] XXIII: 236-37.
[16]*Jokes and their Relation to the Unconscious,* trans. James Strachey, vol. VIII of *Standard Edition.*
[17]"An Infantile Neurosis," pp. 76-77 is the source of the quote. Freud's self-analysis is "An Autobiographical Study," trans. James Strachey, in *Standard Edition* [1924] XX: 1-74. The tablecloth episode is discussed in "The Taboo of Virginity," trans. James Strachey, in *Standard Edition* [1917] XI: 181-206.

Free association linked symptoms to underlying meanings, but on the basis of his collective psychoanalytic experience, Freud was able to show a degree of unconscious expression in material for which the free associations of addressers were unobtainable, particularly written texts and works of plastic art: a book-length *Memoirs of My Nervous Illness* by a state judge, folk-tales, popular fiction like Jensen's *Gradiva*, elements of Shakespeare's plays, a painting by Da Vinci and Michelangelo's "Moses."[18] Ultimately Freud speculated on the psychoanalytic function in the rise of monotheism and civilization itself.[19]

ADDRESSEE: Although symptoms and everyday psychopathologies like jokes and slips of the tongue were communicated to ordinary audiences of acquaintances and relatives, psychoanalysis was intensely concerned with two special audiences: the addresser him/herself, in whose self-monitoring the resistance operated, and the psychoanalyst, through whose presence a cure for psychopathology was possible through the mechanism of the transference. Psychoanalytic symptoms arose as a compromise between a person's needs to express particular ideas and emotions and to keep the same material out of consciousness; the result was a communication in a form so veiled that the communicator was unaware of its meaning, and any attempt to call attention to the underlying meaning provoked active hostility and denial, the same resistance that distorted it.[20] Dreams, which as the subject of Freud's first and greatest theoretical statement had come to be the paradigm of psychoanalytic phenomena, came to be an ideal for study based on their privacy: although they echoed social realities, dreams (as opposed to reports of dreams given to others) were a type of communication in which all others but the addresser were excluded as addressee. Other communications, including those made in public, were shown to be addressed to the self. The irony of such communications was that their exclusion of a wider audience made their meaning no less obscure to the addresser.

---

[18] "Psycho-Analytic Notes;" "Preface to Bourke's *Scatalogic Rites of All Nations,*" trans. James Strachey, in *Standard Edition* [1913] XII: 333-339; "Creative Writers and Day-Dreaming," trans. I. Grant Duff, in *Standard Edition* [1907] IX: 141-53; "The Theme of the Three Caskets," trans. James Strachey, in *Standard Edition* [1913] XII: 289-301; "Leonardo Da Vinci and a Memory of His Childhood," trans. James Strachey, in *Standard Edition* [1910] XI: 35-137; and "The Moses of Michelangelo," trans. James Strachey, in *Standard Edition* [1914] XIII: 209-236.

[19] *Moses and Monotheism: Three Essays,* trans. James Strachey, in *Standard Edition* [1938] XXIII: 1-137. "Civilization and Its Discontents," trans. Joan Riviere, in *Standard Edition* [1929] XXI: 57-146.

[20] See "Some Elementary Lessons in Psycho-Analysis," trans. James Strachey, in *Standard Edition* [1938] XXII: 341.

Freud distinguished these " 'narcissistic' . . . processes . . . in which the satisfaction of [the] instincts is partially or totally withdrawn from the influence of other people" from the "social phenomena" of the "transference neuroses" which encompassed "the relations of an individual to his parents and to his brothers and sisters, to the object of his love, and to his physician."[21] "Physician" meant the psychoanalyst, and in this special mode of social relation was the hope for a cure of the psychopathologies. It would have seemed from Freud's early writings focused on the interpretation of symptoms that cures would be effected when the patient had worked back through free association to underlying meaning. But particular revelations in the course of the therapy did not suddenly effect an end to symptom-formation, Freud found, and in successful therapies the patient had, in addition to discovering the meanings of symptoms, dissolved a projection of the identity of the therapist which he or she had formed in the course of the treatment. The psychoanalyst served as a "transference-object" on whose identity the patient projected those properties of another person which suited his or her pathology. To that illusory persona, representing whatever repressed desires he or she was unable to accept, the patient addressed his or her remarks in the therapy. Freud then realized that the therapist's own projections of desires onto the patient might interfere with the therapy, particularly with its termination, and thus demanded that psychoanalysts complete a training analysis of their own to relieve them from domination by this "counter-transference."[22]

CONTEXT: Freud defined the underlying thought of symptoms in both form and content. The *Interpretation* stated that the latent dream thought was always a wish, and while this was not extended to all areas of underlying meaning, the mark of repressed desire could be seen in them.[23] For example, all forms of paranoid schizophrenia were postulated to stem from a single statement, " 'I (a man) love him.' "[24] "Egoistic day-dreams" were named as a source of the psychoanalytic thread in creative fiction.[25] Obsessive neurotic

---

[21] *Group Psychology and the Analysis of the Ego,* trans. James Strachey, in *Standard Edition* [1921] XVIII: 69.

[22] "Recommendations to Physicians Practicing Psycho-Analysis," "On Beginning the Treatment (Further Recommendations on the Technique of Psycho-Analysis, I)," "Remembering, Repeating and Working-Through (Further Recommendations on the Technique of Psycho-Analysis, II)," and "Observations on Transference-Love (Further Recommendations on the Technique of Psycho-Analysis, III)," trans. James Strachey, in *Standard Edition* [1912-1914] XII: 108-156.

[23] *Interpretation,* p. 598.

[24] "Psycho-Analytic Notes," p. 63.

[25] "Creative Writers," p. 153.

symptoms were said to represent "conflicts in the patients' lives, of the struggle between temptation and moral restraints, reflections of the proscribed wish itself and of the punishment and atonement which that wish incurs."[26] Hysteric symptoms were said to represent "phantasies which unconsciously dominate the subject's emotional life and which have the meaning of fulfillments of secret and repressed wishes."[27]

Freud believed emphatically that the content of these wishes was always sexual, the most controversial aspect of his theory after the initial statement that the behavior he isolated was expressive rather than somatically caused. Whether or not Freud was correct on this issue is a matter independent of his stature as a semiotician: some other content might be placed in the formal structure of wishes and in principle the whole mechanism of symptom-formation and psychoanalytic decoding could operate unaffected. But the motivation for the postulation of the sole sexual source is heavily based on semiotic issues, a matter clarified by his central commentator Jacques Lacan and to a lesser extent Herbert Marcuse.[28] Late works of Freud such as *Totem and Taboo*[29] and *Civilization and Its Discontents* argue that human social life, evolving toward modern civilization, is based on the delay of gratification—the repression of instincts. This is a projection in anthropological terms of Freud's theory of the formation of the human psyche in the supplementation of the Id, the seat of infantile desires, by the Ego, the individualized self arising from the recognition by the child of the separateness of him/herself from what he or she desires, and the Superego, the body of constraints on gratification of desire which are represented by the child's father and lead to civilization. The bridge between pre-civilization and modern civilization, between infant and adult, and between the individual/psycho-developmental and social/anthropological perspective is language. The repression induced by the superego against the desires of the id were claimed to be the source of the psychopathologies, and their symptoms in adults were claimed to be regressions (mediated by the censorship) to the child's proto-linguistic modes of thought with words and other units of adult thought. Hence the exclusivity of sexual underlying material.

CODE: The body of insights on the grammar of psychoanalytic expression makes Freud's treatment of "code" his most thorough of Jakobson's

[26]"The Claims," p. 173.

[27]"The Claims," p. 173.

[28]Jacques Lacan, "The Function of Language in Psycho-Analysis," trans. Anthony Wilden, in *The Language of the Self* (Baltimore, Johns Hopkins, 1968), pp. 1-88. Herbert Marcuse, *Eros and Civilization* (Boston, Beacon Press, 1955).

[29]*Totem and Taboo,* trans. James Strachey, in *Standard Edition* [1912] XIII: 1-162.

six components. Condensation, in which an idea is represented metonymically by one of its parts or aspects, and displacement, in which one idea is represented by another similar to it, were first analyzed in the *Interpretation* as the
constitutive properties of dreams and then shown to underlie all other psychoanalytic expressions. As mentioned above, the two mechanisms were argued
by Jakobson to correspond to Saussure's syntagmatic and paradigmatic axes
of language and thus indicate that ordinary language and psychoanalytic
symptoms have a common dynamic. Freud's work traces countless variations
of the two principles, among which sound substitution and negation are perhaps the most basic. Freud noted that dreams in particular but also jokes and
schizophrenic symptoms had a rebus-like, punning quality based on the condensation of some idea down to the sound of its name, followed by the integration of that sound into others and thus camouflaged. Thus Freud found of
one patient:

> He dreamed that *his uncle gave him a kiss in an automobile.* He
> went at once to give me the interpretation, which I myself would
> never have guessed: namely that it meant auto-erotism.[30]

Negation, the representation of an idea by its opposite, allowed material to
be displaced onto another on the basis of a shared property, a phenomenon
which suggests a binary semantic feature ordering in the unconscious. Freud
claimed that negation explained the common instances of reversal or removal
of affect in dreams and the psychopathologies, for example, the representation of a desired action in a terrifying dream or of rage by a bland emotional
state. Thus, for example, the clumsiness with which Freud's patient mentioned above walked with her lover by her father's office was the result of
negation of an intention:

> She *wanted* [Freud's italics] her father to know occasionally of
> her relations with the lady, otherwise she would be deprived of
> the satisfaction of her keenest desire—namely revenge. So she
> saw to this by showing herself openly in the company of her
> adored one, by walking with her in the streets near her father's
> place of business and the like. The maladroitness, moreover, was
> by no means unintentional. It was remarkable, too, that both
> parents behaved as if they understood their daughter's secret
> psychology. The mother was tolerant, as though she appreciated
> her daughter's 'retirement' as a favor to her; the father was

---

[30]*Interpretation*, pp. 408-9.

furious, as though he realized the deliberate revenge directed against him.[31]

Freud's most detailed, highly structured analysis of code is his demonstration the five forms of paranoia are all "transformations" through negation of a single sentence: " 'I (a man) love him.' " In the five, negation works through orderly combinations of subject-object switching, reversal of affect of the verb, or alteration of one or more features of one of the nominals.[32]

Smaller explanations of the psychoanalytic code in grammatical terms also appear in Freud's work: that a night's dreaming has the structure of a sentence comprised of hypotactic clauses; that some hysteric symptoms are acquired from others through unconscious, deleted inferences; that the first person is the deictic center of all dreams.[33]

CONTACT: Psychoanalysis gave Western medicine its first instance of a therapy achieved through talking—"the talking cure," one of Freud's first patients called it—and thus one of Freud's most central problems was the invention of a mode of contact in which, as he would later understand it, the underlying content could be exposed and the transference could be developed and transcended. The essence of the contact was the "fundamental rule of psychoanalysis," that the patient say everything that comes into his or her head—without censoring it.[34]

What this artifice most resembles is not conventional medical therapy but a linguistic elicitation procedure in field method. Like any attempt to penetrate a code or discover the meaning of a message, Freud's procedure seeks to isolate extraneous information in the contact and to guarantee that the transmission continues until all of what is crucial has been sent. It would not matter that because of the informant's reluctance, the contact would take place only for several isolated hours each week over many years and that ultimately the patient's fantasies about the eliciter might be more important than the underlying message itself. Freud stated, "If one possesses a procedure

[31]"Psychogenesis," p. 160.

[32]"Psycho-Analytic Notes," pp. 63-65. The German text is "Psychoanalytische Bemerkungen über einen autobiographisch beschriebenen Fall von Paranoia (Dementia Paranoides)," in *Sigmund Freud Gesammelte Werke,* ed. Anna Freud et. al., (London, Imago, 1943), VIII: 239.

[33]*New Introductory Lectures on Psycho-Analysis,* trans. James Strachey, in *Standard Edition* [1932] XXIII: pp. 26-27. *Interpretation,* p. 150. *Interpretation,* p. 338.

[34]*Five Lectures,* pp. 31-32.

which makes it possible to arrive at the repressed material from associations, at the distorted material from the distortions, then what was formerly unconscious in mental life can be made accessible to consciousness even without hypnosis."[35]

The semiotic reading of Freud's work manages to capture all of its central concerns except one: it omits those psychodevelopmental constructs which were most controversial among professional and lay readers from Freud's time on. The Oedipus complex, penis envy, and even the triad of the id, ego and superego do not fit in the grids furnished by Jakobson or Saussure—they are not even the sexual "wish" falling under Jakobson's "context"—but instead constitute a gloss on the material which Freud's semiotic mechanism first elicits and then decodes. To read Freud through either of these grids predictably separates his semiotic model from material which is derived from it, but it has the unexpected result of showing that the semiotic material is primary and exclusive of the constructs.

To distinguish the Oedipus complex and other constructs from Freud's semiotic mechanism does not deprive that mechanism of its sexual motivation in context, but the primacy of sexuality may be challenged on other grounds. For Saussure, the signified as well as the signifier in language was arbitrary—unreflective of the sounds of nature, the experience of the body, the emotions or any other element of psychology. For psychoanalytic material to express repressed sexual wishes might make it a type of motivated communication, not language as Saussure conceived it.[36]

A devaluation of the importance of Freudian theory, if not a criticism of it, comes from another element of semiotics, the extension of the communication model into the study of "lower" animals and cell functioning. While for Freud the semiotic mechanism existed to serve the primal mandates of consciousness, albeit repressed consciousness, these new areas of research show communication itself to be primary and fully operative in spheres of life in which no counterpart to human intelligence seems likely. Insects and fish have been shown to govern their individual and social behavior through pheromones, chemical secretions perceived through smell, seemingly the least developed human sense. Research into cell functioning shows the cell to be composed of quasi-independent, interactive organelles whose chemical language is not fully understood, and disease to be a result of an error in judgment by one set of cell parts provoking an inappropriate reaction by other cell parts which proves destructive to the larger

---

[35] "Freud's Psycho-Analytic Procedure," [a contribution by Freud to a psychology anthology] trans. J. Bernays, in *Standard Edition* [1904] VII: 252.

[36] See Ivan Fónagy, "Le signe conventionnel motivé: un debat millenaire," *La Linguistique,* VII (1972): 55-80.

organism.[37] The idea that cells and their parts have their own modes of communication perhaps surviving through the evolution of metazoans from lower forms of life, and that errors in communication are responsible for disease, provides a compelling alternative schema to the psychoanalytic theory of psychosomatic origins of disease, the belief that organic illness might be symptomatic of repressed psychological material. Without a compelling alternative, the popular tendency has been to assume that unless proven otherwise every disease had a psychosomatic origin. An alternate communicative model, one that posits a fully functioning semiotic world inside an organism and independent of whatever consciousness that organism may have, does not refute the discovery of the unconscious in its modes of covert expression but it may put into perspective that discovery, which the neurologist Freud first made in the illnesses of his hysteric patients.

---

[37]Lewis Thomas, *The Lives of a Cell* (New York, Viking, 1974). Harry H. Shorey, *Animal Communication by Pheromones* (New York, Academic Press, 1976). Susan Sontag, *Illness as Metaphor* (New York, Farvar, Strauss and Givoux, 1978).

ERNST CASSIRER AND NEO-KANTIAN AESTHETICS:
A HOLISTIC APPROACH TO THE PROBLEMS OF LANGUAGE AND ART

Emery E. George

The recent revival of interest in semiotics is a happy occasion on which to recall the achievement of Ernst Cassirer (1874-1945), and to offer a capsule summary and critique of his theories on language and art.[1] In the following I would like to stress the originality of Cassirer's contribution, especially since he stands somewhat apart from the mainstreams, both of contemporary aesthetics and of ongoing work in semiotics, and has been identified largely as a suggestive and appealing critic of human culture. Despite this, certain interesting points of similarity and even affinity between Cassirer and the semioticists are worth while pointing out, as I shall try to do in the conclusions to this paper.

1. *The Symbol.* As does his predecessor and teacher Kant, Cassirer places the crux of his problem on the nature of the mind in the forefront of his argument. In the Kantian critique the mind takes the initiative in organizing the universe of sense data into experience to which categories and judgments are universally applicable, concerning which a priori synthetic judgments are possible, and which lends itself to being organized into the objects of intellectual inquiry, scientific, moral, and aesthetic. Early in the *Kritik der reinen Vernunft,* in the preface to the second edition (1787), Kant defines the task and potential of metaphysics "als die veränderte Methode der Denkungsart . . . , dass wir nämlich von den Dingen nur das a priori erkennen, was wir selbst in sie legen."[2] In like manner, Cassirer places at the head of his system the view that man is an *animal symbolicum* (1944, 26); to this extent the methods of the two thinkers agree. Neither the existence of the *ratio* (Kant) nor man's symbolizing capacity (Cassirer) forms the *goal* of a respective theory; each turns out to be a *working hypothesis.* But here the pupil departs from his

---

[1] I wish to record grateful indebtedness to colleagues: to Professors Ladislav Matejka and Wendy Steiner; to the former for several valuable leads and suggestions, to the latter for permission to examine in manuscript her contribution, "American Semiotics since 1945," published elsewhere in this volume.

[2] Kant, 1904, 13; 1922, 19. This is the famous passage which describes Kant's "Revolution der Denkungsart," drawing a parallel with the Copernican revolution in astronomical thought.

master. From the empiricist/rationalist controversy of the Enlightenment
Cassirer both perceives a persisting aporia in method and derives an impetus
for developing a new refinement on Kant's "Revolution der Denkart." No
more than empiricism can explain the mind's capacity to organize data into
the systems of the *ratio,* is rationalism capable of accounting for the existence
of mythical, religious, and especially aesthetic systems in man's total experience. The new Copernican cosmology, which helped Kant formulate his new
epistemology, also forms, according to Cassirer, "the only sound and scientific basis for a new *anthropology*" (1944, 13). The question, new as it is old,
which forms the title of the first part of *An Essay of Man:* "What Is Man?"
reverberates, in one form or another, in Cassirer's historical survey in his
opening chapter: "The Crisis in Man's Knowledge of Himself" (1944, 1-22).
To theories of man there rehearsed, from early Greek thought to Max
Scheler, Cassirer offers, in his next chapter, the famous suggestion that
sounds so much like his answer to Kant: ". . . instead of defining man as an
animal rationale, we should define him as an *animal symbolicum.*" Man is the
unique and unrivaled maker of symbols.

The ability to symbolize and to represent implies the peculiarly human
ability to conceptualize, to think, and to speak. Language, the linguistic symbol, the word, is the human gift and power par excellence. Proceeding at first
strictly on anthropological grounds, Cassirer invokes results of research in
animal versus human intelligence in distinguishing between the ways in which
we know and the way in which animals "know." The key to the far-reaching
difference between the two lies in the distinction between the *sign* and the
symbol; this, Cassirer points out, is a distinction in kind rather than one in
degree:

> All the phenomena which are commonly described as conditioned re-
> flexes are not merely very far from but even opposed to the essential
> character of human symbolic thought. Symbols—in the proper sense of
> this term—cannot be reduced to mere signals. Signals and symbols belong
> to two different universes of discourse: a signal is a part of the physical
> world of being; a symbol is a part of the human world of meaning.
> Signals are "operators"; symbols are "designators." (1944, 32)[3]

[3]Here Cassirer cites the work of Charles W. Morris, "The Foundation of the
Theory of Signs," first published in *Encyclopedia of the Unified Sciences,* and in 1971
in Morris's collected *Writings on the General Theory of Signs* (= Approaches to Semiotics,
vol. 16). In the above quotation, "operator" and "designator" are Morris's terms. Cassirer
could also have had a glance at Morris's paper, "Esthetics and the Theory of Signs"
(Morris, 1939-1940). Although Morris was one of the important early semioticists, his
above-cited work on the sign/symbol distinction was done too late to be considered in
Philosophie der symbolischen Formen.

From this anthropological viewpoint the eclectic Cassirer proceeds to a psychological one; in order to find out what "Man" needs, he studies the needs of the child. In the process of discovering his conceptual world the child must "understand that *everything has a name*—that the symbolic function is not restricted to particular cases but is a principle of *universal* applicability which encompasses the whole field of human thought" (1944, 34-35). More than once throughout *An Essay on Man,* Cassirer spends time with the famous cases of Helen Keller and Laura Bridgman as the classical examples of the necessity for this ongoing task of discovery. But, for handicapped and normal individuals alike, the arena within which this task of discovery through naming is accomplished is *language,* and the principle of symbolism, which Cassirer calls "the Open Sesame! giving access to the specifically human world, to the world of human culture" (1944, 35), is to be identified with this unique tool and gift first.

Man's achievement as a user of language has meant, paradoxically, simultaneous progress (technological, cultural) and regress (a move backward from reality). Man no longer has the nexus with objects of experience that the higher vertebrates have, and this peculiar loss has been lamented by such a critic of the human condition as Rousseau, whom Cassirer quotes: " 'L'homme qui médite est un animal dépravé.' " (1944, 24)[4] To this objection Cassirer answers:

> . . . there is no remedy against this reversal of the natural order. Man cannot escape from his own achievement. . . . Physical reality seems to recede in proportion as man's symbolic activity advances. Instead of dealing with the things themselves man is in a sense constantly conversing with himself. He has so enveloped himself in linguistic forms, in artistic images, in mythical symbols or religious rites that he cannot see or know anything except by the interposition of this artificial medium. (1944, 25)

2. *Language.* Reading Cassirer's monumental *Philosophie der symbolischen Formen,* as well as its one-volume English-language summary, *An Essay on Man,* one is struck by the degree to which this philosopher's central thesis on the peculiar nature of man as a maker of symbols, and cardinally Cassirer's view of language, grows out of his all-pervasive distrust of phenomenological

---

[4]This sentiment is well worth comparing with that expressed by the protagonist in Hölderlin's novel, *Hyperion*: "'O ein Gott ist der Mensch, wenn er träumt, ein Bettler, wenn er nachdenkt, . . .'" (*Hyp.* I, 12, 3-4). That this was the author's own view at the time he wrote the first volume of his novel, and that in this outlook he was strongly influenced by Rousseau, is by now a widely accepted point in the literature.

and empirical research, especially of a historical orientation. This is on the one hand surprising, since Cassirer's "system" itself has been viewed as an appealing central thesis buttressed by monumental and highly detailed scholarship.[5] On the other hand Cassirer's distrust, especially towards the empiricism of linguists, is perfectly consistent with his position that the key to the mystery of the whole is not to be sought in any of its parts, or even in the mere aggregate of its parts. The holistic spirit of Cassirer's enterprise, his concentration on man's symbolic world as a manifold unity, is nowhere felt and grasped better than in his skepticism towards the attempts of historical linguists at explaining what it is that makes language "work." As an early beacon guiding for his own new mode of thought Cassirer looks to Heraclitus, whose thinking reflects fascination with the world of change:

> Yet he is not content with the mere *fact* of change; he seeks the *principle* of change. According to Heraclitus this principle is not to be found in a material thing. Not the material but the human world is the clue to a correct interpretation of the cosmic order. In this human world the faculty of speech occupies a central place. We must, therefore, understand what speech means in order to understand the "meaning" of the universe. (1944, 111)

Not all of the attempts at explaining the origins, stature, and functioning of language occupy the same status of difficulty or even seriousness among the various schools of thought Cassirer looks at (in chapter 8, "Language"; 1944, 109-136). Roughly, we may distinguish three phases of attention to the nature of language, the mythical, the historical, and the structural, and of these only the third phase commands Cassirer's respect. The primitive attempts to explain the origins of language through sound imitation depicted by Plato in the *Kratylus,* something of an outgrowth of pre-Socratic metaphysical positions on the supposed identity between thought and being, the word and the object, are easily dismissed as an untenable metaphysical exercise, along with earlier mythological and later pragmatic views on language held, respectively, by such a nineteenth-century scholar as F. Max Müller and by the Sophists. This may suggest a curious juxtaposition from the viewpoint of chronology alone, but in Cassirer's historical survey on language there is a palpable attitude that the history of a science does not show a straight line of

---

[5] See Körner, 1967, 46, for an observation which is in agreement with my own conclusions: "Cassirer's work depends to a very great extent on the illustrative power of his detailed analyses. . . . philosophical disagreement with his critical idealism is quite compatible with a deep appreciation of his informed scholarship and his sensitive judgment. . . ."

progress, and that happy encounters with kindred minds are independent of time periods.

It is not surprising then that, prior to the work of the structuralists, Cassirer's passionate assent is drawn not by such workers as Jakob Grimm, the brothers Schlegel, Hermann Paul, or Otto Jespersen—not, in short, by the historians of language—but rather by such ahistorically and structurally oriented thinkers as Herder, Wilhelm von Humboldt, and his brother, Alexander von Humboldt. Herder's prize essay, "Über den Ursprung der Sprache" (1772), contains ideas that could not be more in harmony with Cassirer's outlook and temperament. As does Cassirer, Herder holds that the question of the origins of language is not genuinely a historical question; it is, rather, a psychological and an anthropological one. Herder holds that language and man are inconceivable one without the other. The answer to the riddle of language is not ultimate origins locatable in time, but rather what Herder calls the human act of reflection, whereby the mind seizes upon, isolates and concentrates on, certain events of experience. In his third chapter ("From Animal Reactions to Human Responses") Cassirer quotes from Herder's essay (Suphan 5, 34 f.; 1923, 1, 94 f.; 1944, 40), and observes that Herder's theory "did not proceed . . . from an observation of empirical facts. It was based on his ideal of humanity and on his profound intuition of the character and development of human culture. Nevertheless it contains logical and psychological elements of the most valuable sort" (1944, 40). Of the work of Wilhelm von Humboldt Cassirer writes:

> It is impossible, [Humboldt] maintained, to gain a true insight into the character and function of human speech so long as we think of it as a mere collection of "words." . . . The words and rules which according to our ordinary notions make up a language, Humboldt asserted, really exist only in the act of connected speech. . . . Language must be looked upon as an *energeia* rather than as an *ergon*. It is not a ready-made thing but a continuous process; it is the ever-repeated labor of the human mind to utilize articulated sounds to express thought. (1944, 120-121)

Cassirer's sense of breakthrough to scientific work with language that harmonizes with his intuitions concerning the individuality and yet universality of speech acts comes with his discussion of the advance of holistic approaches to phenomena in nature and in man. With no mean degree of fascination Cassirer observes that changes undergone in this respect by the study of language parallel important changes within the sciences. The advance of views in physics and in biology which now hold that the magnetic field or the animal organism (and animal kingdom) are best studied as an entity, no less than the advance of Gestalt theories in psychology, would seem to furnish cause to expect a linguistics to which, likewise, the whole speech act, its contemporaneity and simultaneity, would be more important than its historical development. Cassirer accords due mention to the rise of structuralism and especially to the lectures of Ferdinand de Saussure, to his insistence that speech is the subject not of one but of two disciplines, to his insights concerning the synchronic and diachronic axes of language, to the polarity between *la langue* (the axis of simultaneity) and *la parole* (the axis of succession) (1944, 122).[6] These insights lead Cassirer to his—characteristically theoretical—interest in studies in the structure, function, and classification of languages and language types, to questions of linguistic universals, and to problems of language acquisition. Among structural studies relevant to a philosophical approach to language are phonology, an area in which the study of sound and that of meaning coalesce and yield insights on structures which, to be sure, not all languages share. In addition the question of what languages tend to conserve becomes of keen interest, also, the issue of "categories which are independent of the more or less accidental facts of existing languages" (1944, 127). But here caution is needed. Cassirer distinguishes, once again, between an empirical and descriptive interest in language, and a structural interest. "The variety of individual idioms and the heterogeneity of linguistic types appear in a quite different light depending on whether they are looked at from a philosophical or from a scientific viewpoint" (1944, 129). To the linguist this variety and heterogeneity constitute his very subject matter. Philosophic thought, which aims at discovering overriding laws and uniformities, must shy clear of variety for its own sake.

The final paradox, in fact and in method, comes to the philosopher who tries to account for language in all its unity and diversity. The "unity differentiated within itself," fascination with which Cassirer shares first of all with Heraclitus, is only of partial assistance here, although linguistic diversity can ultimately be of assistance in unraveling the skeins of an adequate theory of art. Cassirer points out that, although the function of language is to communicate, and it should thus unite men, it really separates them. One overhears a connection between Cassirer's interest in the reaction of religion and myth to the diversity of languages and the phenomena of language acquisition at differing ages in an individual's development. There is a fundamental difference between the ease with which a child picks up the language in which it first learns to symbolize, and the difficulty that most adults experience in their attempts to repeat the primordial process by setting about

[6]Here Cassirer accords mention to the work of Trubetzkoy and of the *Circle Linguistique de Prague*, and to phonology as a turning point in linguistics from the diachronic to the synchronic point of view (Cassirer, 1944, 124-126). Illuminating historical studies on this moment will be found in Matejka, 1976.

acquiring a second language. Allowing for variations in aptitude for language study, Cassirer suggests a useful answer to the riddle of this universal difficulty:

> We are no longer in the mental condition of the child who for the first time approaches a conception of the objective world. To the adult the objective world already has a definite shape as a result of speech activity, which has in a sense molded all our other activities. . . . Great efforts are required to release the bond between words and things. (1944, 133)

Although this point concentrates on a point of individual psychology, it does furnish us a clue to understanding some of the important differences that exist between types and groups of languages. Roughly, in such a perspective transferred from the psychological back to the anthropological, the linguistic habits of the adult are to those of the child what the language habits of a technologically advanced society are to those of a primitive tribe. The average adult, whose habits of speech and thought are relatively the more set, may be expected to speak in language tending toward the use of abstractions. This is borne out by the latinate polysyllabism of English as used in the sciences and by bureaucrats at all levels of public life. The speech of the child leans, understandably, toward concretion. By simple extension, the language of a Western society would show high concentration on the generic; the speech of an African tribe, intense interest in the specific. Cassirer cites the work of the Austrian Orientalist, Joseph von Hammer-Purgstall, who in a paper presented before the Academy of Sciences in Vienna, compiled no less than 5,744 different names for the camel in Arabic (discussion in 1923, 1, 258; 1944, 135). Ample additional evidence for the above distinction is to be culled from the languages of tribes which possess individual names for each species of a given tree or animal, but have no generic name for the living thing in question. The issue of classification, in this connection, is a live one in linguistics, but Cassirer's explanation of the phenomenon seems no less sound: "In primitive civilization the interest in the concrete and particular aspects of things necessarily prevails" (1944, 136). Cassirer feels this phenomenon to be "primitive" in the sense of his general theory of language as an instrument for orientation of the individual in his perceptual world. Progress, he holds, is possible only if there is reasonable linguistic dynamism from the concrete pole of language toward the abstract; ". . . each new advance in this direction leads to a more comprehensive survey, to a better orientation and organization of our perceptual world" (loc. cit.).

3. *Art.* The conclusions at which Cassirer arrives in his above-outlined ideas on language are relationally similar but substantially somewhat different from principles that guide him in his theory of the structure and nature of art. Here too it is the organic unity of the work of art, as well as the unity and complexity of the artistic personality, that fascinates the philosopher. But while in the realm of language an improved capacity to symbolize is equated with a tendency toward the pole of abstraction, in artistic endeavor the creator and beholder of art must be seen as gravitating toward concretion. On a scale of abstract to concrete, objective to subjective, art occupies the end: "primitive, concrete, creative," while language and science together are seen to occupy the extreme: "advanced, abstract, critical." "Language and science are abbreviations of reality; art is an intensification of reality. Language and science depend upon one and the same process of abstraction; art may be described as a continuous process of concretion" (1944, 143). Yet in the discrete and at the same time interdependent realms of language, art, and science, other comparisons and contrasts seem equally possible. One such alternate scale suggests that art and language occupy a center, maintaining a balance in the structure of the symbol, while at one end of the scale the *signifié* pulls too far from the *signifiant,* as in mathematical symbolism (science), and at the other, comes extremely close to it, as in the Eucharist (religious ritual).[7]

The body of Cassirer's argument on art is not, once again, devoted to a demonstration that art is indeed symbolic in content and purport. It goes, rather, a step beyond this methodological given, and concentrates instead on defining the nature of artistic creation and experience. Art is a language, and, as such, it gives shape and definition to the relation between our conceptions and the putative reality the latter conceptualize. Instead of being a mere imitative act, art lends concretion and permanence to our symbol-making activity. It is itself an act of making and shaping, embodiment and interpretation. Art conveys a sense of new, intensified reality. Such thoughts on the autonomy of art render invalid both Aristotle's theory of mimesis and the Platonic moral strictures from which Aristotle was for a long time supposed to have rescued art theory. Aristotle, according to Cassirer, formulated his well-known theory on delight in learning "rather as a theoretical than as a specifically aesthetic experience. 'To be learning something,' he declares, 'is the greatest of pleasures not only to the philosopher but also to the rest of mankind, . . .' " (*Poetics,* 4. 1448b 4-5 [Bywater], quoted in 1944, 138). From Aristotle to Batteux and to Rousseau theorists were aware of the

---

[7]Cf. Cassirer's three modes of the one function of symbolic representation: "expressive function" (myth, ritual), "intuitive function" (natural languages), and "conceptual function" (science) (Körner, 1967, 45).

missing ingredient in such a pedagogical account of art. They had to make some allowance for the freedom of the artist, but did not know how to form-ulate or explain away the "disturbance" introduced by the artist's intervening personality. It was given to the young Goethe, of the essay "Von deutscher Baukunst" (1773), to make the transcendent formulation of art's formative function. Goethe speaks of "significant roughness" versus "unmeaning smoothness" (the terms are here quoted from 1944, 140), and formulates the concept of "characteristic art," in which expressive and formative poles are synthesized in the harmonious work of " 'the demigod, creative in repose' " (Goethe quoted, 1944, 141).

The issue of form, the insight on the formative nature of art, arms Cassirer with his characteristically non-Aristotelian answer, both to Plato and to Tolstoi, who insisted that art waters the passions and is thus not beneficial to man's moral life:

> The aesthetic experience—the experience of contemplation—is a differ-ent state of mind from the coolness of our theoretical and the sobriety of our moral judgment. It is filled with the liveliest energies of passion, but passion itself is here transformed both in its nature and in its mean-ing . . . . . . the image of a passion is not the passion itself. The poet who represents a passion does not infect us with this passion. At a Shakespeare play we are not infected with the ambition of Macbeth, with the cruelty of Richard III, or with the jealousy of Othello. We are not at the mercy of these emotions; we look through them; we seem to penetrate into their very nature and essence. (1944, 147)

Cassirer identifies the dialogical and dialectical nature of art, and the fact of audience participation in the creative process. He holds paramount the inner freedom that art gives; art transmutes all the shock values in an *Oedipus* or in a *King Lear* "into a means of self-liberation, thus giving us an inner freedom which cannot be attained in any other way" (1944, 149). Art helps us accom-plish this feat of self-liberation by stressing its own inherent polarities, indeed the entire gamut of forms and emotions, simultaneously. In the best works of art the hard and the soft, the tender and the aggressive, the tragic and the comic, are inseparably wedded. The specific manifold nature of art issues in its enabling us, in work after work, to "pass through the whole gamut of human emotions, . . . grasp the most delicate nuances of the different shades of feeling, . . . follow the continuous variations in rhythm and tone" in order, finally, to "feel the poem" (1944, 149-150). Thus the best art, always both tragic and comic, transcends mere entertainment or satire or moral stricture, to a plane of what Cassirer identifies as "that faculty shared by all art, sym-pathetic vision" (1944, 150).

The complexity of vision and execution, the bond between rationality and emotion, the interest of artist and audience alike in "rough significance," "significant ugliness," or "character," implies that the theoretical model of a work of art is the image of a great crystal in which all the polar axes of theory vivified by experience and energy cross. For this reason Cassirer feels that he must spend a little more time with those "modern" theories, apart from mimetic and emotive ones, in which there is more or less agreement as to the collaboration between mimesis and poiesis, but which still show serious blind spots with respect to the holistic theory of art. It is in their various failures to do justice to "the specific power of the artistic imagination" (1944, 152) that Cassirer sees the failings of a number of aesthetic theories, from neoclassicism onward. He comes down justifiably hard on romantic theories that stress the wonderful and the fantastic as fit subjects for poetic treatment at the expense of the everyday and the probable. Cassirer also points out how romantics everywhere operated on a false assumption that the "lost paradise" of divine or heroic or golden ages is gone for good. This is a fundamental mistake, Cassirer contends, for it misplaces proper emphasis on where the "magic" of the poem lies. To the truly talented poet this "paradise" is never lost, for it is not to be looked for in the external world of subject matter. The imagination is able to invest even the tawdry and the everyday with significance. A good practical example of the romantic fallacy of "fitness of subject matter" is shown in Novalis' bitter disappointment with the more prosaic portions of *Wilhelm Meisters Lehrjahre*; it is also seen in Goethe's own failure when he depicts golden ages and makes symbolic charades replace a good everyday plot (as in *Märchen, Novelle,* and some portions of *Faust II*). One turnabout in theory came with the realists, for example with Émile Zola, who is excellent at depicting the everyday in minute detail. Cassirer points out that realists and naturalists fall back on the old mimetic principle, but while in their insistence on the equivalence of subjects they reap a victory over romanticism, they also neglect "the symbolic character of art. . . . Art is, indeed, symbolism, but the symbolism of art must be understood in an immanent, not in a transcendent sense" (1944, 157).

More recent aesthetic theories are also seen by Cassirer as having their own inimitable "moral blind spots." The play theories of Schiller and the evolutionists, Nietzsche's stress on the Dionysian at the expense of the Apollonian, Bergson's passive capability within creative evolution, and Santayana's aesthetic hedonism—all these systems have in common a characteristic failure to balance the scale, to avoid lopsided judgment on the simultaneous bipolar self-fulfillment of art. They seem comprehensive on the surface, for they all undeniably contribute important partial solutions to the overall problem posed by aesthetic statements. One such excellent "partial solution" is the discovery made by the realists: "The nature of a work of art, . . . does not depend on the greatness or smallness of its subject matter" (paraphrase, 1944, 157). Certainly this is a helpful, even stimulating, theoretical insight. But none of the theories here touched on is holistic in the sense in which Cassirer's view of art, within his total system, is that.

That historic theories, of art or of any other human endeavor, should be seen by later thinkers as lacking in completeness or adequacy in accounting for problems perceived since is no surprise to a thinker of the intellectual generosity of Cassirer. In the end he himself, in stressing the claims to completeness made in his own outlook, goes back to some of the above castigated theories for important clues on the wholeness of his subject as well. One of these clues is Schiller's insight on beauty as "living form"; art, according to Cassirer, possesses a "constructive power in the framing of our human universe" (1944, 167). It is just as significant to live in the "realm of forms" governed by art as it is to concentrate on the realm of our own experience, transmuted as the latter is by our ongoing process of conceptualization. Here we are once again reminded of Cassirer's overriding view of language and art as symbolic systems, and of art as both a kind of language and knowledge of a peculiar and specific kind. If this is so, then Schiller's view on the "forms of beauty" may well prove useful in helping to resolve, once and for all, the old *prodesse/delectare* dichotomy, which latter, to be sure, is oriented toward a recognizably narrow, moralistic view of art, rather than at that sense of autonomy and universal nexus with mental life at which Cassirer's investigations aim.[8]

4. *Conclusions.* In her paper Wendy Steiner writes that the work of Cassirer and of his followers, cardinally of Susanne Langer, has stayed "out of the mainstream of American semiotics." This is undeniably true, and it is not as a representative of contemporary semiotic inquiry that I have tried to present Cassirer here. But our recognition of, and perhaps objections to, the failure of the neo-Kantian aesthete and of his epigones to deal rigorously with the nature of the symbol need not make us oblivious to some surprising similarities in interest, and perhaps even affinities, however partially evidenced, between Cassirer and some contemporary semioticians. Three rather inescapable examples of such similarity and/or affinity may suffice here.

Cassirer and Roman Jakobson should no doubt head this modest list. Long before Jakobson and Morris Halle spelled out their interest in aphasia in *Fundamentals of Language,* Cassirer, in volume 3 of his *Philosophie der*

---

[8]Cassirer's views, of 1925 and 1944, on the autonomy of art are strikingly supported by an earlier (1921) view on the autonomy of the artist. On an important point that it was Hölderlin who may have influenced Schelling in the latter's development as a philosopher, see Cassirer, 1921, 128-132; summarized in Cassirer, 1925, 2, 6.

symbolischen Formen, cited and discussed work on aphasia and on related speech disorders done by the very two British neurologists cited also by Jakobson and Halle, Henry Head and Hughlings Jackson (Cassirer, 1929, chap. 6 [237-323]). To be sure Cassirer's interest centered on such a topic as the roots of propositional versus emotive language per se, rather than on an application of medical aspects of the latter to the metaphor/metonymy question (Jakobson and Halle, 1956, chaps. 3-4 [63-75]). A second interesting similarity between Cassirer and workers in semiotics may be perceived in Cassirer's interest in taxonomic habits present in primitive cultures, and suggestive resemblances between this interest and M. Merleau-Ponty's discussion of color perception and classification in individuals (Merleau-Ponty, 1962, 174-199). Finally it may be worth while pointing to some degree of continuity, even if not contiguity, between Cassirer's grappling with the sign/symbol opposition, and definitions as given in Roland Barthes in his *Éléments de Sémiologie* (Barthes, 1964, 79-172).[9] In all it must be pointed out that Cassirer, partly in his own work and partly in his encouraging the work of Susanne Langer, does share with avant-garde trends in semiotics an interest in symbolism and communication in areas that lie, as Langer has put it, beyond the ken of discursive reason. Especially Langer's analyses of visual art, music, and dance (in *Philosophy in a New Key, Feeling and Form,* and *Mind*) manage to suggest that the "non-mainstream" symbologists were also interested, in their own limited ways, in areas of communication located beyond ordinary language.

Interesting as these similarities may seem, they must not, of course, be allowed to obscure or overshadow blind spots in Cassirer's own system, most important among which are opportunities that Cassirer missed for giving his system additional sophistication, flexibility, and inclusiveness. Prime among these missed opportunities, as I see it, is Cassirer's failure to account, in his phenomenology of art, for the facts and demands of popular culture. That his all-inclusive and valid criterion of sympathetic vision could ever be thought to apply to the structure of a good television Western, or to the musical *Fiddler on the Roof,* is no doubt a suggestion that would have offended this cultivated northern European, so clearly brought up on, and shaped culturally by, his Shakespeare and Goethe, Beethoven and Mahler. It is not too much to suggest that a point of unspoken ideology in Cassirer's total symbolic vision is the contention that art equals culture, and that *culture* is to be thought of as written with a capital *C.* This elitist connotation

---

[9]On Cassirer's accounting for the structure of the symbol, see especially Hamburg, 1949, 77-102. Hamburg stresses Cassirer's indebtedness to Morris, and does not refer to Peirce's even earlier work, for reasons that become clear upon consulting Peirce, 1958, 220-245. Cf. Langer, 1942, 54, and n. 1.

appears not to clash with what the anthropologist means by the word *culture*; in Cassirer symbolizing capacity is viewed from the vantage point of the cultural nutrients that a society's most highly educated members are capable of producing or consuming. In such a way Cassirer is able to maintain consistency between his interest in research in primitive languages and his limiting his phenomenology art to the "best" that any tradition has to offer.[10]

One additional important blind spot in Cassirer's thought (my closing example here) is his refusal to set up a meaningful typology of polarities that could relate linguistic and artistic symbolization processes. If we object that the philosophy of symbolic forms is not a sufficient philosophy of the symbol, then we also have a right to say that not doing rigorous work there could have freed Cassirer's energies for better work in theoretical model building. One misses especially a deeper exploration of the polarities of subject and object which, in art theory for example, could become fruitful in spelling out important differences between the sources of perceptual subjectivity versus the phenomena of nonobjective painting. Better work here would perhaps also have made Cassirer more cautious in his statements regarding the differences between language as used by scientists and language as used by poets (1944, 168).

Part of Cassirer's continuing appeal, beyond questions of contemporary pertinence or usefulness, lies in areas in which this urbane and penetrating mind can still invite productive disagreement. This, it seems to me, is something we can both cherish for its own sake and regard as a side of Cassirer's work that rescues it from being a mere historic artifact.

REFERENCES

Barthes, Roland. 1964. Le degré zero de l'écriture, suivi de Éléments de sémiologie. Paris: Gonthier.

Cassirer, Ernst. 1921. Hölderlin und der deutsche Idealismus. In: E.C., Idee und Gestalt, 109-152. Berlin: Bruno Cassirer.

_____ . 1923-1929. Philosophie der symbolischen Formen. 1 (1923): Die Sprache. 2 (1925): Das mythische Denken. 3 (1929): Phänomenologie der Erkenntnis. Berlin: Bruno Cassirer.

[10]Cf. Gilbert: ". . . the polar pattern of Cassirer's symbol seems a little too balanced and full of grace when approached from immersion in Eliot, Auden, Picasso and Stravinsky" (Gilbert, 1949, 629). No doubt this also holds for any putative relevance of Cassirer's thought to popular art forms. It might be said that Cassirer both came to America too late in life to develop a taste for the Broadway musical, and died too early to experience television. But film and cabaret, among kindred forms, would certainly have been available to him in the Weimar Germany which he fled in 1933.

_____ . 1944. An Essay on Man: An Introduction to a Philosophy of Human Culture. New Haven: Yale University Press.

Gilbert, Katharine. 1949. Cassirer's Placement of Art. In: Paul Arthur Schilpp (ed.), The Philosophy of Ernst Cassirer, 605-630. Evanston, Ill. The Library of Living Philosophers, Inc.

Hamburg, Carl H. 1949. Cassirer's Conception of Philosophy. In: Schilpp, 1949, 73-119.

Jakobson, Roman and Morris Halle. 1956. Fundamentals of Language. 'S-Gravenhage: Mouton. (=Janua linguarum, no. 1.)

Kant, Immanuel. 1902-1955. Gesammelte Schriften, ed. by the Königlich Preussische Akademie der Wissenschaften. I. Abt., 3 (1904): Kritik der reinen Vernunft, 2nd ed., 1787. Berlin: Georg Reimer.

_____ . 1912-1922. Werke. Edited by Ernst Cassirer. 3. (1922): Kritik der reinen Vernunft, ed. Albert Görland. Berlin: Bruno Cassirer.

Körner, S. 1967. Cassirer, Ernst. In: Paul Edwards (ed.), Encyclopedia of Philosophy, 2, 44-46. New York: Macmillan, The Free Press.

Langer, Susanne K. 1942. Philosophy in a New Key. Cambridge, Mass.: Harvard University Press.

_____ . 1953. Feeling and Form. New York: Charles Scribner's Sons.

_____ . 1967, 1972. Mind: An Essay on Human Feeling. Baltimore: The Johns Hopkins Press.

Matejka, Ladislav (ed.) 1976. Sound, Sign and Meaning: Quinquagenary of the Prague Linguistic Circle. Ann Arbor: Department of Slavic Languages and Literatures, The University of Michigan. (=Michigan Slavic Contributions, no. 6).

Merleau-Ponty, M. 1962. Phenomenology of Perception. Translated by Colin Smith. London: Routledge and Kegan Paul.

Morris, Charles W. 1938. The Foundation of the Theory of Signs. In: Encyclopedia of the Unified Sciences.

_____ . 1939-1940. Esthetics and the Theory of Signs. In: Journal of Unified Science (Erkenntnis) 8, 131-150.

Peirce, Charles Sanders. 1931-1958. Collected Papers. Edited by Charles Hartshorne, Paul Weiss, and Arthur Burks. 8 (1958): Reviews, Correspondence, Bibliography, ed. Arthur Burks. 220-245. Cambridge, Mass.: Harvard University Press.

THE ROOTS OF RUSSIAN SEMIOTICS OF ART

Ladislav Matejka

Since the second half of the nineteenth century, the role of signs and symbols in the human community has been among the pivotal topics of Russian intellectuals, whether Hegelians, or Neo-Kantians and phenomenologists, or Marxists.

The concept of sign is particularly prominent in Alexander Potebnja's speculations about the origin of human language and its relationship to human understanding, about language and myth, language and art and, in general, about language in its intrinsic ties to human nature, on the one hand and human cultures, on the other.

In his book, *Language and Thought,* published in 1862, Potebnja discusses the glottocentric character of human languages whereby sounds become signs of thought by means of articulation which is the unique privilege of the human species and clearly distinguishes mankind among all other living species.[1] In accordance with his mentalistic leaning Potebnja insists that the nature of articulation "impregnating sounds with thoughts"[2] is basically a psychological phenomenon which cannot be grasped by physical observations of sound or physiological inquiries into the articulatory processes. It is the psychologically associative ability to connect external, material properties with their non-material, internalized counterparts which, in Potebnja's view, constitute signs and their usage in the human community. The external properites, he asserts, cease to be a component of the sign if they do not produce the inner effect which is understanding. Consequently, his chief interest is in the psychological aspects of communication, in perception and association (*associjacija vosprijatij*[3]) which results in a connection (*sceplenie*[4]) between the external, material form (*vnešnjaja forma*) and the internal, immaterial form (*vnutrennjaja forma*).

The word mediating between the external world and the internal organization of human mind rises to the fundamental concept of Potebnja's linguistic, semiotic and philosophical views. For him, words are not only signs, definable in the lexicographic terms, but tools which are capable of converting concrete images into abstract concepts. Condensation (*sguščenie*) of an image into its essential features (*central'nyj priznak*) results in abstraction (*otvlečenie*). The individual properties of an image are generalized. Detached from a given context, the concreteness of an image turns into an image of an image (*obraz obraza*[5]). The abstract is juxtaposed to the concrete and the general to the individual. Stored in the memory, the words can be activated in the process of communication and used by individuals for the externalization of their personal observations, reflections and feelings while, at the same time, they can be identified and comprehended by other individuals of the same language community. The usage of the word by the speaker objectifies his subjective experience and, vice versa, the hearer subjectifies the word in the act of comprehension. In this process, as Potebnja sees it, the role of context acquires paramount importance. The outer and inner forms, unified in the words, are confronted with the context which serve as a *tertium comparationis*.[6] "The very process of comprehension," he insists, "is a process of comparing."[7] It is precisely the confrontation by means of *tertium comparationis* which establishes the relevant semantic value; changeability of the context determines changeability of the meaning, hinted by the words. By means of *tertium comparationis* the semantic value of the word is continually transposed. Every usage results in a novelty so that language appears as a creative process, comparable to art. "The difference between a word and a poetic act," Potebnja declares," is only the higher degree of complexity of the latter."[8]

Without words, in Potebnja's view, not only human communication but also human thinking would be impossible. The fact that only human beings are capable of using words naturally confines his semiotic interest: articulated words are viewed as a privilege of mankind, a fundamental step in the development of human species and the very basis of human culture, in general, and national cultures, in particular. Potebnja's belief in the paramount role of words in human thinking merges with his conviction that each language determines the thinking of its native speakers in a particular way and, therefore, appears in an intrinsic relationship with the corresponding national spirit. Clearly, this concept of cultural relativism could be traced back to von Humboldt and especially to Potebnja's main source, Hugo Steinthal's "Völkerpsychologie." Subsequently in the twentieth century, this concept played an important role in the neo-Humboldtian school of Karl Vossler which was very influential among the Russian Hegelians; it degenerated, however, under the impact of rising nationalism.

2

Thus, Potebnja's semiotics is not only glottocentric and anthropocentric but ethnocentric as well. In his observations, Potebnja virtually ignores any lesson of "zoosemiotics." For him the outcries of beasts have nothing to do with language and studying the signals of animals only sidesteps the crucial issues of linguistics. In fact, such an approach has been typical for all major trends in Russian semiotics. All of them have been primarily interested in verbal communication, dominated by the phenomenon of articulation which no other species can master.

The semiotic nature of the word in its relationship to the external world on the one hand and to the internal processes of perception and conceptualization on the other has been a thorny issue for philosophers of every brand, the Russian Marxists included. It divided them into numerous factions and caused many vehement controversies. The materialistic and monistic principles of Marxism have been particularly challenged by the problem of qualitative leaps from the matter outside to the concepts inside and especially by the question whether the conscious sensations are copies of the external world or rather something which bears no resemblance to the properties of the external objects and belong to a different world entirely.

Inspired by the nineteenth century empiricists, Georgij Valentinovič Plexanov, one of the classic Russian Marxists, was inclined to interpret the transition from the external world into the human mind as a special processing of signs which have to be learned to be interpreted rightly. In his comments to the first Russian edition of Engels's *Ludwig Feuerbach and the End of Classical German Philosophy*, published in 1892, Plexanov postulates an internalized inventory of signs which he calls hieroglyphs and sees as culturally acquired rather than innate mediators between external matter and the human mind, capable of thinking and understanding:

> Our sensations are in their way hieroglyphs which inform us of what is taking place in reality. The hieroglyphs do not resemble the events conveyed by them. But they can with complete fidelity convey both the events themselves, and—what is the main thing—the relation existing between them.[9]

According to this view, human knowledge of the external world is acquired by reading and interpreting symbols, internalized in the brain and used as a language. Each individual develops his consciousness by mastering the symbols just as he learns his mother-tongue. Thus the mental operation, involved in knowing, is seen as a semiotic process of translating. It is by means of signs, ("hieroglyphs") that the external excitations are transformed into a state of consciousness. Accordingly, sensations and ideas are viewed as products of cultural processes rather than copies of real things and processes of nature.

In Plexanov's papers of materialism and Kantianism (1898-9), the hieroglyphic theory is given a further touch:

The forms and relationships of things-in-themselves cannot be as they appear to us to be, i.e. as they appear to us after having been "translated" in our heads. Our impressions of the forms and the relationships of things are no more than *hieroglyphs*, but these hieroglyphs indicate these forms and relationships well enough, and that is sufficient for us to be able to study the effects which things-in-themselves produce in us, and to influence them in our turn.[10]

Plexanov's position necessarily extends the realm of signs to the entire world surrounding each normal human being. Everything which man sees, hears, feels becomes a semiotic operation of reading and interpreting symbols and transforming them into actions directed towards the desired goals. Sensations become cultural products, acquired by learning, rather than effects of nature wrought on the human mind by external causes. Being signs, conscious sensations, percepts, concepts and ideas need not resemble that what they stand for. They are neither mirror-reflections nor images, because as signs and symbols they can be without any similarity or equivalence to what they represent.

While for Potebnja signs and symbols are chiefly tools of social communication between one human being and another, Plexanov's semiotics pertains to the relation between man and nature. It is nature which imparts information to man. Clearly Plexanov's hieroglyphs are different signs than signs in a verbal system; they are envisaged as instruments of conceptualization and ideation rather than of verbalization. And as such, they became the target of criticism by other Marxists including V.I. Lenin himself. In his semiotic interpretation of the relations between matter and conscious sensation Plexanov was accused of paying tribute to Kantianism which divorced "idea from reality and consciousness from nature."[11]

Following Engels's theory of the mirror-images of the external world in the human mind, Lenin in his *Materialism and Empirio-Criticism* argues that man's sensations and ideas are not conventional signs, symbols and hieroglyphs but copies of real things, images which inevitably and of necessity imply the objective reality of that which they "image." The theory of symbols or hieroglyphs as an explanation of human consciousness is for Lenin an "attempt to draw an absolute boundary between the phenomenon and the thing-in-itself."[12] It represents in his view "distrust of perception and distrust of the evidence of our sense-organs."[13] For him "conventional sign, symbol, hieroglyph are concepts which introduce an unnecessary element of agnosticism."[14] He is, of course, aware that "an image can never wholly compare with the model,". Nevertheless he insists that "an image is one thing, a symbol, *a conventional sign*, another."[15]

Although Lenin's attack on Plexanov's hieroglyphic theory and its German sources does not in any direct way pertain to the general usage of sign and symbols in the communication of man with man, it has hardly helped to promote semiotics among Marxists. Rather it has contributed to their apprehension of dealing with the opposition of concrete *versus* abstract, external *versus* internal and, by the same token, with such antinomies as Saussure's signifying *versus* signified or "la langue" *versus* "la parole" which are essential not only for his concept of linguistics but for his general framework of semiotics as well.

3

In spite of the negative and often hostile attitude of Lenin's followers towards Ferdinand de Saussure's *Course in General Linguistics* and the Saussurianism (*sosurianstvo*), there cannot be any doubt that modern Russian semiotics has been substantially influenced by Saussure and the teaching of the Geneva school. It reached Russia earlier than any other country in Europe. One of its promoters was Saussure's own student, Sergej Karcevskij, who, in 1917, after several student years in Switzerland returned to Moscow and joined the *Moscow Linguistic Circle*. As Roman Jakobson recollects in his *Selected Writings*:

> It was in those years that students of psychology and linguistics in our university were passionately discussing the philosophers' newest attempts towards a phenomenology of language and of signs in general. We learned to sense the delicate distinction between the *signatum* (the signified) and the *denotatum* (the referred-to); hence to assign an intrinsically linguistic position, first to the *signatum* and then, by inference, to its inalienable counterpart as well—that is, to the *signans*.[16]

It was the discussion of Saussure's semiotics in the *Moscow Linguistic Circle* which apparently inspired one of its ardent discussants, Gustav Špet, to use in his *Aesthetic Fragments* (1922-23) his term *semiotika* along with such terms as phoneme (*fonema*) and syntagm (*syntagma*) all of which are typical for Saussure's *Course*.[17] For Špet, a student of Edmund Husserl, *semiotics* is "the ontological science of signs in general"[18] and subsumes "the theory of the word as a sign."[19] It is "a purely rational discipline"[19] which deals with signs and symbols in their abstract aspects in contrast to poetics, "the grammar of poetic language and poetic thought"[20] on the one hand, and to aesthetics, dealing with "the word in *usum aestheticae*"[21], on the other.

The word is for Špet "a sign *sui generis*"[22], distinguishable from other signs such as signals, gestures, symptoms and omina. It is "a complex of sensory data which are not only perceivable but, being tied with meaning or signification, are meant to be understood."[23] In Špet's view "only semiotics can substantiate the difference between a sign and sound."[24] And "only a rigorous phenomenological analysis would be able to determine what distinguishes perception of a sound complex (as a significant sign) from perception of a natural object."[25]

While Saussure's *Course* emphasizes the associative (paradigmatic) aspect of sign, Špet is not interested in the psychological theory of association. "Those theories which are based on association as a psychological explanation of the bond between the word as a sign and that which is meant," he asserts," are merely hypotheses with a zero constructive value."[26] In his view:

> the bond between a word and that which is meant is a specific bond. . . Its specificity is not determined by any sensory complex as such but by that which is meant. This second term of the relation is also an object of *sui generis*. . . [27]

For Špet "the structure of a word is not its morphological, syntactic and stylistic arrangement nor, in general, its surface arrangement (*ploskost'-noe raspoloženie*) but, exactly the opposite, its organic arrangement in depth (*vglub'*) comprising all degrees between the two terms of relations from the object of sensory perception to the eiditic, ideally formal object."[28]

This early structural definition, distinguishing the deep and surface arrangements of language, is further elaborated as follows:

> A structure is a concrete whole; its parts are changeable in both quantitative and qualitative terms but not a single part of the whole *in potentia* can be eliminated without destroying the entirety. *In actu* some 'members' may appear in an embryonic state, not fully developed or degenerated and atrophic. This, however, does not affect the structure. A structure should be distinguished from a composite whether concretely divisible or divisible in abstract terms. A structure is also distinguishable from an aggregate or a complex mass which tolerates destruction or disappearance of any constitutive parts without qualitative change of the whole. A structure can be dismembered solely into the new enclosed structures which can be again reconstructed into the original structure. Spiritual and cultural formations have an essentially structural character so that it is feasible to say that spirit or culture are structural.[29]

Špet's structural potentiality is kept apart from its concrete actualization; accordingly, the word as a potential structure is distinguished from its concrete usage and its functions in the text and context.

In human communication, according to Špet, the word fulfills specific functions which are either "basic, i.e. semantic and synsemantic, or concommitant, i.e. expressive and deictic."[30] As a tool of communication, the word presupposes a human community:

> The word is not only a phenomenon of nature but also a principle of culture. It is its archetype because culture is a cult of understanding and the words are the embodiment of the intellect.[31]

The socio-cultural functions of voice reveal that the speaker belongs to a certain human community and a specific cultural zone bound by the unity of language. It is the knowledge of the given language which determines all socio-cultural functions including understanding. For Špet, to understand means "to extract a text from a context."[32]

However, Špet's analysis makes a specific provision for the role of emotions which have a subconscious ground and, in his view, fulfill natural rather than socio-cultural functions. They characterize subjective and personal aspects of verbal communication:

> Speech is accompanied by the manifestation of spiritual as well as physical states of the speaker; and vice versa, these manifestations are reflected in his behavior including speech. In order to understand the word, it is important to receive it within a context and to locate it within a specific sphere of conversation. This sphere is surrounded by the atmosphere of speaker's self-awareness and world outlook.[33]

Accordingly, the usage of verbal communication is viewed as a complex interaction of nature and culture. In these processes, the orientation of the speaker and hearer focuses on certain strata of the word while other strata recede to the background. In these terms, Špet distinguishes expressivity of the word from its impressivity. Moreover, following Husserl's terminology, Špet recognizes various acts pertaining to diverse roles of the speaker and hearer in their communication.

According to Špet, a special usage of words in a play between logic and syntagmatic relations produces the forms of poetic language. "They are deducible from the logical forms" and constitute "poetic logic and poetic truth"[34] which characterizes "the fantastic and fictitious objects not existing in reality yet logically formed."[35] In Špet's view "the play of the poetic forms may achieve a complete emancipation from real things."[36]

In addition to poetic logic, Špet's poetics comprise "poetic phonetics, phonetic morphology, poetic syntax (*inventio*), poetic stylistics (*dispositio*), poetic semasiology, poetic rhetoric (*elocutio*) etc.[37]

Poetics as a grammar of poetic language and poetic thought is for Špet "a technical discipline."[38] It is, as he explains it, as technical as teaching the technique of drawing, sculpture or the theory of music, and it has no practical use for a poet. Rather, it belongs to the philosophy of art as an ontological discipline and should study "sensory and internal forms of the poetic words (language) regardless whether they are aesthetic or not."[39] "Poetics," Špet emphasizes, "is not aesthetics nor any part or chapter of aesthetics."

Aesthetics in contrast to poetics deals, according to Špet, with aesthetic experience whether it is positive or negative such as enjoyment or disgust. "The existing or imagined object has to be transposed in the mind in order to become an aesthetic object; to establish what is aesthetically beautiful or ugly requires a special orientation (*ustanovka*) which is neither sensual nor rational but *sui generis*.[40] In accordance with his notion of "aesthetic object" Špet distinguishes aesthetic consciousness, aesthetic perception and aesthetic image. However, he vigorously disagrees with Potebnja's psychological approach to the concept of image in verbal art. Referring to the dispute of the Russian Formalists with the followers of Potebnja, Špet says approvingly: "Our anti-Potebnianism (*antipotebnjanstvo*) is a healthy movement; by following Herbart and partly Steinthal and Lazarus, Potebnja discredited the concept of 'the inner form of language'."[41]

Yet, Špet's approval of the Formalists' attack on Potebnja's theory of art as thinking with the help of images did not keep him back from his emotional disagreement with the leading theoreticians of the Russian Formalism for their active involvement in the futuristic experimentations with transense speech.

Špet does not deny that a sound complex, which is artificially detached from its tie to a natural language, can be evaluated in the aesthetic terms but, in his view, such aesthetics is not aesthetics of verbal art. He compares the aesthetics of transense speech to aesthetic experiences with sounds of an unknown language, and categorically warns against those theoreticians who claim that "sounds are essentially tied with one or another modality."[42]

In this connection, however, the rationalism and scientific rigor of his phenomenological poetics are clearly upset by his own evaluative aesthetics which found the experiments of the Russian Futurists a symptom of "decay, corruption and artificial manuring."[43] With obvious distaste for the Futurists he asserts that their "pregnancy is fraudulent"[44] and that "all decadents use the device (*priem*) of focusing to attract attention."[45]

Thus, in Špet's praxis, if aesthetics does not recognize art as art, there is no justification for any poetics either. In his emotional outburst against the Russian Futurists what he finds most disturbing is that the Futurists "proclaim the primacy of poetics over art"[46] and that the theory of art is for them "the impetus, reason and basis of art."[47] Apparently alluding to the theory of *L'art pour l'art*, he finds Russian Futurism "a theory of art without art."[48]

4

The reaction of the Russian Futurists to Potebnja's observations about verbal art not only concerned his attempt to define the essence of verbal art as "thinking with the help of images" but also his insistence that "the form of a poetic work is not sound, the prime external form, but the word, i.e. the unity of sound and meaning."[51] Potebnja's emphasis on the inseparability of sound and meaning in the verbal sign contradicted the Futurists' experiments with sound as an autonomous domain of creativity. Responding from the Futurists' platform, Viktor Šklovskij wrote in 1916 in *Poetika*, the organ of the Society for the Study of Poetic Language (*Opojaz*):

> Potebnja concludes   that poeticality of the word is not manifested by its sound and that the outer form (sound, rhythm) may be disregarded in defining the essence of poetry and of art in general.[52]

For Šklovskij as for early Futurists, whether theoreticians or practicioners, it was precisely the sound arrangement with its external, perceivable form that was regarded as the most essential feature of poetry. They found it challenging to show that poetry uses various devices which shape speech sound in a distinct way and thereby affect perception of the poetic text. "Our approach toward the sound of the word in poetic language and in the language of prose is different,"[53] says Šklovskij and insists that "the organization of a scientific poetics should begin with acceptance of the fact... that there exist two languages, 'prose language' and 'poetic language', each governed by different laws. . . .[54]

In support of this view, Šklovskij's paper "On Poetry and Transense Language", cites German, French and English acoustic phoneticians, psychologists and poets testifying about the values and effects of speech sounds. Šklovskij himself subscribes to the view that "speech sounds in themselves command a special power."[55] Moreover, he is attracted by the theory that "emotions can be best expressed by a special sound language (*zvukoreč'*) which can be without any definite meaning and yet, outside and aside from meaning, can affect emotions directly."[56] Clearly, the center of attention for Šklovskij is not so much the sound organization of Russian poetry as the transrational, sensual, magical aspects of sound in poetry as universal phenomena. Characteristically, the conclusion to his comments on poetry and transense language contains a prophecy that "the day will come when only sounds in poetry will be of interest for poets."[57] This was in full accord with the sound experimentations of the Russian Futurists who, in their most radical attempts to reach universal poeticality, actually ceased being poets of the Russian language. Rather, their poetry came closer to the glossololia, the "speaking-in-tongue" of religious fanatics around the world or to the nonsense poetry of children using speech sounds for their games.

Sound organization as an essential feature of poetry is also the point of departure for the early poetics of Lev Jakubinskij, a student of Baudouin de Courtenay and one of the co-founders of the *Opojaz*. In his paper "On the Sounds of Verse Language," published in *Poetika* in 1916, he sharply distinguishes practical language from verse language. "In practical language," Jakubinskij asserts, "attention is not focused (*ne sosredotočivaetsja*) on sounds, sounds do not emerge into the bright field of consciousness and, serving merely as a tool of communication, have no autonomous value of their own (*samostojatel'naja cennost'*)."[58] On the other hand, in poetic usage, the special arrangement of sounds attracts attention to its own autonomous value which thereby appears in opposition to the practical functions in verbal communication.

The concentration on speech sounds for their own sake (*samocel'*) is connected, as Jakubinskij sees it, with special emotional attitudes. "This is," he asserts, "particularly important for establishing the relationship between acoustic and intelligible aspects of speech in verse language."[59] Accordingly, the poeticality of a versified text is explained as the coordination of two types of emotions, one provoked by sound and the other by meaning. To support the view that the sound of the word can function independently of its meaning, Jakubinskij cites Charles Bally, the editor of the posthumous *Course* of Ferdinand de Saussure. Moreover, he extensively quotes from *Psychology* by William James, the cofounder of the school of American pragmatism. It is here, that Jakubinskij found the impetus for his concept of focussing on speech sounds for their own sake and for making "nude" the phonetic aspect of the word (*obnaženie fonetičeskoj storony slova*) for the sake of special emotional experiences. In this way, James's observations about "sensational nudity"[60], which the Russian translator of *Psychology* rendered as "obnaženie"[61], entered into the lexicon of the Futurists and the Russian school of the Formal method.

An even more radical differentiation between poetic language and practical language appears in Jakubinskij's paper on "Accumulation of Identical Liquids" (1917), where the distinction between the two languages is stated in terms of a sound law of dissimilation. Here Jakubinskij declares that accumulation of liquids retards the tempo of speech, hinders automatization and focuses attention on speech sounds for their own sake. However, in practical language, he asserts all these phenomena are felt as negative and therefore, accumulation of liquids is subjected to the phonetic law of dissimilation. Since his discussion does not use only Russian examples, it gives the impression that dissimilation of liquids in practical language and accumulation in poetic language is a universal law. "Everywhere," he says, "where the sound form is valuable for its own sake and where the element of play with sound is present, dissimilation does not take place... [62] This applies, he feels, particularly, to poetic language: "In poetic language dissimilation does not occur, accumulation is fully tolerated... and can even become a source of special emotions."[63]

Jakubinskij's observations about accumulation and dissimilation of liquids were enthusiastically received by Viktor Šklovskij in his article "Art as Device" (1917) which has been commonly considered the founding manifesto of Russian Formalism. In Šklovskij's view, Jakubinskij's paper with its claim that the law of dissimilation of liquids does not apply to poetic language was "one of the first factual and scientific proofs of the opposition between the laws of poetic language and the laws of practical language."[64] However, much less enthusiastic was Roman Jakobson. In fact, his first contributions to new Russian poetics directly or indirectly attacked not only Jakubinskij's law of dissimilation but several fundamental aspects of Jakubinskij's linguistics and poetics and, by implication, the "psycho-phonetic" trend of the early *Opojaz* in general.

In his *Newest Russian Poetry*, written in 1919, Jakobson accepts Jakubinskij's idea of self-focusing on speech sounds in poetry and even uses his term "concentrating attention on themselves" (*sosredotočivat' na sebe vnimanie*), but modifies it in a fundamental way by separating the notion of emotion from poeticality:

> In emotional language and poetic language, the verbal representation (phonetic as well as semantic) concentrate on themselves greater attention; the connection between the aspect of sound and that of meaning is tighter, more intimate, and language is accordingly more revolutionary, insofar as habitual associations by contiguity retreat into the background... But beyond this there is no necessary affinity between emotional and poetic language.[65]

In Jakobson's view, the laws which govern poetic language are essentially different from those which govern expressions of emotion:

In emotional expression passionate outbursts govern the verbal mass, and precisely that 'turbulent stream of emotion bursts the pipe of the sentence'.. But poetry—which is simply *utterance for the purpose of expression* [*vyskazyvanie s ustanovkoj navyraže- nie*] —is governed, so to speak, by its own immanent laws; the communicative function, essential to both practical language and emotional language, has only minimal importance in poetry... Poetry is language in its aesthetic function.[66]

Jakobson's antipsychological leaning, which was one of the features distinguishing the members of the Moscow Linguistic Circle from those of the Leningrad's *Opojaz*, is best demonstrated by his sarcasm, turned against those who, like Jakubinskij, tried to explain poetic language in terms of emotionality:

One of the commonest applications, or rather, in the given case, justification of poetic language is emotional and mental exper- ience, which serves as a kind of catchall where we may dispose of anything that can't be justified or explained in practical terms, or rationalized.[67]

Although Jakobson also uses the concept of "sensational nudity", borrowed by Jakubinskij from the Russian translation of James's *Psychology* as "*obnaženie*" (and subsequently retranslated into English as "laying bare"[68]), he is not as interested as Jakubinskij in its emotional or hypnotic impact. For Jakobson, "*obnaženie*" is a technical term referring to poetic devices. Thus, for example, "*obnaženie*" of rhyme is "emancipation of rhyme's sound valency from the semantic bond" while "*obnaženie*" of the attribute "simply means to emphasize the attribute as a syntactic fact."

While Jakubinskij in his "Poetics of Glossematic Combinations" dis- cusses the importance of the combinatory axes in poetry, Jakobson empha- sizes that in poetry not only combinations of words but the words themselves appear at the focal point:

The focus upon expression, upon the verbal mass itself, which I have called the only essential characteristic of poetry, is directed not only to the form of the phrase, but also to the form of the word itself.[69]

While Jakubinskij in his paper "On Sound in Verse Language" proposes to deal with the "psychophonetics" of sound in poetry, Jakobson questions whether it is at all proper to talk about sound in poetry:

It is possible to produce verses characterized by an emphasis primarily on euphony. But is this sort of emphasis equivalent to the accentuation of pure sound? If the answer is yes then we have a species of vocal music and vocal music of an inferior kind at that. Euphony operates, however, not with sounds but with phonemes, that is, with acoustical impressions which are capable of being associated with meaning.[70]

Thus Jakubinskij's "psychophonetics", which wanted to examine sounds in their universal capacity, was opposed by Jakobson's phonology which was based on phonemes definable only within the framework of a concrete linguistic system.

Jakobson's emphasis on the phonological rather than "psychophonetic" approach to poetics became even more pronounced in his book *On Czech Verse*, written in 1923. It is here, that he explicitly rejects Jakubinskij's sound law of dissimilation of liquids by pointing out that dissimilation of liquids occurs in both practical and poetic language and that it is only the function of dissimilation which is different. In practical language "it is conditioned" while in poetic language "it is, so to say, goal-directed."[73] Accordingly, poetic language is distinguished from practical language not in terms of different inventories of verbal means but in terms of different functions. Although Jakobson continues to speak about poetic language and practical language, he makes it clear that they do not represent for him two entirely different systems of communication which would require two different analytic approaches. Rather, it is their interrelationship which is the chief target of his poetics while the everyday language serves as a necessary base. By implication, his poetics becomes a branch of linguistics rather than a branch of aesthetics or philosophy of art.

In accordance with his linguistic orientation, the *Newest Russian Poetry* proclaims:

We apprehend each new manifestation of the contemporary poetic language in its necessary relationship with three factors: the existing poetic tradition, the everyday language of the present time, and the developing poetic tendencies with which the given manifestation is confronted.[72]

In connection with Jakobson's phonological approach, which uses phonemes of a concrete natural language as its base, it is noteworthy that the introductory chapter to his *Newest Russian Poetry* refers to Ferdinand de Saussure and embraces his "static method" of analysis. Attuned to de Saussure's sharp separation between the static and diachronic approaches, Jakobson critically turns against the evaluative historical approach not only in linguistics but in poetics as well and proclaims that "scientific poetics will become possible only when it refuses to offer value judgments."[78]

The conflict between Jakubinskij's "psychophonetics" and Jakobson's phoneme oriented poetics caused one of the earliest and perhaps the most profound conceptual crises in the development of the Russian school of the Formal method. It promoted young Jakobson to the leading position as a theoretician of the group and, at the same time, it firmly introduced into Russian Formalism the Saussurian line of ideas, including the concept of phoneme and language as a system.

Jakubinskij did not join the Saussurian trend. His comprehensive paper on dialogue, published in 1923,[74] clearly revealed his Hegelian orientation in general and his admiration for von Humboldt in particular. Subsequently, this paper provided ammunition for the Russian opponents of Saussure and mightily influence the so called Baxtin group which critically turned against the School of the Formal Method and against the Russian Saussurians in general.

A strictly linguistic approach toward poetics, which uses the phonological system as its base and refuses to offer any value judgment, was restated by Jakobson without any substantial changes forty years later in 1960 at the conference on style in Bloomington. In his "Closing Statement" to the conference, Jakobson insists that linguistics is the global science of verbal structure, and, therefore, poetics may be regarded as an integral part of linguistics: "the analysis of verse," he says, "is entirely within the competence of poetics and the latter may be defined as that part of linguistics which treats the poetic function in its relationship to the other functions of language."[75] However, he puts a special emphasis on the fact "that many poetic features belong not only to the science of language but to the whole theory of signs, that is, to general semiotics."[76] As far as the value judgment is concerned, Jakobson's "Closing Statement" expels it from poetics with unchanged vehemence:

> Unfortunately the terminological confusion of "literary studies" with "criticism" tempts the students of literature to replace the description of the intrinsic values of a literary work by a subjective, censorious verdict. The label "literary critic" applied to an investigation of literature is as erroneous as "grammatical (or lexical) critic" would be applied to a linguist. Syntactic and morphological research cannot be supplanted by a normative grammar, and likewise no manifesto, foisting a critic's own taste and opinions on creative literature, may act as substitute for an objective scholarly analysis of verbal art.[77]

5

Recent publication of Nikolaj Trubetzkoy's correspondence with Roman Jakobson has revealed that, in the early stages of their cooperation, Trubetzkoy had profound doubts about the role of poetics as defined by Jakobson in his *Newest Russian Poetry*. He particularly questioned Jakobson's rejection of evaluation and his treatment of a work of art as a linguistic fact outside of social and historical contexts. On the 28th of June, 1921, Trubetzkoy wrote to Jakobson:

> That literature is a factor of social life cannot be disregarded. . . .
> As a matter of fact, the readers do perform aesthetic evaluation of literary products. In order to become a fact of the social order, the given work has to pass the test of taste successfully. Only then does it satisfy the readership and generate imitation, even if only potentially. And strictly speaking, only under such conditions does the given work become a work of literature and enter as a link into the history of literature. . . . In your scholarship, however, Puškin, uncle Mitaj and a highschool girl who tries to write poetry are completely equal targets of investigation.[78]

Aesthetic evaluation also became a fundamental point of Mixail Baxtin's attack in his paper "Problems of Content, Material and Form in Verbal Art," written in 1924. Reacting against the linguistic domination of poetics in the Russian school of the Formal Method, Baxtin rejects all attempts to make poetics a branch of linguistics and categorically proclaims that "poetics, defined systematically, has to be the aesthetics of verbal art."[79] In contrast to Trubetzkoy, however, Baxtin does not highlight the social aspects of verbal art, the role of the community in the acceptance of the work of art and the diachronic approach to literature. In 1924, aesthetics is for Baxtin first of all an evaluative and interpretative activity in terms of aesthetic values which are strictly distinguished from other cultural values such as ethical, political etc. In his opinion, there cannot be any neutral, non-evaluative approach towards art: "when we talk about art," he asserts, "we already define it and evaluate it by the same token."[80]

In striking accord with the idealistic aesthetics of Benedetto Croce, Baxtin in 1924 proclaims the intuitive knowledge of imagination fundamentally different from the logical knowledge of the intellect; accordingly, he distinguishes art from non-art by means of special aesthetic experience which differs from the conceptual form of knowledge. Like Croce, Baxtin sees art primarily as expression rather than communication: "aesthetically significant form is expression of the existential relation toward the world of experience and action, however this relation is neither cognitive nor ethical."[81] Art, in Baxtin's view, "sings and embelishes," it "establishes a concrete, intuitive unity between nature and mankind," it "combines man with nature," it "humanizes nature and makes man natural."[82]

Although Baxtin in 1924 does not explicitly subscribe to Potebnja's definition of art as thinking with help of images, the image is, nevertheless, the fundament of his approach towards art: "the aesthetic component which can be called image is neither a concept nor a word nor a visual presentation but a special aesthetic creativity which is implemented in poetry by means of words and in visual art by means of visual, perceivable material. . ."[83] His preoccupation with the autonomy of aesthetic values, specificity of intuition and immanent aspects of art as expression forces him to divorce the study of verbal art from the social intercourse, on the one hand, and from language, on the other. "By dissolving logic and aesthetic or even poetics in linguistics," he says, "we destroy the specificity of logic, aesthetics and linguistics as well."[84]

Clearly, in 1924 Baxtin was fully attuned to the framework of the idealistic aesthetics of Benedetto Croce and Croce's German followers in the so-called "idealistic neophilology." It is from that position that he confronted the Russian school of the Formal method, accusing it of sheer materialism and slavish dependence on linguistics.

Baxtin's paper "Problems of Content, Material and Form in Verbal Art" was allegedly written in 1924 for A.M. Gor'kij's *Russkij sovremennik*. But it remained unpublished for half a century. Several fragments of that paper first appeared in 1974 in the almanach *Kontekst 1973* under the title "Toward Aesthetics of the Word," without any reference to the time and circumstances of its origin. Since Baxtin in 1974 was still alive and since the heavily edited fragments did not contain any clear-cut temporal markers, the article potentially led readers to believe that this was Baxtin's up-to-date contribution to *Kontekst's* critical attack on modern Soviet literary scholarship from the official party-line. Finally, in 1975, the "Preface" to Baxtin's posthumous volume, *Problems of Literature and Aesthetics* obliquely revealed that the article in *Kontekst 1973* was just an edited selection from a more comprehensive study which originated in 1924. In this connection it is certainly noteworthy that in 1926, only two years after the alleged origin of Baxtin's study, V.N. Vološinov, who for some experts is just a pen-name of Baxtin[86], while for others the name of one of Baxtin's students and intimates[86], published in *Zvezda* a paper, entitled "Word in Life and Word in Poetry." In this paper, he aggressively attacked the very basis of Baxtin's aesthetics of 1924.

While Baxtin in 1924 insists that "an aesthetic analysis has to uncover first and foremost the immanency of the aesthetic object"[87] and "to determine the immanent nature of content in contemplation of art,"[88] Vološinov in 1926 tags all teaching about the immanency and the autonomous nature of art subjective and deceptive. In his view:

> The *aesthetic*, just as the juridical or the cognitive, is *only a variety of the social*. Theory of art, consequently, can only be *a sociology of art*. No "immanent" tasks are left in its province."[89]

The sociological approach is further developed in Vološinov's *Marxism and Philosophy of Language*, published in 1929, where rejection of Baxtin's idealistic aesthetics of 1924 is even more explicit. While Baxtin in 1924 insists on the strict separation of aesthetics and linguistics, Vološinov in 1929 goes to the opposite extreme and subscribes to a radical logocentricity of culture:

> *The word functions as an essential ingredient accompanying all ideological creativity whatsoever*. The word accompanies and comments on each and every ideological act. The process of understanding any ideological phenomenon at all (be it a picture, a piece of music, a ritual, or an act of human conduct) cannot operate without the participation of inner speech. All manifestations of ideological creativity—all other non verbal signs—are bathed by, suspended in, and cannot be entirely segregated and divorced from the element of speech."[90]

While Baxtin in 1924 felt that "by dissolving logic and aesthetics or even poetics in the linguistics, we destroy the specificity of logic, aesthetics and linguistics as well," for Vološinov in 1929 language became a model providing the most profound insight into all aspects of the humanities:

> Nowhere does the semiotic quality and the continuous comprehensive role of social communication as conditioning factor appear so clearly and fully expressed as in language. *The word is the ideological phenomenon par excellence*. The entire reality of the word is wholly absorbed in its function of being a sign.[91]

Thus the concept of signs with its functions in the human community serves Vološinov as the corner stone of his entire philosophy of culture. All the cultural activities of mankind, be it science, religion or art, are approached as semiotic operations, with language as the most essential among them. "Without sign," Vološinov proclaims, "there is no ideology."[92] Creation of signs and their usage for Vološinov define man with his ability to think and to deal with values, whether economical, ethical or aesthetic. In his view, the entire social life depends on signs and their usage and *vice versa*, the existence of signs depends on the human community. Thus, Vološinov's semiotics and mankind presuppose each other.

In accordance with the importance of signs for the human community, Vološinov sees in the world, side by side with the natural phenomena and objects, created by man, "a special world—the world of signs."[93] The concept of signs or more exactly, semiotics, becomes for Vološinov a unifying framework which embraces all the variables of cultural phenomena:

> Within the domain of signs, i.e. within the ideological sphere profound differences exist:it is after all, the domain of the artistic image, the religious symbol, the scientific formula, and the judicial ruling, etc. Each field of ideological creativity has its own kind of orientation toward reality and each refracts reality in its own way. Each field commands its own special function within the unity of social life. *But it is their semiotic character that places all ideological phenomena under the same general definition.*[94]

For Vološinov a sign is a phenomenon of the external world. He is convinced that the localization of signs in the psyche would change semiotics into the study of consciousness and its laws. Therefore, he is unwilling to neglect the physical properties of the sign. Vološinov's emphasis on the material embodiment of sign is particularly striking if compared with Baxtin's views of 1924. While Baxtin in his attack on the "aesthetics of materialism" from the Crocean platform insists that "the artifact is only a physical stimulus of physiological and psychological states"[95] and as such functions only as "a technical apparatus of aesthetic performance"[96], Vološinov in 1929 declares:

> The idealistic philosophy of culture and psychologistic cultural studies locate ideology in the consciousness. Ideology, they assert, is a fact of consciousness; the external body of the sign is merely a coating, merely a technical means for the realization of the inner effect which is understanding. Idealism and psychologism alike overlook the fact that understanding itself can come about only within some kind of semiotic material (e.g., in a speech), that sign bears upon sign, that *consciousness itself can arise and become a viable fact only in the material embodiment of signs.*[97]

However, the most important aspect of the sign for Vološinov is its social function. In fact his semiotics is primarily concerned with the functions of signs in the human community rather than with the essence of sign in the phenomenological sense. In his view, conditions and forms of social communication wholly determine the reality of the sign. "The existence of the sign," he says, "is nothing but the materialization of social communication."[98] It is only in the process of interaction between one individual and another where signs emerge:

> The ideological cannot possibly be explained in terms of either the superhuman or subhuman, animalian roots. Its real place in existence is the special, social material of signs created by man. Its specificity consists precisely in its being located between organized individuals, in its being the medium of their communication. Signs can rise only on *interindividual territory*.[99]

While Baxtin's aesthetics of expression in 1924 is chiefly concerned with the subjective attitude of the artists and therefore emphasizes the role of the addresser in art, Vološinov in 1929 proclaims that "the theory of expression underlying idealistic subjectivism must be rejected."[100] He sees the usage of the word as a two-sided act which is determined equally by whose word it is and for whom it is meant. The stylistic individualization of an utterance reflects, in his view, social interrelationship that constitutes the atmosphere in which the utterance is formed. It is the social context which determines the structure of an utterance:

> The organizing center of any utterance, of any experience is not within but outside-in the social milieu surrounding the individual being. Only the inarticulate cry of an animal is really organized from the inside of the psychological apparatus of an individual creature.[101]

6

Although the concept of sign played an important role in Potebnja's *Language and Thought*, in Lenin's conceptual conflict with Plexanov, in Špet's phenomenological *Aesthetic Fragments* and potentially also in the Russian school of the Formal method, Vološinov's book from 1929, nevertheless, represents the first comprehensive introduction to modern Russian semiotics. Here Saussure's suggestive remarks about the general science of sign are imaginatively developed into an original approach conerned with human culture in its entirely. Yet, Vološinov's semiotics is not truly Saussurian and, as a matter of fact, it directs criticism not only against the Russian Saussurians but against Saussure himself.

While Saussure regards his doctrine of the sign as "a part of social psychology and consequently of general psychology,"[102] for Vološinov the study of signs "does not depend on psychology to any extent and need not be grounded in it."[103] On the contrary, he is convinced that objective psychology has to be grounded in the study of signs.

While Saussure's semiotics is chiefly concerned with the internalized system, "la langue" as a prerequisite of communication, Vološinov is first and foremost interested in its cultural functionality. "From the objective point of view," he asserts, "a synchronic system does not correspond to any real moment in the historical process of becoming.[104] Saussure's *la langue* which as Vološinov sees it, is produced with a good deal of trouble by logical abstracting, represents for him nothing more than an arbitrary scale on which to register the deviations occuring at every real instant in time. It may have, he admits, cognitive or some other practical value but it does not provide any convincing insight into the internalized processes of subjective consciousness and into actual semiotic operations:

> What interests the mathematically minded rationalist is not the relationship of the sign to the actual reality it reflects nor to the individual who is the originator, but the relationship of sign to sign within a closed system already accepted and authorized. In other words, they are interested only in the inner logic of the system of sign itself, taken, as in algebra, completely independently of the ideological meaning that give the sign their content.[105]

Clearly, Vološinov does not believe in a synchronic or static approach in semiotics. In contrast to Saussure, he is not interested in *la langue* but rather in *la parole* or, more precisely, in the interaction of both. For him, the true center of linguistic reality is an individual speech act within the given context. He sees its semiotic function as inextricably fused together with the social situation. At the same time, however, he emphasized that the individual speech act should not be studied as a monologic utterance:

> In each speech act subjective experience perishes in the objective fact of the enunciated word-utterance, and the enunciated word is subjectified in the act of responsive understanding in order to generate, sooner or later, a counter statement. Each word, as we know, is a little arena for the clash and

criss-crossing of differently oriented social accents. A word in
the mouth of a particular individual person is a product of the
living interaction of social forces.[106]

The static nature of Saussure's synchronic model and its artificial
separation from the ceaselessly changing continuum of the creative flow
of language is interpreted by Vološinov as the revival of the Cartesian spirit
in the area of linguistic investigation. As a dialectician, he objects to the
segregating tendency of Cartesian dualism and tries to see evolutionary
forces and systematization as a continuous interaction. Yet he is fully aware
of the impact of Saussure's Cartesianism on his contemporaries. "It can be
claimed," he says, "that the majority of Russian thinkers in linguistics are
under the determinative influence of Saussure and his disciples, Bally and
Sechehaye."[107] And he readily admits that "Saussure's views on history
are extremely characteristic for the spirit of rationalism that continues to
hold sway in the philosophy of language and that regards history as an
irrational force distorting the logical purity of language systems."[108] But
he feels that in contradistinction to the tradition of the Cartesian linguistics,
the Humboldtian linguistics truly encompasses the need for the explanation
of linguistics phenomena. The Humboldtian emphasis on the creative aspect
as the fundamental characteristic of human language is, as Vološinov sees it,
in direct contradiction to interest in the inner logic of the system of sign
itself, taken as in algebra without adequate relation to the actual reality.
Thus, the primary target of linguistic investigation should be exactly that
which reveals the creative aspect of human language. The systematic presentation of the grammar, lexicon, and phonetics is for Vološinov nothing
more than an exercise in logic, segmentation, classification, abstracting and
algebraization. The semiotic nature of human communication cannot be
grasped, as Vološinov sees it, if the novelty of the speech act and its relevance are disregarded as superficial phenomena, as "merely fortuitous re-
fraction and variations or plain and simple distortions of normatively identical forms."[109] According to Vološinov, in Cartesian linguistics in general
and in Saussure's school in particular, the factor of stable self-identity in
linguistic forms takes precedence over their mutability, the abstract over
the concrete, systematic over historicity, the forms of isolated components
over the property of the entire structure. In contrast, dialogue in a broader
sense is seen by Vološinov as an examplary case of verbal interaction displaying as it does, the most essential features of semiotic operation: not only
the speech event with its physical and semantic aspects in relation to another
speech event but also the opposition of the participants of the speech event
and the conditions of their verbal contact in a given context.

In Vološinov's view, the framework of dialogue naturally brings forward the crucial role of intonation for semantics and the inadequacy of grammatical analysis confined within the boundaries of a single, complete sentence. The focus on the binary character of a verbal exchange implies need for taking into account syntactic units that are either more comprehensive or less comprehensive than a single, complete sentence. The concept of utterance as a whole appears as stimulating challenges for syntactic inquiry. At the same time, it becomes apparent that morphologized syntax is a poor tool for handling an utterance as a whole, the syntactic interdependence of utterance structure and, in general, the multifarious manifestation of verbal interaction. Moreover, the study of dialogue in Vološinov's view provides a new approach to the structural characteristics of an utterance and also a basis from which to venture into the mysteries of inner speech and its relationship to human thoughts. "Only by ascertaining the forms of whole utterances and, especially, the forms of dialogue speech," Vološinov argues, "can light be shed on the forms of inner speech. . . [110]"

7

In his prologomena to semiotics, Vološinov proclaimed the philosophy of sign as the only feasible approach not merely to the problems of language and art but to the humanities in general. He conceived semiotics as a framework which could make possible an objective inquiry into the human mind, on the one hand, and human society, on the other. In fact, he even felt that semiotics could enrich and advance the classical doctrine of Marxism. But here he was evidently wrong. While the book of his friend and mentor Mixail Baxtin, *Problems of Dostoevsky's Poetics*, published in 1929, was approvingly received by the Soviet minister of culture himself, Vološinov's book, published the same year, was virtually ignored by everybody in the Soviet Union. Vološinov not only disappeared in the thirties but his name has not been rehabilitated to the present time. Only in Czechoslovakia did Vološinov's views provoke a positive reaction among some members of the Prague Linguistic Circle. They clearly influenced Jan Mukařovsky's semiotic aesthetics and Petr Bogatyrev's semiotics of culture. An echo of Vološinov's views are also detectable in the programatic article of one of the organs of the Prague Linguistic Circle, *Slovo a slovesnost* (Word and Word Culture) where, in 1935, the emphasis on the semiotic approach and the contextual constraints is expressed almost in Volosinov's manner:

Verbal art and art in general provide the prime material for studying the internal structure of the sign itself, for disclosing the interrelationship between a sign vehicle (that is, sound, color, etc.) and its meaning, and for investigating the manifold stratification of meaning. This is due to the fact that the referential relationship of art is attenuated: the work of art is not measur-

able in terms of the veracity of the information conveyed; rather
it is a sign that lives its own life and freely travels between artist
and audience.... The entire dynamics of social development, the
ongoing regrouping and conflict of each of its strata and its
environment, the struggle of classes, nations and ideologies—
all that is intensely reflected in the relation between art and
society and even in the development of art itself, despite the
fact that the changes in the structure of art appear as continuously sequential and ordered.[111]

In the Soviet Union, on the other hand, semiotics has always been
considered from the official party-line as a problematic approach which
potentially conflicts with Marxism and particularly with Lenin's views on
sign and symbol displayed in his ideological conflict with Plexanov.

In recent years the attacks on semiotics of the Vološinov brand and
on some of its followers in the Moscow-Tartu group has been intensified in
various outlets of the   official   ideology and particularly in *Kontekst* which
specializes in criticism of semiotics of art and of modern trends in art theory.
It is only typical for *Kontekst*'s ideological maneuvers that its editors, who
have acquired official acclaim for their criticism of structuralism, did not
hesitate to include into the sequel of attacks on semiotics the heavily edited
fragments of Baxtin's unpublished paper from 1924 without identifying its
origin. In this way, they made Baxtin one of their allies. Among the several
papers directly or indirectly attacking modern semiotics in *Kontekst 1973*,
there is a comprehensive survey of the "crisis" in literary scholarship by
N.I. Balašov who critically puts into the same bag Ferdinand de Saussure,
Edmund Husserl, Sigmund Freud, Roman Jakobson, Luis Hjelmslev, Claude
Lévi-Strauss, Émile Benveniste, Noam Chomsky, Jacques Lacan, Jacques
Derrida, Roland Barthes, Tzvetan Todorov, V.V. Ivanov, V.N. Toporov,
Ju. Apresjan, S. Šaumjan, I. Revzin, Ju. Lotman, B. Uspenskij, I.A. Mel'čuk
and many others, accused of their connection with semiotics and "the
ideological danger of neo-structuralism." Balašov's article ends on a parodic
note quoting from Shakespeare's *Hamlet* a passage about signs and confusion of mind and from Julia Kristeva her apodictic claim: Pour la sémiotique, la littérature n'existe pas...[112] Characteristically, *Kontekst 1973*
is introduced by an editorial preface which uses as its theme a dictum about
historical optimism from a speech by Leonid Breznev, the Secretary General.

One has the right to ask, of course, whether Baxtin was at all aware of
his company in *Kontekst* and whether he himself edited his old paper from
1924 so that it would look freshly written for *Kontekst 1973*. To be sure,
those texts which can be more or less safely identified as Baxtin's own
writing from the last years of his life have nothing to do with Marxism.
Rather, they reveal his old admiration for Karl Vossler and Leo Spitzer
and the idealistic neophilology in general. It is certainly not coincidental

that Spitzer's doctoral thesis on laughter in Rabelais (1910) and his subsequent observations about Rabelais's dionysian humor, "carnival of words", anti-realism, irrealism and hyperrealism[113] found a remarkable response in Baxtin's monumental work *Rabelais and his World*. And Baxtin's paper "Bolder Use of Resources", written for *Novyj mir* in 1970 echoes, it seems, Karl Vossler's thought on the dialectics of opposed cultures and the interplay of the native and the alien in the cultural creativity of man:

> An alien culture reveals itself more fully and deeply in the eyes of *another* culture.... One sense reveals its depth upon meeting and making contact with another, "alien" sense: a kind of *dialogue* begins between them, overcoming the isolation and one-sidedness of the two senses, the two cultures. We put new questions to the alien culture, which it has never asked itself; and the alien culture answers us, opening before us new sides of itself, new depth of sense. Without questions of *one's own* one cannot creatively understand anything other and alien... In an encounter of this kind, leading to a dialogue of two cultures, they do not merge or combine together; each preserves its unity and its *open* wholeness, but they mutually enrich one another.[114]

There is nothing really marxistic in Baxtin's *Kulturgeschichte*. Rather it follows and up-dates Potebnja's cultural relativism which, in its turn, was nurtured by idealistic *Völkerpsychologie*. In an interesting contrast to Vološinov's semiotics, using language as its model, Baxtin in 1970 insists that it is the national culture which has to dominate all aspects of the literary studies:

> First and foremost, literary scholarship must establish a closer connection with the history of culture. Literature is an inseparable part of culture; it cannot be understood outside of the context of the whole culture of a given epoch. It must not be separated from the rest of culture and correlated directly to social-economic factors over the head, so to speak, of culture, as is often done. These factors influence culture as a whole, and only through culture and together with it, do they act on literature.[115]

NOTES

1. A.A. Potebnja, *Mysl' i jazyk* in *È stetika i poètika* (Moscow, 1976), p. 109.
2. *Ibid*. p. 179.
3. *Ibid*. p. 111.
4. *Ibid*.
5. *Ibid*. p. 168.
6. *Ibid*. p. 138.
7. A.A. Potebnja, *Iz lekcij po teorii slovesnosti in Èstetika i poetika* (Moscow, 1976), p.540.
8. *Ibid*. p.541.
9. Cited from V.I. Lenin, *Collected Works*, 14 (Moscow, 1962),p.378.
10. G.V. Plexanov, "Protiv filosofskogo revizionizma," p.178 as quoted by G.A. Wetter, *Dialectical Materialism* (London, 1958),p.106.
11. V.I. Lenin, *Materialism and Empiriocriticism* in *Collected Works*, 14, (Moscow, 1962),p.233.
12. *Ibid*.p.234.
13. *Ibid*.p.235.
14. *Ibid*.
15. *Ibid*.
16. Roman Jakobson, *Selected Writings*, 1 (The Hague, 1971),p.631.
17. Gustav Špet, *Èstetičeskie fragmenty*, 2 (Moscow, 1923). His term *semiotika* could have been inspired by John Locke's *Essay Concerning Human Understanding*, translated into Russian in 1898.
18. *Ibid*. p. 61.
19. *Ibid*. p.10.
20. *Ibid*. p. 67.
21. *Ibid*. p. 7.
22. *Ibid*. p. 8.
23. *Ibid*. p. 7.
24. *Ibid*. p. 61.
25. *Ibid*. p. 9.
26. *Ibid*. p. 8.
27. *Ibid*. pp. 8-9.
28. *Ibid*. p. 11.
29. *Ibid*.
30. *Ibid*. p. 7.
31. *Ibid*.
32. *Ibid*. p. 102.
33. *Ibid*. p. 110.
34. *Ibid*. p. 65.
35. *Ibid*. p. 66.
36. *Ibid*.
37. *Ibid*. pp. 66-67.
38. *Ibid*. pp. 71.
39. *Ibid*.
40. Gustav Špet, *È stetičeskie fragmenty*, 3 (Moscow, 1923), p. 8.
41. *Ibid*. pp. 38-39.
42. *Ibid*. p. 14.
43. Gustav Špet, *È stetičeskie fragmenty*, 1 (Moscow, 1922), p. 46.
44. *Ibid*. p. 45.

45. *Ibid*.p.46.
46. *Ibid*.p.45.
47. *Ibid*.p.44.
48. *Ibid*.p.50.
51. A.A. Potebnja, *Estetika i poètika*, p.178.
52. Viktor Šklovskij, "Potebnja," *Poètika. Sbornik po teorii poètičeskogo jazyka* (Petrograd, 1919), p.5.
53. *Ibid*.
54. *Ibid*.p.6.
55. Viktor Šklovskij, "O poezii i zaumnom jazyke," *Poètika*, p.15.
56. *Ibid*.p.14.
57. *Ibid*.p.26.
58. L.P. Jakubinskij, "O zvukax stixotvornogo jazyka," *Poètika*, p.38.
59. *Ibid*.p.44.
60. William James, *Psychology* (New York, 1900),p.314.
61. V.Džema, *Psixologija*, perev.Lapščina,p.269, as quoted by Jakubinskij.
62. L.P. Jakubinskij, "Skoplenie odinakovyx plavnyx v praktičeskom i poetičeskom jazykax," *Poètika*,p.54.
63. *Ibid*.
64. Viktor Šklovskij, "Iskusstvo kak priem," *Readings in Russian Poetics, Michigan Slavic Materials, 2,p.5*.
65. Roman Jakobson, *Novejšaja russkaja poesija* (Prague, 1921),p.10. Here quoted from Edward Brown's English translation in *Major Soviet Writers*,ed.E.Brown (Oxford, 1973),p.62.
66. *Ibid*.
67. *Ibid*.p.11 and 63 respectively.
68. Cf. for example, Viktor Erlich, *Russian Formalism:History-Doctrine* (s'Gravenhage, 1955),p.162.
69. *Novejšaja russkaja poesija*, p.42; *Major Soviet Writers*,p.73.
70. *Ibid*.p.48 and 77 respectively.
71. *Roman Jakobson, O češskom stixe preimuščestvenno v sopostavlenni s russkim* (Berlin, 1923), p.17; cf. Krystyna Pomorska, *Russian Formalist Theory and its Poetic Ambiance* (The Hague, 1968), p.28.
72. *Novejšaja russkaja poesija*, p.4; *Major Soviet Writers*, p.59.
73. *Ibid*. p.5 and 59 respectively.
74. Lev P. Jakubinskij, "O dialogičeskoj reči," *Russkaja reč'*, 1, ed.L.Ščerba (1923).
75. Roman Jakobson, "Closing Statement: Linguistics and Poetics," *Style in Language*, ed. T.A. Sebeok (Cambridge, Mass., 1960),p.359.
76. *Ibid*.p.351.
77. *Ibid*.p.351.
78. *N.S. Trubetzkoy's Letters and Notes*, ed. by Roman Jakobson, (The Hague, 1975), p.22.
79. M.Baxtin, "Problema soderžanija, materiala i formy v slovesnom tvorčestve," *Voprosy literatury i èstetiky* (Moscow, 1975),p.10.
80. *Ibid*.p.27.
81. *Ibid*.p.33.
82. *Ibid*.p.30.
83. *Ibid*.p.52.
84. *Ibid*.p.43.

85. Fredric Jameson's review of V.N. Vološinov *Marxism and the Philosophy of Language*, Style, 8:3 (1974),p.535.

86. Cf. *Voprosy jazykoznanija*, 2, 1971, pp. 160-162. Also see I.R. Titunik, "The Formal Method and the Sociological Method (M.M. Baxtin, P.N. Medvedev, V.V. Vološinov) in Russian Theory and Study of Literature," in V.N. Vološinov, *Marxism and the Philosophy of Language* (New York, 1973) as well as I.R. Titunik, "M.M. Baxtin (The Baxtin School) and Soviet Semiotics" *Dispositio*, 3, (1976),pp.327-388.

87. M. Baxtin, "Problema...,"p.38.

88. *Ibid*.p.49.

89. V. Vološinov, "Slovo v zizni i slovo v poesii," *Zvezda* (1926),p.246; here quoted from I.R. Titunik's English translation in V.N. Vološinov, *Freudianism: A Marxist Critique* (New York, 1976),p.95.

90. V.N. Vološinov, *Marxism and the Philosophy of Language*, translated by L.Matejka and I.R. Titunik (New York, 1973),p.15.

91. *Ibid*.p.13.

92. *Ibid*.p.9.

94. *Ibid*.

95. M. Baxtin, "Problema...,"p.14.

96. *Ibid*.p.17.

97. Vološinov, *Marxism. . . p. 11.*

98. *Ibid*.p.13.

99. *Ibid*.p.12.

100. *Ibid*.p.93.

101. *Ibid*.

102. Ferdinand de Saussure, *Course in General Linguistics*, translated by Wade Baskin (New York, 1959),p.16.

103. Vološinov, *Marxism*...p.13.

104. *Ibid*.p.66.

105. *Ibid*.p.58.

106. *Ibid*.p.41.

107. *Ibid.p.58.*

108. *Ibid*.p.61.

109. *Ibid*.p.67.

110. *Ibid*.p.38.

111. Cf. "Prague School Semiotics" in *Semiotics of Art: Prague School Contributions*, ed. by L.Matejka and I.R. Titunik (Cambridge, Mass.,1976),p.274.

112. N.I. Balašov, "K kritike novejšix tendencij v literaturovedčeskom strukturalizme," *Kontekst 1973* (Moscow, 1974),p.175.

113. Cf. Leo Spiter, "Die Wortbildung als stilistisches Mittel: exemplifiziert an Rabelais," *Zeitschrift für romanische Philologie. Beihefte*, 29 (1910); "Slovesnoe iskusstvo i nauka o jazyke," *Problemy literaturnoj formy: Sbornik statej O. Val'zelja, R.Dibeliusa, K.Fosslera, L.Spitzera* (Leningrad, 1928); "Zur Auffassung Rabelais," *Romaniscche Stil- und Literaturstudien* (Marburg, 1931), "Le pretendu Realisme de Rabelais," *MP*, 37 (1940), 139-50.

114. M.Baxtin, Smelee pol'zovat'sja vozmoznoštjami," *Novyj Mir*, 11 (1970),p.240.

115. *Ibid*.p.237.

EISENSTEIN AS A SEMIOTICIAN OF THE CINEMA

Herbert Eagle

The films and the theoretical writings of Sergei M. Eisenstein have had an immense influence on the development of cinematic art for over half a century. Hence, it is not at all surprising to find treatment of Eisenstein's contributions in recent works dealing explicitly with the semiotics of cinema (Wollen 1972; Metz 1968, 1971; Lotman 1976). V. V. Ivanov's (1976) recent work on Russian contributions to semiotics deals primarily with the implications of Eisenstein's work—not only for understanding of the sign nature of cinema but with reference to culture and art in general. It is the intent of the present article to complement Ivanov's broad assessment of Eisenstein's insights into myth, literature, the plastic arts, and cinema by attempting a concise and explicit description of Eisenstein's 'semiotics of cinema,' based on the latter's writing and cinematic practice.

1. CINEMATIC ART AS COMPLEX COMMUNICATION

For Eisenstein, a work of art is a complex communication. Akin to mythology, it is "an image-compilation of knowledge of the cosmos" (Eisenstein 1935, 1949: 126), "a construction which . . . serves to embody the author's relation to the content, at the same time compelling the spectator to relate himself to the content in the same way" (Eisenstein 1939a, 1949: 168). In art, the sender attempts to convey his complex conception to the receiver by recreating within the latter an analogous conception. Thus, as Ivanov (1976: 130) points out, Eisenstein's view of art as a process of communication involves the question of pragmatics (in the semiotic sense): the relations of the sender and the receiver to the text. As in cybernetics, Eisenstein conceives of meaning in terms of a change of state in the receiver, that is, in terms of knowledge and of emotions. Eisenstein is quite explicit on the point that meaning, as conveyed in art, is not limited to logical categories. He refers to the complex conception to be communicated as an "inner speech" or as an "emotional state." The nature of a work of art is to model the inner complex through "a compositional structure identical with human behavior in the grip of pathos" (Eisenstein 1939a, 1949: 171).

Eisenstein's identification of "inner speech" as a state existing within the minds of sender and receiver is related to the seminal views of his friend, the psychologist Lev Vygotskij (1962):

> . . . while in external speech thought is embodied in words, in inner speech words die as they bring forth thought. Inner speech is to a large extent thinking in pure meanings. It is a dynamic, shifting, unstable thing, fluttering between word and thought, the two more or less stable, more or less firmly delineated components of verbal thought. . . .
>
> Thought, unlike speech, does not consist of separate units. When I wish to communicate the thought that today I saw a barefoot boy in a blue shirt running down the street, I do not see every item separately: the boy, the shirt, its blue color, his running, the absence of shoes. . . . A speaker often takes several minutes to disclose one thought. In his mind the whole thought is present at once, but in speech it has to be developed successively. . . . Thought itself is engendered by motivation, i.e., by our desires and needs, our interests and emotions. Behind every thought there is an affective-volitional tendency, which holds the answer to the last "why" in the analysis of thinking. A true and full understanding of another's thought is possible only when we understand its affective-volitional basis." (1962: 149-150)

Underlying Eisenstein's approach to cinema, from the very beginning, is the necessity of creating a *sign system* which is capable of communicating the rational and the irrational components of thought, the problem of modeling "inner speech" so that the interwoven fabric of logical and emotional thought is conveyed. Eisenstein echoes Vygotskij's belief that inner speech does not rely only on the logical structures of conventional language systems. Furthermore, Eisenstein rather consistently identifies the non-logical structures of thought with image-thinking or "image-sensual" thinking.

In "image-sensual" structure, a prelogical syncretic form of thinking, a concept is conveyed not by an abstract generalizing sign, but by members of paradigm classes bearing either metonymic or metaphorical relationship to aspects of the complex concept. Eisenstein finds this process present in Bushman language and in primitive religious rituals (1935, 1949: 130-139). Since metonymic relationships underlie the indexical properties of the sign (the signifier is *part* of the signified, in the sense of contiguity in space and/or time and/or causality), whereas metaphorical relationships underlie iconic properties (the signifier is in some way homologous to the signified), Eisenstein's model of inner speech comprises the three principal sign-types of

Peirce's (1932: II, 156-173) typology: symbol (conventional sign, as in verbal language), icon, and index. For Eisenstein, thought processes must be viewed as simultaneously "thematic-logical" and "image-sensual," with the latter clearly in a dominant role. Eisenstein also notes, however, that it is "profoundly incorrect" to ignore "the quality of sliding from one type of thinking to another, from category to category, and more—the simultaneous co-presence in varying proportions of the different types and stages. . . ."

That cinematic art as communication must simultaneously utilize the "thematic-logical" and "image-sensual" aspects of thought may be seen as the cornerstone of Eisenstein's film aesthetics. Like primitive cultural forms (which manifest a "non-differentiation of perception"), film is inherently synthetic and syncretic, utilizing simultaneously the indexical, iconic and conventional properties of its signifiers. Whereas other art forms are limited in one or another aspect of semeosis, cinema unifies the potentials of all the arts:

> For sculpture—cinema is a chain of changing plastic forms, bursting, at long last, ages of immobility.
>
> For painting—cinema is not only a solution for the problem of movement in pictorial images, but is also the achievement of a new and unprecedented form of graphic art, an art that is a free stream of changing, transforming, commingling forms, pictures and compositions, hitherto possible only in music.
>
> Music has always possessed this possibility, but with the advent of cinema, the melodious and rhythmic flow of music acquired new potentialities of imagery—visual, palpable, concrete. . . .
>
> For literature—cinema is an expansion of the strict diction achieved by poetry and prose into a new realm where the desired image is directly materialized in audio-visual perceptions.
>
> And finally, it is only in cinema that are fused into a real unity all those separate elements of the spectacle once inseparable in the dawn of culture. . . . (1940c, 1949: 181-182).

In his films, Eisenstein seeks to interrelate all aspects of the sign system, reproducing, as it were, the syncretism of primitive cultural forms (see Ivanov 1976: 85-88). Primitive man's culture was organic, and Eisenstein perceives this need for organicism in the 20th century. "The forward movement of our epoch in art must blow up the Chinese Wall that stands between the primary antithesis of the 'language of logic' and the 'language of images' " (Eisenstein 1929c, 1970: 41).

Thus, Eisenstein's semiotics of cinema seeks to revive not only the syncretic nature of man's early cultural-aesthetic communication, but its substantial reliance on the 'lower,' sensual centers of the brain for its psychological effect. The implications of modern man's regression to a primary process in art were of some concern to Eisenstein (Ivanov 1976: 71-74), but, he asserts, ". . . the regressive impulse must combine with the realm of progressive applications. Only then is the result . . . beneficial for the development of mankind" (Ivanov 1976: 13).

Ultimately, Eisenstein is not inclined to downplay the importance of 'regressive' primary processes. In fact, the opposite seems to be the case. Eisenstein identifies aesthetic language with the presence of pathos and with the structure of emotionally excited speech (". . . a pathetic structure is one that compels us, echoing its movement, to relive the moments of culmination and substantiation"). In this type of speech, the "image-sensual" aspects dominate. Not only do metaphors arise in our speech during moments of heightened emotion, but it is also metaphor which leads us into new perceptions. Thus, pathetic intensity and communicative intensity for Eisenstein coincide: an emotional leap coincides with a leap into a new understanding. The ecstatic structure associated with such phenomena as, for example, shamanist ritual, encourages a paralysis of conscious will, allowing the image-sensual message to penetrate more effectively (Ivanov 1976: 133-134).

2. THE SIGN NATURE OF CINEMA

Eisenstein, from the time of his earliest work in cinema, analyzes the sign systems which are used to convey "inner speech" with its two dominant modes: natural language and image. He takes as a model the concatenation of conventional signs and iconic signs which characterizes the Japanese system of writing, which employs iconic and conventionalized alphabets at the same time and is therefore "born of the dual mating of the depictive by method and the denotative by purpose" (Eisenstein 1929a, 1949: 32). Arising from an initial set of ideographs (conventionalized iconic images), Japanese ideograms are superpositions of two signifiers to form a third signifier whose concept (signified) is qualitatively different from a mere sum of parts (for example, the combination of the ideographs for 'knife' and 'heart' to form the ideogram 'sorrow'). Eisenstein sees this process at work in other aspects of Japanese culture as well. *Haiku,* for example, functions as an expanded ideogram, an imagistic poem which achieves its effects pictorially (as caligraphy) as well as poetically (Eisenstein 1929a, 1949: 30-31). *Kabuki* theater reduces visual and aural signs to independent elements and then freely recombines them. For example, a verbal text is read by an off-stage narrator while an on-stage actor mimes; simultaneously, elements of make-up represent character traits and emotional moods (Eisenstein 1929a, 1949: 32-36). In order for the visible world to be conveyed conceptually it must be decomposed into signs which can be reintegrated within the receiver. As Eisenstein's contemporary, the literary theoretician and writer Ju. Tynjanov expressed it: "The visible person, the visible thing, is only an element of cinema language when it is given in the quality of a semantic sign" (1927: 61-62).

Eisenstein's attempts to decompose "natural" reality into signs took many forms, focusing attention not only upon objects and persons, but also upon modalities (lighting, color, size of image, sharpness of focus, nature of motion or gesture, etc.). Foregrounding of an object in its sign function is often achieved in Eisenstein's films by the close-up (e.g. the *pince-nez* of the ship's doctor Smirnov in *Battleship Potemkin*). As Tynjanov points out, the close-up "abstracts a thing or detail or face from spatial relationships and from the time flow" (1927: 65-66). By destroying such spatial and temporal relationships between objects, the close-up causes the object to function figuratively: *metaphorically* by association with other members of its potential paradigm classes, or *metonynically* in terms of evocation of the whole by the part. Thus, for example, the famous *pince-nez* in *Potemkin* functions in both these ways: metonymically it recalls Dr. Smirnov and his use of his *pince-nez* to examine the rotten sides of beef and cynically pronounce them fit for consumption; metaphorically, it belongs to a class of objects associated with upper-class and bourgeois intelligentsia, i.e. a class antagonistic to the working class.

In his article on the American pioneer of montage, D. W. Griffith, Eisenstein differentiates his own use of montage from Griffith's (1944, 1949: 237-238). Whereas Griffith uses petty details as metonymies, especially for representing the characters of which they are a part (hence the American term 'close-up'), Eisenstein uses it metaphorically as well: "We say 'an object or face is photographed in 'large scale' *(krupnyj plan)*. . . . We are speaking of the qualitative side of the phenomenon, linked with its meaning . . . not only and not so much to *show* or to *present*, as to *signify*, to *give meaning* . . . to create a new quality of the whole from a juxtaposition of the separate parts."

From whence do these new meanings arise? The juxtaposition of two close-ups (or of any two shots isolated stylistically by some other means, e.g. lighting, positional matching, homogeneity of gesture) gives us two members of a paradigm, in the sense that two semantic units are placed in the same or parallel syntagmatic contexture. Hence, an entire paradigm class comprising these two close-ups is conveyed. Thus, for example, Eisenstein in *October* juxtaposes a Menshevik orator with a playing harp, or a Baroque statue of Christ with an entire series of "gods," from Buddha to primitive carved idols.

These explicit filmic metaphors abound in Eisenstein's films, frequently using 'ready-made' cultural sign material (icons, masks, statues, clothing, architecture). Hence, the new meanings, the new paradigm classes, are created out of elements of their cultural codes and are semantically very rich. In this way we are often presented with syntagms that are narrations in the nominative, narration through things, as Ivanov terms it (1976: 181) or as Ju. Lotman puts it: "Narration can result from the joining of a series of shots showing different objects, or a series in which one object alters modalities" (1976: 59). Such juxtaposition of signs from different cultural spheres dynamizes the prior paradigms, returning each image to its varied sources (Ivanov 1976: 164). Eisenstein asks: ". . . why should the cinema follow the forms of theater and painting rather than the methodology of language, which allows wholly new concepts to arise from the combination of two concrete denotations of two concrete objects?" (1949: 60); ". . . could not the same thing be accomplished more productively by not following the plot so slavishly, but by materializing the idea, the impression . . . through a free accumulation of associative matter?" (1949: 61). The processes which Eisenstein alludes to occur outside of or as a digression from the principal mode of narration, that connected with plot. When Eisenstein's use of such 'narration in the nominative involved objects already encoded in other cultural spheres, he termed it *intellectual montage* (". . . we have taken the first embryonic step towards a totally new form of film expression. Towards a purely intellectual film, freed from the traditional limitations, achieving direct forms for ideas, systems, and concepts, without any need for transitions and paraphrases.") (1949: 63).

Eisenstein's attitude toward the use of human objects as signs, i.e. his theory of acting, closely parallels his use of non-human artifacts. The actor is a complex sign whose potentials are to be brought out through montage. Hence, Eisenstein's 'typage,' the painstaking process of selecting non-actors according to their physical appearance, is a consistent step. The shape of body and face were more essential *sign* considerations in silent cinema than was professional acting experience. For, in any case, the person is to be fragmented through montage, turned into a chain of signs, of "images saturated with secondary meanings" (Lotman 1976: 87). Although the development of sound films led Eisenstein to the use of professional actors, he never abandoned the essential principles of typage. In *Ivan the Terrible*, for example, human gestures and facial movement play a dominant role as signs. Not only did Eisenstein carefully sketch body postures and facial expressions, but faces are disembodied as paintings and icons on the walls of the film set. The architectonics of the *mise-en-scene* (architecture, paintings, shadows, costumes) depends explicitly on sign function; these elements anticipate and reinforce psychology of characters as well as events in the plot. In this respect,

Eisenstein's practice is very close to *kabuki,* as well as to the theoretical positions of the Prague School semioticians of the theater (Bogatyrev 1936, 1938; Honzl, 1940; Veltruský, 1941; Brušák, 1939). As Ivanov (1976: 85) points out, even in his first film *Strike,* Eisenstein had matched characters' faces to the physiognomies of animals which conventionally and/or iconically represented their personality traits.

Even in the traits associated with the Stanislavskij concept of acting (that is, acting as an 'index' of real human behavior), Eisenstein remarks on the inevitable fragmentation into signs:

> The actor is confronted with exactly the same task: to express, in two, three, or four features of a character or of a mode of behavior, those basic elements which in juxtaposition create the integral image that was worked out by the author, director and the actor himself. . . . This rests primarily in the fact that the desired image is *not fixed or ready-made, but arises—is born.* The image planned by author, director and actor is concretized by them in separate representational elements, and is assembled—again and finally—in the spectator's perception. (Eisenstein 1939b, 1942: 31).

Furthermore, the actor, to create in himself these elements, must bring forth for himself a series of representations. "Feeling and experience, like the actions that flow from them, arise of themselves, called to life by the pictures his imagination paints. The living feeling will be evoked by the pictures themselves, by their aggregation and juxtaposition" (Eisenstein 1939b, 1942: 41). Thus, the very same sort of complicated montage with which the filmmaker creates his text also takes place within the actor creating his role and within the spectator recreating the concept.

Eisenstein's awareness of the use of objects and actors as signs is particularly sharp, but even more original and perceptive is his elaboration and practice of the sign-function of paradigms based on modalities. The changes in objects typified by plot, by causally-related movements, is a basic means of paradigm creation in narrative cinema. But other changes in modality can play a significant or even dominant role. In fact, modalities themselves (since they represent changes in time) can function iconically to signify emotions, i.e. the change in modality is homologous to a change in emotion; the complex perturbations of modalities are homologous to the equally complex perturbations of the emotions. This realization is essential to an understanding of Eisenstein's use of modal signs, such as gesture, camera angle, motion of the eye over the surface of frames or into the depth of the frame, lighting, color, and music.

As has been pointed out by V. Ivanov (1976: 29-31), the notion of *gesture* occupies a key position in Eisenstein's use of signs. Gesture is clearly intertwined with human verbal language, together with which it surfaces as a manifestation of inherent syncretic tendencies. Motion of parts of the human body and of intonations of the human voice provides a basis for relating physical gesture to visual movement, on the one hand, and gestural-intonation to music, on the other. Hence, gesture lies at the nexus of verbal, visual and musical phenomena. Furthermore, gesture is closely related to emotions; it is thus the link between expressive elements and pathetic states (". . . Man and the relations between his *gestures* and the *intonations* of his voice, which arise from the same emotions, are our models in determining audio-visual structures. . .") (Eisenstein 1940a, 1942: 71-73). A visual image which possesses indexical and/or iconic signification is assimilated to the *idea* of the creative work through the use of correlations based on movement as expressed in sound or visual phenomena. The impressions derived from different 'lines' are superimposed on the basis of some 'inner synchronization' (which can also be applied antithetically). This inner synchronization is based on movement in its various aspects, for example: (1) musical rhythm and rhythm of cutting (synchronization, syncopation, counterpoint); (2) melodic movement and color movement (tones of music and tones of color, respectively vibrations of acoustic and light waves); (3) the correlation of movement within the shot, camera movement, or movement of the eye in following a sequence of shots with any or all of the rhythmic, melodic and color movement noted in (1) and (2) (Eisenstein 1940a, 1942: 78-83).

In particular, Eisenstein gave much thought to the question of the function of music and color in film, especially in connection with his collaboration with Prokofiev on the musical scores for *Alexander Nevsky* and *Ivan the Terrible* and with his first use of color in *Ivan the Terrible, Pt. II.* After some research, Eisenstein concluded that there is no basis for believing that colors or tones have any absolute meaning in and of themselves. Rather, color associations are conventional, such as that of yellow with love and concord (on the one hand) and its opposites, envy and cowardice (on the other). The conventional meanings develop as paradigms of similarity and opposition, as iconic extrapolations presumably with some fundamental indexical signification at its origin (yellow—and the sun). At the outset, the signifieds of a color-sign are determined only within particular cultural and aesthetic codes. A particular culture may bind a color indexically to a particular *anecdote,* and then proceed to give it an associative chain of meanings. But ultimately, the signified of a color can be definitively determined only within a particular aesthetic text-system: "In art it is not the absolute relationships that are decisive, but those *arbitrary* relationships within a system of images dictated by the particular work of art" (Eisenstein 1940b, 1942: 150), ". . . the emotional intelligibility and function of color will rise from the natural order of establishing the color imagery of the work, coinciding with the process of shaping the living movement of the whole work" (1940b, 1942: 151).

Colors, of course, also function with respect to each individual's image complexes. They may call up an unpredictable array of associations linked in the individual experience (i.e. existentially). However, this does not negate the powers of the aesthetic text in structuring and restructuring color oppositions. In terms of its relationships to other sign systems in the cinematic text, the "inner tonality" of colors should relate to the fundamental concept, to inner speech. Color organization in the film is not an abstract independent line, but one dependent on the meaning of the whole.

Many of the considerations noted above concerning the relational aspects of color-meaning could easily be repeated in discussing the nature of signification in music. Again Eisenstein warns against the purely conventional uses of music, wherein a piece with some general conventional signification accompanies the visual track. Rather, in the famous manifesto written together with Pudovkin and Alexandrov (1928, 1949: 257-261), Eisenstein called for the structural use of music, in conflict with as well as parallel to the visual structures. Here, potential homologies in rhythm, in physical movement, in pitch, in light intensity, in tonality, and in color can be used (modulations and 'intervals' of color can be juxtaposed to musical intervals or physical movements in order to signify modulations of emotions). Here, Eisenstein cites the movement of the hands which often accompanies music and which underlies art forms like ballet. One must deal with such structures as "approachings, recedings, ripples, and reflections. . . . Musical and visual imagery are not commensurable through narrowly representational elements. . ." (Eisenstein 1941, 1942: 164).

Eisenstein's most detailed analysis of the *overtonal* function of music is in its relation to movements of visual contour and to the emotion of tense anxiety in the sequence which precedes the attack of the Teutonic Knights in *Alexander Nevsky:* "We will try to discover here that 'secret' of those sequential *vertical correspondences* which, step by step, relate the music to the shots *through an identical motion* that lies at the base of the musical as well as the pictorial movement" (1941, 1942: 173). In this analysis, Eisenstein demonstrates the homologies between the rising and falling of notes and the trace of the eye's movements within the shot and from shot to shot. The same falling arc of the music, followed by a monotonic plateau, is represented first as a movement of the eye along the graphic surface of the frames, then as a pattern of gradation of light, and finally as a movement into the depth of the frame; ". . . with a systematic distribution of forms, lines or movements, it is just as possible to train the eye for vertical reading, or in any desired direction" (1941, 1942: 174-216). The homology, as described by Eisenstein, seems virtually complete, even to correspondence between repetitions of the same note in a monotonic sequence to the visual repetition of flags, spots, and bands of light within the frame. Eisenstein correlates both the music and the graphic flow to the emotional movement: "If we try to read this graph emotionally in conjunction with the thematic matter of the sequence, checking one against the other, we can find a 'seismographical' curve of a certain process and rhythm of *uneasy expectation*" (1941, 1942: 212). Eisenstein relates this movement gesturally and psychologically to holding one's breath—and then allowing oneself a deep sigh.

In his analysis, Eisenstein relates clashes in the music not only to visual clashes, but also to conceptual clashes: the merciless Teutonic Knights (white) against the humane Russians (black); the galloping attack of the former against the immobile (i.e. non-aggressive) formations of the latter; the living emotional faces of the Russians against the hidden faces of the knights, under Klan-like masks of iron.

In the view of later theorists and semioticians of cinema (e.g. Bazin 1959; Metz 1968), Eisenstein's intense concern with conventional and iconic meanings of the cinematic sign caused him to neglect the indexical aspects of film, its existential and 'natural' relationship to reality, to which the perception of motion photography is linked through an 'inevitable' sequence of physical, chemical and biological processes. Film can achieve powerful emotional effects because suspension of disbelief is so intense: film is received as reality. In Bazin's view, to decompose film into signs as Eisenstein did is to ignore its ability to convey the continuous flow of reality. As Metz puts it: "Whether language or art, the image discourse is an open system, and it is not easily codified, with its nondiscrete basic units (the images), its intelligibility (which is too natural), its lack of distance between the significate and the signifier . . . with its whole sections of meaning directly conveyed to the audience" (Metz 1974a, 59).

Although Eisenstein did not specifically elaborate this aspect of film semiotics in his theoretical writing, one can draw some interesting conclusions about it from his cinematic practice. Eisenstein's films testify to the fact that cinematic art gains by simultaneously asserting and denying its function as index of reality. The indexically-created photographic likeness will always be present, yet, as Tynjanov points out (1927: 56-61), the obviously artificial two-dimensionality and the rectangular boundedness of the frame cannot be avoided. Thus, cinema, by its very nature, asserts itself as an index and simultaneously denies its indexicality, creating iconic and conventional sign structures. This ambiguity and contradiction enriches the potential of film language to create complex communication.

Eisenstein's implicit awareness of the possibility of simultaneous utilization of the indexical, as well as the iconic and conventional potentials of the filmic image is amply illustrated in the film *October,* where Eisenstein used sequences reconstructed with careful attention to documentary accuracy and appearance, as well as sequences of montage which select images (harps, balalaikas, religious idols) not even located in the 'realistic' space of the film, but used to create metaphorical paradigms. Eisenstein's work shows awareness of the sign functions of cinema on diverse levels, with the existence of mutually overlapping signifiers which operate with respect to vastly different codes: from 'continuous' indexical signs to iconic sign-structures of various kinds, from cultural artifacts used as signs with respect to their own cultural systems, to distinctive features such as camera angle, which may be patterned so as to create visual 'rhymes' in the same way that phonemes are patterned in poetry. As Lotman states: ". . . we may compare such a text to a message which is decoded into several languages."

3. ART AS PROCESS

Eisenstein's hypotheses as to the relationship between art and 'inner speech' and the complex interactions of signs in the aesthetic text lead inevitably to an emphasis on dynamism and process:

> A work of art, understood dynamically, is just this process of arranging images in the feelings and mind of the spectator. It is this that constitutes the peculiarity of a truly vital work of art and distinguishes it from a lifeless one, in which the spectator receives the represented result of a given consummated process of creation, instead of being drawn into the process as it occurs. (Eisenstein 1939b, 1942: 17).

For this reason, "a work of art directs all the refinement of its methods to the process." Creating art is creating processes. The image "has to arise, to unfold before the senses of the spectator" (1939b, 1942: 17-18). Although the art work clearly has a tendency to move the spectator to a new condition, the latter's role is by no means a passive one, rather he "is drawn into a creative act in which his individuality is not subordinated to the author's. . . ." Thus Eisenstein's theory of the reception of art may be seen to lie close to that of the Prague Structuralists, as is evidenced by the following remark:

> In fact, every spectator, in correspondence with his individuality, and in his own way and out of his own experience—out of the womb of his fantasy, out of the warp and weft of his associations, all conditioned by the premises of his character, habits and social

appurtenances, creates an image. . . . This is the same image that was planned and created by the author, but this image is at the same time created also by the spectator himself. (1939b, 1942: 33).

Process is at the heart of the perception of signs in particular in the creation and recreation of signs based on structural oppositions. As Eisenstein says: "The classical structure of musical works, of dramas, of films or paintings is almost invariably derived from a struggle of opposites, linked by the unity of conflict." The role of conflict, of opposition, of deautomatization ("making strange") was central to Eisenstein's contemporaries, the Russian Formalists (in particular, V. Sklovkij and Ju. Tynjanov). In his article "Art as Device" (1919), Sklovskij advanced the view that artistic communication was based on 'making strange' *(ostranenie)* and making difficult *(zatrudnenie)* perceptions that have become automatized, thus enabling the receiver to derive new information through an active process. The constant establishment and subsequent frustration of anticipation was advanced by Tynjanov as the organizing principle of the verse text (Tynjanov 1924, 1971). This view is reiterated in the verse theory of the Prague Structuralist J. Mukařovský in the 1930's (Mukařovský 1948), in the continuing work on poetics by Roman Jakobson (1921, 1960, 1971), and in the present-day verse theory of Ju. Lotman, who makes explicit Eisenstein's tendencies in applying the same principles to cinema: ". . . the establishment of norms and deviation from them (automatization and deautomatization) form one of the fundamental regularities of the artistic text. This is demonstrated with particular force in cinematography" (Lotman 1976: 56). Eisenstein's theory and practice of montage is intimately related to this view.

For Eisenstein, montage in the limited sense is the concatenation and superimposition of different types of signs and sign systems. In its broadest sense, however, montage is art in its process of becoming. Related to both ideas is Eisenstein's polemical 'montage as collision.' As a first principle, Eisenstein recognizes that the various sign-functions of the film image can be made manifest only in juxtaposition. Because the still frame as photograph contains potentially infinite properties, it is only in collision with other frames that signs can emerge as distinct by opposition. This process of opposition concerns not only the iconic aspects of the cinematic sign, but also conventionalized oppositions established through the patterning of modalities. How does the spectator *sense* the cinematic phenomenon and react to it? Through montage: the decomposition of the world of objects and modalities and the restructuring of its elements according to new paradigms. Vertical montage (cf. below) implies the simultaneous occurrence of meaning-forming collisions on a multiplicity of levels.

Thus, 'montage as collision' gives Eisenstein a conception of image-language which differs radically from that prevailing in 'classical' narrative cinema. The filmic image is not primarily an index of reality to be used to represent that reality; it is a bundle rich in material which can be made to signify through the structuration of meaning-forming oppositions. As stated above, the essence of cinema is not to show, but to create meaning.

Eisenstein's 'montage as collision' is also 'making strange' in the Russian Formalist sense. In Eisenstein's early theater work, such collisions were produced by 'attractions' which led to the radical interference of one code with another. When an actor expresses his anger through a somersault or his exaltation through a *salto-mortale*, this represents not only the introduction of a new iconic (gestural) code; it also disrupts automatized perceptions with respect to the indexically-based code of the naturalist theater. "Leaps from one type of expression to another, as well as unexpected intertwinings of the two expressions "create a new synthesis of 'real doing' and 'pictorial imagination' " (Eisenstein 1923, 1934a, 1949: 7-8). This same principle accounts for the strong effects of Eisenstein's first film *Strike*; sequences which resemble the later Italian neo-realism alternate with devices from the *commedia del'arte* and the circus. Since aesthetic codes do not emerge *ex nihilo,* but always against the background of prior codes, 'montage as collision' involves simultaneous processes of code destruction and code creation:

> I . . . regard the inception of new concepts and viewpoints in the conflict between customary conception and particular representation as dynamic—as a dynamization of the inertia of perception . . . (Eisenstein 1949: 47).

4. SYNTAGMATICS AND PARADIGMATICS: VERTICAL MONTAGE

Eisenstein uses the term *vertical montage* (or earlier, overtonal montage) to describe the process of concatenation and superimposition of the diverse codes of cinema: indexical, iconic, or conventional; based on patterning of objects, graphic lines, masses, volumes, camera distance, camera movements, motions, gestures, depth of focus, shades of color, tones of music, musical rhythm, rhythm of editing, etc. The result of this process, for Eisenstein, should reflect the dominance of a unified theme, one which governs all the choices in all the participating codes:

> The juxtaposition of these partial details in a given montage construction calls to life and forces into the light that *general* quality in which each detail has participated and which binds together all

the details into a *whole,* namely, into that generalized *image,* wherein the creator, followed by the spectator, experiences the theme. (Eisenstein 1939b, 1942: 11).

As noted above, montage can also be viewed as the dismemberment of an event in reality into signs participating in many codes and the subsequent reintegration of these signs to form a complex unified sign whose essence mirrors that of *inner speech.* And, in fact, Eisenstein's descriptions of his montage sketches strongly suggest an actual articulation of inner speech:

> Like thought, they would sometimes proceed with visual images. With sound. Synchronized or non-synchronized. Then as sounds. Formless. Or with sound-images: with objectively representational sounds. . . .
>
> Then suddenly, definite intellectually formulated words—as "intellectual" and dispassionate as pronounced words. With a black screen, a rushing imageless visuality. . . .
>
> Then racing visual images over complete silence.
>
> Then linked with polyphonic sounds. Then polyphonic images. Then both at once.
>
> Then interpolated into the outer course of action, then interpolating elements of the outer action into the inner monologue. (Eisenstein 1932, 1949: 105).

The above description is not of a projected future state of the art, but a concrete pattern to be realized in actual film work. Eisenstein's notes on his work on *Ivan the Terrible* reflect such a process, albeit not so hyperbolically: drawings of sets, gestures, facial expressions alternate with Eisenstein's writing of the verbal portions of the scenario (Eisenstein 1949: 261-265). The polyphonic ensemble reflects both thoughts and actions in their complex interaction.

What is the syntagmatic process through which these signs are united? It is both horizontal (the development of signs linearly in time) and vertical (the concatenation of signs simultaneous in time). As in Saussure's concept of syntagmatic combination, Eisenstein sees contexture as the basic fact of montage: ". . . two film pieces of any kind, placed together, inevitably combine into a new concept, a new quality arising out of that juxtaposition. This is not in the least a circumstance peculiar to the cinema, but is a phenomenon invariably met with in all cases where we have to deal with juxtaposition of two facts, two phenomena, two objects." (Eisenstein 1939b, 1942: 4). One might compare Eisenstein's statement with Saussure's remarks on the syntagm:

What is most striking in the organization of language are *syntagmatic solidarities*; almost all units of language depend on what surrounds them in the spoken chain or on their successive parts. . . . The whole has value only through its parts, and the parts have value by virtue of their place in the whole. That is why the syntagmatic relation of the part to the whole is just as important as the relation of the parts to each other. (Saussure 1959: 127-128).

What is characteristic of the cinema is that syntagmatic juxtapositions proceed simultaneously on so many levels, levels which are to a degree independent but which at a deeper level must relate to the totality and unity of the concept.

Eisenstein's 'vertical montage' bears resemblance not only to Saussure's concept of syntagmatic concatenation in natural language, but also to Tynjanov's idea of the dual ordering of 'poetic' language. In poetry there is a normal 'syntagmatic' linkage and a rhythmic articulation (on the basis of the succession of verses). The rhythmic articulation is based on the repetition of equivalent units (verses), which provide a given presumption of equality against which significant differences can be perceived. Tynjanov himself extended his theory of verse language to cinema. If shots are considered as relative units of measure in a film (analogous to the verses of metrical form), then "rhythm is the interaction of stylistic moments with metrical ones in the unfolding óf the film. . ." (Tynjanov 1927: 75). Each shot, like the verse, is a compact unit whose various elements are deformed in the sense that each is perceived on the basis of expectations set up by the preceding ones. In Eisenstein's style, as in Majakovskij's free verse, expectations are frustrated very often and the collisions between shots are rich in meaning. Shots are not developed in sequential order but are transformed one into another. "They are transformed just as one verse, one metrical unit, is transformed into another—at a precise boundary. Cinema jumps from shot to shot, like verse does from line to line" (Tynjanov 1927: 74).

Whereas for Tynjanov each shot is a compact unit whose relative values are defined in relation to one another, for Eisenstein the shot itself becomes a dynamic unit internally. The rhythmic ordering described by Tynjanov operates within the shot as well as with respect to it. Eisenstein uses a more flexible term for the basic unit: 'the montage cell.' The montage cell can be smaller than the shot; it may consist of a group of frames in which a certain motion can be perceived and opposed to another motion in the same frames; it may be a group of frames in which the 'motion' of music contrasts with the motion of objects or of lighting. In spite of the fact that the minimal montage cell cannot always be precisely isolated, the principle embodied in the concept of the shot remains valid. Eisenstein and Tynjanov's concept of montage as differential succession is likewise asserted in Lotman's *Semiotics of Cinema* (1976).

The question of processes which take place within shots as well as among them is clearly foregrounded by Eisenstein's choice of the term 'vertical montage.' The obvious source is music, referring to the vertical scoring of parts for different instruments in an orchestral composition:

> Through the progression of the *vertical* line, pervading the entire orchestra, and interwoven horizontally, the intricate harmonic musical movement of the whole orchestra moves forward.
>
> When we turn from this image of the orchestral score to that of the audio-visual score, we find it necessary to add a new part to the instrumental parts: this new part is a 'staff' of visuals . . . where shot is linked to shot not merely through one indication—movement, or light values, . . . or the like—but through the *simultaneous advance* of a multiple series of lines, each maintaining an independent compositional course and each contributing to the total compositional course of the sequence. (Eisenstein 1940a, 1942: 74-75).

As Eisenstein's theories and practice developed, he turned increasingly to the specific problems of vertical montage—in particular, the homologous aspects of various psychological and perceptual processes which could form the basis for similarity and opposition in vertical montage, i.e. the identification and elaboration of distinctive features which would justify transperceptual and transpsychological paradigms.

Taking a concept developed by the Russian Formalists (Jakobson 1971) Eisenstein claimed that in vertical montage one line of syntagmatic development dominates and deforms the others. It provides the basic principle or movement which affects the flow of the other syntagmatic lines, although, in actual fact, the dominant is often only sensed *a posteriori*, after we have experienced the entire syntagm:

If we have even a sequence of montage pieces:

> A gray old man,
> A gray old woman,
> A white horse,
> A snow-covered roof,

we are still far from certain whether this sequence is working

towards a dominating indication of 'old age' or of 'whiteness.'
(Eisenstein 1929b, 1949: 65).

As is clear in the above example, the dominant may reside on an intellectual
level ('old age' involving the abstraction of a concept from the paradigmatic
series) or on a purely sensual level ('whiteness'). Eisenstein also asserts the
importance of the 'secondary stimuli' which always accompany the dominant:
". . . the dominant . . . although the most powerful . . . (is) far from the only
stimulus of the shot" (1929b, 1949: 66). The secondary stimuli, the overtones, emerge as a general value "only in the dynamics of the musical or
cinematographic process." Dominants of a sensual nature generally carry
emotional implications, as a result of indexical or iconic factors or as a result
of prior aesthetic codes. Thus, modulations of grey lighting may be felt as
gloominess, as in the famous 'fog' sequence in *Battleship Potemkin.* The
secondary stimuli which accompany the dominant line of lighting in this
sequence are organized on the principle of "barely perceptible changing
movements" of various kinds, e.g. the rippling of the waves paralleling the
"optical light vibrations" (Eisenstein, 1929b, 1949: 66-70). Vertical montage
may also be based on dissonance or, even more effectively, on the use of
harmony *and* dissonance.

The specific relations of elements of vertical montage to the concept of
the whole is impressively illustrated in Eisenstein's films in general. In *Battleship Potemkin,* for example, Eisenstein consistently uses parallel lines in motion in association with the concept of autocratic, inhuman and relentless
repression. Thus, we have parallel lines in the *Potemkin's* mess hall tables, the
parallel lines of the rifles of the dragoons, their parallel ranks, the parallel
lines of the Odessa steps, and again ranks of soldiers and rifles. (It is interesting that the first indication that the dragoons will not shoot at the condemned sailors is the wavering of their rifles, so that they are at skew angles
to one another rather than parallel). Opposed to this motion of parallel lines
are the more anarchic circular and swirling motions associated with the
sailors' protest against the rotten meat, with their clockwise and counter-
clockwise gathering to revolt, as well as with the mourners on the jetty, who
circle the tent containing Vakulinchuk's body and are later seen extended in
a huge arc on the jetty. Perpendicular lines form a paradigm of images of the
strength of the people when mobilized into action.

Such uses of vertical montage as described above clearly involve the
creation of paradigms within the filmic text, paradigms which link signs within the film to one another semantically. The paradigms in Eisenstein's films
constitute sets of variants related by similarity and dissimilarity (the various
modes that distinctive features like music, color, graphic shape, and lighting
may assume). As in Jakobson's description of verse, "the poetic function

projects the principle of equivalence from the axis of selection into the axis of combination. Equivalence is promoted to the constitutive device of the sequence." (Jakobson 1960: 358). Thus, filmic structure, in Eisenstein's model, represents to a very high degree those very structural characteristics which the Prague Structuralists associated with 'poetic' or 'aesthetic' language.

Eisenstein's pioneering work in the theory of cinema language laid a solid foundation for the semiotic investigations of the present day.

REFERENCES

Bazin, André. 1959. *Qu'est-ce que le cinéma?* Paris: Editions du Cerf.

Bogatyrev, Petr. 1936. "Kroj jako znak" (Costume as a Sign), *Slovo a slovesnost* 2: 43-47. English translation by Y. Lockwood in Matejka and Titunik 1976: 13-19.

_____. 1938. "Znaky divadelní" (Signs of Theater), *Slovo a slovesnost* 4: 138-49. English translation by B. Kochis in Matejka and Titunik 1976: *33-50.*

Brušák, Karel. 1939. "Znaky na čínském divadle" (Signs in the Chinese Theater), *Slovo a slovesnost* 5. English translation in Matejka and Titunik 1976: 59-73.

Eisenstein, Sergei. 1923. "Montaž attrakcionov" (Montage of attractions), *LEF* 3: 70-75. English translation in Eisenstein 1942.

_____. 1928. "Zajavlenie," *Žizn' iskusstva* 5 (August). English translation as "A Statement on the Sound-Film" in Eisenstein 1949.

_____. 1929a. "Za kadrom," afterword in Kaufman, *Japonskoe kino* (Japanese Cinema) Moscow: Teakinopečat,' 1929: 72-92. English translation as "The Cinematographic Principle and the Ideogram" in Eisenstein 1949.

_____. 1929b. "Kino četyrex izmerenij," *Kino* (August 27). English translation as "The Filmic Fourth Dimension" in Eisenstein 1949.

_____. 1929c. "Perspektivy," *Iskusstvo* 1-2: 116-122. English translation as "Perspectives" in Eisenstein 1970.

_____. 1932. "Odolžajtes', " *Proletarskoe kino* 17-18: 19-29. English translation as "A Course in Treatment" in Eisenstein 1949.

_____. 1943a. "Srednjaja iz trex (1924-1929)," *Sovetskoe kino* 11-12: 54-83. English translation as "Through Theatre to Cinema" in Eisenstein 1949.

_____. 1934b. "E! O čistote kinojazyka," *Sovetskoe kino* 5: 25-31. English translation as "Film Language" in Eisenstein 1949.

_____ . 1935. "Vystuplenie na Vsesojuznom tvorčeskom sovešČanii rabotnikov sovetskogo kinematografa," *Za bol'šoe kinoiskusstvo*. Moscow: Gosfotokinoizdat: 22-49, 160-65. English translation as "Film Form: New Problems" in Eisenstein 1949.

_____ . 1939a. "O stroenii vešČej," *Iskusstvo kino* 6: 7-20. English translation as "The Structure of Film" in Eisenstein 1949.

_____ . 1939b. "Montaž 1938," *Iskusstvo kino* 1: 37-49. English translation as "Word and Image" in Eisenstein 1942.

_____ . 1940a. "Vertikal'nyj montaž," *Iskusstvo kino* 9: 16-25. English translation as "Synchronization of Senses" in Eisenstein 1942.

_____ . 1940b. "Vertikal'nyj montaž," *Iskusstvo kino* 12: 27-35. English translation as "Color and meaning" in Eisenstein 1942.

_____ . 1940c. "Gordost," *Iskusstvo kino* 1-2: 17-25. English translation as "Achievement" in Eisenstein 1949.

_____ . 1941. "Vertikal'nyj montaž," *Iskusstvo kino* 1: 29-38. English translation as "Form and Content: Practice" in Eisenstein 1942.

_____ . 1942. *The Film Sense*. New York: Harcourt, Brace & World.

_____ . 1944. "Dikkens, Griffit i my," *Griffit*. Moscow: Goskinoizdat: 39-88. English translation as "Dickens, Griffith and the Film Today" in Eisenstein 1949.

_____ . 1949. *Film Form: Essays in Film Theory*. New York: Harcourt Brace & World.

_____ . 1956. *Izbrannye stat'i* (Selected articles). Moscow: Iskusstvo.

_____ . 1964. *Izbrannye proizvedenija* (Selected works). 6 vols. Moscow: Iskusstvo.

_____ . 1970. *Film Essays and a Lecture*. New York: Praeger.

Honzl, Jindřich. 1940. "Pohyb divadelníhoznaku" (Dynamic of the Sign in the Theater). *Slovo a slovesnost* 6: 177-88. English translation by I. Titunik in Matejka and Titunik 1976: 74-93.

Ivanov, V.V. 1976. *OČerki po istorii semiotiki v SSSR* (Essays on the history of semiotics in the USSR). Moscow: Nauka.

Jakobson, Roman. 1921. Novejšaja russkaja poezija (Recent Russian poetry). Prague.

_____ . 1933. "Úpadek filmu?" (Is the Cinema in Decline?), *Listy pro umeni a kritiku* 1: 45-9. English translation by E. Sokol in Matejka and Titunik 1976: 145-52.

_____ . 1960. "Closing Statement: Linguistics and Poetics," *Style in Language*, T. Sebeok, ed., 350-377. Cambridge: MIT Press.

_____ . 1971. "Dominant" in *Readings in Russian Poetics: Formalist and Structuralist Views*, Matejka and Pomorska, eds., 82-7. English translation by H. Eagle from unpublished text of lectures delivered at Massaryk University in Brno in 1935.

Kuleshov, Lev. 1974. *Kuleshov on Film: Writings*. Tr. R. Levaco. Berkeley: University of California Press.

Lotman, Jurij. 1976. *Semiotics of Cinema* (=Michigan Slavic Contributions 5). Ann Arbor: Michigan Slavic Publications. Translated by M. Suino from *Semiotika kino i voprosy kinoestetiki*. Tallinn. 1973.

Matejka, Ladislav and Krystyna Pomorska, eds. 1971. *Readings in Russian Poetics: Formalist and Structuralist Views*. Cambridge: MIT Press.

Matejka, Ladislav and Irwin Titunik, eds. 1976. *Semiotics of Art; Prague School Contributions*. Cambridge: MIT Press.

Metz, Christian. 1968. *Essais sur la signification au cinéma*. Paris: Klincksieck.

_____ . 1971. *Langage et cinéma*. Paris: Larousse.

_____ . 1974a. *Film Language: A Semiotics of Cinema*. Tr. Michael Taylor. New York: Oxford Univ. Press. Translation of Metz 1968.

_____ . 1974b. *Language and Cinema*. Tr. Donna Jean Umiker-Sebeok. The Hague: Mouton. Translation of Metz 1971.

Mukarovský, Jan. 1948. *Kapitoly z české poetiky* (Chapters from Czech Poetics). 3 vols. Prague;Svoboda.

Peirce, C.S. 1932. *Collected Papers of Charles Sanders Peirce*. Cambridge: Harvard University Press.

Pudovkin, Vsevolod. 1970. *Film Technique and Film Acting*. New York: Grove.

Saussure, Ferdinand de. 1959. *Course in General Linguistics*. New York: Philosophical Library.

Sebeok, Thomas A., ed. 1960. *Style in Language*. Cambridge:MIT Press.

Šklovskij, Viktor. 1919. "Iskusstvo kak priem" (Art as Device) in *Poètika: Sbornik po teorii poetičeskogo jazyka II*. Petrograd: Gostip. English translation in L. Lemon and M. Reis, *Russian Formalist Criticism: Four Essays*, Lincoln: University of Nebraska Press, 1965.

Tynjanov, Jurij. 1924. *Problema stixotvornogo jazyka* (The problem of verse language). Leningrad.

_____ . 1927. "Ob osnovax kino" (On the fundamentals of the cinema) in *Poètika kino* (Poetics of cinema). Moscow-Leningrad: Kinopečat'.

_____. 1971. "Rhythm as the Constructive Factor of Verse" in Matejka and Pomorska 1971: 126-35. English translation by M. Suino of *Problema stixotvornogo jazyka,* 7-17.

Veltruský, Jiří. 1941. "Dramatický text jako součást divadla" (Dramatic text as a Component of Theater), *Slovo a slovesnost* 7: 132-44. English translation in Matejka and Titunik 1976.

Vygotsky, Lev. 1962. *Thought and Language.* Cambridge:MIT Press.

Wollen, Peter. 1972. *Signs and Meaning in the Cinema.* Bloomington: Indiana University Press.

LOTMAN: THE DIALECTIC OF A SEMIOTICIAN

Ann Shukman

One of the most far-reaching and original of Lotman's recent theoretical works is the brief monograph *A dynamic model of a semiotic system* (Lotman 1974). This work is the manifesto of a new development in semiotic theory: "historical semiotics." It was followed up by a series of works by Lotman and Lotman with Uspensky (Lotman 1977a, 1977b, Lotman and Uspensky 1977, among others) on the cultural history of Russia in the light of semiotics. It provided the theoretical framework, at once semiotic and historicist, within which the problem of change, the problem of renewal, could be tackled.

The demarcation of the synchronic from the diachronic was the starting point of structural linguistics. So strong was the appeal of the synchronic approach, so vast the prospects of advancement in theoretical and practical understanding of the nature of language, that in Western Europe and the United States at least, the historical approach was for a time eclipsed. The post-war structuralist boom in theoretical linguistics, in anthropology and related subjects, virtually relegated the diachronic study of language to the modest role of practical learning in classroom and lecture hall. The enrichment of theoretical linguistics in recent years by information theory and the scientific study of communication processes, the stimulus of machine translation, all this closed still firmer the door on historicism and the diachronic approach.

In East Europe matters were somewhat different: the Formalists, living through a period of vast social upheavals and literary experimentation, were always conscious of the dynamism of literary change. The Prague School too never wholly banned diachrony and the study of evolution from the theory of phonology, and the emphasis on language function saved Prague School linguistics from the extremes of the abstract, synchronic approach which were features of Saussurean, Hjelmslevian and some American structuralist thinkers. For Jakobson and Tynyanov in 1928:

> pure synchronism now turns out to' be an illusion: every synchronic system has its own past and future as inseparable structural elements of the system (Jakobson and Tynyanov 1928)

Lotman's development as a thinker shows the passage from historicism, through synchronic abstractions, to a new synthesis in historical semiotics.

THE THESIS

By training as much as by primary inclination Lotman is a literary historian. He was nurtured in the great Russian philological tradition, the tradition that encompassed, and taught the need to encompass, literature together with intellectual trends and social history. Lotman's biography of the Decembrist Dmitriev-Mamonov, his studies of Vjazemskij, Karamzin, and Pushkin's *Evgenij Onegin* (Lotman 1959; 1960a; 1957, 1961, 1966a; 1960b, 1966b, 1975a, respectively), and many other works on eighteenth and nineteenth-century Russian literature are fine examples of the flowering of this tradition. The historicist approach is bred into Lotman and is a fundamental to his mode of thought, as it was also to the Formalists. But the Russian philological tradition has other aspects: it is committed to textual analysis as the primary task of the literary historian, and it is committed to the belief that the literature of any given epoch is supreme bearer of cultural values. The tradition thus looked two ways: to the text and the language of which it is composed, and to the culture in which the text as a work of literature functions.

Lotman, however, looked beyond this. He was a seeker after the general principles, the laws, that govern the structure of a text, the language in which it is composed, its function in a culture, its relationship to the non-literary world. The discovery, in the early 1960s, of structuralism and semiotics provided Lotman with a whole new conceptual framework with which to tackle these traditional problems. The structuralist impact fell into two stages, represented by Lotman's first two books, *Lectures on Structural Poetics* (Lotman 1964) and *The Structure of the Artistic Text* (Lotman 1970a).

ANTITHESIS I: STRUCTURE AND OPPOSITION

The discovery of wholes defined as *structures,* and of structures defined by *oppositional relationships of the elements,* this was the first stage of the revolution in Lotman's thinking. *Lectures* explores the theoretical possibilities opened up by this way of thinking, and in particular by the crucial notion of the *opposition.*

Lectures falls into three main parts: a general theory of art, a theory of poetic language, and a theory of context. For each of these topics the underlying theoretical concept is the notion of the opposition. So art is described as a model of reality, a model which is perceived in contrast to (in opposition to) the object it is depicting; perception is the act of establishing an oppositional relationship between art-object and reality-object. This somewhat naive and restricting approach to art, which in any case is applicable only to the visual arts and then only to the representational kinds (Lotman's example is a prehistoric figurine), was soon to be dropped. Already by the end of the book Lotman has elaborated a typology of art based on the relationship of text to reader-expectations (aesthetics of identity/aesthetics of contrast).

In the second part of *Lectures* Lotman elaborates a theory of poetic language. He starts with the supposition that the devices of poetic language are designed to create, at the different levels of language, various kinds of repetitions or *povtory* (Lotman uses Brik's term). These repetitions, being composed of elements at once both similar and dissimilar, form correlative pairs. On an analogy with the phonological opposition Lotman argues that from this oppositional relationship new meanings are created. The devices of poetry are designed precisely to increase the number of such linguistic forms and so to create a multiplicity of new semantic values. Lotman has held to this theory of poetic language: it is repeated in his second book. *The Structure of the Artistic Text,* and again in *The Analysis of the Poetic Text* (Lotman 1972).

The last section of *Lectures* is concerned with the concept of "text" and "extra-text," that is, the context in which the text has its being. The extra-text may be the literary tradition in which the author is writing (or against which he is reacting), his real historical situation, his ideology; it may also be the expectations, situation and foreknowledge of the reader. In *Lectures* these ideas were only sketched out, but in Lotman's later work on the semiotics of culture and the interrelation of literature with other cultural systems there were to be fully developed.

What is this oppositional relationship that underlies Lotman's thinking in *Lectures*? Ostensibly adapted from the phonological notion of the opposition as developed by Trubetzkoy, Lotman in fact operates with two quite different understandings of the term. In his discussion of poetic language, like Trubetzkoy, he understands that language elements form correlative pairs where there is a basis of similarity; unlike Trubetzkoy, however, Lotman does not attempt a classification of types of oppositional relationships, and moreover he extends his theory beyond the phonological level to encompass all levels of language. When Lotman is discussing questions of artistic perception and of the relationship of text to extra-test, the opposition means something quite different: in these instances it is a generalized relational property—in the former a perception of difference, and in the latter the recognition of an ontological fact.

The oppositional relationship, Lotman declared at the beginning of *Lectures,* is the determinant of any structure; yet it is not so much any given structures that Lotman is here concerned with, but rather with the establishing of a relationary, and in this sense, structuralist, mode of thinking. Poetic language, artistic perception, the nature of text and context these were to be understood in timeless, abstract, relationary terms, rather than as historical variables.

ANTITHESIS II: COMMUNICATION, CODE, SYSTEM

If *Lectures* was a pioneering leap into a structuralist, synchronic (or achronic), mode of thought, *The Structure of the Artistic Text* (Lotman 1970a) was to be the consolidation. Strengthened by a greatly more sophisticated and extensive semiotic theory, Lotman now tackles the problem of art as a language, the problem of the text and its structural axes, the composition of the text and its extra-textual connections.

If the notion of the opposition was the hero of *Lectures,* in *Structure* it is the notion of *system.* All art is structured, all art communicates, all art is therefore systematic, since communication is possible only through system. This is the one pole of Lotman's conception of art: the other is the notion of art as an information-bearing mechanism that preserves and transmits information of a special kind. In this sense art is a language, and the text a particular message, being itself delimited, structured, and expressive. Poetic language can now be analysed in terms of the syntagmatic and paradigmatic axes and the special relationship between these two principles. Lotman adopts the Jakobsonian dictum that "the poetic function projects the principle of equivalence from the axis of selection into the axis of combination" (Jakobson 1960) and rephrases it his way:

The comparison and contrast of repeating equivalent elements, and the comparison and contrast of contiguous (non-equivalent) elements: all the variety of text-construction can be reduced to these two principles (Lotman 1970a: 102-103).

If poetic language is discussed in Jakobsonian terms, the problem of meaning is now tackled in terms from Hjelmslev, while the question of reader reception is discussed in terms of Kolmogorov's theory of probability. Lotman tackles the question of art, text and language in the modern structuralist and semiotic terminology of information, codes, hierarchies, and levels, and perhaps one of the reasons for the interest arosed by this work is the very fact of the amalgamation in it of so many different strands in modern thinking. And the strands all lead in one direction: to a static and universal description of their research objects.

And yet is that what Lotman is after? The terms of reference in *Structure* are familiar, but the logic is not. How can a theory of art as a semiotic system, a language, be propounded without an attempt at a clear definition, even a hypothetical one, of what language is, either in real or in abstract terms? Again, the book leaves us wondering if by text Lotman understands the realization of a system (as in Hjelmslev), or itself a system, or even a clash of systems, and is system in any of these senses comparable with the system-mechanism of communications theory? Again, is one to understand information as the quantifiable entity of information theory, or semantic value? As a theory of art and of the artistic text the book, rich and perceptive though it is, cannot stand. But then is that what Lotman is after, or is it something rather different?

In *Structure* Lotman returns several times to the question of reader-perception (eg. Lotman 1970a: 28-29, 42-43), recognizing that questions of the understanding of works of art are variables determined by cultural and historical background. This leads him to the recognition that *in a historical perspective,* code and message are relative concepts: a work whose innovatory qualities strike its contemporaries may be perceived as a classic (a "code") to later generations. Not only code/message, but also the syntagmatic/paradigmatic axes, rules and restraints are at various points in the book referred to as variables (eg. pp. 28-29, 113, 238-239). But *Structure* was committed to the synchronic (achronic) abstract approach and these ideas were not developed in it.

SYNTHESIS I: THE THEORY OF CULTURE

Lotman is unique among major structuralist thinkers in that for him the distinction between the abstract and the concrete is not emphasized. The Saussurean *langue,* the Hjelmslevian system, the Jakobsonian code are treated by Lotman on the same level as their counterparts (*parole,* text, message), the concrete exemplifications of the abstractions. Lotman's overlooking of this distinction results in some of the uneasiness of his theoretical thinking, the "moveability" of his metalanguage (Vroon 1977: /ix/). The concepts were adopted, the terminology used, but Lotman's essential monism blurred their finer distinctions and the notions swung uneasily in a no-man's-land between construct and reality.

The question of how a semiotic system exists became solved for Lotman with the answer: "within a culture." In 1970 at the Fourth Tartu University Summer School, Lotman put forward the following propositions:

1. That culture, defined as the whole human activity of working out, exchanging and preserving information, should be seen as a unity composed of a number of individual systems.
2. That these individual systems should be studied, in their interrelations with one another and with the whole, in their hierarchical ordering.
3. That culture should be studied in its oppositional relationship to "non-culture" which can be looked on as its structural reserve.
4. That cultures should be studied typologically by various criteria.
5. That culture should be studied in its evolutionary dynamism. (Lotman 1970b).

Theory of literature thus became part of the study of culture, and the problems to be examined were no longer the abstract ones of the nature of the text, the system, etc. but the problem of what text, what system in what interrelationship with other systems and texts, and what *function* they have in a culture.

In a sense, of course, this was a return to the Saussurean conception of the study of "the life of signs in the heart of social life" (Saussure 1916). Or, to use Eco's image, it was the change from studying the surface of the sea which keeps no mark of human intervention to the study of a carefully ordered man-made landscape (Eco 1976: 29). But it had certain extremely original features that make the Moscow-Tartu semiotic group's studies of culture unique.

Culture is to be defined in opposition to non-culture: culture is not a universal set, but a subset, a demarcated domain against a background of non-culture. Culture as against non-culture has the features of being organized, systematic, semiotic, information-bearing; it functions as the "memory" of a collective. Non-culture, on the other hand, is chaos, entropy, and functions as forgetfulness (Lotman and Uspensky 1971). But it is from the relationship of culture to non-culture that cultural change and evolution comes about (see below).

Lotman's cultural typologies are probably fairly well known. He has discussed cultures that are oriented towards "beginnings" and those that are oriented towards "ends" (Lotman 1966c); cultures that are "sign-oriented," such as medieval culture, and those that are oriented against the sign (the Enlightenment) (Lotman 1967); the paradigmatic type of culture and the syntagmatic, the former being closed, concentrically organized, concerned with number symbolism, and the latter, open and historicist (Lotman 1968); cultures that are "text-oriented" and cultures that are "code-oriented" (or expression-oriented vs. content-oriented) (Lotman and Uspensky 1971); culture that is myth-oriented and culture that is science-oriented (Lotman and Uspensky 1973). The methodological approach to these topics is structuralist and relative and uses the notion of the oppositional relationship as its main heuristic tool. But the subject-matter of these typologies are given, historically real, cultures.

SYNTHESIS II: THE DYNAMICS OF CHANGE

The same oppositional mode of thought has led Lotman to a consideration of the *function of non-communication* within a culture. In any actual communication situation, he argues, the codes of addresser and addressee overlap, but do not wholly coincide: partial communication is a given, it is inevitable. But over and beyond this, such partial communication, or non-coincidence of codes, is essential to the functioning of a culture: it is not a question of "noise" or imperfections in the system, but of the very mechanism by which a culture maintains its equilibrium.

Every culture manifests a tendency to self-organization, to a non-contradictory and unified metalanguage. But the opposite tendency is for the semiotic mechanisms within a culture to multiply and diversify. If the one tendency becomes victorious communication is unnecessary; if the other, communication is impossible. In any culture, the random, the individual, the unsystematic (non-cultural) is part of culture's working mechanism, and non-communication and partial communication are as essential to its functioning as communication (Lotman 1973a).

Thinking along these lines has led Lotman to a criticism of Jakobson's well-known six-point schema of the functions of the communicatory situation. Lotman comments on the idealized nature of the schema and goes on:

It is easy to see that the functional emphasis of the schema, while it explains the mechanism for the circulation of already existing messages in a given collective, not only does not explain, but specifically excludes, the possibility of new messages originating within the addresser-addressee chain. Consequently, all scientific constructs which analyse messages within a communicatory chain, while they enrich our understanding of the form of the transmission, accumulation and preservation of information, add nothing to our knowledge of the origin of a new message, that is, our knowledge of the very kernel of the intellectual act. (Lotman 1977a)

Of course, problems of the origin of the new were not at all what Jakobson was concerned with in his schema (Jakobson 1960), but Lotman's remarks are indicative of his attempt to free himself from the established structuralist models and to carry his researches along quite other lines.

The problem then arises of how to describe a culture. If one of the necessary tendencies in a culture is towards a strict and unified self-description (the creation of its own metalanguage), the researcher must adopt a position sufficiently distanced from his research-object so that he can describe both the centralizing, metalingual tendencies of a culture and the opposing a-systematic, individualizing tendencies, while allowing for the fact that all description imposes the quality of orderedness on its object:

> Strict synchronic descriptions, as a rule, ignore the fact of the system's lack of complete internal orderedness, although it is this that gives the system its flexibility and the heightened degree of non-predictability in its behaviour. For this reason the internal capacity for creating information (the inexhaustability of hidden possibilities) of the object is far greater than the description would indicate. (Lotman 1974)

What are the processes by which a culture evolves, what are the factors that give it its dynamism? Lotman gives three answers:

1. The non-systematic (non-cultural) is drawn into the system (culture) and brings about a change in the system. ("It was the stone rejected by the builders that became the cornerstone.") This is the process whereby the non-significant, the irrelevant becomes significant and relevant. Lotman illustrates this with the specific example of how certain slips of the pen in Pushkin's drafts to two of his poems may have been the source of new images (Lotman 1974).

   This process can be looked at also as the interrelation of nucleus and periphery, or again as the interrelation of canon and apocrypha (Lotman 1974, 1977a).

2. The tendency to organization is counter-balanced by the opposite tendency to individualization:

> The striving to increase the semiotic diversity within the organism of culture results in the fact that every meaning-bearing cluster of structural organization shows a tendency to turn into a particular "cultural personality"—a closed immanent world with its own internal structural-semiotic organization, its own memory, individual behaviour, intellectual capacities, and mechanism for self-development / . . . / Bound up with the very essence of the mechanism of culture is the growth of various such closed formations

which greatly contribute to the information-capacity of the given culture and, consequently, the effectiveness with which it orients itself in the world. (Lotman 1977).

Yet, if this tendency goes to extremes,

the mechanism of culture is threatened with a kind of "cultural schizophrenia," disintegration into many mutually antagonistic "cultural personalities"; cultural polyglottism may grow into a semiosis condition like the Tower of Babel. (Lotman 1977).

The other extreme is the culture totally dominated by the metalingual tendency, centralized, over-organized to the point of atrophy. A functioning culture evolves through the interplay of these two tendencies.

3. Imperfect communication gives rise to the need for creative translation or re-encoding from which the new and the original arises. Difficulties in mutual understanding compel the creation of correspondences:

The situation is like that of a literary translation: there is a need for a translation and at the same time there is an awareness that it is impossible to do, this dictates the establishing of correspondences which are either unique or have a metaphoric character. To one element in the text to be translated there corresponds a whole set of elements in the target text, and vice versa. The establishment of a correspondence always implies a *choice*; this act is fraught with difficulties and its outcome is like a godsend or a sudden illumination. It is just this translation of the untranslatable that is *the mechanism for creating a new idea*. It is founded not on a one-for-one transformation, but on an approximate model, a likeness, a metaphor (Lotman 1977a: 16. Lotman's italics).

Lotman's own metaphoric language in expressing his complex thinking should not obscure the importance and originality of these new ideas about the mechanisms of change in semiotic systems. The theory will no doubt be further worked on and the metalanguage perfected. In the meantime Lotman and Uspensky have embarked on a series of "historical semiotic" studies devoted to the history of Russian culture (see Lotman 1973b, 1973c, 1973d, 1975b, 1976; Uspensky 1974; Lotman and Uspensky 1974, 1977a, 1977b). These studies within the general conceptual framework outlined above consider such questions as the interrelation of different semiotic systems (different arts) in a given cultural period, the interrelation of literature and behaviour patterns, the interrelation of types of consciousness (codes) in a given historical period.

With these works one can say that Soviet semiotics has come of age, found its own voice, synthesizing the classical concepts of the structuralist synchronic tradition with its own historicist outlook and opening a new chapter in the development of general semiotic theory.

"Every synchronic system has its own past and future/. . . . . . / every system inevitably represents an evolution /. . . / Evolution itself is necessarily systematic": the prophetic words of Jakobson and Tynyanov in 1928 are now finding fulfilment.

REFERENCES

Baran, Henryk, (ed.) 1976. *Semiotics and Structuralism: Readings from the Soviet Union,* New York.

Eco, Umberto. 1976. *A Theory of semiotics,* Indiana University Press. (Critical Social Studies, London, 1977).

Jakobson, Roman. 1928. (with Ju. N. Tynyanov). "Problemy izucheniya literatury i jazyka," *Novyj Lef,* 12, 1928. (English in *Russian Poetics in Translation,* 4, 1977).

_____ . 1960. "Linguistics and poetics," *Style in Language,* ed. T. Sebeok, M.I.T. Press, 1960, 350-377.

Lotman, Ju. M. 1957. "Evoljutsija mirovozzrenija Karamzina, 1789-1803," *Uchenye Zapiski* TGU, 51, 122-162.

_____ . 1959. "M.A. Dmitriev-Mamonov—poet, publitsist i obshchestvennyj dejatel'," *TRSF* II (*Uch. Zap.* TGU 78), 19-92.

_____ . 1960a. "P.A. Vjazemskij i dvizhenie dekabristov," *TRSF* III (*Uch. Zap.* 98), 24-142.

_____ . 1960b. "K evoljutsii postroenija kharakterov v romane Evgenij Onegin" in: *Pushkin: issledovanija i materialy,* III, 131-173.

_____ . 1961. "Puti razvitija russkoj prozy 1800-kh - 1810-kh gg." *TRSF* IV (*Uch. Zap. TGU* 104), 3-57.

_____ . 1964. *Lektsii po struktural'noj poetike* (*TZS* I; *Uch. Zap. TGU* 160), Tartu.

_____ . 1966a. "Poezija Karamzina" in: *Karamzin: Polnoe sobranie stikhotvorenij,* ed. Ju. M. Lotman (Biblioteka poeta, bol'shaja serija), Moscow-Leningrad, 5-52.

_____ . 1966b. "Khudozhestvannaja struktura *Evgenija Onegina,*" *TRSF* IX (*Uch. Zap. TGU* 184), 5-22.

Lotman, Ju. M. 1966c. "O modelirujushchem znachenii ponjatij 'kontsa' i 'nachala' v khudozhestvennykh tekstakh," *LSh* II, 69-74. (English in *Russian Poetics in Translation*, 3).

————. 1967. "K probleme tipologii kul'tury," TZS III (*Uch. Zap. TGU* 198), 30-38. (English in Lucid 1977).

————. 1968. "Semantika chisla i tip kul'tury," *LSh* III, 103-109 (English in Lucid 1977).

————. 1970a. *Struktura khudozhestvennogo teksta*, Moscow. (English, *The Structure of the Artistic Text*, translated by R. Vroon, Ann Arbor, 1977.)

————. 1970b. "Predlozhenija po programme IV letnej shkoly po vtorichnym modelirujuschchim sistemam," *LSh* IV, 3-5.

————. 1972. *Analiz poeticheskogo teksta*, Leningrad. (English, *The Analysis of the Poetic Text*, Ann Arbor, 1976).

————. 1973a. "Znakovyj mekhanizm kul'tury," *Sb. St.*, 195-199 (English in *Semiotica* 12:4, 1974).

————. 1973b. "Stsena i zhivopis' kak kodirujushchie ustrojstva kul'turnogo povedenija cheloveka nachala XIX stoletija" in: Lotman 1973e.

————. 1973c. "Teatr i teatral'nost' v stroe kul'tury nachala XIX veka" in: Lotman 1973e (English in Baran 1976).

————. 1973d. "Proiskhozhdenie sjuzheta v tipologicheskom osveshchenii" in: Lotman 1973e (English forthcoming in *PTL: A Journal for Descriptive Poetics and Theory of Literature*).

————. 1973e. *Stat'i po tipologii kul'tury (Materialy k kursu teorii literatury* II), Tartu.

————. 1974. *Dinamicheskaya model' semioticheskoj sistemy*, Institut Russkogo Jazyka (*Predvaritel'nye publikatsii* 60), Moscow.

————. 1975a. *Roman v stikhakh Pushkina Evgenij Onegin*, Tartu.

————. 1975b. "Tema kart i kartochnoj igry v russkoj literature nachala XIX veka," *TZS* VII (*Uch. Zap.* 365) 120-142. (English forthcoming in *PTL*).

————. 1975c. "O Khlestakove" *TRSF* XXIV (*Uch. Zap. TGU)* 19-53.

————. 1976. "Khudozhestvennaja priroda russkikh narodnykh kartinok" in: *Narodnaja gravjura i fol'klor v Rossii XVII-XIX vv.*, ed. I'E' Danilova, Moscow, 247-267.

————, 1977. *Kul'tura kak kollektivnyj intellekt i problemy iskusstvennogo razuma*, Nauchnyj sovet po kompleksnoj probleme "Kibernetika" *(predvaritel' naja publikatsija)*, Moscow.

————. 1977b. "Poetika bytovogo povedenija v russkoj kul'tury XVIII veka," *TZS* VIII *(Uch. Zap. TGU* 411), 65-89.

———— and Uspenskij, B.A. 1971. "O semioticheskom mekhanizme kul'tury," *TZS* V *(Uch. Zap.* 284). 144-166 (English, forthcoming, *New Literary History)*.

————. 1973. "Mif—imja—kul'tura," *TZS* VI *(Uch. Zap. TGU* 308), 282-303. (English in Baran 1976, Lucid 1977).

————. 1974. "K semioticheskoj tipologii russkoj kul'tury XVIII veka" in: *Materialy nauchnoj konferentsii (1973): Khudozhestvennaja kul'tura XVIII veka*, Moscow, 259-282.

————. 1977a. "Rol' dual'nykh modelej v dinamike russkoj kul'tury," *TRSF* XXXVIII *(Uch. Zap.* 414), 3-36.

————. 1977b. "Novye aspekty izuchenija kul'tury drevnej Rusi," *Voprosy Literatury*, 3, 148-166.

Lucid, Daniel P. (ed.). 1977. *Soviet Semiotics: An Anthology edited, translated and with an introduction by Daniel P. Lucid*, Baltimore and London.

Saussure, Ferdinand de. 1916. *Cours de linguistique generale.*

Shukman, Ann. 1977a. *Literature and semiotics: A Study of the Writings of Yu. M. Lotman*, Amsterdam.

————. 1977b. "Jurij Lotman and the semiotics of culture," *Russian Literature*, 5:1, 41-54.

Uspenskij, B.A. 1974. "Historia sub specie semioticae," *Materialy*, 119-130. (English in Baran 1976, Lucid 1977).

Vroon, Ronald. "Preface" in Jurij Lotman, *The Structure of the Artistic Text*, Ann Arbor, 1977.

ABBREVIATIONS

LSh III   *III Letnjaja shkola povtorichnym modelirujushchim sistemam: tezisy*, Tartu, 1968.

LSh IV   *Tezisy dokladov IV letnej shkole po vtorichnym modelirujushchim sistemam*, Tartu, 1970.

Materialy   *Materialy vsesojuznogo simpoziuma po vtorichnym modelirujushchim sistemam* 1(5), Tartu, 1974.

Sb. St.   *Sbornik statej po vtorichnym modelirujushchim sistemam,*   Tartu, 1973.

TGU   Tartuskij gosudarstvennyj universitet (Tartu State University).

TRSF   *Trudy po russkoj i slavjanskoj filologii,* Tartu.

TZS   *Trudy po znakovym sistemam,* Tartu.

Uch. Zap.   *Uchenye Zapiski.*

SEMIOTICS IN BOHEMIA IN THE 19TH AND EARLY 20TH CENTURIES:

MAJOR TRENDS AND FIGURES

Peter Steiner and Bronislava Volek

The awareness of semiotics as a discipline capable of providing the humanities and social sciences with a common frame of reference did not emerge in Bohemia until after World War I. At that time, the linguists, estheticians, and ethnographers collaborating in the Prague Linguistic Circle (1926-1948) proclaimed the "problem of the sign" to be "one of the most urgent philosophical problems of the cultural rebirth of our era," because "all of reality, from sensory perception to the most abstract mental construction, appears to modern man as a vast and complex realm of signs" [Havránek et al., 1935: 5].

It was only natural then that at the beginning, Czech semioticians focused more on the future than on the past. Primarily concerned with staking out new territory, they only occasionally looked backward in search of antecedents. But in recent years, with the worldwide acceptance of semiotics, the situation has begun to change and studies devoted to the history of semiotics have started to appear. The discipline is still very young, however, and much more painstaking research will be necessary before a comprehensive history can be assembled. This paper is a modest contribution to this new area of inquiry.

The beginnings of semiotics in nineteenth-century Bohemia are undeniably to be found in the work of Bernard Bolzano (1781-1848), a native of Prague and a professor at Prague university. Forced to retire in 1820, Bolzano devoted his remaining energies to his magnum opus, a four-volume *Wissenschaftslehre* published in 1837, in which he sought to explore the logic of scientific thinking. This search led him to what he called *Zeichenlehre* or *Semiotik*. It was especially in his third volume, entitled *Erkenntnisslehre*, that he defined and promulgated a number of basic semiotic concepts.

According to Bolzano, the sign is "an object. . . through the idea of which we wish to evoke in a thinking being the awareness of some other associated idea" [1930: 67].[1] Signs are used purposively, and thus differ

[1]Here and elsewhere we have rendered the German concept *Vorstellung* as "idea." For an elucidation of this choice see E. Boring [1929: 260].

from indices (*Kennzeichen*) whether physical or biological, for these merely allow one to infer a particular natural state (smoke indicating fire, blushing indicating guilt, and so on).

The cardinal category of Bolzano's semiotics was the concept of "meaning" (*Bedeutung*). As a logician, he was interested above all in the stability of meaning in signs. Therefore he purged meaning of all the vicissitudes of the phenomenal world and characterized it as an "objective idea whose corresponding subjective idea is supposed to be stimulated by the idea of the sign" [*ibid*.: 67]. By distinguishing between the subjective and objective idea, Bolzano separated the phenomenon as part of consciousness from its ideal a priori existence. Meaning as "objective idea" is independent of our consciousness and in its ideality is unchangeable.

To maintain the purity of this concept, Bolzano drew a sharp line between it and another notion termed "sense" (*Sinn*) or "significance" (*Verstand*). In contrast to ideal meaning, sense or significance has reference merely to the intention of the perceiver of a sign which in its subjectivity can easily be   mistaken; thus the   meaning of the sign can be completely different from its sense or significance. The operation of understanding pertains to meaning, for in it we "truly gather from [signs] which ideas their originator wanted to produce," whereas the operation of interpretation applies to sense or significance, for in it we assert that a "sense of a particular sign is such and such" [*ibid*.: 68].

The understanding of signs is not an automatic process for several reasons. Most importantly, every language contains a number of homonyms, signs which signify more than a single idea. Bolzano calls such signs "polysemous" (*mehrdeutig*). But in addition to this inherent polysemy of language, polysemy may also be introduced through signification. We might signify an idea by a sign which we earlier used to signify a different idea. Thus one sign can have two different meanings—one which is original, another which is derived. If a sign signifies its objective idea it was used, according to Bolzano, in its "proper meaning." Otherwise it was used in an "extended" or "improper meaning." These boundaries, however, are not permanently fixed and an improper meaning can in the course of time become a sign's proper meaning.

Moreover, often the perceiver cannot decide which idea the speaker wants to signify by a sign, so that the sign appears "indeterminate" to him. Or sometimes he perceives the sign as a homonym with two or more possible meanings; in contrast to "indeterminate" signs Bolzano speaks here of "fluctuating" (*schwanken*) signs. Or finally, signs may be so opaque that we must guess at their signification, in which case they are "totally incomprehensible" to us. But as Bolzano points out, our understanding of a sign depends to a large degree on the "context" (*Zusammenhang*) in which it appears as well as on the distance between the author and reader in space and time.

Misunderstanding can be further generated by the "improper" usage of signs. In the tropes and figures of speech the relation between the sign and its meaning is not explicit, but indirect. There are two ways in which we can grasp a figuratively used sign. On the one hand, the context in which the sign appears might be sufficient for us to understand precisely what the sign means. Such a usage of the sign is "metonymic" for Brentano. On the other hand, the context might not provide any definite clue about the link between the sign and the idea which it signifies. In this case we are dealing with a "metaphoric" usage.

But even if used non-figuratively, every sign evokes ideas in addition to its idea proper. These connotations of a sign, or in Bolzano's terms, "secondary ideas" (*Nebenvorstellungen*), cannot be completely dismissed because they influence our judgments. If such an influence is detrimental to our judgments we are dealing with an "impure sign," while a sign free of any secondary ideas detrimental to our judgments, on the other hand, is a "pure expression."

Bolzano's typology of signs can be presented as a set of binary oppositions differentiating signs according to their shareability, mode of signification, and mode of perception. In terms of shareability, "universally valid" signs are those objects which are used uniformly by all people to designate an idea. Some signs or sets of signs (most notably national languages), however, are used only by some people and these signs are "conventional" (*üblich*). If an object is associated with an idea because of some feature shared by all people, it is a "natural" sign. Otherwise, the sign is "accidental." In terms of significatory mode, if an "accidental" sign originates in an intentional act and there is no other reason to link it with an idea, the sign is "arbitrary." In contrast to these "immediate" signs which signify an idea directly, there are "mediate" signs signifying other signs. This is the case, for instance, of a written language, in which the written word stands for the spoken word. And finally, in terms of perceptual mode, signs are usually perceived either by sight or by hearing—they are either "visual" or "auditory." In the case of language, Bolzano states that the latter are produced and apprehended in their temporal succession, whereas the former (written language) are organized in a linear fashion stipulated by a particular convention.

Bolzano's remarks about the origin of human language are also sem-iotically relevant. He claimed that there were three distinct stages in its evolution: the language of gestures, the language of similarity, and arbitrary language. The first type of language enabled man to express his inner mental states. Gestures, facial expressions, and various sounds were originally mere indices of mental states and only gradually developed into full fledged signs signifying particular ideas. The imitation of properties of objects external to the psyche, which underlies the second stage of language, enabled people to broaden their communication beyond mere mental states. And from the combination of gestures and imitations arose the knowledge that "a sig-nification of an object does not have to rest on the production of similars. What suffices is to make others comprehend that through such and such a production one wants them to form an idea of a particular object" [ibid.: 83]. Only at this final stage did language become the system of signs we know today.[2]

The philosophical boldness of Bolzano's thought together with his high moral standards and personal charisma secured him a special position in the Bohemian intellectual tradition. Thus, in 1881 the Czech Royal Society of Sciences organized a special meeting to celebrate the centenary of his birth. The keynote speaker at this session was Josef Durdík (1837-1902), a leading Czech esthetician and professor at Prague University. Durdík was too young to be acquainted with Bolzano personally, but according to his own words, he knew many of Bolzano's friends, and his anniversary speech proved that he was familiar with his writings [Durdík, 1881a and 1887: 385].

The selection of Durdík as the main speaker for the celebration of Bolzano's birthday was not, however, motivated solely by such considerations. Despite the fact that Durdík's esthetics was derived prim-arily from Herbart's philosophy, we can detect a certain affinity between his and Bolzano's thought. Mirko Novák, a historian of Czech esthetics, has observed that in several instances Durdík, "not completely faithful to Her-bart, speaks of language and art as a *sign*" [Novák, 1941: 69]. In his dis-cussion of this fact, Novák takes into account only Durdík's distinction between the symbol and the sign, jumping to the conclusion that Durdík's semiotic interest was a manifestation of Hegel's influence in Durdík's otherwise militantly anti-Hegelian system. On closer inspeaction, however, we can see that Durdík's "theory of signs or semiotics" (*znâmkosloví, čili semiotika*) has at least some of its roots in Bolzano's "Semiotik oder

---

[2]For a more detailed discussion of Bolzano's semiotics see E. Walther [1971].

Zeichenlehre."[3]

To understand Durdík's semiotics we must first explain some of his sociological and esthetic ideas. He believed that a human being is always a member of a society and that the essence of every society is what might loosely be translated as the "social consciousness of its members" (*svědomost členův*). To transcend our solitary mental life and communicate with the other members of our society we need a system of signs (*známky*), a language. Moreover, Durdík differentiates between language in the broad and narrow senses. "Since every communication is mediated by signs, the system of these signs is language in the broadest sense of the word: a set of means through which we externalize our internal states." But in the narrow sense language is "the set of audible words and their usage, which facilitate communication among human beings" [1875: 463-64]. Thus, our ideas, to be passed on to others, "must have their signs: through them they appear, are embodied, and expressed. In this way not only does language in the broadest sense of the word arise, but through its help the arts as well" [*ibid.*: 467].

As a Herbartian formalist, Durdík was a principal opponent of content-oriented, romantic esthetics. For him, no object was ever beautiful merely because of its material (or its theme in the case of some works of art), but only because of the relations of the elements which comprised its *form*. In general he distinguished two types of beauty—the sensory and the spiritual. In the case of sensory beauty, what is externalized and communicated are the ideas of shapes, colors and tones. And in turn the "objective shape, objective color (the pigment, the color matter), and objective tone are here the signs of one's own ideas." These signs create systems, so that Durdík speaks of a "language of shapes, colors and tones." Moreover, such signs are "natural" for him because "every perceiver understands them" [*ibid.*: 463]. But sensory beauty is not limited to "natural" signs. There are cases when a composer, for instance, "makes a chord or a musical motif the name or sign of a particular character or phenomenon" (Durdík, 1881b: 492). Such a "semiotic characterization" (*význačnost semiotická*), according to Durdík, stands at the very border of sensory beauty. The true domain of such signification is the other realm of beauty—the spiritual.

The main semiotic difference between sensory and spiritual beauty rests in the fact that the material of the latter—"notional ideas" (*pojmové*

---

[3]Novák points out that there are passages dealing with signs in the work of Robert Zimmermann as well, and wonders whether the influence of Hegel on Durdík was not mediated through him. However, Zimmermann, who was born in Prague and taught briefly at the university there, was a close friend of Bolzano's and his interest in the problems of the sign probably derives directly from him.

představy)—does not have any objective correlate in the phenomenal world, and signs are superimposed upon it more or less arbitrarily. There are two types of signs for "notional ideas": "immediate" signs such as gestures, facial expressions, interjections and onomatopoetic words, which are fairly generally understood and thus close to "natural" signs, and "artificial" signs which do not resemble what they signify and are fixed by a mere convention, for example, "audible words"—the *prima facie* signs of "notional ideas"; or "visible marks"—the "signs of words" and hence "signs of signs" [1875: 464].

But what precisely are these "notional ideas" which Durdík claims are the material of both spiritual beauty and its domain, verbal art? To provide an answer we must first know how Durdík conceived of the relation between mental and physical reality. Insofar as he placed the source of mental life in sensory perception, Durdík was a sensualist. However, he did not completely subordinate reason to the senses. For him consciousness was not a mere passive synthesizer of sensory stimuli but a common substrate around which they could cluster. Through a complex organization of stimuli, "images" (*obrazy*) independent of actual perception arise in our consciousness. And through the secondary process of abstraction we generate out of these "images" an "outline" (*obrys*). "The particular elements of the images from which [the outline] is derived constantly intrude into it and thus more or less change its character. Therefore, every outline is somewhat indeterminate, vascillating; it is all-embracing but incomplete" [*ibid*: 258]. Only through a further abstraction can we eliminate from the outline all secondary features and arrive at a "concept"(*pojem*), the "idea *in itself*, purified of all the secondary features originating in ideation, i.e., in the natural process and its subject" [*ibid*: 258].

Though all three types of mental constructs—image, outline, and concept—are "notional ideas," i.e., ideas expressible only through words, not all of them are equally appropriate as the material of verbal art. Images are too close to our everyday psychic experience, whereas the abstraction of concepts separates them to a large extent from everyday experiences. However, the outline brings together both the emotional vividness of images and the cognitive detachment of concepts. Because of its dual nature, Durdík holds that the outline is most suitable as the material of verbal art.

But as we pointed out above, outlines, like all notional ideas, require a sensory vehicle in order to be externalized and communicated. Since they have no genuine objective correlates in the phenomenal world, signs which are often quite incongruous to them must be superimposed upon them. Thus, verbal art contains two sets of inseparable but distinct phenomena—tangible words and the intelligible outlines they signify. This duality, however, raises one important problem for Durdík's formalist notion that the source of beauty is form: the relations among elements. For now there are two types of elements in verbal art and both of them can be arranged in an esthetic form. Thus Durdík distinguishes between the *outer form* of the poetic work— the organization of its material vehicle—and its *inner form*—the organization of its notional ideas.

The relation between outer and inner form in verbal art reflects Durdík's more general concept of the difference between sensory and spiritual beauty. Since literature is the domain of spiritual beauty, inner dominates over outer form. As Durdík argues, artistic prose does not have an outer form and thus is based solely on the relations among ideas. Nevertheless, it is still to be considered an artistic phenomenon, for in contrast, everyday language and scientific prose lack inner form, and hence could not be art even if someone were to provide them with an outer form by couching them in verse. The dominance of inner form in literature does not, however, imply that outer form is totally irrelevant. The two are semiotically connected and a change in one results in a change in the other. As Durdík argued: "It is because the poet is forced to change his language, his words, and their order for the sake of rhyme and rhythm. . . that he is led to completely new thoughts and unintended images" [1881b: 449].

Durdík's *Poetics*, which he characterized as the "first comprehensive attempt at a poetics grounded in formal esthetics," was to consist of three parts: the relation of verbal art to the other arts, the problem of outer form, and the problem of inner form. He managed to conclude only the first two parts and our sole knowledge of his ideas about inner form in verbal art comes from posthumously published fragments. There we learn that he argued for an inner form of the poetic work, comprised of the relations among its notional ideas. This simple postulate is complicated, however, by the fact that literature is made up of outlines, which are intrinsically unstable entities. They not only tend to change according to their context but are accompanied by what Durdík calls "secondary ideas" (*představy vedlejší*), which may become prominent in some configurations and unimportant in others. Because it is impossible to identify all the possible forms of outlines in verbal art, Durdík reduces their relations to the four basic laws of association: "simultaneity, similarity, contrast, and successivity" [1913: 119]. With each of these laws he associates one of the four basic figures of speech: the *synecdochy* or *pars pro toto* is a relation based on the simultaneity of ideas; the *metaphor* combines ideas because of their similarity; the *joke* (*vtip*) brings together contrasting ideas; and the *metonymy* associates successive ideas [1914: 271-287].

Durdík's writings about poetics, though unfinished, illustrate the advantages and shortcomings of formalist esthetics. They also prove that the formalists did not ignore semantic problems, but rather, failed to develop an effective apparatus to deal with them.

After Durdík, the semiotic orientation of formalist esthetics in Bohemia came to an end. Otakar Hostinský (1847-1910), Durdík's pupil and successor at the university, did not exhibit any direct interest in semiotics.   Mistrust of speculative theorizing led him to concentrate on the material aspect of art, to the analysis of which he freely applied methods from the natural sciences, perhaps with the best results in music.

But the setback semiotic studies suffered in esthetics was more than compensated for in other fields, most notably linguistics. As we have seen, Durdík had shown a keen interest in the linguistic sign, despite the imprecision and intuitive quality of his terms and his impressionistic conclusions. A more precise semiotic treatment of language was attempted by Anton Marty (1847-1914), a Swiss-born professor of philosophy at Prague University. A pupil and close friend of Brentano, Marty treated language mainly as a psychological phenomenon. However, the insights into the workings of language that he gained in his psychological investigations outlasted the general thrust of his work and bear similarity to the semiotic theories of the Prague Linguistic Circle.

Marty's first book [1875] is a critique of what he calls the "nativist" theories of the origin of language propounded by Steinthal, Wundt, and others, according to which language was a kind of "reflex motion" (*Reflexbewegung*). The nativists considered onomatopoetic associations in the broadest sense the origin of linguistic signs. "Broadest sense" is important here, since according to some "nativists" (e.g., Steinthal), the resemblance between the "idea" (*Vorstellung*) and the sound did not have to be direct, but could be mediated through an emotion.

Against this "instinctive" theory Marty advocated a teleological view according to which language is a phenomenon that originated from the human need for communication. The formation of language had thus, according to Marty, an intentional and conscious, though unplanned character. A sign could realize a meaning either through its resemblance to the object designated or through an association to it which was present either by chance or custom. But because such immediately appropriate signs were hard to come by, it became necessary to use a secondary associative power of signs as well in order to express the ever-increasing number of meanings (*Bed-*

eutung, Inhalt, Mitzuteilende, Funktion). An example of such a secondary association might be the designation of an object by the name of an object associated with it, this resulting in the creation of a homonym. The transposed use of linguistic devices stands at the center of Marty's theory of the formation of linguistic designation, and the notion he developed to describe it was "inner linguistic form."

For example, a sign for some extralinguistic reality (*bow-wow* as a sign for the barking of a dog) can be used in a secondary stage for the dog itself. Then the idea of barking changes from the meaning of a sign to a mere "secondary idea" (*Nebenvorstellung*), i.e., an associative connection between the sound sequence (*Ausdrucksform*) and the meaning, i.e., the mental content that should be evoked in the hearer by the sound sequence. The goal of the associative connection is thus to evoke its meaning (the idea of the dog). The auxiliary idea is not a meaning since it is not itself meant, but becomes an inner linguistic form, an "Etymon." The inner form originates, Marty held, in order to serve communication and so is the main vehicle of language formation.

Different sound sequences can stand for the same content (synonyms) and can be connected by different inner forms. The form appears thus as something unstable and changing, whereas the meaning is stable, a material that is formed [1884: 67 f.] .

However, according to Marty, signs need not be formed through an Etymon, as is the case, for example, with a cry of pain. There need be no inner form in signs of "sheer thinking" either, such as representations of concepts, the most striking case being numbers, which represent the concept of numbers. These signs can be totally arbitrary, e.g., algebraic signs. Their only resemblance to signs with Etymons would be that they form a system, and so the idea of such a sign could be connected with a secondary idea of its position in the system, and this idea might suggest the first idea. Nevertheless, Marty says, this is only a shadow of real inner form.

Marty distinguishes two different types of inner form: the "figurative" (*figürliche*) and the "constructive" (*konstruktive*), to the first of which we shall devote most of our attention. Figurative inner linguistic form (which Marty sometimes terms "image" [*Bild*]), is related to meaning in two ways. First, image and meaning may stand in a relation of analogy or resemblance. Resemblance is to be understood either as a partial sameness, or a small difference sufficient to trigger associations; analogy is understood as a sameness between things that are different in an absolute sense.

We find analogy, e.g., in an expression like "ass," "pig," "goose" when applied to persons, when we speak about "sweet talk," or when we call a lion "the king of beasts." Within this group belong all metaphors.

Secondly, image and meaning may stand in a relation of another kind, namely contiguity, as in the metonymy or synecdoche. This may be a relationship of cause and effect ("to buy a Rembrandt"), of *pars pro toto* ("sail" for "ship"), of accident for substance (similar to the *pars pro toto* relationship when an object is designated by its states, actions, dispositions, or abilities), of a member for its class ("roses" for "flowers") [1908: 501 ff.].

Marty attributes the origin of figurative inner form to imitation, of which there are two kinds. The first is imitation involving phenomena of the same nature, (e.g., speech sounds may imitate nonlinguistic sounds). These primary imitative expressions can then be used indirectly for the designation of something else that stands to the imitated thing as a part to a whole or as a cause to an effect, i.e., in a relationship of regular association. In this way a contiguity relationship is formed, which is unlimited and hence can construct a great number of immediately understandable signs [1875: 85-90; 1884-1892: 210 ff.; 1908: 678 ff.].

The second type of imitation is that in which the sounds of signs imitate phenomena of a different nature. Marty describes analogies between different types of idea contents (*Vorstellungsinhalten*) as they appear in the metaphors of a natural language, e.g., when we speak of high or deep tones. Deep tones and dark colors are related, according to Marty, not only in the similar feelings that they evoke, but in their very natures.

Figurative inner linguistic form appears in syntax as well. For Marty, syntax means combinations of signs that as a whole have a meaning or "auxiliary meaning" (*Hilfbedeutung, Mitbedeutung*) which cannot be found in the elements themselves. Syntax here is conceived broadly, not only as rules of combination that construct sentences; it plays a role even in the construction of nouns [1875: 107; 1893: 92; 1908: 532 ff.]. Syntax is thus understood as a form, a method of expression. The figurative inner linguistic form appears here in cases where autosemantic devices (i.e., those with independent meaning) undergo a transposition and become synsemantic devices (those without independent meaning). For example, in the past perfect, "Ich habe ihn gelobt," the image of possession in "habe" provides the figurative inner form for the designation of the perfect; but today this fact is recognizable only genetically. Another case of figurative inner form in syntax is the metaphoric use of synsemantic devices (e.g., cases and prepositions in other than a locative meaning can have locative ideas as an inner form: "sich vor etwas furchten").

Marty distinguishes carefully between the genetic aspect of figurative inner form (i.e., what can be discovered only through "genetic reconstruction" and the descriptive (synchronic) aspect: inner form exists only insofar as it is alive in the mind (*Bewusstsein*) of the understanding subject [1908: 150].

The sign in Marty's theory is thus most often constituted of sounds (outer form), auxiliary ideas (*Begleitvorstellungen, Hilfvorstellungen, Nebenvorstellungen*) which are not meant but only lead the hearer toward the meaning (the inner form), and finally the meaning itself, which is the idea of the designated extralinguistic object. This conception of the sign follows from Marty's deep concern for the distinction between form (*Form*) and material (*Stoff*) in the semantic relation. To understand a meaning as material and the linguistic means of its expression as form, it is especially important to distinguish between the outer form, which is perceptible by the senses, and the inner linguistic form, which can be experienced only internally (analogically, like meaning itself). Both meaning and inner form are thus mental phenomena, whereas outer form is a sensory phenomenon. This particular characteristic, namely the exclusively psychic accessibility of inner form and meaning, was the reason for the lack of a consistent distinction by both W. von Humboldt [1907: 86 ff.], who introduced this term into the philosophy of language, and his successors, Steinthal and Wundt. Marty on the other hand gives the concept of inner form an unambiguous content, different from meaning.

What general laws are there for the choice of a specific figurative inner linguistic form? Practically any idea can be one if it is more easily accessible than the meaning that is to be expressed. Therefore it is usually an idea that is nearer to sensory perception than the idea that is meant [1910: 103--04, 106 ff.]. The only condition is that a figurative inner linguistic form should be appropriate; that is, it should lead to a meaning, even if only indirectly [1893: 73].

The consequence of the ability of linguistic signs to shift referents is homonymy, i.e., expressions that have the same outer form but a different meaning and inner form. Marty argues that not every homonymy is based on a figurative inner linguistic form, i.e., on an intentional transposition. Homonymy can happen as a result of a simple lack of differentiation between two objects which are then designated by the same sign [1908: 520]. The opposite of homonymy—synonymy—Marty characterized as a difference in outer or inner forms where the meaning stays the same. Sound sequences and inner forms that express similar meanings or have different emotional coloring are not considered synonymic. And, according to Marty, synonymy and homonymy are extensively, but not exclusively, conditioned by the effects of figurative inner linguistic form.

In contrast to the figurative, the second kind of inner linguistic form, as we noted above, is the constructive. The first is simultaneous, while the second is successive and emerges not on the level of individual words, but only in sequences of words as an accompanying phenomenon of outer form, a secondary idea (*Nebenvorstellung*). Secondary ideas evoke a certain expectation concerning the meaning of the whole. On the one hand they can prepare for it; but on the other, they may act as an obstacle to understanding. The field of the constructive inner linguistic form is thus syntax. For example, the expectation suggested by the idea of the German "Es gibt" in "Es gibt einzellige Organismen" is fulfilled; but in the sentence "Es gibt keine Zentauren," on the contrary, it is not. In both cases, Marty considers the expression "Es gibt" syncategorematic, i.e., lacking in independent meaning. Such are some of the effects on meaning of the constructive inner linguistic form [1908: 144 ff., 211].

We have devoted most of this section so far to inner linguistic form because of its crucial role in Marty's thinking. Its importance is a result of its role as mediator between sound sequences and meaning. To complete this summary of Marty's semiotics, then, we might look briefly into his notions about this latter factor, meaning.

According to Marty, meaning is a psychic phenomenon evoked in the hearer. If it is independent it can be of three kinds, a triple distinction borrowed from Brentano [1873, 1911]. First, it may be a conceptual or notional idea (*Vorstellung*) which is present in idea-suggestive expressions (*Vorstellungssuggestive*); these are mainly substantives or their equivalents, that is, expressions that are able to fulfill the function of a subject in a predicative relation. Secondly, an independent meaning may further a judgment (*Urteil*) contained in utterances (*Aussagen*). And thirdly, it may be an emotional phenomenon expressed by the so-called emotives (*Emotive*). Emotives are understood very widely as wishes, commands, questions, and so forth.

According to Marty, utterances and emotives are fundamentally different kinds of signs from nouns. The latter name "real objects" and mean "immanent objects" [1908: 385]. Utterances and emotives, on the other hand, do not name, but they mean and express their real object immediately. That is, there is an existential relationship between the real object and such a sign; "the perception of the sign is a motive for the presupposition of the object" [1908: 281]; meaning and being-a-sign (*Zeichensein*) are, in such cases, one and the same thing. Marty here sets up an analogy to the unintentional cry of pain, a basic indexical situation: "In the same way that the cry of pain does not name or utter, the utterance "es regnet" stands in relation to the fact that I judge so" [285]. The only difference is that the cry of pain is unintentional, whereas the act of judgment is an intentional act. Meaning in the narrow sense of the word is something that is intermediate and primarily intended by the communication. Signs usually function in an intentional speech in more than one way, "meaning" on the one hand and "expressing" on the other.

In addition to independent meaning, Marty investigated synsemantic expressions as well [1908: 204 ff., 226 ff., 476 ff., 532 ff.], although we shall not go into them here. He was thereby reintroducing into linguistics the ancient classical distinction between categorematic and syncategorematic signs, a distinction that has proved to be extremely fruitful in the work of the linguists that followed him. Investigating with others the semantics of the sentence, Marty also helped to clear the way for the understanding of functional sentence perspective [1897: 309-364]. He was thus a central figure on the road to modern linguistics, and had a decisive influence on the Prague Linguistic Circle. One striking connection, for example, is his conception of the dynamism of the linguistic system; his concept of the homonymity and synonymity of linguistic signs found a special parallel in Sergej Karcevskij's notion of the dual asymmetry of the linguistic sign [see Karcevskij, 1929]. And in the study of poetry, the concept of language as an unstable equilibrium which is constantly disturbed by homonymic and synonymic extensions of meaning found its best application [see Mukařovský, 1938, 1940: 133 ff.]. Through his teleological conception of the language system, his groping toward a universal grammar, his descriptive orientation in linguistics, and his emphasis on semantic problems, Marty can be seen as a major forerunner of Prague Structuralism.

The last figure of our survey is Otakar Zich (1879-1934), whose esthetics was psychologically oriented. His ideas bear on our topic in two important ways. First, his work on theatre and music, though not semiotic

in the strict sense, served as an impulse for semiotic redefinitions by the
Prague Structuralists. The members of the Circle concerned with theatre
or music—whether Bogatyrev, Mukařovský, Sychra, or Veltruský—felt compelled to take Zich's penetrating observations into account. Secondly, Zich's
analyses of literature had an immediate semiotic relevance, for he treated
the word—the material of literature—as a sign (značka), a unity of sound and
meaning. His "On Poetic Types" [1917-1918] in particular had an influence
on Mukařovský's early work.

Let us begin with Zich's theory of music and theatre. Here he differentiated three stages in the perception of music [1911]. The first is
"musical perception" in the proper sense of the word, i.e., the perception
of "musical sounds." Even this primary experience is not merely acoustic
or physiological for Zich, but psychological. As he argued, "the difference
between a 'tone' and a group of 'tones,' i.e., a chord, is not. . . essential
as far as the physical impulse is concerned. . . but only from a psychological
point of view" [1911: 3]. This primary impulse is augmented in the psyche
by the "reproductive complementing and modifying of musical perceptions"
[ibid.: 25]. An illustration of this point is the difference between our perception of a musical pause and a break. A break comes at the end of a composition or of some of its parts. Its only function is to signal that musical
perception has come to an end. A pause, on the other hand, is as important
a part of our musical perception as the tones themselves. Following Reimann,
Zich calls the pauses "minus values" and discusses in detail the role of the
retrospective prolongation of previous perception during a pause as well as
the anticipation of what will follow.

In the third stage a "semantic idea" (významová představa, Bedeutungs-
vorstellung) is added to the perception;[4] we not only perceive tones and modify them in our consciousness, but we also attribute some meaning to them.
To illustrate more precisely what he means by this opaque term, Zich speaks
of the perception of a painting. If we perceive a color patch we complement
it and modify it and arrive at some configuration. But only if we attribute
to it some "semantic idea" that clearly delimits it from other configurations—
for instance, that it is a grape—will we complete our perception. Zich is quite
vague about the nature of this "semantic idea," but perhaps we can understand it as the perception of an object qua object. As long as we do not

---

[4]For a somewhat more detailed discussion of the concept, "semantic idea"
see O. Sus [1958].

endow the perceived and modified impulses with meaning, we do not recognize them as a configuration and our psychic experience does not stand
for any object in the phenomenal world. For Zich, this meaning-attributing
activity is the basic property of our consciousness, prior to such secondary
meaning-attributing acts as the verbal representation of semantic ideas. As
he insists: "Every idea of ours does not have to have its appurtenant word
but each can become a 'semantic idea' " [*ibid.*: 39].

This is especially true of the semantic ideas in music which are virtually inexpressible in words and profoundly altered if such an attempt
is made. Zich differentiated three kinds of semantic ideas in music: the
objective (*věcný, dinglich*) or musical, such as musical themes or motifs,
particular harmonies or rhythms; the material, i.e., the tones in their absolute quality, intensity and timbre; and the technical, such as the genre,
period or individual style of a composition. These three types of semantic
ideas are not completely separate from each other. Though, for instance,
a particular musical theme will not be seriously altered if performed on two
different instruments, some of the instruments will be better suited to it,
and when performed it might evoke the image of this instrument in our
minds.

Now we can perhaps see the appeal of Zich's esthetics for the Prague
structuralists. Despite its explicit psychologism, the theory is adaptable to
the semiotic frame of reference. For Zich held that every esthetic experience has two distinct aspects, a primarily sensory aspect—the perception
and modification of the object—and a primarily mental aspect—the meaning-
attributing act completing the perception. From the semiotic point of view,
the sensory aspect can be seen as the material vehicle of the esthetic sign
and the mental aspect as the meaning of the sign.

But it was Zich's writings about theatre, and acting in particular, that
the Prague Structuralists found especially stimulating. Zich described the
theatrical experience as follows. If we sit in the theatre we perceive acoustic
and optic impulses. We modify and complement them and finally attribute
to them a semantic idea; for instance, we recognize that this set of perceptual
impulses is Macbeth. However, this is only part of our recognition. At the
same time that we conceive of the person on the stage as Macbeth, we recognize equally well that he is not Macbeth but an actor who represents
Macbeth, or better, creates the image of Macbeth. This is especially true if
the actor is famous and we have encountered him previously in other roles.
We thus attribute another semantic idea to our sensations. Since the first
semantic idea is an image of Macbeth, Zich calls it the "imagistic [*obrazová*]
semantic idea"; the other, that of the actor, he calls "technical."

But this distinction still does not fully exhaust the complexity of

dramatic art. As we saw in Zich's essay on music, there is a third kind of
semantic idea involved, namely the "material semantic idea." To show that
it applies to theatre as well, Zich advances the following parallel. "An *artist*
creates out of a specific *material* a *work* which represents *such and such*.
For example, a *sculptor* creates out of *marble* a particular *statue* representing,
for example, *Heracles*. An *actor* creates *out of himself* a particular *figure*
representing for example *Macbeth*" [1931: 54]. What at first glance seemed
a simple "idea" of Macbeth is in fact a twofold entity: the "dramatic character" [*dramatická osoba*], i.e., Macbeth, is the image evoked by the material
vehicle which Zich terms the "dramatic figure" [*herecká postava*]. He represents these notions in the following way:

Artist	Material	Product	Image
Actor	The Same Actor	The Figure	The Dramatic Character [*ibid.*: 57]

This scheme indicates the peculiar nature of acting in which the artist and
material are identical. But it also heightens the difference between the "product" and the "image" or what the structuralists in their semiotics of acting
would call the "signans" and "signatum" of the histrionic sign [see Veltruský, 1976: 555].

   Zich's observations about the relation of art to reality were also important to the Prague semioticians, particularly his distinction between the
representational and non-representational arts. Whereas in the perception of
the former we always juxtapose art to reality, in the perception of the latter
such an association is only secondary. The discussion of semantic ideas in
music and theatre demonstrates this difference. In music, Zich spoke of
"objective or musical semantic ideas" whereas in theatre he spoke of "imagistic semantic ideas." The reason for this difference is clear. Music as a
non-representational art does not refer directly to reality and its themes
and motifs are objects in themselves without reference to extra-musical
reality. This, of course, does not mean that the perceiver cannot associate
them with reality. But if he does so, he does so only indirectly on the basis
of general laws of association: *similarity* (music resembles human speech
or the sounds of nature), or *contiguity* (the associations are arbitrary, due
to social conventions or individual experience) [see Zich, 1911: 54-67].

   In theatre, a representational art *par excellence*, the situation is completely different. Here the relation of the work to reality is so strong that
it is possible to confuse one with the other. However, every theatrical pro-

duction contains enough signals to tell us that what we see is not life but art. This triggers in us a special "mental set [*příprava mysli*] evoking an 'imagistic conception' [*obrazové pojetí*] —what we could call an artistic illusion" [Zich, 1921: 202]. Nevertheless, our recognition of the objects in theatre comes about because what we see resembles reality or in other words is an image of reality. Consequently, Zich terms theatrical semantic ideas imagistic. The theatrical illusion can be upset in many ways. As an example, Zich analyzes the marionette theatre with its deep gap between the dramatic figure and the dramatic character. According to him, our perception of marionettes can be dominated either by their unnatural guise (so that we see them as comically grotesque), or by their likeness to people (so that we see them as mysterious, like statues which come alive) [1923]. Bogatyrev's critique of this particular study of Zich [1937-1938] was one of the first attempts of the Prague structuralists to discuss the semiotic ramifications of artistic perception—a topic which gained prominence in Prague during the forties [see, for example, Mukařovský, 1943].

In contrast to Zich's work on music and theatre, his studies of literature operate directly with the concept of the sign. In the most famous one [1917-1918], Zich divided the perception of the poetic text into three stages. The first, called the "sensory factor," pertains to the sound of poetic language; the second, the "immediate reproductive factor," relates to the meaning of words generated directly by their sounds; the third, the "mediated reproductive factor," is the group of images evoked by the meanings of words and sentences" [*ibid.*: 7-8].

Let us begin with the "sensory factor." Like many other students of poetry of his day, Zich was primarily interested in isolating the musical quality of poetic language. But in contrast to many of them (e.g., Sievers, Ejxenbaum), he rejected any attempt to root this quality in intonation and treat it simply as melodics. Poetic musicality is a "phonic rather than a tonic quality," he argued. It is a "*phonic quality* created by the grouping of speech sounds according to particular *rules*, which are grasped intuitively" [*ibid.*: 25]. By formalizing these rules, Zich arrived at four basic types of speech sound organization in poetry: the *frequent* or *selected* repetition of vowels and consonants; the *temporary omission* of some vowels and consonants; the *repetition of a vocalic sequence in syllables*; and the *repetition of speech sound groups* [*ibid.*: 15].

In addition to speech sounds, the sensorily perceptible stratum of poetry consists of rhythm—the division of the continuous speech flow into segments. According to Zich, there are two main criteria for this division. First, there is *logical* segmentation based on the *meaning* of the utterance; it divides an utterance into words and sentences. On the other hand, *metrical* segmentation exists apart from the meaning of the utterance and divides it on the basis of *sound*, creating units such as feet and lines. Though Zich considered "metrical rhythmicization more or less independent of the logical" [*ibid*.: 16], in actual poetic speech these two principles always interact. The scope of this interaction is indicated by the scale: prose..... rhythmical prose.....free rhythmical verse.....strictly rhythmical verse.

Zich's analyses of the sound stratum of verbal art were quite similar to some of the early Russian formalist studies of the essence of poetic language written at about the same time. However, Zich went beyond the formalists in considering the word not merely a sound configuration, but a sign—a unity of sound and meaning. As he insisted, "human language—the material of poetic works—has *two aspects*: phonic and semantic. They are closely connected and we cannot separate them without violating the essence of language" [*ibid*.: 109]. By depriving language of either of these aspects we turn it into two different systems: gesticulation or music.

Following the sensory factor is the second stage in our perception of verbal art, that of the "immediate reproductive factor," which is comprised of the meanings of words—the ideas or concepts conventionally linked to particular sound configurations.

The third stage is constituted by the "mediated reproductive factor," the images evoked in us by the meanings of words and sentences. This stage differs essentially from the other two. Whereas sound and meaning are indispensable to the existence of verbal art, sensory images are not. As we know from our own experience, "there are great poetic works which do not have imagistic values at least in some of their parts...and yet do not suffer because of this lack" [*ibid*.: 110]. For this reason Zich declares that images are not essential to the poetic work. This assertion, of course, was not completely new in his time. Already at the turn of the century the psychologists belonging to the Wurzburg School (Marbe, Mayer, Orth, etc.) had demonstrated experimentally their thesis of "imageless thought" and this idea had relevance for students of literature as well   [see Meyer, 1901:8] To some extent it also parallels Zich's earlier observations about the secondary nature of extra-musical associations in the perception of music. But in seeing literature as an interplay between sound and meaning, Zich was a forerunner of the early structuralist concept of verbal art [see Mukařovský, 1928].

This cursory look at Zich's ideas brings us to the end of our survey. During Zich's lifetime the Prague Linguistic Circle was founded and modern semiotics came into existence in Bohemia. But it would be wrong to assume that this development was motivated purely by domestic impulses. Without any doubt the ideas of Saussure, Husserl, and Buhler were more instrumental sources of structuralist semiotics in Bohemia than the local tradition. However, when these ideas arrived in Bohemia they took root in a soil that was fully prepared for such an intellectual development. The native tradition of semiotics, in the persons of Bolzano, Durdík, Marty, and Zich, left a fertile heritage, the importance of which we are only now beginning to appreicate.

REFERENCES

Bogatyrev, P. 1937-38. "Príspevok ku skúmaniu divadelných znakov," *Slovenské smery umelecké a kritické*, 5.

Bolzano, B. 1930. *Wissenschaftslehre*, vol.3, 2nd ed. (Leipzig).

Boring, E. 1929. *A History of Experimental Psychology* (New York).

Brentano, F. 1874. *Psychologie vom empirischen Standpunkte* (Leipzig).

_____. 1911. *Zur Klassifikation der psychischen Phänomene* (Leipzig).

Durdík, J. 1875. *Všeobecná aesthetika* (Prague).

_____. 1881a. *O filosofii a činnosti Bernarda Bolzana. Řeč na oslavu stoletých jeho narozenin* (Prague).

_____. 1881b. *Poetika jakožto aesthetika umění básnického* (Prague).

_____. 1913, 1914. "Útvary básnické," *Česká mysl*, 13, 14.

Havránek, B. et al. 1935. "Úvodem," *Slovo a slovesnost*, 1.

Humboldt, W. von. 1907. *Gesammelte Schriften*, vol. 7, part 1 (Berlin).

Karcevskij, S. 1929. "Du dualisme asymétrique du signe linguistique," *Travaux du Cercle linguistique de Prague*, 1.

Marty, A. 1875. *Ursprung der Sprache* (Würzburg).

_____. 1884. "Über subjektlose Sätze und das Verhältnis der Grammatik zur Logik und Psychologie," see *Gesammelte Schriften*, vol. 2, part 1.

_____. 1884-92. "Über Sprachreflex, Nativismus und absichtliche Sprachbildung," see *Gesammelte Schriften*, vol. 1, part 2.

_____. 1893. "Über das Verhältnis von Grammatik und Logik," see *Gesammelte Schriften*, vol.2, part 2.

_____. 1897. "Über die Scheidung von grammatischen, logischen und psychologischen Subject resp.Prädikat," see *Gesammelte Schriften*, vol. 2, part 1.

_____. 1908. *Untersuchungen zur Grundlegung einer allgemeinen Grammatik und Sprachphilosophie.* vol. 1 (Halle).

_____. 1910. *Zur Sprachphilosophie. Die "logische," "lokalistische" und andere Kasustheorien* (Halle).

_____. 1916, 1918,1920. *Gesammelte Schriften*, vols. 1;2, part 1; part 2 (Halle).

Meyer, Th. 1901. *Das Stilgesetz der Poesie* (Leipzig).

Mukařovský, J. 1928. *Máchův Máj. Estetická studie* (Prague).

_____. 1938. "Dénomination poétique et la fonction esthétique de la langue," *Actes du Quatrième congrès international des linguistes*, ed. L. Hjelmslev, et al. (Copenhagen).

_____. 1940. "O jazyce básnickém," *Slovo a slovesnost*, 6.

_____. 1943. "Záměrnost a nezáměrnost v umění," see *Studie z estetiky* (Prague, 1966).

Novák, M. 1941. *Česká estetika od Palackého po dobu současnou* (Prague).

Sus, O. 1958. "Sémantický problém 'významové představy' u O. Zicha a J. Volkelta," *Sborník prací filosofické fakulty Brněnské university*, F2 (Brno).

Veltruský, J. 1976. "Contribution to the Semiotics of Acting," *Sound, Sign and Meaning*, ed. L. Matejka (Ann Arbor).

Walther, E. 1971. "Einleitung," *Rot*, 43.

Zich, O. 1911. "Estetické vnímání hudby. Psychologický rozbor," *Věstník Královské české společnosti nauk: Třída filosoficko-historicko-jazykozpytná: Ročník 1910* (Prague).

_____. 1917-18. "O typech básnických," *Časopis pro moderní filologii a literaturu*, 6.

_____. 1921. "Estetická příprava mysli," *Česká mysl*, 17.

_____. 1923. "Loutkové divadlo," *Drobné umění-Výtvarné snahy*, 4.

_____. 1931. *Estetika dramatického umění. Teoretická dramaturgie* (Prague).

ON THE RELATION OF VERBAL AND NONVERBAL ART
IN EARLY PRAGUE SEMIOTICS : JAN MUKAŘOVSKÝ

Thomas G. Winner

It was only in the 1930's, some two thousand years after the beginning of semiotic thinking, that aesthetic questions began to be addressed in a systematic manner. While many questions that we find considered in Plato and Aristotle, such as the problem of naming and of mimesis, may be seen as touching upon important areas later to be taken up by semiotic aesthetics, such as the critical question of iconicity, and while Peirce and Saussure had envisaged a broad field of semiotics that would encompass all possible communicative systems, both verbal and nonverbal, the questions of the arts and the interrelationship of the main arts to each other and to other cultural systems, were not addressed by Peirce and Saussure and received little attention in earlier semiotic writings.

It was thus not until the second and third decade of the present century that questions of the semiotics of the arts were treated systematically; this occurred simultaneously with the elaboration of a new, overall semiotic theory, following, and elaborating, Saussurian postulates, based fundamentally on the model of natural language. In the work of the Moscow Linguistic Circle and the OPOJAZ in the 1910s and 1920s, and especially the Prague Linguistic Circle in the 1920s and 1930s, Saussurian linguistic theories were expanded in the direction of a general semiotics of verbal communication. A new epistemological approach to problems of aesthetic perception and creation, and to the problem of the structuration and signification of aesthetic texts was elaborated by a group of highly original scholars: linguists, aestheticians, and folklorists. Most of these early works in aesthetic semiotics were concerned with verbal communication, and it was not until the late 1930s that semiotic theories of the nonverbal arts were evolved in the Prague Linguistic Circle, setting the stage for elaborating theories of inter-art translation. It is of this development that this paper will treat.

The investigation of the nonverbal arts and their relation to the verbal arts has had a distinguished history in the Czech lands in the works of Otakar Hostinský (1847-1910) and Otakar Zich (1887-1934). Hostinský's work lay primarily in the field of musicology, and he was particularly interested in the Wagnerian concept of opera as a *Gesamtkunstwerk* (Hostinský, 1971).

While Hostinský's aesthetic view emanated from Herbartian aesthetic formalism, with its emphasis on the formal structure of music, he also attempted
to connect the language of music with that of the other arts and with social
phenomena in general (e.g. Hostinský, 1873). Hostinský's gifted pupil, Otakar
Zich, worked in the area of general aesthetics, musicology, drama and verse.
In all these areas, he considered the task of aesthetic studies to be the examination of the artistic construction of the work of art as well as its specific
function and signification. Anticipating the work of modern semiotic structuralism, Zich saw the structuration of the work of art as a live and dynamic
process, and the work of art itself as a hierarchical system in which the levels
are related to each other in dynamic, ever-changing processes (e.g. Zich,
1931). Again anticipating the later work of Roman Jakobson and Jan Mukařovský, Zich concerned himself with the significant question, later to be taken
up by semiotic pragmatics, of the reception of the work of art (Zich, 1910)
in a manner that can be labeled pre-semiotic. While some interesting work on
Hostinský and Zich, these two pioneers in modern aesthetics, has been done,
especially by the Czech aesthetician Oleg Sus, a systematic study of these
very important figures is still very much needed today in order to redress the
balance on the history of semiotic theory.

While early structural semiotic studies were primarily based on the
model of natural language, that is in the arts on verbal art, the possibility
of a study of other communicative systems, their interrelationship and their
relationship to culture in general, was given in the late 1920s in a new poetic
stance that questioned the immanence and closedness of structures that had
been implied by Herbartian aesthetics and adopted as a battlecry by the
Russian Formalists. Already in 1923, Roman Jakobson had implicitly questioned the immanence of the work of verbal art by demonstrating how certain
formal features of Czech verse must be seen as functioning within the total
system of the Czech language (cf. Jakobson, 1923). And in 1928, Jakobson
and Tynjanov had discussed poetry and oral art in terms of social function
and in terms of their relative dependence upon cultural norms. In their now
celebrated joint statement of 1928, Jakobson and Tynjanov challenged, for
the first time explicitly, the isolation of the work of art from other cultural
phenomena, and replaced the concept of immanence and closedness with
that of autonomy. At that time, they defined the work of art as autonomous,
because it is organized according to its own internal laws of structuration
and evolves according to these. Thus the work of art must not be reduced to
other phenomena. Nevertheless, the work of art is never totally closed and
isolated, but exists in rather complex relations to other structures (Jakobson
and Tynjanov, 1928:37). We may consider this a key statement that leads

fruitfully into later investigations of interrelationships of individual works of art, or sets of works of art, to their senders, to real and potential receivers, as well as to other artistic works and sets of artistic works, making possible semiotic inter-art and intra-art comparative studies.

While his most voluminous work was to be on the verbal arts, Zich's talented student, Jan Mukařovský, significantly advanced not only the semiotic study of the nonverbal arts, but also investigated the problem which became focal for the work of the Prague Linguistic Circle, that of the interrelation of the arts to each other. In the early 1930s, Mukařovský sought to defend the Formalist view of closedness of systems, but, in 1934, in a review of the Czech translation of Šklovskij's influential *Theory of Prose*, Mukařovský decided against this assumption and, for the first time, spoke of art as one aspect of social communicative phenomena, with the latter defined as multiple structures, each of which has its own autonomous evolution, but all of which interact in complex ways (Mukařovský, 1934:349). Shortly after the Second World War, Mukařovský began to explain the interrelations of structures as composing a dynamic hierarchy, and, finally, a "systems of systems," a position which significantly anticipates that of the much later Moscow-Tartu School which sees all culture as a complex semiotic system for the storage and transmission of information. Mukařovský writes:

> ... Structuralism, which more than any other scientific orientation is aimed at the totality of phenomena-since structure itself is by definition a totality-had to touch, during its evolution, increasingly on problems lying outside the structure of the work of art: as soon as a certain view was obtained about the composition of the artistic structure and its movement, structures of a higher order began to become outlined behind it, structures of which the structure of a given art is only an element. It becomes clear that if we want to understand the evolution of a certain branch of the arts, we must examine that art and its problematics in connection with the other arts. . . . Furthermore, art is one of the branches of culture and culture as a whole, in turn, forms a structure, the individual elements of which (for example art, science, politics) are in mutual, complex, and historically changeable, relations to each other (1946-47: 50).

Mukařovský's and Jakobson's semiotic approach to the various arts in the 1930s laid a new basis for comparative studies. In the 1930s both scholars wrote about the nonverbal arts as well, covering film, music, the visual arts, architecture, as well as the theatre.

The Visual Arts

The early proponents of semiotic aesthetics, Jakobson and Mukařovský, both by professional training closer to verbal than to nonverbal communication, were soon attracted also to the other arts. Mukařovský's interest in the verbal arts was complemented by his writing on the visual arts, architecture, the theatre and film, while Jakobson added to his repertoire of linguistic and poetic studies his trenchant observations on the visual arts, music and film. In two recent interviews, Jakobson speaks of the fundamental influence which the nonverbal arts had on the development of his semiotic direction, and states that his association with the Cubo-Futurist painters and his exposure to modern music had a more seminal influence on his semiotic thinking than the theoretical writings of scholars. He names among those artists who have exercised their most profound influence upon him the most significant representatives of he European avant-garde in the verbal, visual, and musical arts: Picasso, Braque, Xlebnikov, Joyce and Stravinsky (Jakobson, 1967a:281). Clearly, if one were to search for a common feature of the art of the 1910s, 1920s and 1930s, one of the salient aspects uniting them would have to be the close interrelation of all the arts. This is true especially of the visual and the verbal arts. We know that many futurist poets were also active as painters (e.g. David Burljuk, Elena Guro, V. Majakovskij, and A. Kručennyx, to name only a few), and that futurist poetry itself was highly syncretic, frequently combining the auditory and lingual with the visual aspect of the poem, through particular arrangement of the line and/ or letters and, at times, even the use of special paper on which the verse was printed. The hegemony of the visual arts in the first two decades of our century, noted by Grygar (1973), is expressed aptly by Xlebnikov, when he says: "We want the verbal arts to follow boldly in the footsteps of painting" (Xlebnikov, 1940:334). This same close interconnection between the visual and the verbal arts is characteristic of the Czech avantgarde during the 1920s and 1930s, when Jakobson and Mukařovský were active in the Prague Linguistic Circle. Suffice it to remember that Karel Teige, the foremost theoretical spokesman of the Czech avantgarde, first entered this sphere of art as a painter, strongly influenced, as Effenberger has pointed out (Effenberger 1974: 6, 10), by analytical cubism.

While Roman Jakobson's remarkable contribution to the theory of visual art was to come much later (1964, 1967b, 1970) in his important discussions of the problem of linearity and simultaneity in both visual and audial semiotic systems, remarks about the visual arts are sprinkled throughout his writings of the 1930s. Perhaps the most crucial early Jakobsonian contribution to the area of the interrelation of the arts occurs in his article on Pasternak's prose (1935), where he talks, in historical terms, about the hierarchical relation of the arts to each other and the relative value culture places on the individual arts: the visual arts dominate in the age of Classicism, Romanticism is oriented towards music, while the visual arts are the dominant value of the Futurists (1935:358-9).

Having dealt with Roman Jakobson's keen observation on the interrelation of the art elsewhere (Winner, 1975), I shall limit myself here to an account of the crucial contribution of Mukařovský to this area of investigation. Mukařovský worked in all nonverbal artistic areas, with the exception of music. We have trenchant essays on film (1933, second half of 1930), the theatre (e.g. 1937a), architecture (1937b) and many essays on the visual arts. His essays on the visual arts and on film are of particular significance, for they lay the groundwork for which broad inter-art research in contemporary semiotics. Here I am proposing to discuss his work on the visual arts as his most important and most productive contribution to the nonverbal arts.

Mukařovský's first attempt to inquire into the visual arts, and to define, at least in an initial manner, the relation of the arts to each other, appears in an essay published in 1935 which has quite unjustly been neglected in the critical literature. In this essay, recently translated under the title "Dialectic Contradictions in Modern Art", Mukařovský attempts to define certain dichotomies in modern art, and to confront the question of the common denominator of modern art.

The problems of meaning in modern art had first been stated in structural terms by Jakobson, in his essay on futurism (Jakobson, 1919) in which he emphasized the new stress on internal relations within the work of art and the abandonment of static space and linear time in cubist aesthetics, leading him to talk, more than four decades later, of a violent shift in modern art in the relations between signifier and signified on the one hand and sign and denotate on the other (1965:11). Mukařovský approaches this problem in a similar manner, but with a slightly different perspective. For him, the important element uniting modern art is the fact that through manipulation of the perceiving individual the work of art is most intensely experienced as a sign (1935:129), and he raises some important questions regarding the relation of art to the individual. Clearly, Cubism, which is no longer organized along the line of the temporal and spatial perceptions of one unifying point of view and which substitutes a multiple perspective, acts to suppress the individual as a focal mechanism in the unification of the work of art. Similar patterns pertain in the verbal arts that experiment with various time structures (e.g. Joyce, Broch, Faulkner, Belyj), and in modern music that has abandoned the single perspective implied by the diatonic scale with its dominant harmonies and stable tonal and rhythmical relations. The Surrealists' intense interest in the individual's subconscious would seem to return to the individual as the mediator between art and reality.But, as Mukařovský sees it, the Surrealists have abandoned the traditional socio-psychological individual of Romanticism who is activated by a conscious will. Instead, the personality is reduced, as he says, to biological forces (the *id*), or the subconscious, no longer constrained by cultural norms or conscious superegos, and not even integrated into an ego. Free of such inhibitions, we see nature, not culture—an interesting insight into the whole nature/culture dichotomy so important in later cultural semiotics. Mukařovský's thesis then is that in all modern art the individual is suppressed as a unifying agent; that all modern art is thus essentially multi-perspectival. And Mukařovský holds that the lack of a unifying perspective causes the dialectical oppositions inherent in all arts to be perceived in a sharper manner. Mukařovský lists seven contradictions, inherent to all art, but sharply dramatized in modern art:

1. *The aesthetic function/other functions*. There is always a tension between a work of art perceived in its aesthetic function and perceived as dominated by another function. This opposition pervades all art. The aesthetic function can be stressed at the expense of all other functions (for instance the "pure painting" of the Suprematists in which color and line remain entities which are "self-valuable" to the extreme, leading to a painting of pure form, similar to the poetry of "pure sound" of dada and the Russian *zaum* poets). But there is also the opposite perspective. One can think of art in which the aesthetic function is seemingly entirely suppressed, and where the suppression is itself a focal aspect of the art. Here we might use as examples pop-art paintings with which Mukařovský was not familiar in his time, for instance Warhole's tomato soup cans. This suppression of the aesthetic function becomes an aesthetic value in itself (*Ibid.*, 136).

2. *Art/Individual Psychic Life*. In the pragmatic sphere, Mukařovský notes, art may create tension by virtue of its being an expression of the mental state of the Addressor, the Receiver, or both. This is opposed to the more traditional role of art as an objective sign, mediating between the members of a collective.

3. *The Work of Art as an Autonomous Sign/The Work of Art as a Referential Sign*. The work of art oscillates between "truth" and fiction. Whether we can say that a work of art is "true" or not becomes, itself, a most important aspect of the inner structuration of the work of art. The problem was investigated with great care in one of Mukařovský's later and most ambitious essays on aesthetic function, aesthetic norm and aesthetic value (1936). The antimony between the autonomous, as opposed to the referential, function of the artistic sign is a basic issue in modern art. Such an oscillation dominates in Cubist painting that breaks up objects by destroying

their actual outline, but on the other hand emphasizes objectivity by allowing the work of art to be viewed (of course synechdocically) simultaneously from many perspectival points in order to make its unity felt as a crystallizing point in space, independent of the personal perspective of the viewing subject. In Surrealism this contradiction is even more striking, if less subtle, because Surrealism presents us with seemingly realistic objects, but suggests, by placing these objects into nonhabitual and nonreal contexts, that these things are merely metaphors of a nonobjective meaning of the whole (*Ibid,* 141). Nor is this antimony lost in Suprematism. Even though Suprematism is seemingly completely nonobjective, in another sense in a Suprematist painting the artistic sign becomes an object itself. A Suprematist painting becomes an object among objects to such a degree that one can think of serial productions of the painting, and this of course leads to the art of the 1950s and 1960s and 1970s, and especially to pop-art.

4. *Material as Such/Material as Part of Artistic Structure.* The work of art can exploit material either positively or negatively. That means it can either violate the material or actualize it. In this sense, modern art is again highly dialectical, drawing attention to the nature of the material and thus letting it stand in opposition to artistic structure. Hence, as Mukařovský remarks (*ibid.,* 142), the predilection of modern art for unusual materials. Again, examples from contemporary art would be the large area of "found art" such as the juxtaposition of utilitarian objects to the artistic structure which they imply (Duchamps, Kolář, and the entire problem posed by the modern concept of collage or montage).

5. *Art/Nonart.* Modern art is preoccupied with ways to express the antithesis between art and other products of human activity. For example, the painting by René Margritte which represents a simple, completely realistically painted, tobacco pipe and the subscript which, in the careful writing of a French school primer, says "ceci n'est pas une pipe", clearly is a meta-painting stressing this tension. Similarly, the famous bicycle wheel by Duchamps, his bottle rack, or his "shocking" pissoir, express other human products, yet presents them as art, forcing the viewer to reflect on the apparent absurdity and contradiction.

6. *Contradictions Between the Various Arts.* Every art implies a path towards another art, stressing components dominant in another art. (Thus, poetry and music are linked by the stress on rhythm and sound.) The interrelations between the arts can be extremely complex. Mukařovský cites Wagner's concept of opera as a total work of art as something directly in-

fluenced by structural concepts of the verbal arts, whereas some literature
(e.g. Thomas Mann), is in turn strongly influenced by music.

In a lecture presented at the opening of an exposition of two Czech
Surrealist painters, Jindřich Štyrský and Toyen (1938), and announced as a
talk about Surrealism, Mukařovský touched on the general noetic and
aesthetic principles active in the art of the twentieth century in a manner
thoroughly anticipating modern Moscow-Tartu theories of the semiotics of
culture and of the interrelation of art and ideology as well as science. In a
brilliantly conceived article, published in 1973, V.V. Ivanov (1973), basing
himself on the writings of the scientific conceptions of time and space by
the Russian philosopher Pavel Florenskij elaborated a complex system, in
which he related the concepts of relativized time and space, focal problems
of modern art, to concepts of modern physics and contemporary philosophy.
Already thirty-five years before this, Mukařovský had posited that the revolutionary new scientific concepts of time and of space, as well as the totally
novel view of causality, were fundamental to the avantgarde arts of the
1920s. It is not surprising that Mukařovský found in Surrealism, flourish-
ing in Czechoslovakia, the indicators of this artistic, philosophical insight.
He concentrates on the painting of the two principal representatives of
Czech surrealist painting, Štyrský and Toyen. Here the surreal, bodiless
heads, the empty clothes which already by their plasticity anticipate the dead
bodies that they will enshroud, the face which is at the same time a burned
book, the "femme introuvable" by Margritte and the five left hands, like
the elements of a cubist canvas, are synechdoches. In both Cubism and
Surrealism, these parts represent a totality. But while in Cubist paintings the
many synechdochal planes create a multiperspectival point of view, in the
painting of Surrealism, the "torso", by its incompleteness, implies its own
separation from the reality role of the object depicted. Thus the "part"
changes from a simple object into a phantom, because it is represented as
separate from its practical and objective relationships. This dreamlike separation from reality means that the art object obtains an indefinite relation
to space and time: "There is no other up and down, forward and backward,
than that which the thing itself determines by its own motion" (310). Mukařovský maintains that Surrealist painting and Surrealist poetry, unlike the
art of the Cubists, stress not the sign, but the things and objects signified
by the sign. The thing represented, rather than the sign itself, according
to Mukařovský, are signs, since such objects take over the role of something
which stands for something else (311). Thus, the thing represented becomes
a new sign in its own right, which "stands for" some reality outside of it.

We may ask what really Mukařovský means by this statement. Cubist
painting portrays, among other things, the purely formal relation of fundamental shapes, colors, etc. to each other. Oppositions as color harmony

versus contrast, motion versus static, up versus down, far versus near, triangles versus cubes and cones, are all relatively independent aesthetic principles. After we have seen Braque's violins, we have a certain apprehension of spatial arrangements and musical atmosphere, but our view of violins as objects of use or of everyday life is not fundamentally changed. But René Margritte's "The Red Model" (1935), which represents a pair of boots which are half boots and half naked feet, does not place in the foreground formal aesthetic oppositions. But the painting may alter our perception of objects like boots and feet; for the grotesque combination of the uncombinable disturbs our perception of things "out there", and forces us to conceive objects in the "world out there" in a slightly metaphorical way.

3. Thus we may conclude by observing that already in the 1930s and 1940s, giant strides were being made towards semiotic syntheses of the arts as inter-related structures, laying the basis for modern semiotic comparative studies which relate the various arts to each other and to other cultural sets. For Mukařovský's comparative art used as its data not individual works seen as independent values, but rather entire evolutionary sets seen in polar relation-ships (1941:1). Mukařovský's suggestion that the relation of structures belong-ing to different arts is analogous to the relations between literatures of diff-erent national languages (*ibid.*:3) foresaw many later trends in inter-art and intra-art semiotics. However, the criterion of material, which Mukařovský felt. was so important in distinguishing the arts (*ibid.*), seems hardly adequate today for his ambitious purposes. As he wrote, the various arts are distinguished from each other primarily by the material of which they are constructed: language for the verbal arts, stone in sculpture, color and shapes in painting, tone for music, etc. Reacting against the traditional division of the arts into time arts (literature, music), spatial arts (the visual arts) and syntheses of these two (theatre, cinema, etc.), Mukařovský omitted these criteria entirely. What he is telling us, indirectly at least, is that the material is the only difference sep-arating the arts from each other. And no matter what the material, that is what art we are considering, they all engage the same aesthetic processes, they all present the same dialectical oscillations, and the same freedoms from trad-itional time and space structures. Thus here also, we may see Mukařovský as a pioneer. For he clearly anticipated many problems taken up in semiotic writings of the 1960s and 1970s regarding the relationships of spatial and temporal structures in the arts, linear and non-linear texts, sequentiality and non-sequentiality. Thus, as Jakobson, Lotman, and others have more recently demonstrated, simultaneity is not absent from the so-called linear texts, such as musical and literary texts, and temporality is an important aspect also of the so-called spatial, non-temporal arts, such as painting.

In his broad attempts to relate the arts to each other and to culture in particular, Mukařovský has anticipated much that modern semiotic theory has developed in the 1960s and 1970s. It was perhaps Mukařovský's particular genius to sense the importance of simultaneous and shifting points of view, changes of function in art, changes in the relation of signifier and signified, and of sign to denotate, as they affected the dynamics not only of the work of art itself, but also of the interpretor. Such an open-minded and insightful approach stimulated further semiotic investigations and continues to provide cues for new advances.

REFERENCES

Effenberger, Vratislav. 1974. Od "stavby básně" k surrealistické semiologii. Unpublished manuscript.

Grygar, Mojmír. 1973. Kubizm i poèzija russkogo i češskogo avangarda, in *Structures of Texts and Semiotics of Culture,* edited by Jan Van Der Eng and Mojmír Grygar. The Hague-Paris (Mouton): 59-101.

Hostinský, O. 1871. *Richard Wagner.* Praha.

_____ . 1873. *Darwin a drama.* Praha. Lumír.

Ivanov, V.V. 1973. Kategorija vremeni v iskusstve i kul'ture XX veka. In *Structures of Texts and Semiotics of Culture.* Edited by Jan Van Der Eng and M. Grygar. Paris-The Hague (Mouton): 103-150.

Jakobson, Roman. 1919. Futurizm. *Iskusstvo* (Moscow) August 2. Cited from Jakobson, *Questions de la poétique,* edited by Tzvetan Todorov. Paris (Seuil): 25-30.

_____ . 1923. *O češskom stixe, preimuščestvenno v sopostavlenii s russkim.* Berlin. Reprinted as Brown University Slavic Reprint, edited by Thomas G. Winner.

_____ . 1935. Randbemerkungen zur Prosa des *Dichters* Pasternak. *Slavische Rundschau.* Praha. VII:357-74.

_____ . 1964. On Visual and Auditory Signs. *Phonetica XI. E Zwirner gewidmet,* 216-220.

_____ . 1965. Vers une science de l'art poétique. In *Théorie de la littérature. Textes des formalistes russes.* Edited and translated by Tzvetan Todorov. Paris (Seuil): 9-13.

_____ . 1967a. Questionner Jakobson. Jean Pierre Faye. *Nouvelle revue française.* Cited from *Le récit hunique.* Paris 1967:273-285.

_____ . 1967b. About the Relation Between Visual and Audial Signs. *Models for the Perception of Speech and Visual Forms*. Edited by W. Watten Dunn. Cambridge, Mass.:1-7.

_____ . 1970. On the Verbal Art of William Blake and other Poet-Painters. *Linguistic Inquiry*. I.1:3-23.

_____ & Jurij Tynjanov. 1928. Problemy izučenija literatury i jazyka. *Novyj LEF* (Moscow).

Mukařovský, Jan. 1934. K českému překladu Šklovského Teorie prózy. *Čin* VI: 123-30. Cited from *Kapitoly z české poetiky* I:344-50.

_____ . 1935. Dialektické rozpory v moderním umění. *Listy pro umění a kritiku* III. Cited from *Studie z estetiky*. Praha 1966:255-65'

_____ . 1936. *Estetická funkce, norma a hodnota jako sociální fakty*. Praha (Borový). Cited from *Studie z estetiky*. Praha 1966: 17-54.

_____ . 1938. K noetice a poetice surrealismu v malířství. *Slovenské smery umelecké a kritické*, roč. V. 1938. č.6-8:226-30. Cited from *Studie z estetiky*. Praha 1966:309-311.

_____ . 1941. Mezi poezii a výtvarnictvím. *Slovo a slovesnost* VII: 1-16.

_____ . 1946-47. Problémy individua v umění. University Lecture. Printed from ms. in *Cestami poetiky a estetiky*. Praha. (Československý spisovatel.)

Winner, T.G. 1975. Grands thèmes de la poétique jakobsonienne. L'Arc (Paris) No. 60. *Roman Jakobson: Sémiologie, Poétique, Epistémologie*:55-63.

Xlebnikov, V. *Neizdannye proizvedenija*. Pod red. N. Xardžieva i T. Gric. Moscow.

Zich, O. 1910. *Estetické vnímání hudby*. Praha.

_____ . 1931. *Estetika dramatického umění*. Praha.

TOPICS IN ISRAELI POETICS AND SEMIOTICS

Nomi Tamir-Ghez

An Israeli school of poetics, with a consistent theoretical framework, emerged in the 1960's. Its main concern was theory of literature and poetics, with emphasis on combining structural poetics with analysis of individual texts and works by particular authors, historical poetics, and later—general semiotics and semiotics of culture. The school centered around its founder and major figure—Benjamin Hrushovski —whose lectures on the language of poetry and theory of the literary text (delivered in the mid 1950's and early 1960's) served as the main impetus for the new trend. Hrushovski's approach of systematic poetics in the formalist-structuralist and phenomenological tradition soon gained enthusiastic followers. Several members of this group became the core of the Department of Poetics and Comparative Literature, founded by Hrushovski in 1966 at Tel-Aviv University. In 1968 the journal *Ha-Sifrut* (Literature) was launched, and became the major organ of literary theory and poetics in Israel. In 1975 Hrushovski established The Porter Institute for Poetics and Semiotics at Tel-Aviv University, and later founded *PTL*, an international Journal for Descriptive Poetics and Theory of Literature (the first issue appeared in January 1976).

As will become clear later in my discussion, some of the basic theoretical assumptions of the group can be traced back to influences of Russian Formalism (mostly in its later stage) and Czech Structuralism (e.g. emphasis on the dynamics of the text; awareness of literature as a system of norms, or poly-system, etc.). However, following the phenomenology of the literary object as proposed mainly by Roman Ingarden, the text is conceived as a complex structure which has to be "actualized" or "concretized" by the reader in order to become an aesthetic object.

In the 1950's Hrushovski's work was devoted mainly to studies in poetics, showing the systematicity of literary phenomena that seemed at the time to be only individually organized in each specific text (focusing on prosody and figurative language). Searching for systems of norms in poetic texts, he demonstrated that even for something as "free" as free verse one can formulate a systematic theory (see Hrushovski , 1954, 1960). Later he shifted his main interest from the language of poetry to the literary text, or more precisely to the *system* of the text (in Mukařovský's sense of the term). Because of this affinity to the principles of Czech Structuralism the Israeli group called itself for a while "Neo-Structuralism."

In the early 1960's Hrushovski developed the outline of his unified theory of the literary text. This theory has served, and still does, as a background for many studies done by members of the group. Some of these studies consist of applications of the theory or of development of some of its aspects. Naturally, some of the group went in new directions. However, even in works of such scholars the influence of Hrushovski's teachings is prominent and widely acknowledged.

Because of limited space, I will only briefly consider here a few of the major studies and theories developed by the Tel-Aviv group. Unfortunately, many important studies done by members of this group, as well as by other Israeli scholars interested in semiotic problems (e.g. philosophy of language, linguistics) will have to be discussed on another occasion. For a fuller account of the early years of Israeli semiotics see Ben-Porat and Hrushovski (1974). See also Kaufman (1974) for a bibliography.

Theory of the Literary Text

Hrushovski's ambitious "Unified Theory of the Literary Text" aims at accounting for the unique and complex nature of the literary object.[1] Most literary theories until quite recently dealt with isolated aspects of the text, typically with either the "lowest" units of the text—the sound stratum (prosody) and isolated words and phrases (stylistics)—or with the large structures which are abstracted from the text—plot, characters, ideas, etc. Hrushovski's theory, on the other hand, deals also with the wide in-between no-man's land, and shows how we arrive from the printed page to the larger structures, or, in other words, what is involved in the process of reading and understanding a literary text.[2]

The text is seen as a highly complex network of patterns of different types (a pattern being a link of two or more elements in the text, constructed by any means whatsoever). The elements or materials which are linked by the reader to construct any pattern can be either *continuous*

---

[1]For an outline of the theory see Hrushovski (1976a), and Ben-Porat and Hrushovski (1974: 13-23).

[2]This subject, which Hrushovski has been studying and commenting upon since the early 1960's, was recently taken up also by other theorists, who usually enlist logical procedures and theories such as the "possible worlds theory," presuppositions, implicatures, etc. in order to solve the problem (see, for example, van Dijk, ed., 1976). It seems to me that Hrushovski's theory offers a more comprehensive answer.

(as in meter) or *discontinuous* (as in rhymes), and they can be either of *homogeneous* or of *heterogeneous* material; rhymes or alliterations are made of homogeneous elements ("inherent" aspects of sound), while a pattern such as a plot is made of heterogeneous materials—event-statements, dialogues, descriptions etc.[3] Moreover, not all the links are formally or explicitly indicated by the text. The reader is usually faced with many gaps, ellipses, unlinked units, which he has to link and fill in through an active and complex trial-and-error process.

The patterns in any text are organized on two levels: (1) the level of the text-continuum; (2) the reconstructed level. Characters, plot, ideas, time, space, etc. are built by the reader from discontinuous elements in the text and are reorganized according to their inherent principles (e.g. reorganization of time elements in a chronological order). It is this reconstructed level which is usually dealt with in literary theories, though critics rarely distinguish between what is given in the text and what is added and reconstructed by the reader.

Ideas, characters, plots, are presented to us, though, through a language continuum which unfolds step by step, from one sentence to another, from one paragraph to another. This level of the text has been practically overlooked in previous theories. While the text-continuum is aimed at providing material for the construction of a "world" (by the reader), it has its own rules of progression and organization. The author has to justify shifts from sentence to sentence and from scene to scene. The result is a high degree of organization of the text-continuum, quite different in character from the organization of the reconstructed level. The general principle of the unfolding of the literary text is the "principle of unprincipled progression": unpredictable shifts from description to ideas to dialogue, from generalizations to details, etc., and back again. The text is usually divided into many small segments with a whole network of "motivations" for the introduction and closure of the segments, with shifters from one segment to another, with transitions from one semantic focus to another, etc. Some of the "motivations" or justifications of the segmentation are formal (e.g. the division of a novel into chapters or a poem into strophic groups), but mostly segments are based on "semantic groupings." Hrushovski (1976a: 23-29) deals at length with the different modes and forms of segmentation, and analyzes the first chapters of *War and Peace* as an example. Although we cannot discuss all the details here, there are basically two kinds of techniques

[3]For a fuller account of the different types of patterns and principles of linking elements see Hrushovski (1976a: 4-5) and Ben-Porat and Hrushovski (1974: 18-20).

for presenting the text continuum: (1) overall principles of segmentation, overlapping with each other and dividing the whole text into smaller parts; (2) principles of step-by-step transitions. In addition to the ordered segmentation there are dynamic uses of chains of semantic and other material running through parts of the text.

A most important part of the theory is the description of the relations of units of the two levels.[4] It is crucial to realize that the segments—the units of the text-continuum—differ from the units of the reconstructed level. On the reconstructed level we are dealing with literary patterns (rhyme, metaphor, plot, etc.) which are constructed from at least *two* language elements. In the text continuum there is no language material or segments which belong exclusively to one pattern. This means: (1) no "pure" literary units are to be found on the level of the text. Literary units emerge only as a result of abstracting material from dispersed places in the text, and connecting them according to some principle. Thus a rhyme is a pattern of sound, abstracted from the other aspects of the words (e.g. their meaning); (2) every unit of the text contimuum (word, sentence, scene) may serve as a *junction* where different patterns intersect. In other words, every such unit may contribute to a number of heterogeneous and discontinuous patterns. Every pattern on the reconstructed level abstracts from the text continuum those aspects which are relevant to its nature.[5]

Integrational Semantics

The two levels of the literary text—the text continuum and the reconstructed level—involve both semantic and non-semantic material. Hrushovski proposes his theory of integrational semantics to account for the decoder's processing of the semantic material. This theory is not limited to the literary text, but applies to the process of encoding and decoding of meanings in general.

Meaning of sentences and texts is not simply a result of combining the designations of the words and adjusting them according to the specific context. Rather, it relies on pieces of information outside of the text, which the addressee is sent to collect. The addresser does not simply add new information to what is already known to us, but *manipulates* information which we already have or may have to acquire. Meaning is the product of the integration of new semantic elements with the ones already known.

[4]Barthes, for example, realizes the importance of distinguishing between these two levels, but admits that "we do not know how the two correspond to each other" (Barthes, 1973: 31).

[5]For another approach to the theory of the literary text, see Even-Zohar (1972). The two approaches are, on the whole, complementary.

Any semantic processing involves, therefore, the interaction of three levels: (1) The *senses* (designations) of words and of sentences composed of these words—an information which is derived from our knowledge of the *language* (lexicon and syntax); (2) A *field of reference* (FR), and specific frames of reference (fr) within it. The FR acts as a store of information—taken from our knowledge about the *world*—which is used to comprehend in full what is conveyed by the senses of the words. An fr is a continuum of any kind, in time and space, in theme, idea etc.; (3) *Regulating principles*, representing the attitudes of the *speaker* (irony, point-of-view, kind or genre of text, etc.). These principles tell us in what way to understand the senses of the words (a speaker's tone of voice or facial expression may indicate that when he says "you are great!" he actually means the opposite).

What distinguishes the literary text from other texts is the fact that it creates an Internal FR (IFR) (we cannot go beyond the text to verify whether the characters really exist, whether they really loved each other and so on). This does not mean, however, that the literary text does not refer also to external fields of reference—it can, and often does, refer to history, human nature etc. Hence literary statements are *true* statements referring to an IFR.

Literary Pragmatics

Many of the studies of the Israeli group, both in theoretical and descriptive poetics, rely upon and emphasize the relationship text/reader, and the reading process. As was briefly mentioned above, the literary object is conceived as dependent for its existence on the reader, who "concretizes" it. The complex process of "concretization" involves such procedures as linking dispersed materials, constructing patterns, filling-in gaps, etc. Since literature is an "art of time", the text is conceived as a *continuum* of signs which unfold not simultaneously but successively, and its realization as a process which takes place in time. Hence, special attention is given to the complex and dynamic structuration of the text-continuum and to its effects on the actualization process. A series of papers published since the mid 1960's, mainly in *Ha-Sifrut* (e.g. Perry and Haefrati, 1966; Perry and Sternberg, 1968; Perry, 1968/9, 1977; Sternberg, 1974) deal with related subjects such as the ways of gradual meaning-construction in texts, the relations between meaning and order of presentation, corrections and retrospective re-structuring in the reading process, manipulation of the reader's expectations, tensions between separate points in the continuum, emphasis or suppression of information for rhetorical purposes etc.

Perry and Sternberg (1968) concentrate on the necessary procedures for the actualization of the fictive world projected by the text. Using a biblical narrative they show that the literary text is constructed as a well-organized *system* of gaps, which the reader fills in through the construction of hypotheses. This phenomenon ranges from simple linkages, almost automatically carried out by the reader, to very complex linkages, which are constructed consciously, laboriously, with constant corrections and modifications. The gap-filling process is by no means arbitrary. Rather, it is directed and limited in various ways by the text, by cultural conventions and rules of human perception. Moreover, stories can be distinguished from each other and characterized on the basis of the type of gap-filling system they employ: the information withheld can be central or peripheral, the suppression of information can be temporary or permanent, it can be used for tension, irony or other rhetorical purposes and so on.

The process of gap-filling does not merely enrich the meaning of the text, but it is necessary for the understanding of the internal field of reference (events, characters, etc.). In some cases (such as the biblical narrative of David and Bathsheba, or Henry James's *The Turn of the Screw*) the text deliberately exploits the reader's inability to choose between two (or more) systems of gap-filling. In such texts these "multiple systems of gap-filling" often serve as the main compositional principle. This ambiguity on the level of events in prose is parallel to ambiguity on the word level in poetry.

Perry (1977) opens his book with a long introductory chapter which discusses the main characteristics of the process of semantic realization of the literary text. He describes the dynamics of the semantic continuum in poetry, that is the aesthetic and rhetorical motivations for the order of material-presentation in poetic texts, and the effect which the continuum has on the reader. Perry emphasizes the fact that the reader starts integrating semantic material from the very first stages of the reading process. Consequently, he formulates rules concerning (1) the effect of initial stages of the reading process on the following stages; (2) specific predictions and expectations which are raised in one stage of the reading about further specific points in the text-continuum; (3) retrospective activity in the reading process, which involves additional patterning and re-patterning of semantic material. Re-patterning is the most drastic retrospective activity, and one which makes conspicuous the nature of the process of semantic integration. Perry's work is devoted specifically to this phenomenon, which he studies in the poetry of Bialik—a Hebrew poet who recurrently uses "inverted poems" (in Perry's terminology).

Literary Systems and Contacts

Following the work of Russian Formalism in its late stage—especially Jurij Tynjanov's concept of literature as a system correlated with other, extra-literary systems, Even-Zohar suggests in a series of articles (1970, 1973, 1976, 1978) that the variety of literary and semi-literary texts of any given culture should be seen as an aggregate of systems, or as a *poly-system*. The major opposition in the polysystem is that of "canonized" ("high") versus "non-canonized" ("low") systems, where both "original" and translated literature participate (on the status of translated literature within the literary polysystem see Even Zohar, 1978: 21-27). The main principle governing the behavior of this opposition is assumed to be the alternation of primary and secondary patterns (activities/models). A "secondary" activity is that which takes the initiative in creating new items and models for the repertoire, while the "secondary" is conceived as a derivative, conservative and simplifying activity. With the help of these categories of stratification and typology, it is assumed that a whole range of questions about the synchronic and diachronic existence of literature can be discussed in a more fruitful way than that pursued by traditional histories of literature. The relations between center and periphery, and the primary/secondary models established alternately in them, thus become a major clue for the understanding not only of what is traditionally called the diachronic aspects of the literary polysystem, but of its dynamically synchronic aspects as well.

Generally, literary structures on all levels are never adopted by the non-canonized system before they have become a common stock of the canonized one, and when adopted by the periphery these structures are typically "made simple." The oppositions between various literary systems function as an optimal literary and cultural balance within the literary polysystem, where the canonized system is thus constantly vitalized by a (positive) struggle with the non-canonized.

Moreover, it is assumed that no literary polysystem is historically isolated from other literatures. Hence, interliterary contacts are an indispensable part of any historical description. In his "Universals of Literary Contacts" (1978: 45-53) Even-Zohar formulates some basic principles concerning such contacts: for example, literatures are never in non-contact; contacts are mainly unilateral; a Source-Literature (the one whose norms are appropriated by the Target Literature) is selected by prestige and dominance; contacts are not necessarily maintained with the major (primary) systems of the Source-Literature, but often through epigonic intermediaries; when selecting an item to be appropriated, the target literature may filter out some of its components, and it does not necessarily keep its original function; appropriation tends to be simplified, regularized, schematized.

In a recent article, Even-Zohar (1978: 39-44) extends his view of literature as a polysystem to cultural history. Having reached the conclusion that "all literary systems strive to become polysystems," i.e. multi-stratified, he maintains that the same is true for all cultural systems.[6]

Translation Theory

Work on translation theory started as a separate branch of poetics to deal mostly with the textual procedures taking place between a source text (ST) and a target text (TT). Even-Zohar (1971) strives to clarify where the peculiarity of literary translation lies. His main hypotheses are: (1) Through translation a text is decomposed, disclosing in the process the textual relations prevailing within it; (2) This process of decomposition discloses the inevitable incompatibility of the set of textual relations in the ST and these in the TT. The major *loci* where discrepancies are most strikingly manifested are the *textemes:* textual units which are constrained by the literary repertoire and by the proper textual relations (order, concatenation, position), in addition to common linguistic constraints. Such textemes are often ignored by translators, who replace them by non-textemic units; (3) As a result, we can distinguish between a TT produced according to the norms prevailing in a target system (which may differ from, or even negate, the norms constraining the ST), and a TT produced through (at least partial) neutralization of the target system. The first is labeled *equivalent* and the second *adequate* translation(with no value-judgement intended).

One result of Even-Zohar's research is the hypothesis that when eliminating such peripheral facts as "mistakes," and when taking for granted the objective differences between languages, it becomes clear that translational decisions are first and foremost determined by norm-governed models, dominating the target literature system (and not by idiosyncracies of the translators). In other words, it is "higher," rather than "lower" levels which constrain translation. Surveying literature translated into Hebrew (mainly from German and English) between 1930 and 1945, Toury (1978) redefines the concepts of equivalence and adequacy, and demonstrates how a complex set of norms dominating the literary system at the time determines to a large extent the translators' decisions (see also Toury, 1976a, 1976b). It was thus confirmed that translation procedures are an integral part of an aggregate of procedures within the literary polysystem. The study of translational norms is therefore seen now as part of a study of the general role of norms in the behavior of text production within a literary polysystem.

Summary

I hope that this brief and incomplete survey may give the reader an

---

[6] A discussion of literary systems from a different point of view was offered by Hrushovski (1976b), but cannot be commented upon here for lack of space.

idea of directions taken by some of the Israeli scholars. The theoretical
approaches described here typically suggest *hierarchical* models, where the
order is conceived not as stable and architectonic, but as dynamic and reversible. In Hrushovski's theory of the literary text, the different patterns
are viewed as creating a complex network of reversible hierarchies. The whole
network may be subordinated at any point to the pattern which most
interests the reader at the time, or to the demands of the text at a specific
point. Perry and Sternberg emphasize the dynamic character of the reading
process, the existence of multiple systems of gap-filling, each organizing
details in the text in a different hierarchy. Perry devotes special attention
to "inverted poems" that force the reader to re-organize and reinterpret
the semantic materia already processed. Even-Zohar (and Toury) emphasizes
the dynamic character of the whole literary system, describing it as a
(stratified) heterogeneous structure ("polysystem") with constant shifts
between the centers and the peripheries. This feature is shared by many
studies of this group, and is most characteristic of its whole approach: the
theoretical models offered for a given aspect of literature are intended
to be flexible enough to deal with (and reflect) the complex and dynamic
nature of the literary phenomena.

REFERENCES

Barthes, Roland. 1973. "Analyse textuelle d'un conte d'Edgar Poe." in Chabrol, C.,
     ed. *Sémiotique narrative et textuelle* (Larousse), pp. 29-54.

Ben-Porat, Z. & B. Hrushovski. 1974. *Structuralist Poetics in Israel (Papers on Poetics
     and Semiotics 1)*. The Porter Institute for Poetics and Semiotics, Tel-Aviv Univ-
     sity.

Dijk, Teun A. van., ed. 1976. *Pragmatics of Language and Literature*. (North-Holland).

Even-Zohar, Itamar. 1971. *An Introduction to the Theory of Literary Translation*.
     Ph.D., Tel-Aviv University.

_____ . 1972. "An Outline of a Theory of the Literary Text." *Ha-Sifrut* 3: 427-
     46. (In Hebrew (with English summary).

_____ . 1973. "The Relations between Primary and Secondary Systems in the
     Literary Polysystem." in *Proceedings of the VIIth ICLA Congress, Ottawa*.
     (in press; also in Even-Zohar, 1978).

_____ . 1976. "Interferences in Dependent Literary Polysystems." in *Proceed-
     ings of the VIIIth ICLA Congress, Budapest 1976*. (in press; also in Even-Zohar,
     1978).

_____ . 1978. *Papers in Historical Poetics. (Papers on Poetics and Semiotics 8).* The Porter Institute for Poetics and Semiotics, Tel-Aviv University.

Hrushovski, Benjamin. 1954. "On Free Rythms in Modern Yiddish Poetry." in Weinreich, U., ed. *The Field of Yiddish.* pp. 216-66.

_____ . 1960. "On Free Rythms in Modern Poetry." in Sebeok, T.A., ed. *Style in Language.* (MIT Press), pp. 173-92.

_____ . 1976a. *Segmentation and Motivation in the Text Continuum of Literary Prose: The First Episode of 'War and Peace'. (Papers on Poetics and Semiotics 5).* The Porter Institute for Poetics and Semiotics, Tel-Aviv University.

. 1976b. "Toward a Theory of Systems in Literary History." Paper read at the International Symposium on Semiotics and Theories of Symbolic Behavior, Brown University, Providence. (forthcoming in the proceedings of the symposium, Peter de Ridder Press).

Kaufman, Channa. 1974. *A Selective Bibliography of Semiotics and Related Fields in Israel in Recent Years. (Papers on Poetics and Semiotics 3).* The Porter Institute for Poetics and Semiotics, Tel-Aviv University.

Perry, Menakhem. 1968/9. "The Inverted Poem: On a Principle of Semantic Composition in Bialik's Poems." *Ha-Sifrut* 1: 603-31.*

_____ . 1977. *Semantic Dynamics in Poetry: The Theory of Semantic Change in the Text Continuum of a Poem. (Literature Meaning, Culture 3).* The Porter Institute for Poetics and Semiotics, Tel-Aviv University.*

Perry, M. & J. Haefrati. 1966. "On Some Characteristics of the Art of Bialik's Poetry." *Akhshav* 17/18: 43-77.*

Perry, M. & M. Sternberg. 1968. "The King Through Ironic Eyes: The Narrator's Devices in the Biblical Story of David and Bathsheba and Two Excursions on the Theory of the Narrative Text." *Ha-Sifrut* 1: 236-92.*

Sternberg, Meir. 1974. "Retardatory Structure, Narrative Interest, and the Detective Story." *Ha-Sifrut* 18/19: 164-80.*

Toury, Gideon. 1976a. "The Nature and Role of Norms in Literary Translation." in: Holmes, J.S. et al., eds., *Literature and Translation: New Perspective in Literary Studies.* Acco: Leuven.

Toury, G. 1976b. "Translational Norms and the Concept of Equivalence." in *Proceedings of the VIIIth ICLA Congress, Budapest 1976* (in press).

_____ . 1978. *Translational Norms and Literary Translation into Hebrew, 1930-1945. (Literature, Meaning, Culture 6).* The Porter Institute for Poetics and Semiotics, Tel-Aviv University.*

* in Hebrew (usually with English summary)

SEMIOTICS IN ITALY

Teresa de Lauretis

It was no accident that the first Congress of the International Association for Semiotic Studies (IASS, founded in 1969) was held in Milan, in June 1974. Not only was its chief organizer Umberto Eco, then secretary of IASS and internationally known exponent of Italian semiotics; but a widespread interest in semiotic research had existed in Italy since the early 60's, in a large variety of fields (de Lauretis, 1977a, 1975).

Like any other cognitive system, semiotics is subject to historical determinations, or rather overdeterminations. Although it is certainly not a question of establishing "the origins" of semiotics in Italy, an understanding of the sociocultural forces that shaped its particular development and thus have made possible to speak of an Italian semiotics is necessary. I will therefore attempt to give an overview of the development of semiotic theory and practice in Italy, outling its ideological concerns and main areas of investigation as they have been defined and redefined in relation to a changing historical situation over the past fifteen years. An immediate advantage offered by historical hindsight is the possibility to confront the confusion, or the simplistic assimilation of semiotics and structuralism.

I.   When, under the title "Strutturalismo e critica," Cesare Segre (1965) published the responses of fourteen scholars to a questionnaire intended to assess the impact of post-Saussurian linguistics on Italian literary studies, it became apparent that structuralism was considered mainly as a "critical instrument" capable of renewing a critical tradition steeped in historicism and almost entirely lacking in formalist textual approaches. After the bankruptcy of Crocean idealism, the influence of philosophies like existentialism or neopositivism had not significantly affected the area of literary studies. In a stifling intellectual climate, structuralism meant first of all a rigorous textual method, a scientific habit of thought and a new practice of criticism, all the more appealing since Italy had had no experience comparable to Anglo-American New Criticism or to Russian Formalism. Understandably, then, structuralism appeared to be exempt from the teleological overtones of both Croceanism and deterministic Marxism.

Structuralism took hold, in the early-to-mid 60's, primarily in the works of linguists and medievalists, art historians and estheticians who favored the analytical study of texts: against the Crocean concepts of art as intuition-expression, and of the work of art as a juxtaposition of poetic and non-poetic moments, the text came to be seen as a system whose internal coherence rested on the total inter-relation of its linguistic, thematic and stylistic (rhetorical) elements. Thus the critic was no longer to evaluate the content of the text or to explain the text by external factors of norm, esthetic tradition or history; instead, agreed the structuralists, the role of criticism was to describe the formal modes of internal coherence that constituted the structure of the text. Single works, especially poetry in the Jakobsonian mode, but also narrative and drama were analyzed phonologically and syntactically, in relation either to the poetic universe of the author, or to other works within the genre, or to an entire cultural period (de Lauretis, 1971). A number of new scholarly journals appeared, specializing in structural theory and analysis of literature, such as *Strumenti critici* published by Einaudi in Turin and *Lingua e stile* published by Il Mulino in Bologna. Among existing journals, *Paragone, Lettere italiane, Sigma, Nuova corrente* and others also devoted much space to the new critical views. Since 1973 *Strumenti critici* has included in every issue a current bibliography of studies in structuralism and semiotics in Italy.

The sudden success of structuralism was accompanied by two different types of opposition: the reaction of traditional critics who found their view and practice of criticism radically challenged by a new terminology, complete with graphs and formulas, which threatened the time-honored distinction between art and science; and the more serious opposition by Marxist critics who leveled their critique at the epistemological and ideological implications of the "structural method." The major objections of the Marxist critics to literary structuralism (Luperini, 1971) were: a) its view of a text as a self-contained totality that could be studied in isolation from   other social and cultural processes; b) the idealist implications of positing an *a priori* structure immanent in the text; and c) the tautological fallacy of a purely "descriptive" criticism solely directed at verifying the existence for formal structures assumed to be inherent in the object. By denouncing the illusion of an objective, "scientific" criticism and its conception of the text as a self-contained system that could, indeed must be studied in itself rather than in relation to historical and social formations, the Marxists critics opened to questions the ideological premises and textual choices of structural criticism. Critical discourse itself, they insisted, is subject to the very social forces and cultural constraints that operate in language and literary expression.

These essential questions and the ensuing dialogue or debate were crucial to the development of semiotics in Italy. In the changing historical situation, which culminated in the political events of May 1968, structuralism as such came to denote a rigid and narrow view of the critical activity, while its early innovative charge and conceptual tools were assumed, developed, and sharpened by semiotics.

Semiotic research, of course, had been carried out before 1968, along with structural analyses of texts. Semiological studies, as they were then called following Saussure and French usage, were primarily concerned with non-literary and non-verbal sign systems such as advertising, comic strips, television and the mass media, architecture, cinema, and so forth. Umberto Eco's *La struttura assente*, certainly the most comprehensive formulation of early Italian semiotics, consists of five sections representative of the range and vitality of the semiotic project: A. notions of general semiology; B. visual signs and codes; C. architectural signs and codes; D. a critical discussion of structuralism as both methodological and philosophical construct; E. a survey of the entire semiological domain. The last two chapters, in particular, indicate another important aspect of semiological studies, namely their theoretical component. Unlike literary structuralism, which relied on the theoretical framework already developed by structural linguistics, Lévi-Strauss' structural anthropology, Greimas' structural semantics, and the work on narrative structures from Propp to Todorov, semiotic research had to develop a set of conceptual tools, a theoretical "language" to approach communicative processes based on non-verbal, non-literary, or mixed media for which little or no critical inquiry existed.

The difficulties encountered by semiologists dealing with cinema and theatre in light of the Saussurian *langue/parole* model are a good example. Since Christian Metz's 1964 essay "Cinéma: langue ou langage?" (reprinted in *Essais sur la signification au cinéma*), attempts to adapt Saussurian categories to the semiological investigation of cinematic language met with no success: certain characteristics of verbal language, such as the double articulation or the homogeneity and arbitrariness of linguistic signs, simply could not be posited for cinema, which on the contrary was shown to be characterized by a plurality of heterogeneous codes (Eco, 1968) and by "natural" signs (Pasolini, 1972). It was only with the discovery of Peircian semiotics that cinematic signs could be described in their iconic, indexical and symbolic aspects (Bettetini, 1971; of particular importance is the original research done in Italy on visual communication and iconism—see *Versus*, 3 and Eco, 1976). In other words, the need to account for the specific modes of cinematic signification more accurately than was possible with Saussurian linguistics moved the research toward other theoretical models such as Hjelmslev (Garroni, 1968, 1972; Grande, 1974, 1975) and Peirce (Eco, 1968, 1972, 1976; Bettetini, 1971). A similar process was to take place a few years later with the development of a semiotics of the theatre (Ruffini, 1974; Bettetini, 1975; Bettetini and De Marinis, 1977).

II.   In *Produzione del senso e messa in scena* Gianfranco Bettetini states
that the crisis in the traditional concept of sign, as unitary entity or
elementary unit capable of conveying meaning, is at the basis of the transition from early semiotic research, restrictively focused on the formal aspects
of signification and on the sign systems, to its current   concerns with the
operations of meaning production and their ideological and economic
supports.

Like psychology and linguistics, semiotics initially sought to establish
itself as a scientific discipline, a universal science of signs, in a climate of
persisting positivism and under the empiricist banner. Thus the methodological necessity to define levels of analysis and criteria of pertinence,
which is a legitimate requirement of all theoretical research, was confused
with the so-called "scientific neutrality." Had it remained within the dominant scientific tradition, semiotics too would have come to identify methodological needs with ontological foundation. Fortunately, semiotics was just
getting on its way in the late 60's when the problematic of ideology erupted
in the human sciences and opened to question all their operations—from the
initial choice of hypotheses to the reading of the "data" and to the social
impact, utilization or manipulation of the "findings." This third Copernican
revolution (as Bettetini calls it) placed the subject of ideology squarely at
the center of any research into social structures and relations; voiding
the claims of scientific neutrality, it stressed the role of ideology in
"overdetermining not only the communication models used in infrasocial
exchanges, especially in the area of mass communication, but even the
instruments designed to analyze their structures and their effects" (Bettetini, 1975:13).

If the older and more established human sciences continued, for the
most part, along a strictly experimental path, without seriously questioning their own practices, semiotics was still relatively unofficial—open territory, as it were. And so it was able to subject its epistemological premises
to self-criticism—for example the notion of sign, the ideological implications of a purely "descriptive" intentionality, and the fragmentation of
the social sphere into discontinuous systems. By abandoning altogether the
hypothesis that a text or a message could be studied in itself and by means
of a metalanguage (that is to say, that a language could be isomorphic with,
and therefore able to translate, either "reality" or a metalanguage), semiotic
research ceased to be a kind of linguistics applied to verbal and/or non-
verbal messages; from the formal study of signification systems, it turned
to examining the modes of sign production and the previously ignored
area of meaning (the semantic field).

Communication and signification, Eco maintains in his recent *Theory of Semiotics*, function in a complex and dialectical relationship. One cannot really conceive of signification systems (the phonemes of a language, road signals, a set of semantic contents like the system of kinship, etc.) outside the social purpose of communication. Vice versa, it is impossible to study communication processes independently of the underlying systems of signification. Which also means that the elements of each system must be, and in fact are, understood by someone, i.e. they must be correlated to a culturally assigned content or meaning. The rules that establish the correlation between a physical or material sign-vehicle and a content are historically and socially determined, and therefore changeable. These operational rules (and *not* the sets of elements constituting each system) are what Eco calls codes (1976:49). The codes, as socially established relationships between signs and meanings, change whenever new or different contents are culturally assigned to the same sign-vehicle or whenever new sign-vehicles are produced. A different interpretation of a text (a sign for Eco can be any significant unit, from a single word to a string of signs, a text or even a macrotext, depending on one's level of analysis) or a new text sets up a new content, a new *cultural unit* that becomes part of the semantic universe of the society that produces it. In studying codes, semiotics also studies the production of signs, which requires labor, both physical and intellectual, of different types for different signs. The expenditure of physical or intellectual energy in order to produce signs is, of course, interrelated with the social utilization of semiotic labor and thus with the social relations of sign production. For Eco, semiotics is a critical discipline "concerned with signs as social forces" (1976:65).

With the redefinition of its object in view of a materialist but nondeterministic practice, Eco's theory steers clear of the somewhat naive claim to scientific (objective) status that previous semiotic works had inherited from structural linguistics and, in Italy, from the dominant Marxist tradition (cf. Colletti, 1973)—a claim still evident in the work of Ferruccio Rossi-Landi. Postulating a homology between linguistic production and material production based on the homology between message (*enoncé*) and industrial artifact, Rossi-Landi (1968) then applies deductively the labor theory of value and the Marxist concept of alienation to linguistic production, equating value with meaning (*Linguistics and Economics*, 1975:5, but completed in 1971). By considering "human language as the principal object of linguistic science" and "economic exchange as the principal object of the science of economics" in a unitary way, Rossi-Landi intends "to begin a semiotic elaboration of the two social processes which we can identify provisionally as 'the production and circulation of goods (in the form of commodities)' and as 'the production and circulation of sentences (in the form of verbal messages)'." The role of semiotics, he concludes, is to mediate between the dimension of the modes of production and the dimension of ideologies. Since, however, according to Rossi-Landi, both the economy (modes of production) and ideologies are to be treated as sign systems, *hence postulated as homologous to language*, it seems to me that, by his own formulation, semiotics is not a *mediation* but a kind of universal key to the entire spectrum of phenomena, which are thus homologized by, precisely, semiotics. He does, in fact, speak of semiotics as "the general doctrine and science of signs and of their systems" (1975:203).

In Eco's formulation, probably the most coherent and far-reaching to date (cf. de Lauretis, 1977b), semiotics seeks not a scientific knowledge of material reality, but rather a critical knowledge of what might be called the sociohistorical construction of reality, i.e. the conditions of production, circulation and consumption of social discourses (in the broadest sense) from which representations, beliefs and values are engendered. How did the theoretical and ideological shift from early semiological studies to contemporary semiotics in Italy come about? The re-reading of Peirce, who had been known earlier mostly through the work of Morris (introduced in Italy by Rossi-Landi in 1953), marked a crucial theoretical step forward in this direction. However, to claim that the European discovery of Peirce singly caused "the crisis of the sign" and the demise of structuralism and Saussurian semiology around 1968 would be a gross, idealist oversimplification. It was, most likely, the events in the real world that made people look for new models, more useful interpretants of the writing on the walls: "A rightful attention to the problems of meaning and the complementary discourse on neutrality and on the non-innocence of formal structures were not brought about simply by the internal difficulties that the object analyzed kept posing to a structuralist methodology, but were also urged by external events which in turn forced [semioticians] to re-think the problematic of ideology and to study its interconnections with all communication phenomena" (Bettetini, 1975:22).

The external events referred to were those of 1968 in Europe, the student movement in the United States, the crisis of all types of bourgeois rationalization, the recall of the values of the imagination and poetic productivity. Such events, which could not be foreseen by previous semiotic practice, certified that the contradictions of our social system existed in reality, and were evident to many people and groups; they were described not only at the theoretical level by a few prophets, semiotically or otherwise, but at the level of a new social consciousness, in the light of a new idea of possible relations between people and between people and things. The crisis denounced by the cultural revolution could not be reduced to a crisis of the semantic field, where ideology had conveniently been tucked away. It obviously had to affect the entire process of meaning production inclusive of the semiosic activity by which signs and codes are elaborated and transformed—a production that continuously intersects both expression and content planes, and that is itself historical and ideological. In other words, the emphasis shifted from the sign systems as machines or mechanisms that generate messages to the work performed through them, which constitutes and/or transforms the codes, the subjects using the codes (i.e. performing the work), and, however slowly, the systems themselves. Thus, the subject of the semiosic activity is no longer the transcendental subject of structuralism, "the human mind," but an historical subject, and therefore a class subject (at least as long as the theoretical concept of class is a useful interpretant of social reality).

The claim I have made in the preceding pages, along with Eco, Bettetini and many others, that semiotics today is a critical discipline concerned with all social communication must be substantiated by semiotics' continuing willingness to deal, both in theory and in practice, with the emerging needs, demands, private-political practices of a given society and with the social discourses that express them. I can only point, in this limited space, to some desirable directions for semiotic research within the Italian context. Just as a qualitative shift in the socio-political conception of productive forces after '68 may be seen as directly related to the current semiotic concern with sign production and code operations, other social issues have emerged in post-1977 Italy that may transform or shift, however radically, the theory, practice and object of semiotics: the issues of group autonomy vs. institutional organization, individual needs vs. social productivity, the unconscious, pleasure, sexual difference, and so forth. Thus a theorization of subjectivity in its historical forms, in relation to the cultural apparati of social reproduction and to various countercultural modes of communicative behavior will have to become, crucially, a central concern of semiotic discourse.

BIBLIOGRAPHY

All issues of *Versus: Quaderni di studi semiotici*, edited by Umberto Eco and published by Bompiani, Milano, may be profitably consulted; in particular, the special issue 8/9 (maggio-dicembre 1974) is devoted to a rich international semiotics bibliography edited by Ugo Volli, Patrizia Magli, and Omar Calabrese, indexed by country and by discipline: the chapter on Italy contains a general section, "La semiotica in Italia," ed. by Omar Calabrese and Patrizia Magli, pp. 145-176, plus a "Bibliografia degli scritti italiani di semiotica del cinema," ed. by Alberto Farassino, pp. 178-184. An annotated bibliography of basic semiotic works on the theatre and on drama, expertly compiled by Marco De Marinis and Patrizia Magli, appeared in

Versus, 11 (maggio-agosto 1975), pp. 53-128. A useful bibliographical selection may be found on pp. 156-165 of Francesco Casetti, *Semiotica* which also includes a general critical essay on the present state of semiotics and selected passages from basic works intended for pedagogical use. In addition to the previously mentioned issues of *Strumenti critici* since 1973, see also the Prepublications/Working Papers put out by the Centro Internazionale di Semiotica e di Linguistica, Università di Urbino (Professor Pino Paioni, Secretary).

The following is a selected list of works cited or referred to in this essay.

REFERENCES

Avalle, D'Arco Silvio. 1970. *L'analisi letteraria in Italia. Formalismo-Strutturalismo-Semiologia.* Milano: Ricciardi.

_____ . 1975. *Modelli semiologici nella "Commedia" di Dante.* Milano: Bompiani.

Barberi Squarotti, Giorgio. 1966. *Simboli e strutture della poesia del Pascoli.* Messina-Firenze: D'Anna.

Bettetini, Gianfranco. 1968. *Cinema: lingua e scrittura.* Milano: Bompiani.

_____ . 1971. *L'indice del realismo.* Milano: Bompiani.

_____ . 1975. *Produzione del senso e messa in scena.* Milano: Bompiani.

Bettetini, G. and De Marinis, M. 1977. *Teatro e comunicazione.* Firenze: Guaraldi.

Brandi, Cesare. 1968. *Struttura e architettura.* Torino: Einaudi.

_____ . 1974. *Teoria generale della critica.* Torino: Einaudi.

Casetti, Francesco. 1974. " 'Nuova' semiotica, 'nuovo' cinema," *Ikon,* 88/89 (gennaio-giugno),pp.275-346.

_____ . 1977. *Semiotica: Saggio critico, testimonianze, documenti.* Milano: Accademia.

Colletti, Lucio. 1973. "Marxism: Science or Revolution?" in Robin Blackburn, ed. *Ideology in Social Science.* New York: Vintage, pp. 369-377.

Corti, Maria. 1969. *Metodi e fantasmi.* Milano: Feltrinelli.

_____ . 1976. *Principi della comunicazione letteraria.* Milano: Bompiani.

Corti, Maria and Segre, Cesare, eds. 1970. *I metodi attuali della critica in Italia*. Torino: ERI.

de Lauretis, Teresa. 1971. "Metodi strutturali nella critica letteraria italiana," *MLN*, 86 (January),pp. 73-88.

_____ . 1975. "The Shape of the World: Report on Structuralism and Semiotics in Italy," *Books Abroad*, 49 (Spring), pp. 227-232.

_____ . 1977a. "Interview with Umberto Eco," *Canadian Journal of Research in Semiotics*, 4 (Spring-Summer), pp. 107-114.

_____ . 1977b. "Semiosis Unlimited," *PTL: A Journal for Descriptive Poetics and Theory of Literature*, 2, pp. 367-383.

De Marinis, Marco and Magli, Patrizia. 1975. "Materiali bibliografici per una semiotica del teatro," *Versus*, 11 (maggio-agosto), pp. 53-128.

Eco, Umberto. 1968. *La struttura assente*. Milano: Bompiani.

_____ . 1971. *Le forme del contenuto*. Milano: Bompiani.

_____ . 1972. *La structure absente*. Paris: Mercure de France.

_____ . 1973. *Il segno*. Milano: ISEDI.

_____ . 1975. *Trattato di semiotica generale*. Milano: Bompiani.

_____ . 1976. *A Theory of Semiotics*. Bloomington: Indiana Univ. Press.

Faccani, Remo and Eco, Umberto, eds. 1969. *I sistemi di segni e lo strutturalismo sovietico*. Milano: Bompiani.

Garroni, Emilio. 1968. *Semiotica ed estetica*. Bari: Laterza.

_____ . 1972. *Progetto di semiotica*. Bari: Laterza.

Grande, Maurizio. 1974. "Appunti per la definizione del ruolo di alcuni procedimenti formali del film," *Filmcritica*, 242/255.

Luperini, Romano. 1971. *Marxismo e letteratura*. Bari: De Donato.

Pasolini, Pier Paolo. 1972. *Empirismo eretico*. Milano: Garzanti.

Patrizi, Giorgio. 1974. "La critica del segno: appunti per una ipotesi politica della semiologia" in *Marxismo e strutturalismo nella critica letteraria italiana*. Roma: Savelli, pp. 211-237.

Ponzio, A. 1976. *La semiotica in Italia*. Bari: Dedalo.

Rossi-Landi, Ferruccio. 1968. *Il linguaggio come lavoro e come mercato* Milano: Bompiani.

_____ . 1972. *Semiotica e ideologia*. Milano: Bompiani.

Segre, Cesare. 1965. "Strutturalismo e critica" in *Catalogo Generale 1958-65*. Milano: Il Saggiatore, pp. i-lxxxv.

_____ . 1969. *I segni e la critica: fra strutturalismo e semiologia*. Torino: Einaudi.

_____ . 1974. *Le strutture e il tempo*. Torino: Einaudi.

A. J. GREIMAS AND NARRATIVE SEMIOTICS

Lawrence Kritzman

For students of narrative, the literary scholarship of the 1960's elaborated an unlimited number of theoretical models of "plot structure" based on renewed epistemological and methodological presuppositions of what constitutes a "text." Often, the foundation of a "grammar of plot" was derived from a formal theory of grammar. Many theoreticians of the period turned to the linguistic models of Saussure and Chomsky in order to elucidate the relationship between abstract text structure and literary competence or performance. Working within this tradition, A.J. Greimas based his theoretical presuppositions on Saussure's notion of a *langue* which underlies *parole*, a concept roughly analogous to Chomsky's competence/performance dichotomy which suggests that sentences are generated by a system of rules or norms found in their "deep structure." In his analyses, Greimas proposes a narrative grammar defined by a finite number of constructs capable of accounting for individual text performance. As a result, one is obliged to consider the surface structure of a story simply as a manifestation of a highly conventionalized narrative form. In essence, then, the Greimasian study of narrative ultimately becomes the study of text competence.

The methodological framework which Greimas postulates in *Sémantique structurale*[1] begins with the Saussurean and Jakobsonian concept of binary oppositions. According to this theory, the function of the elementary sounds of speech are determined by their phonemic differences or distinctive features. Both Saussure and Jakobson abandon the atomistic study of a sound-object as an isolated entity and transform phonetic matter into a phonemic system. Greimas adapts this model and applies it to his study of semantics. Elementary concepts of meaning start at a level of thought prior to language. In effect, our perception of both implicit and explicit oppositions in the universe engender what Greimas terms the "elementary structure of signification." "Nous percevons des différences et, grâce à cette perception, le monde prend forme [...] la signification présuppose l'existence de la relation: c'est l'apparition de la relation entre les termes

[1] A.J. Greimas, *Sémantique structurale* (Paris: Larousse, 1966).

qui est la condition nécessaire de la signification" (*Sémantique structurale,*
p. 19)·[2] In Greimas' system, meaning is generated by the oppositions that
we perceive between two semes or minimal semantic units: black and white,
fat and thin, are defined by our sense of mutual semantic differences based
on a relational type of perception. The binary patterning that Greimas
proposes, establishes theoretical constructs for elucidating the semantic
and thematic description of a literary corpus.

Greimas argues that all narratives can be explained in terms of three
basic binary oppositions from which all the roles in stories are derived.
Each opposition constitutes an "actantial model" consisting of two semantically differential actants. An actant can be a character (*acteur*) or group
of characters, a thematic unit, or an anthropomorphic entity that has been
transformed from an abstract structure to a more complex series of relationships on the surface level of text. Actants are not beings nor are they psychological essences; characters and themes are simply defined by their actantial
role based on what they "do" within the framework of a story. To be sure,
each actant is defined according to its "phonemic" function and participation
in the narrative. And these functions, in turn, are regarded as being isomorphic with the fundamental semantic structure of the sentence. In short, the
deep structure of a narrative is based on a permanent "enunciation-spectacle"
(*énoncé spectacle*); the actors and the content of a story may vary, but the
actants never change since "sa permanence est garantie par la distribution
unique des rôles" (p.173).

Instead of working his way inward, penetrating the solidified surface
of the text, and thereby reducing the action of individual stories to a slightly
more abstract grouping, the Greimasian model starts from the general
structural conditions for the generation of all narratives. In other words,
Greimas' method is deductive and teleological, positing an algorithm of
the semantic oppositions that a text must realize in the course of its transformation. This theoretical framework is indeed best described by Frederic
Jameson's comparison of Greimas' model to what Sartre terms a "progressive-
regressive" method.[3]

In general Greimas aims at reconstructing the theoretical principles
set forth fifty years ago in the metalanguage of Propp which was based

---

[2]The source of Greimas' argument is Merleau-Ponty's *Phenomenology of Perception* in which the latter describes the operational procedures involved in the
perception and transformation of a natural object into a scientific object.

[3]Frederic Jameson, *The Prison House of Language* (Princeton: Princeton
University Press, 1972), p. 125.

on taxonomic closed inventories of characters, functions, and narrative sequences.[4] What attracts Greimas to the work of Propp is primarily the syntagmatic features of his model as well as his interest in the part or "function" characters play in plot development. In his *Morphology of the Fairy Tale* Propp calls the active relationship in which characters (*acteurs*) engage "functions," and he defines them in terms of their significance in the course of the action. Propp studied a wide variety of stories (100 Russian fairy tales) and attempted to generalize a set of seven invariable spheres of action; Greimas' actantial model synthesizes them into three sets of binary oppositions capable of accounting for the proliferation of more complex relationships. Whereas Propp's actantial categories were based purely on a homogenous classification of syntagmatic functions in and for themselves, Greimas' model derives its structural importances from its emphasis on the differential value established between reduced structures of content; each actantial category is defined in terms of its functional relationship with an opposing actant.

The first and most fundamental opposition is between Subject and Object. This binary pair implicitly articulates the basic structure of quest or desire underlying all narrative and includes two of Propp's spheres of action: the hero and the sought-for-person. A second actantial category constitutes the opposition between Sender (*Destinateur*) and Receiver (*Destinataire*). In his discussion, Greimas criticizes Propp for his failure to clearly delineate these categories. First of all, according to Greimas, Propp mistakes the father of the sought-for-person for an aspect of the object of the quest, and not as the Sender. Secondly, Greimas asserts that the Proppian sphere of action "dispatcher" (*mandateur*) is a misnomer since the *acteur* who instigates the hero's quest is essentially the beneficiary of the latter's action.

Greimas also observes that there are stories in which the second actantial model subsumes an inverted form of the primary binary opposition. For example, in a banal love story which ends in the marriage of the Subject and the Object, the Subject becomes the Receiver and the Object is transformed into the role of Sender. Thus the equation:

$$\frac{\text{Him}}{\text{Her}} \quad \approx \quad \frac{\text{Subject} + \text{Receiver}}{\text{Object} + \text{Sender}}$$

[4]Vladimir Propp, *Morphology of the Folktale* (Austin: University of Texas Press, 1970). For a more complete discussion of the metalanguages of Propp and Souriau, consult Robert Scholes, *Structuralism in Literature* (New Haven: Yale University Press, 1974), pp. 104-106.

However, Greimas also points out that in more complex stories, such as in the *Quest of the Holy Grail*, four separate *acteurs* can be equated with four different actantial roles.

$$\frac{\text{Subject}}{\text{Object}} \approx \frac{\text{Hero}}{\text{Grail}} \qquad \frac{\text{Sender}}{\text{Receiver}} \approx \frac{\text{God}}{\text{Humanity}}$$

The third and final category is Helper (*Adjuvant*) versus Opponent (*Opposant*). This actantial pair is capable of working for or against the realization of the narrative quest of the Subject. Moreover, it subsumes four Proppian spheres of action: Helper (helper and donor) and Opponent (villain and false hero). Thus Greimas' model appropriates Propp's seven spheres of action in the following manner:

Greimas	Propp
(Subject	Hero
(Object	Sought-for-person
(Sender	Father of the sought-for-person
(Receiver	Dispatcher
(Helper	Donor; Helper
(Opponent	Villain; False Hero

For Greimas, every narrative sequence in a text contains two actants that are engaged in basic actions of disjunction and conjunction, separation and union, struggle and reconciliation. The identification of a principal action within the plot structure of a text is achieved only be the delineation of a central thematic change associated with the development of the plot. Furthermore, suggests Greimas, a narrative should be defined as the transfer of an object, value or entity from one actant to another within a temporal framework.

In his study, Greimas illustrates how the elements of a story's narrative combine a tripartite list of syntactic structures to form a basic set of predicates capable of accounting for all possible changes of relationships that may occur in a text. With respect to the syntagmatic structure of narrative in general, Greimas observes three patterns related to his actantial model: (1) Contractual syntagms involve the acceptance or the refusal to do something. This relationship implies a contract between a hero and a superior power who possesses the authority to reward or punish. (2) Performative syntagms refer to narrative sequences in which the subject undergoes the actual performance of action such as in the series of "tests" which the Chevalier must undergo in the courtly novel before he is deemed "worthy" of the lady's hand. (3) Disjunctive syntagms involve movement or displacement.

Greimas views most narrative as the transformation or the movement from a negative to a positive contract or vice versa. This principle confirms Jonathan Culler's hypothesis that contractual sequences are central to plot development, and that the two other syntagmatic predicative categories are derived from it, and consequently must play a secondary role.[5] Yet what is most troubling in Greimas' model is his failure to provide us with specific information on how or why we are to identify those syntagmatic structures that are essential to plot development. Specific theories about the nature of narrative can only be understood in the larger context of theoretical questions asked not only about the relationship of language to literature, but also, more importantly, about how the reader is to impose constraints on the process of the identification and naming of narrative action.

The Semiotic Square

In two essays in *Du Sens*, one on semantics, the other on narrative grammar (*énoncés narratifs*), Greimas proposes the theoretical prolegomena for the future study of a specific text (Maupassant's "Deux amis").[6] He distinguishes between two levels of analysis, deep and surface structures, shifting his emphasis here to the transformation of surface manifestations seen from the perspective of a basic taxonomy. Greimas describes a formal apparatus based on a generative model which explains how a narrative grammar syntagmatically temporarizes the semantic content of a text. It is indeed this procedure that indicates a change in Greimas' theoretical perspective from structuralist description to the semiotic production of meaning.

In "Les Jeux des contraintes sémiotiques," Greimas elaborates on his theory of the "elementary structure of signification," arguing that production of meaning in narrative can only be effected in relationship to an organized signifying whole. He demonstrates how the basic semantic structure of a discursive order may be expressed in a four-term homology of "oppositions" and "contradictions" ($S1: S2:: \overline{S1}: \overline{S2}$), a scheme Greimas calls the semiotic square. A complete system of meaning may be generated from any point in the following structure:

[5]Jonathan Culler, "Defining Narrative Units," in *Style and Structure in Literature*, edited by Roger Fowler (Ithaca: Cornell University Press, 1975), pp. 131-2.

[6]A.J. Greimas, *Du Sens* (Paris: Seuil, 1970). The two primary essays I shall discuss are "Les Jeux des contraintes sémiotiques," (with Francois Rastier), pp. 135-155 [originally in *Yale French Studies*, 41, "Game, Play, Literature" (1968] and "Éléments d'une grammar narrative," pp. 157-183 [originally in *l'Homme*, 9 (1969)].

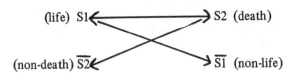

The elementary structure of signification is seen in terms of two opposing semes, such as in life to death, that are anterior to any discursive investment. Greimas argues that each of these semes taken separately implicitly constitutes the existence of contradictory semantic values which are negative transformations of the starting term, S1, and its binary opposition, S2. In other words, Greimas' mechanism possesses the potential of germinating a complete system of rules from an isolated "static" concept.

If, when using Greimas' semiotic square, we take S1 to be the starting point, then $\overline{S1}$ must be regarded as a non-S and S2 simply the opposite of S1. Therefore the two contrary semes S1 and S2 considered separately generate two contradictory items $\overline{S1}$ and $\overline{S2}$; as such, each one of the elements in the semiotic square articulates two other items in terms of contradictory and contrary elements. Thus each system comprises rules that can be defined positively in terms of presupposed binary oppositions, and negatively in terms of what they are *not*. Furthermore, these binary patterns engender two types of disjunction or what Greimas terms "homologized contradictions" that contribute to the elaboration of structural relations: disjunctive contraries (S1 and S2) and the disjunction of contradictions (S1 and $\overline{S1}$; S2 and $\overline{S2}$).

Greimas' analysis of the sexual relations of European culture attempts to illustrate his proposed constitutional model. The various elements of sexual behavior—conjugal love, incest and homosexuality, adultery by the man and adultery by the woman—are not in themselves meaningful entities; they have no intrinsic value. Here Greimas once again uses the binary opposition as a heuristic device, the principle from which the sexual hermenutic is elucidated. He begins with Lévi-Strauss' principle that human societies are divided between culture and nature or rather the acceptance versus the rejection of proposed rules of conduct. Thus the primary opposition:

Culture (permissible relations) vs. Nature (unacceptable relations). If indeed one opposes what the dominant ideology considers to be "permitted relations" (S1) to unacceptable or natural relations, we end up with an opposition between prescribed sexual behavior (S1: matrimonial relations) versus forbidden or abnormal relations (S2: incest). In other words, the primary opposition appears to be one of prescriptions versus interdictions. In addition, the function S1 stands opposed to those relationships which are not prescribed or permissable according to the Western matrimonial code; S1 therefore represents the positive definition of the rules, $\overline{S1}$ their negative definition. That is to say, the third term ($\overline{S1}$) is a simple negation of the first term, a phenomenon which is manifested in cases of female adultery. The last item that makes up the semiotic square ($\overline{S2}$) can be read as a negative transformation of "abnormal" sexual relations into "normal" or acceptable relationships, as in cases of male adultery. By articulating this model of society's so-called sexual code, one is able to elucidate a series of conflicts and transformations that exist *in potentia*. The model of Western sexual behavior thus formulated by Greimas is:

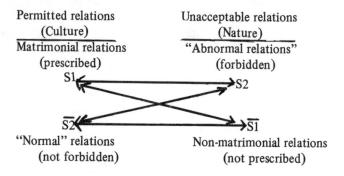

Permitted relations
(Culture)
Matrimonial relations
(prescribed)
S1

Unacceptable relations
(Nature)
"Abnormal relations"
(forbidden)
S2

$\overline{S2}$
"Normal" relations
(not forbidden)

$\overline{S1}$
Non-matrimonial relations
(not prescribed)

Indeed, the discovery procedure set down by Greimas' epistemological language permits the linguistic description of systems that are not essentially linguistic in nature. In other words, the fundamental inventory of semic categories serves as constitutive model for analyzing all possible discursive orders.

Narrative syntax

In a second article "Éléments d'une grammaire narrative," Greimas formulates a program based on discursive linguistics and semiotics, investigating how the syntactical features of texts articulate the transformation of its semantic contents. The generation of meaning, a phenomenon marked by the transfer or exchange of a value or an object from one actant to another, can only be achieved by certain basic narrative features (*énoncés narratifs*).

> La génération de la signification ne passe pas, d'abord, par la production des énoncés et leur combinaison en discours; elle est relayée, dans son parcours, par les structures narratives et ce sont elles qui produisent le discours sensé articulé en énoncés (p. 159).

Meaning itself is a narrativized form of the elementary structure of significance. The essential problem therefore becomes one of delineating the
connection between syntagmatic and semantic levels, or rather how narrative syntax appropriates the semantic elements of a text.

According to Greimas, narrative grammar contains an elementary morphology composed of the semiotic square and a fundamental syntax that
operates on the static elements of his model. The function of narrative
syntax therefore will be to transform dynamically the surface enunciation
of these taxonomic categories by the processes of conjunction and disjunction; this model thus delineates the descriptive procedures that enable
a narrative to move from one level to another by means of positive and negative transformations.

The fundamental syntactical generating feature is "doing" (*faire*).
As a semiotic action, doing presupposes a subject; as a message it is "ob-
jectified" and implies a sender and a receiver (p. 168). A simple narrative
action will therefore be brought about by the predicative force of a subject,
or rather the appropriation of a function by an actant or semantic value.

This primary action is further elucidated by modal features (*énoncés
modaux*) such as the verb "to want" (*vouloir*) whose subject contains within
it both the desire and the capacity to transform a virtual state into an essential reality: the acquisition of the object of the quest. In other words, the
verb *vouloir* functions as an orientated narrative potentiality "qui instaure
l'actant comme sujet, c'est-à-dire comme opérateur eventuel du faire" (pp.
168-9). The optative modalization of narrative syntax is significant insofar
as it redoubles everything that will actually happen; it causes us to see that
the syntactical function of "doing" consists in the transformation of a
virtual program into one that is realized by an actantial value.

Two other important modal features are the verbs "to know" (*savoir*)
and "to be able to" (*pouvoir*). In stories primarily of a psychological
nature, the author permits the reader to enter into the mind of a character, enabling the former to elucidate the possible "causal functions" of
an ulterior action. Knowing something (e.g. when the subject acts according to ruse or deception) or the consciousness of being able to bring about
an action have potential consecutive and consequential functions within
the development of plot. Whereas descriptive features (*énoncés descriptifs*)
relate the "doing" of an actant, modal features anticipate a hypothetical
or future action in which the performing subject will be in possession of
the desired object.

Two groups of syntactical "performances" emerge from Greimas'
narrative grammar: 1) those which allow for the acquisition and transition of modal values; and 2) those characterized by the acquisition and
transfer of objective values. In the first group the subject is an "implied"

operator capable of creating virtualities; in the second category performances are actually realized. Greimas proposes that essential change in narrative is achieved by a number of performatives and modalities whose
syntactic trajectory is arranged in the following way:

to want....> to know....> to be able to....> to do
(vouloir)   (savoir)   (pouvoir)   (faire)

In essence, the ultimate transferral of the value object represents the logical
consequence of an *a priori* modal performance. A "syntactic operator" is
followed by a performance that actualizes the syntactic operation.
Practical analysis

Critics of narrative semiotics have claimed that theoreticians are
unable to apply their methodologies to so-called "serious" literary texts,
but in *Maupassant: la Sémiotique du texte* (Exercises pratiques),[7] Greimas
applies the rigorous rules of his epistemological language to the short story
"Deux amis." In general he devotes increased attention to the following
areas: the relationship between a story's discursive level and its semantic
structure; the various temporal features that engender a "gap" in the text
from which the narrative is to be formed; the spatial markers that reify
the dynamics of the semiotic square; and the cognitive modal feature
"knowing" or "recognition" which serves as catalyzing agent in the
acquisition of the desired object.

The story is simple. Morissot and Sauvage meet in Paris during the
Franco-Prussian war. Their friendship is based on the relationship that they
have formed during their weekly fishing excursions. One Sunday, after
having had a few drinks under an "empty sky," they decide once again to
go fishing. However, given the wartime situation they must obtain permission to cross the battle lines. They arrive at the river and spend an en-
joyable day in renewed "friendship," despite the cannon fire they hear
from nearby Mont-Valérien. Suddenly some German army officers arrive
and threaten to kill them unless they tell the secret pass-word which enabled them to cross French lines. Morissot and Sauvage refuse. They are
shot and tossed into the river.

In analyzing this tale, Greimas proceeds in much the same manner
as Roland Barthes in *S/Z*.[8] Greimas divides Maupassant's story into twelve
fundamental sequences. He examines the "textual organization" of each
sequence by subdividing it into minimal units of reading, such as isolated
sentences or groups of words that have a function different from that of

[7]A.J. Greimas, *Maupassant: la Sémiotique du texte (Exercises pratiques)* (Paris:
Seuil, 1976).

[8]Roland Barthes, *S/Z* (Paris: Seuil, 1970).

neighboring textual "fragments." But unlike Barthes who dislocates the "signified" and thereby views writing as a kind of autonomous play of *différances* in which meaning is constantly deferred, Greimas aims in his fretting out of these narrative segments to demonstrate the text's semantic homogeneity within *a* structure assigned to it by his formal grammar. The goal then is to delineate a "meaningful" and coherent whole in the narrative. Maupassant's story thus appears as "une invitation à la condensation du discours, afin qu'arrivé au bout de sa peine... le texte se présente... comme un schéma de comprehension simple, un tout de signification" (p. 224).

The semantic constraints that Greimas imposes on the text are mediated by a symbolic dialectical interplay between the dimensions of heights and depths, as depicted in the semiotic square:

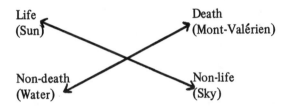

Life
(Sun)   Death
                                 (Mont-Valérien)

Non-death   Non-life
(Water)   (Sky)

He traces the symbolic transformation of the physical landscape which appears to be isomorphic with what he terms the "noological" (inner) transformation of the two friends. At first the sun is associated with a life giving force. In the second part of the story, however, the sky appears as an empty and deceitful space (non-life) which essentially motivates the tragic quest of Morissot and Sauvage. The cannon fire that the two friends hear when fishing is regarded by Greimas as being associated with death. However, the last scene in which the characters are killed and thrown into the water functions as a negativization of death because the friends ultimately are brought together in the object of their quest: the water where they used to go fishing. Thus the semiotic square permits Greimas to elucidate the figurative elements of the fictional universe in terms of opposites and contradictions. In essence, he distinguishes two axiological levels of content: 1) euphoric or positive connotations associated with Existence, and containing the semantic items life (Sun) and non-death (Water) [the sun penetrates the water in which the friends are submerged at the end of the story]; and 2) dysphoric or negative connotations associated with non-existence, encompassing the terms death (Mont-Valérien) and non-life (Sky).

Greimas is careful to point out that narrative change is not merely a question of the semantic constraints articulated in the four-term homology. Closely associated with plot development are temporal features or "aspectual

structures" which create "gaps" in the narrative, opening "durative" situations which terminate in the course of plot development. For example,
the first sentence of the story ("Paris was blockaded, starving and at last
gasp") reveals, according to Greimas, that Paris is in a state of degradation,
characterized by the notions "death" and "non-life". An initial tension is
created by the binary oppositions "dying" and "living" expressed in the
lexemes "starving" and "at last gasp". These lexemes are indeed figurative
expressions that denote the durative aspect of the narrative state, as well
as their virtual transformation into punctual features. In short temporal
markers possess an implicit "tensitivity" which establish the narrative *telos*
to be brought about through syntactical modulation.

Living					logical level /life/⟵⟶ /non-life

aspectual level /dur./→/+tens./⟶/term./

Dying					logical level /non-death/⟶/death

aspectual level /dur./→/+tens./⟶/term.

Greimas' aspectual structures not only account for the temporal development of the logical semantic structures of story content, but more importantly, they affirm that these supplementary features permit the conciliation
of both structural and discursive transformations.

Greimas also assigns particular importance to spatial markers in the
text. From the outset he indicates that Maupassant's story maintains its
consistency from the syntagmatic expansion of the referential values
assigned to the semiotic square. In light of this, spatial indicators are
predetermined by the semantic constraints imposed on the text. For example, the second sentence of the story ("The sparrows were becoming
scarce on the roofs, and the sewers were being depopulated") contains
within it the dysphoric elements "non-life" and "death". This sentence
functions anaphorically by logically reiterating the tension expressed in
the lexical items of the first sentence ("starving" and "at last gasp"). To
be sure, the spatial references explicitly stated in the text about "sparrows
on roofs" implicitly generates an opposition derived from what is usually
considered to be the habitat of rats. Thus the formulation:

roofs	:	"Sparrows"	:	high	aerial being
(rats)		sewers		low	chthonian being

An analogy is established in the story in which scarcity of sparrows is associated with non-life as is scarcity of rats associated with death.

$$\frac{\text{sparrows}}{\text{living}} \quad \sim \quad \frac{\text{air}}{\text{non-life}}$$

$$\frac{\text{rats}}{\text{dying}} \quad \sim \quad \frac{\text{earth}}{\text{death}}$$

The remainder of the text develops these presuppositional semantic givens (air:non-life :: earth:death) which subsequently reappear in Maupassant's tale in the form of spatial markers that are essential referential recurrences of previously articulated semantic values (Sun:Sky :: Mont-Valérien:Water).

In this study Greimas seeks to reorganize his previously articulated hierarchy of modal values by placing the primary syntactic function "wanting" in a subordinate position to "knowing" or "recognition". The ability to carry out narrative performances are predetermined by actantial cognition. To be sure, this does not mean that "knowing" is a dynamic feature of narrative. Rather it would be more precise to say that the modalities of knowledge and ability are presuppositions that initiate the modal value "to want". "La reconnaissance rend possible un nouveau programme narratif, elle ne l'instaure pas" (p. 156). Thus cognitive performance now becomes an *a priori* function that instigates the narrative program; it has as its consequence the attribution "the ability to do".

Greimas enlarges upon this modal feature by defining what he terms narrative knowledge (*savoir narratif*). This phenomenon involves a character's internalized competence or memory of a previous action in the story. For example, the Prussian officer realizes that Morrisot and Sauvage have been able to cross the lines to reach the river because they are aware of the secret password. The officer's recognition of this fact enables him to transform his knowledge into a virtuality, threatening the friends with their lives in exchange for the password. Thus the logical presupposition that leaving implies returning endows the operator with a "knowing-how-to-do" that permits him to recognize his ability to bring about the performance for which he has been created. The acquisition of this modal value by the anti-subject (the Prussian officer) ultimately brings about the story's denouement.

Greimas' study of Maupassant's "Deux amis" appears to be incomplete however. Although he elaborates in detail both the semantic values assigned to the semiotic square and the syntactic trajectory the story takes, one is left with the impression that he is unable to illustrate how these two levels interact. From the beginning of his analysis, despite apparent ruptures on the text's discursive level, all thematic material is regarded as a systematic variation of the same abstract structure, a definitive and invariable set of functions frozen into a conceptual terminology. To be sure, Greimas limits the manner in which the text is to signify. In doing so, surface manifestations such as dialogue and description are not viewed as possessing any intrinsic differential signifying value, and consequently their only function is to justify the needs of a reductionist model. As a result, meaning is regarded as an isolated and static concept which limits the possible transformative movement of the narrative; the significance that the syntagmatic features carry appear to function independently of their thematic substance. Moreover, the cognitive performance that Greimas considers as primary to the consecutive and causal development of the text is only introduced very late in his analysis of the tale. Although this syntactic feature catalyzes the unfolding of the discourse, all that it apparently accomplishes is an indirect reification of the semiotic square. Indeed, the litmus test that   Greimas' narrative competence has yet to undergo must provide us with a clearer picture of the interrelationships between syntagmatic motivation and semantic development. It is in this area, I believe, that Greimas' most enriching future research lies.

KRISTEVIAN SEMIOTICS

Towards a Semanalysis

J. Féral

Kristeva's semiotics can only be understood in light of the threefold triangulation of language-system, text, and subject; and these elements in turn through the *dynamic* relationships they entertain simultaneously with one another, in the social, ideological, and historical continuum to which they stand in dialectical rapport.

Dynamics and dialectics: pressed to define the central concern of Kristevian semiotics, one comes perhaps closest by evoking a non-rigid system which takes into account the *dialectical logic* inherent in any signifying practice, for Kristeva's primary interest is to get beyond the *static* dissections of an unbending structuralism to a signifying *polyphony*, ultimately to get beyond Saussure's dyadic sign.

Thus, Kristeva's theory establishes itself in opposition to any kind of formalism. It aspires to surpass the limitations and inadequacies of the Saussurian model resulting from the fact that the theory of the sign (Peirce's as well as Saussure's) participates in the conceptual framework of *representation* and *communication*. Any linguistic theory that has grown out of the ideas of Saussure and Peirce is representational in that the sign, by definition, stands in place of something else—an object or abstraction—which it both refers to and represents[1]; in so doing, it points to the absence of that thing to which it refers, a void filled by its deceptive presence. Linguistic theories are also communicative because the sign is automatically included in the communicative circuit triggered by the subject. It functions as the link in the chain which carries a given message from Sender ("destinateur") to Receiver ("destinataire"). As for the communication itself, restricted to the domain of utterance/enunciation ("énoncé"/"énonciation"), it tends by the very nature of its structure to suppress all that which is actively transformational, limiting itself to the linearity of surface structure and admitting of only one disposition, that of the speaker; in contrast, the Kristevian theory of communication is topological, in that, since it is ground-

---

[1]The object however (i.e. referent of the sign) is put aside and forgotten, and the sign is thus reduced to its simple duality, signifier/signified.

ed in the concepts of *volume* and *netword* ("réseau"), it deals with *discontinuity* and the *plurality* of disposition. This study will demonstrate how these concepts constitute a topology of the text, or more precisely, of the *writing* ("écriture").

Inadequacy of text, inadequacy of structure: when one conceives of language as a sign system (and this indeed is what structuralism does), it is reduced to a logical construct composed of elements internally dependent on one another. The sign, limited by its binary nature, is finite and fixed. It can be neither modified nor transformed. And when integrated into a supporting structure, it becomes structure as well. Yet Barthes warns of the frozen quality of structure, emphasizing "its *static nature*, because it immobilizes perceptual levels, its *didacticism*, because it imparts knowledge, its *habit of creating finitude*, because speech organizes the world as a series of choices and amputations."[2] [..."son *statisme* puisqu'elle immobilise les niveaux de perception, son *didactisme* puisqu'elle a une fonction de connaissance, sa *finitisation* puisque la parole organise le monde en une série de choix et d'amputations."]

In such a system, links between sign and structure are of only one type: *causal*, yet this reinforces the linearity of the structure's topology and characterizes it as a single-directional construct, neither reversible, nor capable of being transformed.

Kristeva points out, however, that a signifying relation need not necessarily be structural. Although it sometimes functions as communication, it can also serve to unveil what she calls the extra-linguistic ("hors-langue"), which arises from the ideological component ("idéologème")[3] of the dis-

---

[2]*Le système de la mode*. Paris: Le Seuil, pp. 23-7.

[3]*"Idéologème"*: a function which binds together a society's translinguistic practices through condensation of the dominant mode of thought. Cf *Séméiotiké, Recherches pour une sémanalyse*. Paris: Le Seuil, 1969, pp. 60-62.

Moreover, Kristeva writes: "We shall call the intersection of a given textual organization (semiotic practice) with the utterances (sequences) it incorporates in its own space or assigns to the space of exterior texts (semiotic processes), an *"idéologème"*. p. 114 ["Le recoupement d'une organisation textuelle (d'une pratique sémiotique) donnée avec les énoncés (séquences) qu'elle assimile dans son espace ou auxquels elle renvoie dans l'espace des textes (pratiques sémiotiques) extérieurs, sera appelé un *idéologème*."]

text/history), because of its very determinism, is inadequate and inapplicable to "poetic language."[6] In fact, Saussure's sign, as it is necessarily dydic (signifier/signified), does not take into account concepts of continuity (this, because it is composed of distinct components) and movement. Monological, setting the *0* against the *1*, it implies that mutually exclusive oppositional terms are preeminent.

In the poetic text, distinctions between the signifier and signified become inoperative; therefore, it is necessary to find new instruments with which to work.

Insofar as this undertaking is concerned, the Kristevian method is influenced on the one hand by the writings of *M. Bakhtin*, in all that touches upon the dynamic model of text, and on the other, by those aspects of *mathematical theory* and *generative linguistics* that deal with the scientific formulation of such a model. The temptation to which Kristevian semiotics succombed in its early stages—the temptation of science—is no doubt attributable to the belief of the time that the text, despite its specificity, could constitute a scientific specimen, and that only the inadequacy of the research instruments applied to it excluded it from the domain commonly held to be scientific. Formulae, due to their abstractness, allow one to make-up for such a lack. Nonetheless, by the time *La Révolution du Langage poétique* was written, the inadequacy of such proceedings and the theoretical traps they tend to create had become evident to Kristeva.

From Bakhtin, Kristeva borrows the contextualization of any signifying practice, and particularly that of the text, in an historical or social frame. Attempting to replace the *static* subdivision of texts by a model in which the literary structure does not merely *exist*, but *elaborates* itself in relationship to another structure, Bakhtin chose the "status of the word" as minimal structural component. By this, he meant that the word was no longer to be considered as a *point* of fixed meaning, but as a *place*—a place where various textual surfaces and networks, such as those of author, of Receiver, of past or present cultural contexts, cross.... Following this example, Kristeva replaces the working component of the sign with *dialogical* components[7] which are semantic and polyphonic: these are double

---

[6]The notion of poetic text goes beyond that of mere poetry, incorporating texts such as those of Mallarmé, Lautréamont, Bataille, Céline, Sollers. . . which Kristeva often cites and has analyzed as well.

[7]Kristeva uses the term *dialogism* ("dialogisme") in opposition to *monologism* ("monologisme"), when referring to the narrative, as an expression of the duality of its language and logic, the latter being analogical rather than causal, and based on nonexclusive oppositions—in short, a transfinite logic. (pp. 152-53)

components that actualize both the ONE and its OTHER (the sign, however, becomes caught in its model, ONE/NON-ONE), constituting a formalistic rupture with the norm and positing the relationship between non-exclusive oppositional terms. By rejecting in this way the sign as well as the linguistics it grows out of, the Kristevian theory dismisses the kind of semiotics founded on "the sign, and thus on the concept of meaning as predetermining and presupposed." [... "le signe, donc sur le sens comme élément prédéterminant et présupposé."] For her, such systematic and monological semiotic practice is "conservative and limited, its elements oriented toward the denoted. It is logical and explanatory: it takes itself to be law, linked in a one-to-one relationship to an object, it represses any rapport with the Receiver...."[8] .. [... "conservatrice, limitée, ses éléments sont orientés vers les denotata. Elle est logique, explicative: elle s'identifie à la loi et renvoie par une liaison univoque à un objet, en refoulant ses rapports avec le destinataire...."] By turning aside such concepts, Kristeva is rejecting the structuralism of Todorov, Bremond, of Propp and the Slavic formalism from which, nonetheless, she has borrowed the notion that any signifying practice must be inscribed within the social context giving rise to it.

Kristeva's method substitutes a new semiotic for the old, a "dialogical or paragrammatic"[9] semiotic capable of taking into account the articulations, transformations and variations through which the dialectic of language is realized. Thus, reductionist structural links are exploded in order to introduce the added dimension which is missing from structural linguistics.

---

[8]Id., p. 196.

[9]Cf "Thus, *paragrammatic* space—the poetic space which we find on the edge of the *void*, on the slope opposite that of the speaker... is the neuralgic locus of our culture where junctures take place between the idea of the sign as normative utterance and that functioning which has no need of a logical subject to operate. This implies that the *paragrammatic* (and we paraphrase Lacan here) is for us a concept which has been formed in the path of that which functions to link the de-constitution of the subject with its constitution, the de-constitution of the utterance with the constitution of the text, the de-constitution of the sign with the constitution of writing." (p. 274) ["Ainsi l'espace *paragrammatique*—l'espace de la poésie que nous trouvons sur le versant opposé à celui du sujet parlant, aux abords de ce *vide*... est l'espace nevralgique de notre culture où s'operent les jonctions entre la pensée du signe en tant que parole normative, et ce fonctionnement qui n'a pas besoin d'un sujet logique pour s'exercer. Ceci pour dire que le *paragrammatisme* est pour nous (et nous nous permettons ici de paraphraser Lacan) un concept formé sur la voie de ce qui opère pour lier la déconstitution du sujet à sa constitution, la déconstitution de la parole à la constitution du texte, la déconstitution du signe à la constitution de l'écriture."] Thus the literary text, twofold writing-reading, is made up of a network of connections.

The task is twofold:

1. Semiotics first constitutes itself as a science of discourse and initially needs to anchor itself in the formal entity of the sign.
2. But it will be necessary to submit this notion of sign to critical examination. Meaning will need to constantly fall back on its own origin, reflecting upon it and transforming it. This system can only exist, then, as a criticism of semiotics itself, opening outward toward another realm, stepping into the *ideological*. And as such, this science constitutes a semanalysis ("sémanalyse").[10]

It should be noted, however, that we are not speaking in terms of system here. Semanalysis cannot be defined as a closed, completed edifice, as a structured and universal method of analyzing a finished product. Heir to the Freudian, Marxist attitudes which disturb the status of the subject and its discourse, semanalysis takes up the question of text as *production* as well as that of the transformation of meaning that results from it. Marked by *dialectical*, rather than formalistic logic, neither contenting itself solely with linguistic methods, nor with logical presuppositions, semanalysis takes both as its points of departure, emphasizing the text as subjectivity as well as communication. This explains the recourse to mathematical theory in early Kristevian discourse.

The theory is influenced by mathematical formalism since mathematics are free of the constraints of logic that conceives of the sentence in terms of subject and predicate; the mathematical optic works to lessen the severity of monological science (0-1) and emphasizes the dialectical nature of the language-system.[11]

The theory is influenced by generative linguistics as well since it sees language as a *dynamic* system of relations. The primary objectives of this formalizing process are 1. to point to the fact that beneath all that has to do with content and expression lies a translinguistic, algebraic locus, where relationships are traced that create governing laws before the fact, that there are also networks of a certain meaning above and beyond those of the expressed contents; 2. to attempt to extract the historical, epistemo-

[10]Id., cf pp. 18-19.
[11]Id., cf p. 174.

logical, and ideological implications from such a network. In Kristevian theory, such insistence on textual *dynamism* is linked to the notion of the locus of the subject. Therein lies its originality, as it tends to see the text in terms of *production* and writing as *practice* ("pratique").[12]

Semanalysis has come to replace semiotics, then, emphasizing that it is important not to "oppose the study of the signifying processes by the sign, but rather to break-down that sign, to open up an exterior within it, a new space of malleable, combinatory loci, the space in which meaning is created."[13] [. . . "bloquer l'étude des pratiques signifiantes par le signe, mais de le décomposer et d'ouvrir dans son dedans un nouveau dehors, un nouvel espace de sites retournables et combinatoires, l'espace de la signifiance."] Such a theory of textual signification envisions the sign as a mirror which reflects the *engendering* process ("engendrement") internal to it. In other words, without dismissing the fact that the text constitutes a system of signs, semanalysis opens another space within it: that in which "signifiance"—the process through which meaning is created—takes place. Without ceding to the illusion that it can leave behind the very realm of the sign that makes it possible, semanalysis sets out to reveal the existence of a combinatory process which constitutes an operation, a form of *production*, rather than simply to *describe* a structure.

Semanalysis underlines the fact that the text, more than a simple *linguistic* phenomenon reducible to the sum of juxtaposed structures and signs tied one to the other within a linear construct, engenders the language-system and the *I* who conveys that language. Thus, it is an object that has been made dynamic, the privileged space where the language constitutes itself as process.

In order to account structurally for such a conception, Kristevian theory, borrowing from the terminology of Šaumjan-Soboleva, divides the text into two loci: the *geno-text* and the *pheno-text*: the pheno-text being the locus of words, sentences, and successions of sentences arising from the symbolic of subject and that obey syntactic and lexical rules; the geno-text, on the other hand, being "an abstract level of linguistic functioning that, rather than reflecting sentence structures, precedes and exceeds them." [. . . "un niveau abstrait d'un fonctionnement linguistique qui ne réflète pas les structures de la phrase, mais les précède et les excède."] The geno-text generates not a structure, but a *signifier* which, in turn, manifests itself in the structures of the pheno-text.

The geno/pheno-text distinction henceforth obliges critical discourse to take on a dualistic view, to define two levels of utterance: that of the

[12]Id., cf p. 191.
[13]Id., cf p. 279.

linguistic phenomenon and of the structures growing out of the sign and capable of being *described* and formulated in structural terms; that of the process which *engenders* meaning, whose sign alone cannot fully reveal its network and manner of functioning. On the one hand, we are dealing with surface, on the other volume: Kristevian theory takes on the task of demonstrating the infinite complexity of the latter. And it betrays a predilection for the concept of geno-text as well, putting aside the structured subject ensnared in the law, for a different, ever mobile subject which engenders and re-engenders itself in and beyond the words.

By doubling the aspects of the text in order that they form a dialectical relation one with the other and in order that they may demonstrate how the subject engenders itself, Kristeva is able to account for signifying practices such as those of Sollers (cf. *Nombres*, analyzed in *Séméiotiké*), Lautreamont and Mallarmé (cf. *La Révolution du langage poétique*), and Céline, all of whose discourse dislocates the unifying mirror of meaning and breaks ground for a translinguistic site where the trial of the subject takes place. In so doing, such discourse, which Kristeva (following Bakhtin) terms carnival-like, goes beyond the latter's logic to open a space where the concepts of difference and multiplicity come into play, to forge a path toward the infinite. The text, as "mise en abîme", lends itself to a nonlinear, infinite reading that situates subject and text in historical context, and by so doing, creates a subversive process through which it repeatedly strikes blows against its institutions.

Today, Kristevian theory continues to support these concepts, though the mathematical formalization of the text proved with time to be inoperative and inexact and has been discarded. Despite the multitude of formulae, and their varying levels of sophistication, writing has continued, by its very nature, to produce creative *residue* which resists inclusion in such formulae. And it is of this very residue that the pleasure we take from the text ("le plaisir du texte") is born.

Translated by Susan Huston

SPEECH ACT THEORY AND ITS APPLICATIONS
TO THE STUDY OF LITERATURE

James A. Fanto

The discipline of semiotics includes as one of its fields of specialty pragmatics, which studies the use of sign systems. Speech act theory belongs to the purview of pragmatics because it describes how speakers employ the linguistic system of their community. The central tenet of speech act philosophy is, however, that any use of the language counts as part or all of a purposive action in a situation. When the speech act theorists have formulated rules for language use, therefore, these rules take the form of conventional procedures that a speaker must follow to accomplish an act and comprise many nonlinguistic, contextual features: the intentions of the speaker and hearer, their knowledge of one another, and the circumstances in which the particular usage of the language, the utterance, occurs. According to the speech act philosophers, each speaker understands how to perform an action in speaking or writing because of his knowledge of these rules established by his community, whereas the hearer recognizes the action his partner is accomplishing for the same reason. In this essay, I will first trace the development of this Anglo-American contribution to pragmatics by explaining several basic concepts of speech act theory. How literary critics have applied this theory to literature will next occupy me. My conclusion will then survey the work of those who have criticized speech act theory and its literary applications.

In its development, speech act theory defined itself as an opponent of two schools of modern disciplines. It denied, on the one hand, analytic philosophy's claim to submit all sentences to a true/false criterion. Speech act theory, moreover, pointed out the shortcomings of formal linguistics, which studied syntax and phonology and neglected the use of language, relegating it to the nontheoretical level of performance. In founding speech act theory, J. L. Austin opposed the analytic philosophers, while John R. Searle developed it as a correction to problems in linguistics.

Austin's William James Lectures at Harvard in 1955, later published as *How to Do Things with Words,* constitute the seminal work of speech act theory. The reader of these lectures follows Austin's critique of analytic philosophy that culminates in the establishment of a new theory of language. At the book's beginning, Austin observes that philosophers cannot appropriately consider all sentences descriptions of states of affairs in the world or representations of psychological states of mind and thus call them true or false. Consider, for example, the following sentences:

(1) The cat is on the mat.
(2) Sam smokes habitually.
(3) I name this ship the *Queen Elizabeth.*
(4) I bet you a dollar it will rain tomorrow.

Sentence (3) is not a true or false description of a christening; indeed, it describes nothing at all. When a speaker utters it in a particular situation, he performs part of the act of christening. Sentence (4) does not report a psychological state of mind in the speaker; the utterance accomplishes the act of betting. Austin's first move, then, is to present several sentences to which the analytic philosophers' true/false criterion does not apply.

This insight leads Austin to distinguish two classes of sentences. He calls sentences, such as (1) and (2) above, "constatives" because they describe states of affairs and therefore conform to the true/false criterion. The other class of sentences he labels "performatives." In uttering them the speaker does not report a state of affairs but performs an action, brings into existence a new state of affairs. Austin characterizes the world-creating nature of performatives by his expression, "saying makes it so." He realizes, moreover, that for an utterance to become a performative an appropriate speaker has to say it in a correct context. A man who utters sentence (3) outside the conventional ceremony while striking a ship with a bottle would not, for example, be described as performing the act of christening. Austin thus concludes that rules for the successful execution of performatives exist.

Austin then establishes a new criterion for performatives: he calls them felicitous or infelicitous depending upon whether the speaker utters the particular sentences according to rules or conditions. Austin sets out these felicity conditions in the second lecture of his book:

(A. 1) There must exist an accepted conventional procedure having a certain conventional effect, that procedure to include the uttering of certain words by certain persons in certain circumstances, and further,

(A. 2) the particular persons and circumstances in a given case must be appropriate for the invocation of the particular procedure invoked.

(B. 1) The procedure must be executed by all participants both correctly and

(B. 2) completely.

(Γ. 1)   Where, as often, the procedure is designed for use by persons having certain thoughts or feelings, or for the inauguration of certain consequential conduct on the part of any participant, then a person participating in and so invoking the procedure must in fact have those thoughts or feelings, and the participants must intend so to conduct themselves, and further

(Γ. 2)   must actually so conduct themselves subsequently. (14-15)

These rules, however, are not all on an equal footing. If the speaker does not fulfill one of the first four conditions, he will fail to produce a performative. His act will be infelicitous. In a Christian country, to take one of Austin's examples, a man cannot divorce his wife by saying to her, "I divorce thee." He has not met Austin's first felicity condition. Yet a speaker can neglect to satisfy the last two conditions and still accomplish a performative. I can promise to do something for you, but I can really intend not to carry it out and refuse to perform the stipulated action at the appointed time. One could not say that I had never promised, but that I had abused the procedure for promising.

This distinction between the felicity conditions is an important sign of the nature and limitations of Austin's thought and of speech act theory in general. By stating that the first four conditions are essential, Austin means that a speaker accomplishes a performative once he has fulfilled these conditions. According to Austin, moreover, a speaker who invokes the felicity conditions takes responsibility for the intentions presupposed by them. If he performs the conventional procedure for promising, for example, he makes a public expression of an intention to do some future action for his addressee. Austin admits that a speaker may possess thoughts and feelings that contradict his stated intentions; furthermore, he acknowledges that a speaker may fail to accomplish the future action predicated by the performative. By excluding the final two conditions from the essential conditions, however, Austin indicates that a speech act has nothing to do with such intentions and its consequences: a performative takes place regardless of them as long as the speaker fulfills the conventional procedures. For if a man could void his performative by stating later that his real intentions were not those stipulated by the felicity conditions, society, Austin implies, would break down. Austin's phrase, *"our word is our bond,"* sums up the social, ethical, and legal aspects of his thought inherent in the distinction between the conditions. Speech act theory after Austin, as we will see, conforms to its founder's division of the conditions. It focuses on the procedures that constitute a speech act and the intentions attributed to the speaker because of his invocation of the procedures. It resolutely ignores unspecifiable intentions and the consequences of any performative.

In the course of *How to Do Things with Words* Austin gradually erases the boundary between the performatives and the constatives until the former class completely absorbs the latter. Every utterance, he discovers, is an action constituted by conventional procedures that include contextual information. To abolish the independence of the constative, Austin shows that the context determines the true/false criterion itself. His well-known example is the phrase, "France is hexagonal." Austin observes that whereas some people, such as a general, would call this statement true, others, like geographers, would label it neither true nor false and would identify it as "rough." Austin concludes, therefore, that the true/false criterion does not represent an absolute standard applying to all constatives. He says that one must "realize that 'true' and 'false,' like 'free' and 'unfree,' do not stand for anything simple at all; but only for a general dimension of being a right or proper thing to say as opposed to a wrong thing, in these circumstances, to this audience, for these purposes and with these intentions" (145). An absolute true/false criterion and the pure constative become only theoretical constructs: "This is the ideal of what would be right to say in all circumstances, for any purpose, to any audience, etc. Perhaps it is sometimes realized" (146). Since the constatives belong to the general category of the performative, a speaker must fulfill the ˛licity conditions mentioned above to accomplish a successful constative. For example, one must utter the sentence, "France is hexagonal," before particular people, preferably not geographers, in order to produce a felicitous constative.

Once having abolished the constative/performative distinction, Austin presents a new formalization of all utterances. He proposes that a speaker performs three acts in uttering a sentence: the *locutionary,* the *illocutionary,* and the *perlocutionary acts.* The *locutionary act* entails three theoretically distinct parts: the "phonetic act" describes the noises a speaker utters; the "phatic act" involves the saying "noises of certain types, belonging to and as belonging to, a certain vocabulary, conforming to and as conforming to a certain grammar"; finally, the "rhetic act" deals with the usage of words with a "certain more-or-less definite sense and reference" (95). The *locutionary act,* as one can see, embraces phonology and syntax as well as traditional semantics. To borrow an example from Austin, one could describe the *locutionary act* of the utterance, "Shoot her!," as follows: "He said to me 'Shoot her!' meaning by 'shoot' shoot and referring by 'her' to *her*" (101). The *illocutionary act* is a new name for the performative. Each *illocutionary act,* moreover, possesses an "illocutionary force," Austin's definition of a meaning, different from "sense and reference," that a speaker communicates to his addressee. This force belongs to the *illocutionary act* by virtue of what makes it an act: the following of the felicity conditions by the speaker. The hearer receives this "force" the moment he recognizes that the speaker is invoking conventional procedures constituting a particular act. To continue the same example, one could identify the *illocutionary act* of the utterance, "Shoot her!," by the following description: "He urged (or advised, ordered, etc.) me to shoot her." Finally, the *perlocutionary act* involves the production of "certain consequential effects upon the feelings, thoughts, or actions of the audience, or of the speaker, or of other persons" by the speaker's saying something (101). The speaker may intend his utterance to produce these effects, but he cannot control them. The *perlocutionary act,* accordingly, pertains to rhetoric. Austin thus describes the perlocution of the above example as "He persuaded me to shoot her" or "He got me to (or made me, etc.) shoot her."

In proposing this novel formalization of language, Austin has two purposes in mind. His account of the language acts provides a basis for theoretical analysis and does not claim to describe the genesis of the acts. That is, according to Austin, one does not first perform a locution, then add to it an illocutionary force, and finally arrive at the perlocution. All three acts occur simultaneously in the utterance of any sentence. Secondly, he intends to establish the *illocutionary act* as the primary object of language study and of speech act theory in particular. Grammarians can abstract the locution from the illocution for syntactic and traditional semantic analysis, and rhetoricians can study the perlocution or the effects of the *illocutionary act.* Both must, however, recognize the primacy of the illocution, the speaker's performance of an action in uttering words in a context. The heirs of Austin would, like their master, concentrate on theorizing further the *illocutionary act,* while paying little attention to the locution and devoting almost none at all to the perlocution.

John R. Searle, a philosopher at the University of California, Berkeley, is the most well-known of Austin's disciples and has formalized the insights of his master in articles and especially in the book, *Speech Acts: An Essay in the Philosophy of Language* (1969). Like Austin, Searle defended ordinary language from the criticisms of the analytic philosophers. Yet he has also developed speech act theory as a response to formal linguistics that neglected the use of language to communicate meaning. According to Searle, theorists of formal linguistics, such as Chomsky and his precursors, believed that they could not adequately formalize the usage of language as they could syntax. They thus considered language use an unsuitable object of study for linguistic theory and dismissed it to the level of performance. In opposing this theoretical exclusion, Searle drew support from Chomsky's own students, the generative semanticists, who brought language usage, contextual features, and semantics into the deep structure description of a sentence and thus into linguistic theory (Searle, 1972). By rigorously formalizing Austin's insights about speech acts Searle was, in effect, proving to formal linguistics that human use of language was a suitable object of theoretical knowledge.

In *Speech Acts,* Searle sets out to produce a theoretically precise account of Austin's felicity conditions. He begins to explain the conditions by introducing a distinction between two types of rules, regulative and constitutive. According to Searle, regulative rules "regulate a pre-existing activity, an activity whose existence is logically independent of the rules," whereas constitutive rules "constitute (and also regulate) an activity the existence of which is logically dependent on the rules" (34). Regulative rules, notes Searle, regulate "brute facts": physical movements, weight, and raw feelings. Constitutive rules, on the other hand, constitute and regulate "institutional facts": for instance, games or procedures in a ceremony. Men, therefore, create "institutional facts," while "brute facts" belong to a world existing independently of human activity.

An example adapted from Searle will prove helpful to make these distinctions clear. Imagine that a particularly intelligent man who is unfamiliar with American football walks into a stadium while a game is in progress. We then ask him to compose laws about what he sees. As Searle explains, the man might formulate from his observations the following laws: "For example, we can imagine that after a time our observer would discover the law of periodical clustering: at statistically regular intervals organisms in like colored shirts cluster together in a roughly circular fashion (the huddle). Furthermore, at equally regular intervals, circular clustering is followed by linear clustering (the teams line up for the play), and linear clustering is followed by the phenomenon of linear interpenetration" (52). These laws are inductive generalizations based on the man's observations of the "brute facts" of physical motion and regulative because they do not constitute, but only regulate, these "facts." If we then ask a football fan to characterize what he sees, his description will differ considerably from the laws of the first observer. He will speak of huddles, passes, penalties, touchdowns, and of a game played by teams on a field. Moreover, observes Searle, a football fan's remarks would seem tautological: that is, his description of the "facts" are indeed the rules that bring the facts into existence in the first place. For example, the fan's account of the "fact," touchdown ("He ran with the ball across their goal line."), resembles a rule book definition of how to score a touchdown: "a touchdown is scored when a player has possession of the ball in the opponents' end zone while a play is in progress" (34). Searle calls such rules constitutive because they both constitute and regulate "institutional facts."

Searle then identifies the illocutionary or speech act as an "institutional fact" and, consequently, Austin's felicity conditions as constitutive rules. The felicity conditions thus constitute and regulate the speech acts: a speaker follows them in order to produce an illocutionary act, and one describes this act in terms of these conditions. In refining Austin's account of the felicity conditions, Searle presents his own detailed version of them and extracts from them four basic rules that produce the illocutionary force of any utterance. An example borrowed from *Speech Acts,* the illocutionary act of promising, will suffice to demonstrate the enactment of the rules. If a speaker wants to promise, he must first fulfill a *propositional content rule.* That is, in uttering a sentence he must predicate some future action on his part. In the sentence, "I promise to pay you five dollars," the propositional content would be the phrase, "I will pay you five dollars." The speaker must then satisfy the *preparatory rules.* Such rules would include the following contextual information: in the case of our example, the hearer would prefer the speaker's paying him five dollars, and the speaker believes that the hearer would prefer this action. Another *preparatory rule* states, moreover, that it would not be obvious to both the speaker and the hearer that the former would pay the latter five dollars in the normal course of events. The speaker must next observe the *sincerity rule*: the "I" of our example must sincerely intend to pay his interlocutor five dollars. The hearer, of course, cannot verify the speaker's intentions. Yet the utterance of this sentence in a particular context stands for a public avowal of the intention to promise sincerely. Finally and most importantly the speaker complies with the *essential rule.* According to this rule, the utterance of our example sentence counts as the speaker's action of putting upon himself the obligation to pay five dollars to his addressee. The hearer, then, receives the illocutionary force of this speech act, that is, he understands its meaning, when he recognizes the speaker's intention to promise. And he perceives this intention by noticing that the speaker is fulfilling the above rules constituting the illocutionary act of promising. In other words, once the hearer detects the speaker's intention to perform a speech act, the speaker accomplishes the act and communicates his meaning to the hearer.

Searle significantly includes intentionality in his formalization of the constitutive rules for illocutionary acts because he believes that pragmatics must take into consideration man's purposes for using language, purposes often neglected by formal linguistics. Like Austin, however, Searle can handle only those intentions for which a man accepts responsibility by uttering certain sentences in particular contexts. As I mentioned earlier, Searle realizes that the hearer can never confirm whether the speaker really fulfills the sincerity rule for an illocutionary act. The hearer just supposes that the speaker means what he says, if the speaker satisfies the other rules. Searle's concept of intentionality, then, does not extend beyond these conventional intentions.

After Searle finished his revision of Austin's felicity conditions, he then proceeds to reevaluate his teacher's classification of illocutionary acts. In the concluding lectures of *How to Do Things with Words,* Austin categorizes illocutionary acts according to verbs. He groups, for example, in his "verdictive" class, which "consists in the delivering of a finding, official or unofficial, upon evidence or reasons as to value or fact, so far as these are distinguishable" (153), such verbs as acquit, convict, rule, estimate, and grade. Searle criticizes Austin's taxonomy for the identification of illocutionary acts with verbs and presents his own classification in his important essay, "A Classification of Illocutionary Acts" (Searle, 1976). He distinguishes five kinds of illocutionary acts:

> *Representatives.* The point or purpose of the members of the representative class is to commit the speaker (in varying degrees) to something's being the case, to the truth of the expressed proposition. ("I state that it is raining.")
>
> *Directives.* The illocutionary point of these consists in the fact that they are attempts by the speaker to get the hearer to do something. ("I order you to leave.")
>
> *Commissives.* Those illocutionary acts whose point is to commit the speaker to some future course of action. ("I promise to pay you the money.")
>
> *Expressives.* The illocutionary point of this class is to express the psychological state specified in the sincerity condition about a state of affairs specified in the propositional content. ("I apologize for stepping on your toe.")
>
> *Declarations.* It is the defining characteristic of this class that the successful performance of one of its members brings about the correspondence between the propositional content and reality, successful performance guarantees that the propositional content corresponds to the world. ("I appoint you chairman.") (adapted from Searle, 1976, 10-16)

Rather than by verbs, Searle separates illocutionary acts mainly on the basis of their illocutionary point, a new name for the essential rule. Yet Searle enumerates other characteristics, many developments of the conditions and rules formalized in *Speech Acts,* that differentiate illocutionary acts. The direction of fit between the words and the world, for example, distinguishes one act from another. A speaker performing a commissive intends to get the world to match up with his words. To illustrate this, let us consider once more our example sentence of promising. The speaker predicates a future action (the world) that will ultimately correspond to his utterance (words).

Searle's list of distinguishing features also includes such circumstances of the context as the social status of the conversational participants. Certain directives, in fact, presuppose the superiority of the speaker. A private, for example, cannot felicitously command a general. Searle's classification, then, formalizes well the differences between illocutionary acts.

While formulating this theory of pragmatics, Austin and Searle said little about fiction or literature. In *How to Do Things with Words,* Austin acknowledges the existence of "parasitic" discourse or the "etiolations" of language, such as speech in plays, fiction, poetry, quotation, and recitation (93), yet he leaves it out of his discussion. Searle deals with only "serious" utterances in *Speech Acts* and excludes from theoretical consideration such utterances as "play acting, teaching a language, reciting poems, practicing pronunciation, etc." (57). Fortunately for students of literature, Searle regarded nonserious discourse as an important enough problem to devote an essay to it in *New Literary History,* "The Logical Status of Fictional Discourse" (Searle, 1975b).

In this essay, Searle decides to fix the necessary and sufficient conditions for fictional discourse, which includes jokes, anecdotes, and some literary works. According to Searle, the speakers and hearers of fictional discourse agree to a nonsemantic "horizontal" convention that lifts the speech acts in fiction from the world and suspends the normal commitments required of the speaker. In other words, the speaker of fictional discourse pretends to perform speech acts and goes through the motions of making them. To illustrate this distinction between fictional and serious discourse, Searle analyzes two assertions, one taken from a newspaper and the other from a novel. The newspaper reporter, he says, is making an assertion in conformity to the felicity conditions of asserting: for instance, the reporter commits himself to the truth of the proposition contained in his assertion and must be able to produce on demand evidence for its truth. The fiction writer, on the other hand, utters a sentence that normally commits a speaker to the truth of the expressed proposition. He does not, however, commit himself to its truth, believe in its truth, or feel compelled to provide evidence for it. His audience, moreover, understands which illocutionary act he is performing and does not hold him responsible for this act because of its knowledge of the horizontal convention.

Searle makes two other points in this article that would interest a literary critic. For Searle, the author is pretending to perform the speech acts of fictional discourse. Being a professional philosopher, Searle is unaware that students of literature have been accustomed during the past years to identify the speaker of fiction as the narrator or persona, seldom as the author himself. Searle admits, moreover, that an author occasionally produces serious assertions in fictional discourse. If an author, for example, refers to something or someone of the real world in the proposition of the assertion, in Searle's view he makes a serious assertion, and the reader will accordingly hold him responsible for the felicity conditions of asserting. Since Searle admits that serious speech acts appear in fictional discourse, critics have suggested that he does not establish the necessary and sufficient conditions for such discourse (Fish, 1976). His horizontal convention, they say, only explains whether a particular utterance is fictional or not.

Whereas Searle's particular account of fictional discourse did not influence many literary critics, students of literature were attracted to the central concept of speech act theory, which leads Searle to consider the author as the speaker of fictional discourse: each use of language is an act by an individual with specific intentions. That this concept assumed such importance for several American critics becomes clear when one examines the recent history of literary theory in this country. New Criticism, which reigned in American literary life for about thirty years, labeled any concern with the historical author and his intentions the "intentional fallacy." This movement proposed instead the doctrine of textual self-sufficiency. Studies inspired by formalism and structuralism echoed this doctrine, dismissing the biography of an author as extra-literary data. Not surprisingly, then, literary historians and critics who were interested in the author's meaning were quick to claim speech act theory as an ally because of its emphasis on intentionality. On several occasions, E. D. Hirsch has called speech act theory a useful corrective to modern theories of textual self-sufficiency (Hirsch, 1975a; 1975b). In an article appearing in *New Literary History*, "Motives, Intentions, and the Interpretation of Texts," Quentin Skinner attacks Wimsatt and Beardsley by drawing support from Austin's theory (Skinner, 1972).

Yet this application of speech act's concept of intentionality to literature is metaphorical. As I pointed out earlier, speech act theory limits itself to those intentions specified by a speaker's invocation of felicity conditions established by his linguistic community. The theory cannot handle unconscious intentions or conscious purposes not identifiable by the conventional procedures for making speech acts. When Hirsch and Skinner use speech act theory as evidence for a view of complex authorial intentions controlling the genesis of a text and informing the text itself, they are pushing the theory beyond its self-imposed limitations. Hirsch, in fact, realizes these limitations and prefers other philosophical formulations that give more freedom to authorial intentions than does speech act theory according to Austin and Searle (Hirsch, 1975a, 574-77).

Once a critic detaches intentionality from its strict definition in speech act theory, his application of this concept to literary studies can take whatever shape he selects. One method calls for a critic to use the concept to justify a search for the author's intentions in biographical data and in the history of ideas of his time. Several critics, who all seem inspired by E. D. Hirsch, have chosen this method. This group of critics would certainly include Michael Hancher, editor of *Centrum,* a journal that frequently publishes articles on speech act theory and literary criticism. Hancher, in fact, often explains the theory to an audience of literary critics. He wrote, for instance, an essay in *College English* in which he analyzes the speech acts in poems by Shakespeare and Robert Frost as a method of describing the basic concepts of the theory (Hancher, 1975). He has, moreover, reviewed the recent trends of the application of speech act theory to literature in an essay/review published in *Modern Language Notes* (Hancher, 1977).

Hancher's own method of applying speech act theory to literature appears in another *MLN* essay, "Three Kinds of Intentions" (Hancher, 1972), and presents, as I said, an extension of the concept of intentionality. In this essay, Hancher accuses Wimsatt and Beardsley of confounding different kinds of authorial intentions in their attack on the "intentional fallacy." There are, he argues, three types of intentions: the *programmatic* or the author's desire to produce some kind of literary text, such as a poem or novel, the *final* or the author's wish to accomplish something by writing, say, to become rich, and the *active* intention to be understood as acting in some way. He exemplifies this last kind of intentionality by his comments on Hopkins's "The Windhover": "For example, I may at the moment of completing a certain poem intend and understand the whole action of that poem to be (and want others to understand it to be) my celebrating the metaphorical presence of the Passion of Christ as it is recognized in the flight of a windhover" (Hancher, 1972, 830). The "intentional fallacy," notes Hancher, pertains to the *programmatic* and *final,* not to the *active,* intentions. Speech act theory, according to him, lends support to the importance of the *active* intentions because of its emphasis on the speaker's intention in the production of illocutionary acts. If the analogy between Hancher's *active* and speech act intentions were complete, however, one would expect to find him listing rules that would enable the reader to move automatically from the literary text to its author's intentions. Yet he does not formulate such rules. As it is, the analogy permits Hancher to justify his close readings of texts and research of biographical information as a search for clues to the author's *active* intentions. And his form of literary criticism resembles the methodology of traditional literary history.

Like Michael Hancher, other critics have used the speech act concept of intentionality to allow them to discuss what a writer thought he was doing in composing a literary text. One of Hancher's colleagues at the University of Minnesota, Marcia Eaton, who has compiled a bibliography on speech acts (Eaton, 1974) and who is collecting references for an updated version, affirms that a reader must try to recapture the author's intentions behind the words of the fictional characters, if necessary, by referring to extra-literary information (Eaton, 1970). In the article cited above, Quentin Skinner extends the speech act concept of intentionality to include "what a writer may have *meant by* writing in that particular way. It is equivalently to be able, that is, to say that he must have *meant* the work *as* an attack on or a defense of, as a criticism of or a contribution to, some particular attitude or line or argument, and so on" (Skinner, 1972, 405). Skinner, too, has recourse to the author's statements about his intentions and to other literary historical data in order to identify the author's meaning in writing a particular work. Since these critics, like Hancher, offer no rules for specifying the author's intentions, they extend the concept of intentionality to the point where it bears little resemblance to its formulation in speech act theory.

Other critics who have borrowed concepts from speech act theory have made a more rigorous analogy between their methods of literary analysis and the theory itself. These critics adopt, as did Hirsch and Hancher, the concept of intentionality to justify their interest in authorial intentions. They also borrow, however, the notion of felicity conditions so as to provide a reader with a rule-governed method of identifying these intentions. For them, conventions such as genre rules for literary forms become the felicity conditions of literature and therefore in Searle's terms constitutive rules. They suggest, then, that these conventions lead the reader to the author's intentions.

This particular application of speech act theory characterizes the work of Robert Brown and Martin Steinmann, both affiliated with *Centrum* and Hancher's colleagues at Minnesota. Brown first defines Searle's horizontal convention of fictional discourse as one of the felicity conditions of literature: literature is composed of pretended speech acts. He alters, however, this convention, allowing no serious speech acts to break the unity of fictional discourse. He explains, moreover, that the author himself does not make the pretended speech acts in fiction, but pretends to report the speech acts of fictional characters. Brown also identifies the genre rules of literature as felicity conditions: "It treats poetic meaning as continuous with meaning in everyday language, but still allows us to formulate sufficient conditions to differentiate distinct types of language acts. Such conditions would formalize the *conventions* known to speakers and hearers which constitute their sense of genre, or at the highest level, their intuitions about differences between poetry and everyday language use" (Brown, 1974, 65). According to Brown, a reader works from these felicity conditions back to the author's intentions or meaning. Steinmann, too, labels the genre conventions the felicity conditions of literature (Steinmann, 1974; 1976).

Although the essays of Brown and Steinmann are meant to be programs for future studies, they do not provide a method of detecting the authorial intentions, which would interest a literary critic, because their application of speech act concepts is metaphorical. Whereas Searle, as we saw, considers his horizontal convention of fictional discourse nonsemantic in character, by making it a felicity condition of literature Brown and Steinmann suppose that it is semantic. What meaning, however, does a reader receive from his awareness that the author of fiction intends the sentences as reports of fictional speech acts other than the knowledge of this authorial intention? A similar limitation of intentions arises from describing genre rules as felicity conditions. The only intentions a reader perceives because of his knowledge of genre conventions are the author's intention to compose a novel or a poem and, perhaps, his intention to violate certain genre rules. These literary felicity conditions will not tell a reader why an author violated a particular genre convention or why he chose to write a particular kind of literary text. The intentions specified by such conditions resemble the conditions themselves. The meaning of a speech act, on the other hand, differs in nature from the felicity conditions that constitute it. In a promise, for instance, the speaker's uttering certain words in a context indicates his intention to accept the obligation of performing some future action for his hearer. Once again, therefore, the analogy between speech act theory and a literary methodology is imperfect. Several critics, moreover, have questioned the correctness of the comparison of genre conventions to felicity conditions, identifying the former as regulative, not constitutive, rules (Hancher, 1977; Fish, 1976).

Wolfgang Iser, the prominent theorist of the phenomenology of reading, also proposes an analogy between the felicity conditions of speech acts and the conventions of literary genres as a method of locating the author's intentions (Iser, 1975). Iser, however, extends still further the concept of felicity conditions in his studies of literary texts. As I mentioned earlier, in speech act theory each linguistic community establishes the felicity conditions that constitute the "institutional facts" or speech acts. Since these conditions include contextual features, one could say that they are connected to particular contexts. A speaker, for example, could not promise unless he satisfied the preparatory rules concerning contextual information: he believes that the hearer would prefer his performance of the predicated future action. Now Iser makes an analogy between the felicity conditions and other social conventions, such as ways of perceiving the world or religious views, that function in everyday situations. He then proposes that an author lifts these conventions out of their ordinary contexts and displays them in a literary text. A reader, accordingly, wonders why the author has exhibited these conventions that he normally takes for granted in his life. According to Iser, the genre conventions of the particular literary work help the reader in his search for the author's reasons for such a display. Yet this borrowing of speech act concepts again results in their transformation into a methodology that hardly resembles the original theory. The felicity conditions of a speech act, I repeat, allow a hearer to identify automatically the speaker's intentions, while Iser's genre rules only guide the reader in what seems an arduous pursuit of the author's meaning in displaying real world conventions in a literary text. Indeed, as Iser observes, the genre rules can even thwart a reader's search for intentions in innovative examples of a particular genre. As Stanley Fish has pointed out, Iser's methodology is interesting but has nothing to do with speech act theory (Fish, 1976).

Critics who are primarily interested in identifying the historical author's intentions have no monopoly on speech act theory, for the advocates of textual self-sufficiency have also used its concepts in their studies of literature. These opponents of intentionality admit only one authorial intention: the author intends his work to be taken by the reader as a report of imitation speech acts. In other words, such critics would accept Brown's refinement and extension of Searle's horizontal convention of fictional discourse. Once they state that this convention is in force whenever men write or read literary works, however, they see no reason to talk any longer about the author and his intentions. The text, composed of imitation speech acts performed by fictional characters, is for them self-sufficient and needs only a reader to activate it. When a reader takes up a literary work, they say, he brings along his knowledge of felicity conditions for the performance of real world speech acts. As he reads the sentences, therefore, he fills in the context presupposed by them. For example, if a character in a novel says the sentence, "I promise to pay you five dollars," the reader knowing that the utterance of this sentence normally counts as the act of promising supplies the necessary conditions to make it felicitous: he attributes to the speaker the belief that his addressee will prefer his performance of the action predicated in the proposition, the sincere intention to put himself under an obligation to his hearer, and so on. With his speech act competence, then, the reader creates to a great extent the world and characters of a literary text. Barbara Smith, who has occasionally written on speech act theory (Smith, 1975), has proposed an application of the theory to literature that resembles the one described above. Monroe Beardsley, one of the author's of the "intentional fallacy," has also employed speech act theory in his study of literature. Like Smith, he describes a literary text as a display of illocutionary acts uttered by fictional characters for the reader's imaginative involvement (Beardsley, 1970).

The main problem with this application of the theory to literature lies in the distinction these critics make between a normal conversation and the reader's activity in a literary situation. They suggest that in a face-to-face conversation the intentions of the speaker are so evident because of his physical presence and because of the context that he easily communicates his meaning to the hearer. In speech act terms, however, a speaker has no advantage in communication on account of his presence before the hearer. He must follow the conventional procedures for producing speech acts and hope that the hearer will recognize his intentions from his actions. The hearer, moreover, fills in information about a speaker—his intentions and presuppositions—from the latter's utterances in a way similar to a reader's creation of a fictional character from the text's sentences. The hearer, in effect, builds up an idea of the speaker's mind as he listens to his utterances and interprets other signs, such as movements, gestures, and intonation. A face-to-face conversation, then, gives the hearer no more certainty about the speaker's real thoughts and feelings than does a literary text about its fictional characters. Both the hearer in a normal conversation and the reader of literature depend upon the speech act felicity conditions that attribute certain intentions to the minds of a speaker.

Like Smith and Beardsley, Richard Ohmann also regards literature as made of imitation speech acts or what he calls "quasi speech acts." Yet Ohmann, who was one of the first literary critics to write about the possible applications of speech act theory to literature, formulates in addition a theory of stylistics from his description of the imitation speech acts. In one article, "Instrumental Style: Notes on the Theory of Speech as Action" (Ohmann, 1972a), he devises a complicated classification of illocutionary acts to facilitate his characterization of an author's style. Although he never performs in detail a stylistic analysis, however, he implies that one would accomplish it by enumerating the speech acts in a text and interpreting, for example, the predominance of one or two classes of speech acts. Ohmann labels, for instance, a passage of Carlyle "authoritarian" because of the presence of many "Influencers" (Searle's directives). Yet nothing in speech act theory provides Ohmann with support for his desire to interpret lists of speech acts. The illocutionary act, as I have said, possesses only one meaning, its illocutionary force: the hearer recognizes that the utterance of a particular sentence in a context counts as a certain action. To refer to Ohmann's Carlyle passage, the presence of many directives only signifies that many utterances in the text stand for attempts by the speaker to get his audience to perform some future action. Speech act theory cannot decide whether such a text is authoritarian or not. One must conclude, therefore, that by trying to link lists of speech acts with an interpretation Ohmann is pushing the theory beyond its limited competence and, in fact, supplying his own interpretation. While Ohmann performed a great service by publicizing speech act theory in literary circles with his numerous articles, his application of the theory to stylistics, as Fish has observed, bears little resemblance to the original theory.

When presenting his speech act version of stylistics, Richard Ohmann includes in his analysis transformational grammar (Ohmann, 1972a). This combination of speech act and other linguistic theories characterizes the work of the speech act theorists themselves. John Searle, for example, often uses transformational grammar to describe the syntax of particular illocutions (Searle, 1976). Several journals have recently published articles whose authors have studied literary problems or texts from a theoretical perspective uniting speech act theory with other forms of linguistic analysis. In the journal, *Poetics,* edited by Teun A. van Dijk, Dorothy Mack has written an article describing her efforts to clear "metaphoring," which includes metaphors and similes, from Austin's charge that it is parasitic on normal discourse (Mack, 1975). She first analyzes the deep structure of "metaphoring" sentences and then shows that they fulfill Austin's felicity conditions. In a subsequent article published in the same journal, Edward Levenston refines Mack's deep structure description of "metaphoring," while praising her speech act analysis of this literary problem (Levenston, 1976). Another review, the *Journal of Literary Semantics,* occasionally prints articles combining speech act theory with other linguistic formulations in the study of literary texts. While demonstrating how generative semantics can help one analyze a text, Elizabeth Traugott draws parallels between its concern with rules of language use and speech act theory's felicity conditions (Traugott, 1973). In the same journal, Ronald Tanaka has drawn attention to the need for a literary methodology that would include speech act theory, syntax studies, and semantics (Tanaka, 1972). Tanaka's article is, in fact, typical of the above essays, except Mack's, because it serves as a program for future studies rather than as a thorough analysis of a literary text or problem.

In the course of this essay, I have discussed the main tradition of speech act theory, as Austin and Searle developed it, and its applications to the study of literature. Literary critics, however, have begun to borrow concepts from the work of another ordinary language philosopher, H. P. Grice, during the past few years, and his work will likely attract more attention in the near future (Tanaka, 1972; Hirsch, 1975a; Hancher, 1972; 1977). Grice's main work, *Logic and Conversation* (1967 William James Lectures), remains unpublished, although parts of it have been printed as articles. Like Austin, Grice also formulated a theory of language use to oppose philosophers who criticized ordinary language. Yet Grice's adversaries regarded ordinary language as imperfect because its reasoning devices were deficient in comparison with those of formal logic. Grice countered by stating that a man could not only use conversational language rationally, but also when using it he was following principles that dictated the overall rational behavior in man.

Since Grice conceives of conversation as purposive, rational behavior, he formulates rules that explain men's conduct in their talk exchanges. First of all, he says, speakers and hearers assume a "Cooperative Principle" (CP), defined as follows, to be in force throughout their conversations: "Make your conversational contribution such as is required, at the stage at which it occurs, by the accepted purpose or direction of the talk exchange in which you are engaged" (Grice, 1975, 45). The CP encompasses four rules or Maxims:

> I. *Maxims of Quantity*
>   1. Make your contribution as informative as is required (for the current purposes of the exchange).
>   2. Do not make your contribution more informative than is required.
>
> II. *Maxims of Quality*
>   1. Do not say what you believe to be false.
>   2. Do not say that for which you lack adequate evidence.
>
> III. *Maxim of Relation*
>   1. Be relevant.
>
> IV. *Maxims of Manner*
>   Supermaxim: Be perspicuous.
>   1. Avoid obscurity of expression.
>   2. Avoid ambiguity.
>   3. Be brief (avoid unnecessary prolixity).
>   4. Be orderly.
>
> (adapted from Grice, 1975, 45-6)

This CP and the Maxims, then, reflect Grice's conception of the rationality of human conversations.

Grice next uses the CP and Maxims to explain *implicature,* a process whereby a speaker means more than he says and a hearer infers this meaning. According to Grice, this process demonstrates well the logic of conversation in ordinary language. To explain *implicature,* Grice first lists the possible violations of the Maxims:

1. He may quietly and unostentatiously VIOLATE a maxim; if so, in some cases he will be liable to mislead.
2. He may OPT OUT from the operation both of the maxim and of the CP; he may say, indicate, or allow it to become plain that he is unwilling to cooperate in the way the maxim requires. He may say, for example, *I cannot say more; my lips are sealed.*
3. He may be faced by a CLASH: he may be unable, for example, to fulfill the first maxim of Quantity (Be as informative as is required) without violating the second maxim of Quality (Have adequate evidence for what you say).

4. He may FLOUT a maxim; that is, he may BLATANTLY fail
to fulfill it.

(adapted from Grice, 1975, 49)

According to Grice, when a speaker makes any of the first three violations, he often endangers the CP, and the conversation cannot proceed. If, for example, a speaker utters the sentence, "My lips are sealed," the conversation usually ends. *Implicature,* on the other hand, properly belongs to the fourth violation, flouting. In this case, says Grice, a speaker fails to fulfill a Maxim while maintaining the CP in order to communicate some meaning in addition to what he has said. And the hearer infers this meaning because he recognizes that the speaker is flouting or exploiting some Maxim, not violating it in one of the other three ways, in accordance with the purposes of the conversation (CP).

An example of flouting will demonstrate Grice's concept of the logic of conversation. He explains the flouting of the first Maxim of Quantity with a story of a student who asks his professor to write him a letter of recommendation for a philosophy job (Grice, 1975, 52). The professor complies and sends a letter that reads as follows: "Dear Sir, Mr. X's command of English is excellent, and his attendance at tutorials has been regular. Yours etc." The receiver of the letter, somewhat puzzled by the professor's response, decides first of all that the sender is not opting out, because he took the trouble to write the letter. The professor is, therefore, maintaining the CP. The receiver believes, moreover, that the professor cannot be unable to say more since he knows the student well. And the professor should realize that a letter of recommendation demands more information. The receiver of the letter thus concludes that by refusing to write a more detailed account of the student's abilities, the professor is flouting the Maxim of Quantity to implicate a meaning that he is reluctant to write down. The professor, infers the receiver, implies that the student in question will be no good at the philosophy job.

Grice's other examples of *implicature* will probably interest students of literature. Under flouting of the first Maxim of Quality Grice lists irony, metaphor, meiosis, and hyperbole, whereas his examples of the flouting of Maxims of Manner include ambiguity and obscurity. Literary critics, in fact, have already begun to apply his explanation of such examples of *implicature* to the study of literary texts (Hancher, 1977).

The first book on speech act theory and literature, Mary Louise Pratt's *Toward a Speech Act Theory of Literary Discourse,* proves that Grice's work is attracting the attention of literary critics (Pratt, 1977). For Pratt borrows Grice's formulation of the CP and Maxims as the main theoretical basis for her book. Here I will briefly summarize her application of Grice's concepts to literature, while skipping over her interesting remarks on the value of sociolinguistic theories for literary analysis, remarks that echo the work of other critics (van Dijk, 1976). She first uses Grice's concept of a point or purpose of a conversation. When Grice formulated his CP and Maxims, he was describing in particular the behavior of participants in a conversation whose purpose was to communicate efficiently information. He did not, however, rule out other purposes for other conversations. Taking this hint, Mary Pratt proposes that the point of the "conversation" between an author of a literary text and his readers is the display of unusual and interesting experience.

Pratt proposes, moreover, that *implicature* often occurs in these literary conversations. She explains that the CP, which directs, as we remember, the conversational participants to follow the point of the talk exchange, is especially protected in these conversations because of the selection process for literary works. That is, editors and critics have selected for publication only those works that maintain the purpose of the display of unusual experience. Since the reader knows of this selection process and has the editors' assurance that the purpose is maintained throughout a published text, he immediately interprets any Maxim violations as floutings by the author to implicate some additional meaning. Pratt's complex explanation of how this *implicature* actually works in practice prevents me from discussing it in detail. According to her, it occurs in two ways. On the one hand, the literary text presents a conversation between the narrator and the reader. Whenever a reader detects any Maxim violation by the narrator, he interprets it as an authorial flouting to communicate some meaning. When Tristram Shandy, for example, does not cooperate in the conversation with his readers by refusing to talk about important details in his life, a reader should interpret this opting out of a Maxim of Quantity as a flouting by Sterne. Pratt also extends the Maxims to govern the type of discourse that a fictional narrator is producing. Thus, to take the same example, Tristram's refusal to be informative counts as an opting out of the Maxim of Quantity as it applies to the rules of autobiography. That is, a writer of autobiographies is supposed to supply many facts about his life to his readers. Once again the reader should consider this Maxim violation a flouting on the author's part to convey some unspoken meaning.

Yet the authorial meaning that Pratt infers from her examples of *implicature* in literary texts is disappointing because it does not follow logically from the Maxim violations that she describes. In other words, her analogy between Grice's conversational *implicature* and the same process in literature is not complete. To illustrate the problems of her use of Grice's concepts, let us consider how she moves from the Maxim violations of the narrator to the author's meaning. The author, she says, maintains the CP for literature and accordingly displays unusual experience, which turns out to be for Pratt the violations of conversational Maxims and discourse rules by the narrator. By presenting such unusual experience, she infers, the author often expresses his dissatisfaction with the literary genre he is using. For example, by portraying an unreliable narrator who violates the conventions of conversation and the autobiography, Sterne signals his displeasure with the rules of the novel, which call for a reliable narrator, and, perhaps, his desire to revise these rules. Yet one could replace this meaning supplied by Pratt with a number of other interpretations because it does not logically and necessarily follow from the description of the narrator's violations, which would be required if her analogy with Grice's *implicature* were complete. Her application of Grice's theory cannot offer her the logical necessity of meaning in literary texts that she desires because she has pushed the theory beyond its limited competence. Grice's theory possesses explanatory power on account of its focus on a specific, one might say ideal, situation, in which two individuals converse in a rational manner. The theory simply cannot handle the two levels of discourse that Pratt perceives in a literary text, conversations between the narrator and the reader and between the author and the reader. Grice, moreover, did not design it to explain a violation of genre rules, such as those of an autobiography. Just as critics failed to discover a foolproof method of detecting authorial intentions by a methodological analogy with speech act theory's concept of intentionality and its felicity conditions, Pratt does not provide a recipe for discovering a text's meaning by her extension of Grice's CP and Maxims to the literary situation.

A sign of literary critics' interest in speech act theory is the controversy that it and its literary applications have provoked, a controversy that continues to this day. For the purposes of this essay, I am leaving aside philosophical discussions and concentrating on the debate among literary critics concerning the theory's value. The American critic, Stanley E. Fish, best represents those who are critical of the theory while recognizing the value of its contributions to the study of language. One can divide Fish's treatment of the theory into three stages. In 1973, he published two essays, "How Ordinary Is Ordinary Language" (Fish, 1973a) and "What Is Stylistics and Why Are They Saying Such Terrible Things About It" (Fish, 1973b), in which he drew support from speech act theory for his attack on contemporary disciplines. The first article constitutes a criticism of the ordinary/poetic language distinction established by formal linguistics and poetics. Linguists, Fish argues, describe ordinary language in purely formal terms, excluding from it human purposes and intentions, which they relegate to poetic language, the province of literary critics. Since speech act theory, as we have seen, introduces intentionality into the description of all language, Fish employs it as an ally to break down the ordinary/poetic language dichotomy. In the second article, speech act theory proves helpful to him in his criticism of stylistics, a discipline which, according to Fish, employs formal analysis to extract meaning from a text. Borrowing speech act theory's concept of meaning or illocutionary force produced by purposive language use, Fish develops a theory of reading: for him, the reader creates the meaning of a literary work through the purposes he has in mind while reading it. Fish therefore denies that meaning is inherent in a text and discoverable by formal analysis, as the stylisticians suppose.

From using speech act theory as a weapon against formal linguistics and stylistics, Fish turns in his article, "How to Do Things with Austin and Searle: Speech Act Theory and Literary Criticism," to examine how critics are applying the theory and to point out its own shortcomings. I have already mentioned Fish's criticism of Ohmann and Iser that appears in this article. His main criticism, however, falls upon the theory itself and the distinctions made by it, such as "brute"/"institutional" facts, regulative/constative rules, serious/nonserous discourse, especially visible in Searle's article on fictional discourse. Fish objects to the left terms of these distinctions because they suggest a world existing independently of man's activities and a method of describing objectively this world. By returning to *How to Do Things with Words* for support, he points out that every utterance depends upon the context and purposes of the speaker and the hearer, and that no fact can be specified apart from human intentions. According to Fish, therefore, no rules are regulative, if regulative means objective and free from human purposes; no discourse is serious, if this implies statements holding true for all times, situations, and peoples; no facts are "brute," if this term signifies facts not constituted by man's perception and language. He admits, however, that certain discourse lays claim to a serious status, because men use it for what they define as ordinary life. Fish originally presented a shortened version of this paper at a colloquium on speech act theory and literature that included as participants E. D. Hirsch, Barbara Smith, and Martin Steinmann. Michael Hancher has published the contributions to this colloquium and the discussion following it in an issue of *Centrum* ("Discussion," *Centrum,* 1975). The differences in the speech act theories of the participants significantly appear in the discussion's debates.

In his most recent theoretical essay, which he presented at the 1977 Summer Session of the School of Criticism and Theory at Irvine, California, Fish again makes John Searle's writings a target of criticism (Fish, 1978). Searle had formulated a theory of indirect speech acts, a concept that bears much resemblance to Grice's *implicature,* in an essay published in 1975 (Searle, 1975a). An indirect speech act, according to Searle, has an illocutionary force different from the literal meaning of the utterance of a sentence. If, for example, one hears the sentence, "Can you pass the salt?," one takes it literally as a question about one's abilities but actually as a request. To account for this phenomenon in which a speaker means more than what he says, Searle proposes the theory of the indirect speech act. Fish, in short, opposes this theory because it implies that some meaning, the literal meaning of the utterance, preexists the purposive use of a sentence by a speaker in a given context. Such a formulation, according to Fish, contradicts the major insight of speech act theory that there is no meaning apart from the illocutionary act, except when one separates the locution for analytical purposes. For Fish, therefore, Searle's example sentence literally means a request because the hearer understands the speaker to be using it to perform the action of requesting. In all of his essays on speech act theory, but significantly in this last one, Fish's criticism of the theory, its developments, and its literary applications grows out of a desire to remain faithful to the original insights of Austin.

With the publication of the semiannual journal, *Glyph,* by Johns Hopkins University, the controversy between proponents of speech act theory and its critics has received much publicity in American literary criticism. In the first issue of their journal, the editors of *Glyph* published a translation of an article on speech act theory by Jacques Derrida, a well-known French philosopher. Following this article they printed a short response by John Searle (Searle, 1977). The second issue of the journal then included a nearly hundred page reply to Searle by Derrida, "Limited Inc" (Derrida, 1977a). Derrida's interest in speech act theory is all the more striking because, except for linguists, most French intellectuals have ignored until quite recently the theory's existence. The French philosopher's critique of the theory is complex and takes for granted an awareness of the issues debated by continental philosophy and of Derrida's own particular method of analysis, deconstruction. He is, in short, disturbed by the same speech act dichotomies that trouble Fish: ordinary/poetic or parasitical language, serious/nonserious discourse, literal/nonliteral or implied meaning. In his first article, "Signature Event Context," which was translated from a paper delivered in 1971, he probes at the assumption underlying the speech act distinctions: the consciousness of participants completely informs language in some situations, as for example in the face-to-face conversation, thus enabling them to communicate fully their meaning. This assumption, suggests Derrida, leads speech act theorists to regard as secondary instances of language use, such as writing and fiction, that do not share the features of this ideal communication situation. Since Derrida concentrates on Austin's works in his first article, Searle defends his former teacher in his reply by explaining the theoretical necessity of Austin's attention to serious speech. He also notes what he believes are confusions in Derrida's terminology. Derrida's reply, which Johns Hopkins has also published in its French version, constitutes a step-by-step refutation of Searle's critique. In developing the criticisms of Austin's version of speech act theory, Derrida focuses, too, on Searle's writings besides the contribution to *Glyph,* such as *Speech Acts* and the essay on fictional discourse. Literary critics await the next issue of *Glyph* to see whether Searle will devote any more time to this continental criticism of speech act theory.

Whether this controversy continues or not, literary critics will likely use speech act theory in their analysis for the next few years. As I have shown, its concepts can support different and contrasting approaches to literature. Some critics borrow its concept of intentionality to support their attempts to identify the historical author's intentions. Others extend the notion of felicity conditions to include genre conventions and agreements between the author and reader about the nature of speech acts in literature. Analysts describe texts using a taxonomy of illocutionary acts or Grice's CP and Maxims. In the course of this essay, I have tried to indicate some of the dangers of pushing the theory beyond its limitations. For the theory cannot, I believe, provide a critic with a fail-safe method of locating an author's intentions, the meaning behind genre violations, or a theory of stylistics. It does, however, offer us a new view of ordinary language: according to it, each use of language is a purposive act by an individual in a particular context. Literary critics would do well to consider the value that speech act theory has conferred upon ordinary language before trying to apply its concepts to the study of literature.

REFERENCES

Austin, J.L. *How to Do Things with Words: The William James Lectures Delivered at Harvard University in 1955*. Ed. J.O. Urmson and Marina Sbisà. 2nd ed. 1962; rpt. Cambridge, Mass: Harvard Univ. Press, 1975.

Beardsley, Monroe C. *The Possibility of Criticism*. Detroit: Wayne State Univ. Press, 1970.

Brown, Robert L.,Jr. "Intentions and the Contexts of Poetry." *Centrum*, 2 (1974), 56-66.

Cole, Peter and Morgan, Jerry L.,eds. *Speech Acts (Syntax and Semantics, 3)*. New York: Academic Press, 1975.

Derrida, Jacques. "Limited Inc abc. . . " *Glyph*, 2 (1977a), 162-254.

————— "Signature Event Context." *Glyph*, 1 (1977b), 172-97.

van Dijk, Teun A. "Philosophy of Action and Theory of Narrative." *Poetics, 5 (1976)*, 287-338.

"Discussion." *Centrum*, 3 (1975), 125-46.

Eaton, Marcia. "Good and Correct Interpretations of Literature." *Journal of Aesthetics and Art Criticism*, 29 (1970), 227-33.

_____ . "Speech Acts:A Bibliography."*Centrum*, 2 (1974), 57-72.

Fish, Stanley E. "How Ordinary Is Ordinary Language." *New Literary History*, 5 (1973a), 41-54.

_____ . "How to Do Things with Austin and Searle: Speech Act Theory and Literary Criticism." *Modern Language Notes,* 91 (1976), 983-1025.

_____ . "Normal Circumstances, Literal Language, Direct Speech Acts, The Ordinary, The Everyday, The Obvious, What Goes Without Saying, and Other Special Cases." (forthcoming in *Critical Inquiry*).

_____ . "What is Stylistics and Why Are They Saying Such Terrible Things About It?" *Selected Papers from the English Institute: Approaches to Poetics.* Ed. Seymour Chatman. New York: Columbia Univ. Press, 1973. 109-52.

Grice, H. Paul. "Logic and Conversation." In Cole and Morgan above, 41-58.

Hancher, Michael. "Beyond a Speech-Act Theory of Literary Discourse." *Modern Language Notes,* 92 (1977), 1081-98.

_____ . "Three Kinds of Intentions." *Modern Language Notes.* 87 (1972), 827-51.

_____ . "Understanding Poetic Speech Acts." *College English,* 36 (1975), 632-39.

Hirsch, E.D., Jr. "Stylistics and Synonymity." *Critical Inquiry*, 1 (1975), 559-80.

_____ . "What's the Use of Speech-Act Theory?" *Centrum,* 3 (1975), 121-24.

Iser, Wolfgang. "The Reality of Fiction: A Functionalist Approach to Literature." *New Literary History,* 7 (1975), 7-38.

Levenston, Edward A. "Metaphor, Speech Act and Grammatical Form." *Poetics,* 5 (1976), 373-82.

Mack, Dorothy. "Metaphoring as Speech Act: Some happiness conditions for implicit similes and simple metaphors." *Poetics,* 4 (1975), 221-56.

Ohmann, Richard. "Instrumental Style: Notes on the Theory of Speech as Action." *Current Trends in Stylistics.* Ed. Braj. B. Kachru and Herbert F.W. Stahlke. Edmonton, Canada: Linguistic Research Inc., 1972a. 115-42.

_____ . "Literature as Act." *Selected Papers from the English Institute: Approaches to Poetics.* Ed. Seymour Chatman. New York: Columbia Univ. Press, 1973. 81-107.

_____ . "Speech, Action, and Style." *Literary Style: A Symposium.* Ed. Seymour Chatman. New York: Oxford Univ. Press, 1971. 241-59.

————. "Speech Acts and the Definition of Literature." *Philosophy and Rhetoric*, 4 (Winter 1971),1-19.

————. "Speech, Literature, and the Space Between." *New Literary History*, 4 (1972), 47-64.

Pratt, Mary Louise. *Toward a Speech Act Theory of Literary Discourse*. Bloomington: Indiana Univ. Press, 1977.

Searle, John R. "Chomsky's Revolution in Linguistics." *New York Review of Books*, 29 June 1972, 16-24.

————. "A Classification of Illocutionary Acts." *Language in Society*. 5 (1976), 1-23.

————. "Indirect Speech Acts." In Cole and Morgan above (1975a), 59-82.

————. "The Logical Status of Fictional Discourse." *New Literary History*, 6 (1975b), 319-32.

————. "Reiterating the Differences: A Reply to Derrida." *Glyph*, 1 (1977), 198-208.

————. *Speech Acts: An Essay in the Philosophy of Language*. 1969; rpt. Cambridge: Cambridge Univ. Press, 1974.

Skinner, Quentin. "Motives, Intentions, and the Interpretation of Texts." *New Literary History*, 3 (1972), 393-408.

Smith, Barbara H. "Actions, Fictions, and the Ethics of Interpretation." *Centrum, 3 (1975), 117-20.*

————. "Poetry as Fiction." *New Literary History* 2 (1971), 259-81.

Steinmann, Martin, Jr. "Cumulation, Revolution, and Progress." *New Literary History, 5 (1974)*, 477-90.

————. "Perlocutionary Acts and the Interpretation of Literature." *Centrum, 3* (1975), 112-16.

————. "Poems as Artifacts." *Proceedings of the VIIth International Congress of Aesthetics*. Bucarest, 2 September, 1972. Bucarest, România: Editura Academiei Republicii Socialiste Romania, 1976. 541-43.

Tanaka, Ronald. "Action and Meaning in Literary Theory." *Journal of Literary Semantics, 1* (1972), 41-56.

Traugott, Elizabeth C. "Generative Semantics and the Concept of Literary Discourse." *Journal of Literary Semantics,* 2 (1973), 5-22.

WHAT IS WRONG WITH THE THEORY OF LITERATURE ?
(Some recent considerations on the field of literary studies)

Walter Mignolo

I

One possible view of the situation in the domain of literary studies within the last thirty years has a preoccupation for systematization and generalization as a central focus. Without any pretension of giving an historical and systematic account of this discipline, but in order to establish a background for the ensuing discussion, it will be useful to underscore three different orientations. Orientations that, on one hand, are not clearcut conceptual areas and, therefore, allow the analysis of cross-reference and interference of aims, concepts, chronological distribution, etc.; and, on the other hand, inspite of cross-references in aims and concepts, allow an intuitive identification of "distinctive features." Thus, taking "theory" and "science" as concepts the three orientations have in common, each one could very roughly be identified as follows:

a) As is well-known, A. Warren and R. Wellek make a claim in their classic work (1948) for an *organon* of methods, called literary theory, as "the great need of literary scholarship today." The implementation of this aim is thought of as: 1) the organization of the field of study by differentiating and interrelating three activities: theory, criticism and history; and 2) the division of the domain of study in "intrinsic and extrinsic" approaches. Without forcing too much an analogy (permitted by the very loose use of the term "theory"), one can say that the aim of the book is directed more toward a *science* of literature; and that the science aimed at is a *descriptive* science of literature.

b) The second orientation, exemplified by R. Jakobson among others, may be called the "immanentist" orientation (Lázaro Carreter, 1976: 17-18). The explicit aims (as given by Jakobson himself (1960-73)) or the implicit ones (S. Levin, 1963, 1976; J. Trabant, 1970) lie in establishing a definition of literariness. The result is an analytical concentration on the linguistic properties of "verbal works of art" where the main tools are provided by different schools of linguistics. The immanentist approach is heavily oriented toward substantive aspects of the

study of literature, and less attention is paid to methodological and
epistemological concerns.

c) The third orientation manifests its "distinctive features" in the strong
stress put on metatheoretical questions (e.g. concept and theory formation) and on epistemological ones (e.g. the philosophical foundation of
a racional-theoretical science of literature based on (analytical) philosophy of science (T. van Dijk, 1971, 1972a, b; J. Ihwe, 1972,
1973a, b; 1976; S. Schmidt,1973b, 1974, 1976),G. Wienold, 1972,
1973)[1]

It is this last orientation my comments will be concerned with, and my
interest could be couched, to use Toulmin's terminology (1972:1-35; 200-
241), as a concern with general aspects of conceptual formation and conceptual change in a discipline—in this case, "literary studies." Those aspects are
illustrated by the introduction of a methodological and epistemological discussion into the field of literary studies, absent in its history. One of the
major "attractions" of this conceptual change is that the discipline is not
only open to consideration of "how to analyse literary texts," but is also
concerned with the analysis of *discourse about* (interpretation, explanation,
explication) literary texts. As a result, my comments will be devoted more
specifically to this aspect of a "new direction" in literary studies.

II

One of the distinctive assumptions that characterizes the proposals for
a theoretical science of literature (TSL)[2] based on (analytical) philosophy of

---

[1]I will refer to this orientation as TSL, encompassing the terms "theoretical,"
"science" and "empirical" frequently used by the authors I'll be commenting. The earlier
considerations on the term *Poetics,* by T. A. van Dijk (1972a: 169-70) should not be
confused (cfr. Lázaro Carreter, 1976) with the uses of the term in the context of the
orientation summarized in b). The conception of Poetics in van Dijk is clearly oriented
toward TSL (pp. 174-84). Apparently, both orientations trace their roots in the earlier
Russian Formalism: for the first, see T. Todorov (1971: 931); for the second, J. Ihwe,
1973a and b).
[2]I am neither attempting a full picture of the aspects discussed in this direction
nor a review of several works on it, but rather some observations on a few concepts
(e.g. the object of TSL; theory and interpretation, explanation, explication and interpretation, essentialist definition of literature). For a more complete account and an extensive bibliography, see G. Wienold, 1978. I am also not taking into account other
possible orientations based on similar principles as, for instance, the working project of
literary theory developed by A. J. Greimas et al. (see the first report by H.-G. Ruprecht,
1978).

science,[3] is the fact that the notion of literature is no longer a non-controversial concept which designates some given "object" (T. van Dijk, 1972a:167) to be described by literary theoreticians; neither is it a question of *defining* its specificity—literariness (R. Ohman, 1971), but rather a very problematic notion that cannot be taken for granted in a construction of a theoretical science of literature.

J. Ihwe (1973a), in what must be considered an important contribution in the direction we are concerned with, raises the question of an "empirical content of the study of literature" and by so doing throws doubt upon the concept of literariness as the designating concept of the object of literary studies. Taking the general field as point of reference, Ihwe characterizes the empirical content of the discipline in the past as "description and evaluation ('interpretation') of given objects—of 'verbal works of art,' 'literary texts,' or however one cares to name these objects" (p. 310). In his view, the organization of the discipline is based on a very simple operation: "the set of 'verbal utterances' is, in this perspective, divided up into two complementary subsets: 'literature' and 'non-literature.' What counts as 'literature' is laid down by the very categories (criteria) that were used in the delimitation of the phenomenon 'literature' itself" (p. 310). Ihwe concludes that the empirical content is delimited by an essentialist definition (i.e. *real definitions* in K. Hempel's terminology (1952)). Essentialist definitions are, at least in the case of literature, on one hand, *normative* ("what is to be counted as 'literature' is (. . .) laid down once and for all"; p. 310); and, on the other hand, as a consequence of its normative character, essentialist definitions aim at the *universal* (as illustrated by the history of attempts at defining literature) while being, in fact, restricted to the *particular* criteria used in the delimitation of the phenomena. There is, therefore, no point in asking which of the essentialist definitions of literature is the best or the correct one—as essentialist and normative definitions they are equally valid and they constitute the very history of literature itself. From a different perspective, we may say that the history of (the empirical content of) literature is the history of two main activities: one consisting of *definitions,* the other of descriptions and evaluations developed from the *presupposition* that the objects talked about are *literary* (poetic, a work of art, etc.).

At this point we certainly have the right to ask what is wrong with the interpretation, description and (essentialist) definition of literature. One

---

[3]The use of the expression "analytical philosophy of science" in this paper does not make the distinction (which is not necessary for this exposition) between "analytical philosophy" and "philosophy of science": the first having as its domain the sentences of science, while the second emphasizes the facts of science (J. O. Urmson, 1956).

possible answer, taken from Ihwe himself, is that the picture just presented constitutes a "quasi-study of literature" (p. 312) and that it is difficult to see in what sense it might claim to be "scientific." But this answer does not do justice to Ihwe's proposal because in reading the entire article we realize that the "picture just presented" does not refer to the totality of the field in its history, but is instead restricted to recent orientations that call for "scientificity" without discussing the rather weighty implications of the word. I suppose that a different type of argumentation would be necessary for the claim of "scientificity" in the philological tradition where the term "science" is taken as denotation for a well-founded facts description. In other words, a tradition that does not demand *generalizations* (i.e. law-like statements) but, on the contrary is based on the belief that a "scientific study of literature" is the "ascertaining and discovery of facts" (G. von Wright, 1971:1).[4] It would appear that Ihwe is not concerned with this branch of scientific activity but rather with the one aiming at "the construction of hypotheses and theories" (von Wright, ibid.).

With this proviso in mind, we can move to more specific aspects derived from the questions about the "empirical content of literary studies," and to restrict them to proposals claiming "scientificity" and aiming at generalizations in terms of "theoretical sciences." The alternate proposal that J. Ihwe sets up, after the "picture just presented," gives foundation and justification to his criticism:

> The picture just presented here of what I have called the 'quasi-study of literature,' as I cannot see in what sense it might claim to be 'scientific,' is at the same time meant to be a first circumscription of a certain *partial* area of the *observational range* of the study of literature, when I pose the question of the empirical content of the study of literature in the following way: I understand this question to ask precisely after that which so far has always been presupposed as 'given' and posited as 'phenomenon *per se*,' respectively; as the question of how it comes to be that a 'verbal utterance' *has the (valid, accepted) status* of an instance

---

[4]For example, this statement from R. Curtius (1948): "Just as European literature can only be seen as a whole, so the study of it can only proceed historically. Not in the form of literary history! A narrative and enumerative history never yields anything but a cataloguelike knowledge of facts. The material itself it leaves in whatever form it found it. But historical investigation has to unravel it and penetrate it. It has to develop analytical methods, that is, methods which will decompose the material (after the fashion of chemistry with its reagents) and make its structures visible. The necessary point of view can only be gained from a comparative perusal of literatures, that is, can only be discovered empirically. *Only a literary discipline which proceeds historically and philologically can do justice to the task*" (pp. 15; italics mine).

of 'literature.' I take the central phrase of my answer, 'to have the (valid, accepted) status' to be the central, if one will, 'pragmatic' notion of the study of literature: it implies, in my analysis, that we have to indicate *for whom* a 'verbal utterance' counts as 'literature,' and furthermore that this is true at a *certain point in time* and *in a certain situation.* (pp. 312-313)

After this first characterization of the empirical content of literary studies, it will be pertinent to ask: a) how the empirical content should be handled, and b) what the status of "interpretation" would be from the point of view of an empirical science of literature which has, as a central assumption, the question "how it comes to be that a 'verbal utterance' has the (valid, accepted) status of an instance of literature." We will comment on a) and b) in the following two paragraphs.

II.a. Thus, if literariness is questioned, what is left? With what could we replace it in order to have "organizing principles" guiding our research? What must we look for if literariness is no longer to be sought after? It seems to me that the concept of literariness can be broken down into two aspects: the *question* ("What makes a verbal message a work of art?") appears to be still very pertinent; but the *answer* ("The poetic function projects the principle of equivalence from the axis of selection into the axis of combination") raises several doubts. Doubts that Ihwe has worded as follows:

> One of the most striking findings is that the question of literarity ('poeticity,' etc.) of verbal utterances cannot be answered on the level of linguistic structuring: it has been proved impossible to derive, in any systematic way, differentiating critera in terms of any of the field discussed in this connection. (. . .) Positively viewed, this means that 'textqualities' as they are postulated by such expressions can only be established adequately if their origination with regard to the whole area of *linguistic structuring* is illuminated. (1973a: 336)

At this point, the concept introduced by Ihwe of "languaged-centred discipline" seems of cardinal importance. This concept makes clear, first of all, that the notion of literariness has to be developed taking into consideration the totality of the "verbal universe of discourse" (i.e. literariness cannot be derived by partial and arbitrary choices, defining literary structures in opposition to historiographic discourse or to "conversational languages," and "literary acts" cannot be derived from "speech acts" but rather counted as a sub-class of all (possible) "language acts," as a component of the set "verbal

universe of discourse"). "Textquality" (as a function attributed by a person
to verbal actions and structures) becomes, thus, a central concept for the
organization of the "verbal universe of discourse." Secondly, the concept
"language-centred discipline" makes clear that the "verbal universe of discourse" implies its complementary class: the "non-verbal universe of discourse." Therefore, if language-centred disciplines have as their domain the
verbal universe of discourse, they will be a sub-class of all "sign-centred
disciplines" (semiotics) which deal with the *manipulation* of signs, both
verbal and non-verbal, for human interaction. This perspective mentioned by
Ihwe (1973a: 332-333) is not developed because the empirical content of
TSL has to be delimited in the "verbal universe of discourse." However, the
concept of language-centred discipline gives a more accurate picture for treating the problem than the one given by the opposition "literature/non-
literature," and the consequent reduction of non-literature to some partial
and arbitrary component of the "verbal universe of discourse." [5]

Textquality becomes thus the central concept, of which literariness
may be viewed as one of the possible *semantic contents* of the abstract
operation designated by it. Not surprisingly, one of the central assumptions
of TSL relies on the concept of textquality: [6]

> The theory of grammar specifies how verbal utterances may, in
> general, be organised as 'texts'; literary theory specifies—in the
> case under discussion—how verbal utterances may be organized as
> 'texts' of a specific type (or of specific sub-types). (Ihwe, 1973a:
> 326).

---

[5] However, modern poetry makes evident that not everything in "literature" is
solved within the verbal universe. Poets themselves have raised questions against "linguistic methods" (S. Yurkievich, 1977). On the other hand, scholars have started paying
attention to the nonverbal in "poetry" (Haroldo de Campos, 1977; G. H. F. Longree,
1976). It seems necessary, therefore, to extend the domain of language-centered disciplines regarding "literature" toward a more general "sign-centered discipline." And perhaps, this extension could be logically done by the introduction of the (semiotic)
notion of "universe of discourse" (L. Prieto, 1966: ch, II; 1976: ch. I). The universe in
question will be thus conceived as *sign processing*; more precisely, "the production and
reception of verbal and non-verbal signs for human interaction." As far as the notion of
sign is concerned, I'm not thinking of the signified/signifier relation, but mainly of its
pragmatic and (instructional) semantic dimensions: for instance, the notion of "semic
act" in L. Prieto (1966; 1976), where the sign production is conceived as an "instructional act"; also E. Itkonen, where the instrumental dimension of sign interaction is
emphasized (1974: 130-7).' Or yet the conception of sign in an "instructional semantic"
reviewed by S. Schmidt (1973a: 4.6.2).
[6] Assuming that "quality" (properties) implies the identification of (the class of)
objects possessing it.

To deal with the central assumption of TSL implies the need of introducing the notion "Verbal utterances as texts of a specific type." In other words, how can the question about verbal utterances organized as "texts" of a specific type be handled? Ihwe employs the expression *processing*[7] as "a general concept for the characterisation of all those individual processes which form the field of observation of the language-centred disciplines" (1973a: 316). The question which next arises is: "What then is to be the meaning of the statement: 'Person P processes a verbal utterance A' in terms of the study of literature?" (p. 316). Ihwe goes on to propose an *elementary observational situation* (a set whose elements are time intervals, space, socio-cultural contexts, psycho-physical conditions and verbal utterances), from which he derives a *rule* that gives the expression *processing* an evaluative function. This evaluative function may be considered a basic "organizing principle" for the notion "textquality" (p. 339). The rule, in a simplified version, reads as follows: Person P is prepared to assign the verbal utterance A at a specific point in time, at a specific point in space, within a sociocultural context, and under psycho-physical conditions, a determined value F (p. 318).

If the preceding rule is valid for the processing of all kinds of utterances belonging to the verbal universe of discourse (i.e. assignation of textquality to verbal utterances), then the "field of observation of the study of literature is (. . .) a very complex social sub-process" (p. 315). Consequently, if the rule aims at capturing a social sub-process, it must be completed by introducing a new concept, such as that of "sphere of action of P." The value-assignment will thus be dependent upon the sphere of action; and the sphere of action will be characterized (I am giving again a simplified version of Ihwe's formulation) by the ability of P to employ: (a) the linguistic system of a language L; b) the stage.of a language L (where the diachronic aspects of textquality are ıken into consideration); (c) types of verbal utterances in a language L, ıaracterized in relation to (a); and (d) means of forming types of verbal 'erances in the language L, also in relation to (a) (1973a: 323-4).

Because of space and time restraints, it will be necessary to disregard consequences Ihwe derives from these basic formulations as well as his iderations on epistemological aspects which will be referred to in III. ıver, it would be appropriate to emphasize two points regarding the 'rical content of literary studies": (1) If it is accepted that essentialist ions of literature are normative and don't compete in the attribution ıntic contents (i.e. textqualifying operations, according to the "value-ion rule"), then a TSL can neither be based on any of the existing ıst definitions nor propose a new one. On the contrary, the question literature," if pertinent at all, cannot be answered by definitions d by the theoretician, but rather by building up abstract frames of ıeıerence from which the "processing of verbal utterances as literary" will be

[7]For more details on the notion of processing in literary studies, see G. Wienold 1972 and 1976.

handled as text-processing and text-qualifying operations; and whereby (essentialist) definitions of literature will become indicators of different ways of (text) processing and (text) qualifying as "literary"; (2) although the scope that is assigned to the notion "literary studies" is unclear in relation to TSL, both notions at times appear to be synonyms. If this is the case, it will be necessary to show whether or not the two can be equated. If the answer is affirmative, it will imply that literary studies has to become, in its totality, a "scientific discipline," in the sense of TSL. If the answer is negative, a TSL must be seen as one alternative in the discipline of literary studies where other conceptions of theorizing may be introduced (e.g. hermeneutically based theory), although non-scientific from a TSL point of view; and where interpretation can neither be barred from the field because of its "quasi-scientific" character nor reduced to scientific claims (see section II.b).

What is important in these considerations is not to confuse the means by which methodological and epistemological levels are implemented according to the knowledge to be obtained (i.e. according to the functional goals of the discipline) with the ideological level and the results we expect from stressing ideological concerns (E. Veron, 1971). The need for this distinction could be justified with pragmatic considerations about intellectual disciplines where ideology is seen not as a special kind of message but as a level in every type of message (V. Volosinov, 1930: 9-16; C. Geertz, 1964), including "scientific" and "metascientific" discourse (Th. Herbert, 1966-68; E. Veron 1971). If this is the case, we face an ideological maneuver when the means whose function is the obtaining of knowledge is converted into the means used to minimize or disqualify competing alternatives. This is neither to say, nor imply, that the methodological and epistemological assumptions in TSL are the only ones employed with an ideological purpose; even less that by controlling the ideological dimension a "neutral knowledge" will be attainable. For the first case the results could be reached, not only by appealing to the "ideal of science" but also with such "non-scientific" notions as "subject," "dissemination," "transcendental pragmatics," etc. In the second case, non-neutral knowledge—it is known—could be attainable, because the scholar at every step of his work faces several alternatives where the selection of one has not only epistemological but also ideological ramifications. Nevertheless, it could be fruitful if the two levels were, as far as possible, distinguished, making clear when concepts are being manipulated with the purpose of contributing to the "growth of knowledge" and when we are using them with ideological function: not with the purpose of consolidating our methods and philosophical assumptions, but for the disqualification of what is considered an opposing position. Briefly, the ideological operation will be at work when we construct a conceptual framework to propose not *one* but *the* alternative (see section III.a.3.).

II.b. More recently, J. Ihwe (1976) has proposed a reconsideration of the "logic" of interpretation, first, as a "cultural tradition of making interpretation of literary texts" and, second, as an activity, respectable in its own right, to which 'scientific' claims are not pertinent" (pp. 330). Regarding these statements in connection with what was previously commented upon, the incertitude about where a TSL stands in relation to interpretation may appear; and even more so when we read, in this article, that Ihwe—refuting the possibility of giving scientific foundations to interpretations—refers to himself as having promoted this erroneous belief in the past. The argumentation is, indeed, ambiguous. On the one hand: "In the preceding (. . .) I concluded that the philosophy of science can give nothing to the *practising literary critic*" (1976: 352, italics mine). However, the following page: "So my answer to my initial question is, that in the precise sense of 'crucial' and in the precise sense of 'philosophy of science,' the philosophy of science cannot play a *crucial* role in one of the possible domains of the *science of literature*" (p. 353; last italics are mine). Based on these quotations, criticism as interpretation and criticism as science of literature seem to be understood as the *same* activity. It would also be possible, employing Ihwe's argumentation, to distinguish interpretation from (a search for) TSL and to consider them as two different activities within the field of literary studies.

Interpretation, as it seems to be construed in Ihwe's article (and in the most general denotation of the term), could be viewed as the *elaborated reconstruction of the experience of reading verbal works of art.* Where *elaborated* stands for an "institutional activity" (J. Ihwe, 1976) comprising "fresh" interpretation of recent verbal works of art" as well as "re-interpretation" of ancient ones. Although the notion of interpretation requires a more careful explication, the above few comments are satisfactory for the point in discussion. The view that no scientific foundation is pertinent for interpretation seems essentially correct, as does the conclusion that for interpretation philosophy of science cannot play a *crucial* role. What will be needed, however, is a characterization of "interpretive statement" making clear the role of interpretation in literary studies and its place vis-a-vis TSL. Summarizing some of the conclusions by Ihwe, although not employing his terminology (the reader interested in more precision should consult his article), should help to better visualize an alternate end and, perhaps, to point out some of the consequences. Ihwe's general characterization of the activity of "making interpretations" follows:

> The ethos of the institutionalised occupation with "works of art" we may say, is founded on the assumption that a work of art has 'objective' properties of this kind. 'Objective' properties here literally means 'properties of the object' (the novel, the

drama, etc.). And the main aim of institutionalised occupation with 'works of art' (which I will hereafter call 'interpretation') is, according to the standard defense of 'interpretation' as a respectable public occupation, the discovery and illumination of properties of objects which are 'works of art.' " (1976: 343)

Such an activity, Ihwe continues, is based on two major presuppositions: (a) that the predicates used by the interpreter (constructed on a basic vocabulary: plot, iambic pentameter, verse, etc.) denote "natural" properties of verbal constructs; and (b) that such properties, if not only at least crucially, characterize literary "works of art" (1976: 344). Things look different if it is accepted that "ascribing a meaning to a conventional sign is a *construction* of a meaning" (p. 345) and, therefore, the meaning neither *is in* nor *belongs to* the object. By viewing (a) in these terms, then (b) becomes an "artificial construction" upon the first (presupposed) principle. But where do those presuppositions come from? It seems natural (Ihwe continues) to think "the application of a specific vocabulary that literary critics develop cannot be characterised as an exercise of their freedom but only as the exercise, or reinforcement, of a specific system of norms" (p. 345). This is not far from saying that the reconstruction of a system of norms provides the "organizing principles" for an essentialist definition of literature. If a system of norms "controls" the ascription of meaning, it is easy to infer that the question about the *right* interpretation is meaningless[8]; at least if the question is understood as an empirical one, "because a *right* interpretation claims to give true, or at least correct, statements about the specific 'objective' properties of a 'work of art' (p. 345). This is perhaps why, from a TSL standpoint (or from a logical-positivistic conception of science) it is possible to state that "to give interpretation is not to perform a scientific exercise" (p. 345). And perhaps this is also why it makes sense to view the function of literary interpretations as giving "recommendations about how to process works of art" (p. 347); and as, therefore, an activity which is essentially normative ("to give recommendations primarily means that the attention of the addressee is focused on specific properties of a work of art, namely, literary properties. This means, furthermore, that these literary properties get a specific weight, and this means in turn that they are related to specific emotional and/or cultural values" (p. 348)).

Before changing slightly the direction followed until here, a summary of the two pictures in front of us shows: (a) textqualifying operation as a

---

[8]However, for a different perspective and opposite view, see E. D. Hirsch, Jr. (1967: 174-208).

substantive aspect of TSL and (b) the making of interpretations as a normative activity whose function is to "give recommendations." Pursuing point (b)—always with the goal of clearing up its relations with point (a)—it is tempting to say, even though it may not be entirely in accord with Ihwe's proposal, that if (c) interpretation is the appropriation and use of "verbal utterances," both operations are located in the reception process. Therefore, (d) the interpreter, as a receiver executing—by his interpretive act—a recommendative act, can be construed as the *person P* of the *elementary observational situation* discussed above (section II.a.). This means mixing two propositions not clearly related in the two articles by Ihwe commented on so far. Nevertheless, a reading of the two proposals seems to ask for a reformulation of the role of interpretation and TSL in the field of literary studies. Pursuing the "attractive," and perhaps risky suggestion advanced, the system of norms guiding an interpretation can be called—borrowing a concept from H. Verdasdonk and C. J. van Rees (1977)—*poetic concept* (PC). As the argument developes, a reconsideration of the rule of "value-assignment (stated and commented on in section II.a.), to include PC as (a component of the set) guiding value-assignement in literary interpretation, could be suggested. This (reconsidered) rule reads roughly as follows:

> Person P is prepared to assign the verbal utterance A, a determined value F, in the sphere of action of P, under the guiding principle of PC.

Perhaps the notion PC needs more clarification. For Verdaasdonk and van Rees (1977: 69) a PC is "a system of essential definitions with regard to (i) the function of literary texts; (ii) the literary techniques necessary for the accomplishements of this function; (iii) the nature of literary texts." Or, in a more concise formulation, a "PC consists of real definitions stating the essence of literature and the function of literary texts, and determining the techniques that are relevant" (pp. 69). Reading still a few more lines will show some similarities between, on one hand, PC and Ihwe's "system of norms"; and, on the other, between "poetic statements" based on PC and "making interpretations" based on a system of norms:

> In qualifying the characterization of a PC as essentialist, we deny that the statements, derived from or based upon it, are empirical in nature; nor has a PC anything in common with a set of testable hypotheses. The poetic statements aimed at determining and describing textual properties make use of terms ('unity,' 'plausibility,' etc.) that, besides their vagueness, are evaluative to such an extend that, instead of 'describing,' it would be better to

speak of their aim as 'normative stipulation of textual properties' " (Verdaasdonk and van Rees, 1977: 69).[9]

What is of interest in this proposal is the need to distinguish between the
notions "reading of a text" and "scientific study of literature" (pp. 71).
Although the article in question emphasizes the first, and the second is generally stated ("For our purpose the difference between the two approaches
can be localized at one point: claims handled in the scientific analysis of
literary texts must have the nature of hypotheses that are testable and therefore open to refutation" (pp. 70)), the distinction seems to be a useful one,
even though the supporting reasons do not look too convincing. The expression, for instance, "scientific analysis of literary texts" may be meaningful
not because scientific analysis, as opposed to reading (interpreting), is open
to refutation and has the form of testable hypotheses (i.e. it is hard to
imagine how such an hypothesis can be proposed without relying on one or
the other PC as essentialist definition and guiding principle for conceiving
literature), *but because,* one can argue, *such an analysis will be bound to the
elementary observational situation instead of PC.* The argument is based on
the fact that the *elementary observational situation* makes clear that for TSL
(or "scientific analysis" in the terminology of Verdaasdonk and van Rees) the
question is not *the analysis of literary texts* (activity characterizing interpretations or reading of a text) but *the ways of analysing literary texts* (e.g. text-
processing and text-qualifying). If this is valid, then the inclusion of PC in the
elementary observational situation could be (logically) justified. In this respect, the "scientific analysis" (or the developing of a theory—P. Achinstein,
1968—in our case TSL) will not assign "literary properties" to verbal constructs; instead TSL (or "scientific analysis") will start from the fact that:
(a) literary properties, LP, in a text T, are value-function, VF, according to
I-statements founded on PC_X; (b) PC_X supports the validity of an I-statement
assigning LP to T.

If nothing else, this formulation could be a way of opening other views
on the distinction between "reader" and "analyst," raised by those who—
from a TSL perspective—think it is important but missing in the hermeneutical conception of the reception process:

> The hermeneutical thesis of the humanities is incapable of es-
> tablishing a subject-object cognitive situation comparable to that
> of the physical sciences on the grounds that *meanings* constituted
> by men and not *objects of nature* are the objects of investigation.

---

[9]The concept of "literary metalanguage" in J. Lotman, 1976, should be mentioned in this context. A more extensive analysis on this topic is in W. Mignolo, 1978.

This thesis neglects the necessary separation between "experiencing understanding" of a text through individual reception process and the attempt of a scholar of literature to: (a) interprete texts in a systematic way on the basis of explicit textual grammars and with recourse to law like assertions from the physical and social sciences (. . .) and (b) to make the process of experiencing understanding as a text-processing operation the object of empirical research (S. Schmidt, 1976: 252).

III

The last observation points out that one of the main aspects derived from the discussion on TSL and on interpretation, from TSL's point of view, is the analysis of *discourse* (e.g. set of statements) *about literature,* as much its *form* (e.g. interpretative, descriptive, explanatory, etc.) as its *foundation* (e.g. analytical philosophy of science, hermeneutics). Some expansion of this point may help to clarify the reconsideration of the field of literary studies derived from TSL.

III.a. Returning to Ihwe (1976), we will retain his expression "deontic space of the science of literature" defined as:

> We can define the domain of 'interpretation' as 'deontic space.' By 'interpretation' I mean here, as before, the institutionalized occupation with 'works of art' (. . .). Now I want to show how the *normative* character of statements of interpretation (. . .) transmits itself to all of the areas of the study of literature in which statements, in one way or another, play an important role, which are based on statements of interpretation.

> Being based on an I-statement ('statements of interpretation') is *one* criterion for a literary critical statement to be a D-statement ('deontic statement'). By a 'literary critical statement' I mean any statement which, first, deals with 'works of art' and, second, a statement which the utterer is prepared to defend as a *publically valid* statement. By 'D-statement' I mean a 'statement within the deontic space of the science of literature" (pp. 346).

What Ihwe is trying to capture with the notion of D-space are those statements which belong to the class 'literary critical statements' (L-statements), identified as those dealing with "properties of works of art" (in the sense discussed in section II) and not, for instance, those that belong to the class of L-statements, but not to D-space (e.g. statements about the author, the society, etc.). What is somewhat bothersome here is the status of D-space within the science of literature: if D-statements are statements within the D-space of the science of literature, how can we reconcile (after what was said in section II.b.) *science* with *interpretation*? To follow this line of thought, *science* could be replaced by a more "neutral expression" such as *study* or even, perhaps, by *facultative* (Lt.: *facultas,* A branch of knowledge; a branch of learning at the university. *Webster's Dictionnary*), and to talk about "facultative statements about literature." "Science" is problematic because it is one of the concepts in question in the "facultative space" (F-space, as designation of the discipline of literary studies) needing the same specifications as I-statements, in such a way, for instance, of making possible the characterization (in F-space) of the sub-set of I-statements and the sub-set of S-statements (scientific statements).

Thus, the first sentence of this section could be reworded by saying that in the F-space two sets of problems can be distinguished: one dealing with the (epistemological) foundation of TSL (S-statements) and the other with the reconstruction of I-statements. If this division is meaningful, it is so from the point of view of TSL. What is more general is that the discipline (F-space) is formed by configurations of distinctive (and opposed) sets of statements (intra and inter paradigmatic relations in a discipline, cfr. R. Botha, 1968), and that a discipline is not a homogeneous space but the heterogeneous conceptual configuration of its own history.

S. Schmidt (1976, 1973b and c) offers several insights into t¹ (analytic) philosophy of science which are aimed at showing that, for a coi temporary scholar of literature, it is necessary to decide which direction o inquiry should be taken and which standard of critical rationality should be striven for in argumentation in literary studies (1976: 256). The scholar faces an option, according to Schmidt, between the acceptance that "understanding is based on a great many presuppositions and employing this uncontested fact as 'a stimulus for a systematical investigation of such presuppositions," while attempting—at the same time—"to make them as far as possible intersubjectively explicit" (1976: 256). To make presuppositions explicit, *presuppose,* therefore, a philosophy of science oriented foundation of literary studies:

> On the one hand this is a question of whether or not it is possible
> to conceive a theoretically founded, empirically working science
> of literature with intersubjectively verifiable results and what
> such a science should consist of; and, on the other hand, it would
> be important for philologists to finally elaborate what until now

has only been promised them as a 'logic of humanities' (this logic, not a 'different' but a common, formal one) by hermeneutic theorists (1976: 257).

From this standpoint, the problem becomes *what kind* of statement *could (should?)* be constructed in the F-space as S-statements? And things seem to come full circle because the *normative* statements about what a TSL should be or look like imply the analysis of normative I-statements (quasi-scientific) which we already dispose of in the F-space in order to show that they do not fulfill the conditions of scientificity which S-statements are expected to satisfy (i.e. the notivation for a theory; P. Achinstein, 1968). But the F-space is not necessarily "covered" by the expectations of the scholar adopting a "critical view" toward the field and having whatever frame of reference to justify his criticism. It seems more adequate to say, going back to Schmidt's quotation, that while the philologist *may* elaborate on the logic of humanities ("this logic, not a 'different' but a common, formal one," p. 257), he *does not have to*. Which, in its turn, means that the organization of the F-space by the TSL-oriented scholar does not have to be thought of as *the* organization of the F-space: what can be labelled "science of literature" as a philologically-founded and descriptive science, does not necessarily have to follow "recommendations" from the TSL-oriented scholar. Briefly, the construction of TSL does not by force eliminate other alternatives about methodology and the ideological level in the F-space (cfr. Section II.b. and III.b.a3.).

III.b. It is perhaps time to close this paper by summarizing some of the main problems that certain works aiming, in the last six or seven years, at the foundation of TSL have brought into the discipline of literary studies. The intended reorganization of the field, as was briefly mentioned, reintroduced the hermeneutical tradition of making interpretations and, consequently, created a polemic at the methodoepistemological and ideological levels. Our summary will begin where Section III.a. left off: the "logic" of science and the "logic" of humanities interferring in the field of literary studies. One way of presenting those aspects parallels, on one hand, the earlier opposition between *explanation* vs. *understanding* and, on the other hand, raises the question about the status "literary statements" (interpretive, critical, theoretical) may have regarding either pole of the opposition. It is not the objective here to review the criticism raised by the analytical philosophy of science against hemeneutics, or vice versa.[10] Instead, based on argumentation from

---

[10] For a general view, see G. Radnitzky, 1968. For criticism by the philosophy of science toward hermeneutics, I refer to the summary and bibliography in S. Schmidt,

both sides, a few problems that must be solved in the construction of TSL and in the reconstruction of literary statements in the F-space will be pointed out.

a) The problem of understanding, as conceived by hermeneutitians, is related to "tradition" (cfr. H.-G. Gadamer, 1960: 157-61, K.-O. Apel, 1967: 20). But it seems evident that prior to this type of understanding comes "understanding *understanding*" (i.e. a general cognitive problem is prior to one specific—and perhaps sophisticated—kind of understanding).[11] Now if, from the point of view of a TSL-orientated scholar, one possible goal is to know how people assign values to verbal utterances, it then seems obvious that the fundamental problem is the understanding of the verbal object (sentence, utterance, text, discourse) in distinction to how people understand non-verbal objects (non-verbal signs, human actions, natural events, etc.). It follows that the TSL-oriented literary scholar has to rely on "cognitive knowledge" (cognitive theories; cfr., W. B. Weimer and D. S. Palermo, 1974; W. Kintsch, 1974; D. A. Norman and D. E. Rumelhart, 1975), where language is one of the aspects of cognition as "understanding *understanding*." [12]

If the starting assumption is that understanding verbal objects is a cognitive problem, *what kind of verbal discourse we must construct to account for cognition of verbal objects* must follow. When we go from general aspects of cognition to the understanding of verbal objects with the ascription of literary text-quality, the spectrum has several colors. Dividing it in just three parts, it appears that:

1976. In a "humanistic" context, although taking a philosophy of science position, the lengthy discussion by D. Freundlieb, 1975; and some insights of A. Lefevere, 1977. For criticism of the philosophy of science and analytical philosophy by hermeneuticians, see K.-O. Apel, 1967. Perhaps it is worth remembering, in this anglo-saxon conflict the classical book by E. Betti, 1955, especially those pages concerning "metodologia ermeneutica" (Vol. I: 291-342) and those concerning "interpretazione filologica" (Vol. I: 350-390). Also, P. Ricoeur (1969) on the relations between hermeneutics and semiotics (pp. 31-63; 80-100; 233-264). For a discussion on the hermeneutical bases of literary knowledge, see E. Forastieri, 1978.

[11]I'm assuming, contrary to the hermeneutical perspective that sees understanding and interpretation as the same operation (H. G. Gadamer, 1960: 291), that they may profitably be "divided," meaning by interpretation not the (possible) cognitive operation involved in understanding, but the verbalized results (i.e. the socialization through signs of the individual (non-communicable) experience of understanding).

[12]Of interest for TSL orientation, the works by T. A. van Dijk 1977 and van Dijk and W. Kintsch (1977). [For non-verbal understanding the recent Sol Worth (1978)]

a1) The distinction between interpretation and TSL (or between I-statements and S-statements), and the introduction of the notion "system of norms" or PC as a frame of reference for interpretation, creates a serious obstacle. The TSL-oriented scholar has tried to solve it with the opinion that a systematic account, based on text-grammars ("interpret text in a systematic way on the basis of explicit textual grammars and with recourse to law-like assertions from the physical and social sciences," S. Schmidt, 1976: 252; also J. Ihwe 1973; T. van Dijk 1972a) would guarantee more "scientific" than interpretive results. It is difficult to come to terms with this belief. Taking seriously the notion of "system of norms" and "essentialist definitions," there are two available options: (a) the description of a "literary work of art" on the basis of an explicit text grammar *may be* systematic, but *will also be* interpretative, because it *presupposes* that object *x is* a literary work of art, and that object *x has* properties *x'*, necessarily *identified* with "neutral" properties of text structure, as described by text grammars; (b) the other alternative, clearly explicit, for instance, in M. A. K. Halliday (1967: 56-60) is that descriptions of literary texts, linguistico-theoretically based, will *just* be *linguistic* descriptions. Which means that these descriptions will not count as statements in the F-space, but rather as statements in, so to speak, the "L (inguistic)-space." In the F-space it seems really to be no alternative: any "description" of literary works of art will be interpretative, whatever the instruments used or the foundation employed. This aspect can be conceived as the "pragmatic problem of F-space."

a2) The second part of the spectrum is in turn twofold:

a2.1) What will be (if all descriptions of literary texts are interpretative, according to a1) the conditions a statement has to fulfill in order to be a S-statement and not an I-statement? Since the characterization of S-statements will depend on its distinction from I-statements, this could be named the "theory building and reconstruction problem";[13]

a2.2) What will be the conditions a statement has to fulfill in order to be an I-statement? This could be referred to as "the making interpretation problem."

It is clear that TSL-oriented scholars could very well reconstruct interpretation; is less clear how much right they have to "give recommendations"

[13]On "reconstruction" of statements about literature, see H. Gottner 1976a, 1976b.

about how to interpret. These recommendations appear more appropriate for the interpreter-practician reflecting on his own activity. Although an hermeneutician could claim that the *control* and decisions about interpretation is an hermeneutical activity insofar as literary interpretation involves tradition and tradition is an hermeneutical business, it would be misleading to think that only hermeneutical theories of interpretation are valid (cfr. "the pragmatic problem of F-space"). On the other hand, the function and validity of statements *about* interpretation, from a TSL point of view, are pertinent as far as those statements make clear the operational dimensions of S-statements (cfr. "theory building and reconstruction problem"). In this case, a TSL-oriented scholar will be more concerned with, for instance, *explanatory* and *explicatory* statements (as possible kinds of S-statements), than with interpretative ones; and the "moment" of theory building will be differentiated from the reconstruction of I-statements. To expand on what is meant by explanatory and explicatory statements in the context of F-space, a few words about the status E. Itkonen (1974) (in discussing transformation-generative brammars) attributes to both notions, will be in order.

Instead of using the opposition *understanding* vs. *explanation*, Itkonen choses *understanding* vs. *observation* (pp. 122-29). He argues that in dealing with human behavior it is not adequate to break the action in atomistic parts and to *observe* them. Actions are not observed, but understood; and to understand an action is to understand a pattern. In its turn, understanding a pattern, without breaking the action into atomistic parts, implies understanding the *intention* of the action. Itkonen then argues the need for a distinction between *rules* and *regularities* (pp. 83-90): regularities, in the domain of nature, are observed; actions in the domain of human behavior, are understood; and they are so because actions are "rule-governed" and to understand a rule is to be able to perform the action described by that rule. Which, obviously, is not the case with regularities of events. Consequently, if *causal explanation* is pertinent in the case of regularities observed in nature, *teleological explanation* (as a *practical syllogism*; on this notion and causal and teleological explanation, see G. von Wright, 1971 and 1976) would be the relevant way of explaining linguistic actions (Itkonen, 1974:295-306). Conversely, not all in linguistics is limited to explanation of linguistic actions, for *something* also has to be done with the structure of sentences. Itkonen considers this "something" *linguistic descriptions* and proceeds to analyse them as *linguistic explications.* By linguistic explications he understands statements dealing with *what* and *how* questions (while explanations account for *why* questions; pp. 301). The function of linguistic explication is to convert the *atheoretical* knowledge of the native speaker into the theoretical knowledge of the theoretician (pp. 259-276). According to this view, it seems plausible to argue against what was said in (a1); proposing that, at the same level as in

linguistic theory, TSL may have explicative statements which are not interpretative in character. The objection is not clear however, because linguistic
explications do not involve textqualifying operations. Instead, any "literary
description" (as text-description), before fulfilling the same conditions as
linguistic explications, will have to solve the problem that "literary descriptions" (which as such presuppose textqualification) has an ambiguous status
regarding their character of *description as explication* or *description as
interpretation.* This is why, again, the "reconstruction" problem goes hand in
hand with the "theory building" one.

a3) Last but not least, because these few comments have been centered on
the consequences derived from TSL-oriented proposals, not too much
attention has been paid to the strong accent on the "deal of science"
guiding-principle. The belief of TSL-oriented scholar in science and the
implications about the reduction of the field of literary studies to the
"ideal of science," ask for a few remarks to complete the preceding
picture of a "new direction" in literary investigations.

The earlier claims by Ihwe (1973a: 315-16) for an "empirical pragmatics" of the language-centered disciplines to handle problems of "the
appropriation and *use* of 'verbal utterances' according to their suitability to
play a certain role in specific contexts or strategies of behaviour," reflects on
the *appropriation* and *use* of "intellectual means" and of "strategies of behavior" in scientific activity. In brief, the need for an empirical pragmatic of
scientific activity is clearly a concern in recent trends in the philosophy of
science (for instance, the "intellectual ecology" in S. Toulmin; 1972: 316ff;
or the "sociological paradigm" in Th. S. Kuhn, 1974). Without going too far
in this direction, it will be sufficient to point out that a science is a social
activity governed by "rules": those concerned with the "techniques" for
investigation (instruments for data recollection, measurement, hypothesis
formation, etc.), and those for "expressing" the results of the investigation in
a "pertinent" form (a scientific discourse). Accordingly, the "scientificity"
of a statement is, first, a problem of scientific discourse; and, second, a
problem that could be solved according to the (arbitrary) norm of "scientificity" the community of researchers in one discipline has already established as *conditions of scientific statements.* Now, if the problem is one-
sided in natural and formal sciences (the "growth of scientific knowledge" to
dominate the institution chasing "common" and "pre-scientific" knowledge
(e.g. astrology) from it), *ghosts* and *alchemists* are still alive in the "humanities" as an institution. Methodologico-epistemological arguments, as was
pointed out in section IIb., are very often confused with ideological ones. It
would be a doubtful ideological operation to disregard "non-scientific

activity" in F-space in the name of the *ideal* (for whom?) of scientific knowledge. In the field of literary studies (F-space) where both scientific and non-scientific statements (start to) interact, an empirical pragmatic of F-space may indeed be helpful (and may conserve time) in the conflicting "growth" of literary knowledge.

REFERENCES

Achinstein, Peter. 1968. *Concepts of Science* (Baltimore: John Hopkins University Press)

Apel, Karl-Otto. 1967. *Analytic Philosophy of Language and the Geisteswissenschaften* (Dordrecht: D. Reidel Publishing Co.)

Betti, Emilio. 1955. *Teoria Generale della Interpretazione* (Milano:Giufrée).

Botha, Rudolf. 1968. *The Function of the Lexicon in Transformational Generative Grammar* (The Hague: Mouton).

Campos, Haroldo de. 1977. "Ideograma, anagrama, diagrama (Umaleitura de Fenollosa" in *Ideogramma, lógica, poesia, linguagem*, Haroldo de Campos (Ed.) (Sao Paolo: Cultrix)

Curtius, Ernest Robert. 1948. *European Literature and the Latin Middle Ages* (Translated from German by W.R. Trask) (New Jersey: Princeton University Press, 1973.)

Dijk, Teun A. van. 1971 "Some Problems of Generative Poetics", *Poetics*, 2, 5-35.

_____ . 1972a. *Some Aspects of Text Grammars* (The Hague: Mouton).

_____ . 1972b. "On the Foundations of Poetics", *Poetics*, 5, 89-123.

_____ . 1977. "Frames, Macro-structures and Discourse Comprehenion" in *Cognitive Processes in Comprehension*, Carpenter, P and Just, M. (Ed.) (New Jersey: Erlbaum).

Dijk, Teun A. van and Kintsch, Walter. 1977. "Cognitive Psychology and Discourse. Recalling and Summarizing Stories", in *Trends in Texlinguistics*, Dressler, Wolfgang, U. (Ed.) (New York: De Gruyter).

Freundlieb, Dieter. 1975. "Hermeneutics versus Philosophy of Science: "A Critique of K.O. Apel's Attempt at Philosophical Foundation of the Humanities", *Poetics*, Vol. 4, 1(13), 47-106.

Forastieri, Eduardo. 1978. "La base hermenéutica del conocimiento literario", in *Dispositio*, Vol. III, 7/8.

Gadamer, Hans-George. 1960. *Wahrheit und Methode* (Tubingen: J.C.B. Mohr)

Geertz, Clifford. 1964. 'Ideology as a Cultural System" in *Ideology and Discontent* D' Apter (Ed.) (N.Y.: The Free Press)

Gottner, Heide. 1976a. Analysis of the Problem of Relevance in the Study of Literature", *Poetics*, 17, 35-56.

_____ . 1976b. "Structures of Theory in the Study of Literature", PTL, II, 2 : 297-312.

Halliday, M.A.K. 1962. "Descriptive Linguistics in Literary Theory" in *Patterns of Language*, Halliday and A. McIntosh (Eds) (London:Longmans, 1966): 56-69.

Hempel, Carl G. 1952. "Fundamentals of Concept Formation in Empirical Science", Vol I/II, *Foundations of the Unity of Science* (Chicago: Univ. of Chicago Press)

Herbert, Thomas. 1966. "Réflexions sur la situation théorique des sciences sociales et spécialment de la psychologie sociale", in *Cahiers pour l'Analyse*, 2.

_____ . 1968. "Pour une théorie générale des idéologies", *Cahiers pour l'Analyse*, 9.

Hirsch, E.D. Jr. 1967. *Validity in Interpretation* (New Haven: Yale University Press)

Ihwe, Jen. 1972. "What's Wrong with the 'Theory of Literature'? On the role of Linguistics in the Study of Literature", in *Linguistische Bericht.*

_____ . 1973a. "On the Validation of Text-Grammars in the 'Study of Literature'," in *Studies in Text-Grammars*, J. Petofi and H. Rieser (Eds.)

_____ . 1976. "The Philosophy of Literary Criticism Reconsidered On the "Logic" of Interpretation" *Poetics* 5, 339-372

Itkonen, Esa. 1974. *Linguistics and Metascience* (Finlandiae: Studia Philosophica Turkuensia, Fasc. II)

Jakobson, Roman. 1960. "Concluding Statement: Linguistic and Poetics", in *Style in Language*, Th. A. Sebeok, (Ed). (Cambridge:MIT), 350-77.

_____ . 1973. "Postscriptum" in *Question de Poétique* (Paris:Du Seuil).

Khun, Thomas S. 1974. "Second Thoughts on Paradigms", in *The Structure of Scientific Theories*, F. Suppes (Ed.) (Urbana: III. Univ. Press) 459.

Lázaro Carreter, Fernando. 1976. "Introduction: La poetica", in *Estudios de Poetica* (Madrid: Taurus)

Levin, Samuel R. 1962 *Linguistic Structures in Poetry* (The Hague: Mouton)

_____ . 1976. "Concerning what kind of Speech Act a Poem is", in *Pragmatics of Language and Literature*, T.A. van Dijk, (Ed.) (Amsterdam: North Holland)

Lefevere, André. 1977. "The Growth of Literary Knowledge", PTL, Vol. 2. 33-64.

Longree, Georges H.F. 1976. "The Rhetoric of a Picture-Poem", PTL, Vol.1, No.1, 63-84.

Lotman, Jury. 1976. "The Content and Structure of the Concept of 'Literature'," PTL, Vol. 1, No. 2, 339-356.

Kintsch, Walter. 1974. *The Representation of Meaning in Memory* (New Jersey: Lawrence Erlbaun Associates).

Mignolo, Walter. 1978. *Elementos para una teoría del texto literario* (Barcelona: Crítica-Grijalbo)

Norman, Donald A. and Rumelhart, David E. 1975. *Explorations in Cognition* (San Francisco: W.H. Freeman)

Ohmann, Richard. 1971. "Speech Acts and the Definition of Literature", *Philosophy and Rhetoric* ", Vol. 4, No.1, 1-19.

Prieto, Luis. 1966. *Messages et Signaux* (Paris: P.U.F.)

_____ . 1976. *Pertinence et Pratique* (Paris: Minuit)

Radnitzky, George. 1968. *Contemporary Schools of Metascience* (Goteborg: Akademiforlaget)

Ricoeur, Paul. 1969. *Le Conflit des interpretations* (Essais d'Herneneutique) (Paris: Du Seuil)

Ruprecht, Hans-George. 1978. "Pour un projet the Théorie de la Littérature: Document de Travail", *Dispositio*, Vol. III, 7/8.

Schmidt, Siegfried. 1973a. *Texttheorie*. (Munchen:Fink)

_____ . 1973b. "On the Foundation and the Research Strategies of a Science of Literary Communication", *Poetics*, 7, 7-35.

_____ . 1974. "Literaturwissenschaft Zwischen Linguistik und Sozialpshuchologie", in *ZGL*, 2.1., 49-80.

_____ . 1976. "On a Theoretical Basis of a Rational Science of Literature" PTL, Vol. 1, No. 2, 239-264.

Todorov, Tzevetan. 1971. "L'Héritage méthodologique du Formalisme", in *Poétique de la Prose* (Paris:Du Seuil) 9-31 (original version: 1964)

Toulmin, Stephan. 1972. *Human Understanding* (New Jersey: Princeton Univ. Press)

Traban, Jurgen. 1970. *Zur Semiologie des Literarischen Kunswerks. Glossematik Und Literaturtheorie* (Munchen: Wilhelm Fink Verlag)

Urmson, J.O. 1956. *Philosophical Analysis* (Oxford:

Verdaasdonk, H. and C.J. van Rees. 1977. "Reading a Text vs. Analyzing a Text", *Poetics*, 6, 55-76.

Veron, Eliseo. 1971. "Ideology and social sciences: a communicational approach" *Semiotica* 3 (1), 59-76.

Vološinov, V.N. 1930. *Marxism and the Philosophy of Language* (Translated by L. Matejka and I.R. Titunik) (N.Y. - Seminar Press, 1073)

Wiemer, Walter B. and Palermo, David, S. (Eds). 1974. *Cognition and the Symbolic Processes* (N.Y.: John Wiley and Sons)

Wienold, Götz. 1972. *Semiotik der Literatur* (Frankfurt: Athenaum)

_____ . 1973. "Experimental Research on Literature: Its Need and Appropriatness", *Poetics*, 7, 77-85.

_____ . 1976. "The Concept of Text Processing, the Criticism of Literature and Some Uses of Literature in Education", in *The Uses of Criticism*, P. Foulkes, (Ed); (Bern: Lang) 111-31

_____ . 1978. "Textlinguistic Approaches to Written Works of Art", in *Current Trends in Textlinguistics* (N.Y.: Walter de Gruyter) 133-54.

Worth, Sol. 1978. "Man is Not a Bird", *Semiotica*, 23:1/2, 5-28

Wrigth, Henrik Von. 1971. *Explanation and Understanding* (London:Routledge and Kegan Paul)

_____ . 1976. "Replies" in Essays on *Explanations and Understanding*, J. Manninen and R. Tuomela (Eds.) (Dordrecht: Reidel Publishing Co) 371-416.

Yurkievich, Saúl. 1977. "Crítica de la razón lingüística", *Dispositio*, Vol. II, 5/6.

DISTINGUISHING SEMIOTICS FROM LINGUISTICS AND THE POSITION OF LANGUAGE IN BOTH

Irmengard Rauch

I

"My language is the sum total of myself"—Peirce's stunning 1868 definition of language, or the reverse, of man (Peirce 1960: 5.314) proves cogent in the midst of the perennial (cf. e.g. Ramat 1975) identification problem of semiotics and linguistics. In the same paragraph Peirce writes: ". . . man is the thought . . . thought is a sign . . . sign *is* the man himself." Does this mean that, as far as language is concerned, Peirce's sign theory has swallowed language up, and that linguistics for Peirce is accordingly a non-entity? Not at all. In his classification of the sciences Peirce (1931:1.183, 186, 189, 191, 200) derives semiotics from logic, a normative science branching from philosophy, while he assigns linguistics to classificatory psychics or ethology branching from the psychical sciences which, in turn, branch from idioscopy.

Conversely, a present-day philosopher, Moravcsik, inadvertently defines linguistics, writing "In modern times, language . . . has become the object of scientific study . . . , linguistics . . . an empirical science" (1975:11). Moravcsik warns however (12):

> One can raise an enormous variety of questions about language. Language is used for a great diversity of purposes, it affects many different aspects of personal and interpersonal activities, it has its physical qualities in terms of sound patterns, it evokes reactions from people, etc. It is senseless to expect that there should be one unitary science that would answer all these questions. Its answer would be a unitary science of matter that would combine all of what we call today the natural sciences. Such gigantic systematisation is at most programmatic; certainly no science starts out with such pretensions.

On the linguistic side, early in this century Saussure saw linguistics as ". . . only a part of the general science of semiology. . . ." (1959:16), which, however, ". . . can become the master-pattern for all branches of semiology although language is only one particular semiological system" (68). His definition of language is:

Language is a well-defined object in the heterogeneous mass of speech facts. It can be localized in the limited segment of the speaking-circuit where an auditory image becomes associated with a concept. . . . It is a system of signs in which the only essential thing is the union of meanings and sound-images, and in which both parts of the signs are psychological (14-15).

Interestingly, Saussurean tradition lives on in the classical generative concept of language in which ". . . a language associates sound and meaning in a particular way. . ." (Chomsky 1972:115). It is thus tempting to attribute to Saussure himself the understanding of language as strictly verbal language and, as a result, the assignment of language to the aegis of linguistics.

In the Neotransformational era, language is just now beginning to be reinterpreted. Particularly incongruous, however, are those linguistic enterprises which include animal communication but which, in turn, exclude it from the concept language (cf. e.g. Marshall 1970). Narrowing in on the very present, as recently as 1976 in *Psycholinguistics: Introductory Perspectives* by Joseph F. Kess we read "The essence of language, which distinguishes it from the communication systems of other animals, is the quality of abstraction" (and) "The study of language as a characteristic behavior of the human species is embraced by the field of psycholinguistics" (1). In his 1977 *Introduction to Linguistics,* Ronald Wardhaugh confidently states: "Linguists are in broad agreement about some of the important characteristics of human language, and one definition of language widely associated with linguistics may be used to illustrate areas of agreement. This particular definition states that *language is a system of arbitrary vocal symbols used for human communication*" (3). At this point and in striking contrast we now hear Charles J. Fillmore (1977:IX) say: ". . . either the scope of linguistics must reach beyond language strictly defined, or the concept language must be extended to include the rich and powerful symbolic systems of the kind we see described here [American sign language] ."

Possibly it is redundant to predict what sorts of definitions we should expect in the future concerning the primacy controversy of linguistics and semiotics, since the cumulative past delineations of the respective domains of the two disciplines have not at all succeeded in clarifying either the disciplines or language itself. It would seem then that Peirce's definitions of language (cf. Rauch forthcoming), semiotics, and linguistics, from which it can be extrapolated that language is the shared object of two separate disciplines, have been overlooked. Indeed, linguistic attempts such as those of Weinreich 1963, Shapiro 1969, and Anttila 1972 to treat linguistic data within a strongly semiotic framework have not provoked a revolution in linguistic method. Conversely, the application of linguistic analogues in such semiotic modalities as music (cf. e.g. Ruwet 1972) and art (cf. e.g. Uspensky 1976) remain limited.

If semiotics and linguistics are independent disciplines, a fact which is not accountable to language, then wherein lies their independence? All opining as to their respective domains can be curtailed by a serious look at their working tools, and if working tools can be found which are distinctive to only one discipline, then Alston's (1971:295-6) apocalyptic statement is rendered impotent: ". . . If and when semantics is developed and integrated into structural linguistics along with grammar, the differences between the two sorts of inquiry [philosophy and linguistics] in methods and status of conclusions, though not in ultimate aim, may well be reduced to the vanishing point."

II

Let us examine a working tool which is distinctively linguistic, and one which is distinctively semiotic. We propose here that a principle such as the principle of MINIMAL OPPOSITION is a distinctively linguistic tool, while a principle such as the principle of SECONDNESS is a distinctively semiotic tool since they are applicable with generality only in their respective disciplines. There are many examples of the formulation of an emic construct in various semiotic modalities: Edward T. Hall's proxemics (1972) which does not specify a *proxeme* since as Hall writes (269): ". . . it is concerned more with proxetics than proxemics. . . ."; in film semiotics the *videme* ("Image-Event"), *cademe* ("camera shot"), and *edeme* ("editing shot") of Sol Worth (1969:299-300) are, according to Lange-Seidl (1977:18) ". . . in reality abbreviations for technical procedures, not minimal units isolated theoretically in the sense of structuralism"; finally, Kenneth L. Pike's *behavioreme* ("A unit of behavior such as the church service or the football game . . ." (1954: 57) is criticized by Greenberg (1973:55) because ". . . a religious ceremony, while in a very broad sense meaningful, does not send messages, as it were, with such precision that we can say when the message is the same or different."

On the side of semiotics the phenomenological principle of SECOND-NESS can be demonstrated to be a decidedly semiotic tool. Although Peircean Firstness, Secondness, and Thirdness are found in linguistic treatments under the cover of icon, index and symbol, the pure dynamics of the three phenomenological categories are not exploited fully by linguistic method. To demonstrate this let us consider a case of linguistic change in contemporary American English. In his 1970 *Language* article "Aspect and variant inflection in English verbs," Randolph Qurik discusses the results of a series of tests aimed to substantiate his hypothesis that in both British and American English the so-called irregular weak verbs display, on the one hand, a voiceless dental inflection to signal perfective (momentary) aspect and, on the other hand, a voiced dental inflection to signal imperfective (continuous) aspect, for example *spilt* in "When I shouted, he *spilt* his coffee" versus *spilled* in "The water *spilled* out all day until the ceiling gave way." Quirk is convinced that the results of his experiments corroborate a speaker distinction between perfective -*t* and imperfective -*ed* which are associated with the past participle and preterite respectively, and that in fact (310) "we might infer a corresponding direction of analogical influence," that is, the participial -*t* penetrates the preterite paradigm. Anyone familiar with Quirk's article is aware of the tenuousness of his results, which prompts him to invoke even diachronic Middle English data, lending some support to the claim of analogical influence of the participle upon the preterite.

It is surprising, however, that Quirk's experiments consider only written data and only the dental suffix to the complete neglect of the accompanying vowel alternation which occurs in three of the eight verbs included in his results: *dreamt, leapt, knelt,* beside *spoilt, spillt, learnt, spelt, burnt.* (Quirk excludes *smell* and *lean* on the basis of poor test design, 307.) When Quirk's data (Figures 2a, 2b of page 305; 4a, 4b of page 309) are studied with a view toward the vowel alternation, a clear-cut correlation between non-alternating root and suffix -*d* and alternating root and suffix -*t* emerges. This correlation is particularly strong in American English in which, using Quirk's statistics, *dreamed, leaped, kneeled* can be found to be more objectionable than *spoiled, spilled, learned* and *burned* in the -*ed* perfect (Figure 2a—most objectionable: *kneeled* 20%; *dreamed* 18%, *leaped* 12%; *spelled* 12% and all others less than 12%). In the -*ed* preterite *dreamed* and *kneeled* are the most objectionable while *leaped* joins the non-alternating group (Figure 4a—most objectionable: *kneeled* 15%, *dreamed* 12%; all others less than 12%, *leaped* 4%). Conversely, *knelt, dreamt,* and *leapt* are, but for *spoilt,* the least objectionable of the eight verbs in *t*-perfect (Figure 2b—least objectionable: *knelt* 27%, *dreamt* 39%, *leapt* 51%; except *spoilt* 47%, all others more than 51%); and, with the exception of *burnt,* the verbs *knelt, dreamt,* and *leapt* are also the least objected to in the *t*-preterite (Figure 4b—least objectionable: *knelt* 17%, *leapt* 38%, *dreamt* 51%; except *burnt* 40%, all others more than 50%).

Of the three root alternating verbs the order of objection to -*ed* suffix from least to most in both the perfect and preterite is *leaped, dreamed, kneeled;* correspondingly the reverse order might be expected for the *t*-suffix, and this is, in fact, the case in the perfect, thus least objectionable *knelt,* then *dreamt,* and most objectionable *leapt.* In the *t*-preterite, *dreamt* and *leapt* change places, thus least objectionable *knelt,* then *leapt,* and most objectionable *dreamt.*

Two conclusions can be drawn from these observations. Firstly: the iconic association of the *t*-suffix with the alternating root regardless of whether the suffix signals tense or aspect, or both, is accountable at least in part for the spread of the *t* suffix (thus e.g. *knelt* is a relatively late alternate, nineteenth century, as compared to the fourteenth century *dreamt* and *leapt*). Secondly, the *-t* suffix relative to the verb *leap* is in an indexical relationship, that is, regardless of the spelling, the voiceless dental alone is possible, contiguous to a root in voiceless consonant by general phonological rule. The neutralization of the *-ed* and *-t* suffixes with *leap* accounts for *leap* joining the non-alternating roots in the perfect, *have leaped, have leapt,* as well as in the preterite imperfective *leaped*. At the same time, the strong alliance of *leapt* in the preterite perfective (where *leapt* in fact is less objectionable than *dreamt*) corroborates the neutralization of *-t, -ed* by showing that the onus of the distinction between *leaped* and *leapt* in the preterite resides in the alternating root alone.

III

In observing the occurrence of the irregular *-t* preterites in contemporary American English, we witness the effect of a Firstness association identifying the alternating root with the *-t* suffix, and the effect of a Secondness association COMPELLING the *-t* suffix alone to be joined to a voiceless root final consonant. Linguistic method sorts out the minimal opposition between voiceless and voiced dental; it also shows voice as automatically constrained by environment. Semiotic Secondness, however, identifies the automatic constraint as COMPULSORY in contrast to the similarity between the alternating root and the *-t* uffix (Firstness), which is only POSSIBLE and not compulsory. Without doubt then, the potency of the Secondness correlation is strongly predictive and explanatory. From this point of view, it is difficult to understand why Anttila (1972:95) describes the paradigm of Latin *wōk- / wōkw-* 'voice,' which regularizes in favor of *wōk-* (nominative), instead of the oblique cases according to Latin habit, as an example of ". . . the irregularity of analogy (one cannot predict the direction) . . . ," while maintaining that the change is regular in itself, since Latin prohibits interconsonantal *w* which would result in **wōkws*. It must be admitted that one can predict this particular Latin analogy after all.

We can conclude that semiotic method provides a tool for strengthening the predictability factor in linguistics, which, in turn, strengthens the position of linguistics as a science. (Cf. Wells 1947:24: "When it [linguistics] becomes predictive not only of the past but also of the future, linguistics will have attained the inner circle of science.") Semiotic method demonstrates its explanatory power—a characteristic of any scientific theory (cf. L. Jonathan Cohen 1975:25: "One criterion of appraisal for a semiotic theory . . . is its ability to assist the impartial resolution of . . . controversies"). And lastly, semiotic method is acquitted of the frequent charge that it does not have distinct working tools, but rather a tool box containing an accumulation of tools from the other sciences (cf. Moravcsik quoted above: "It is senseless that there should be one unitary science. . . ."). Accordingly, language, while enjoying crossfertilization by semiotics and linguistics, nevertheless requires the individual treatment of each discipline.

REFERENCES

Alston, W.P. 1971. "Philosophical Analysis and Structural Linguistics." *Philosophy and Linguistics*, ed. by Colin Lyas, 284-296. London: Macmillan St.Martin's Press.

Anttila, Raimo. 1972. *An Introduction to Historical and Comparative Linguistics*. New York: Macmillan.

Chomsky, Noam. 1972. *Language and Mind*. Enlarged edition. New York: Harcourt Brace Jovanovich, Inc.

Cohen, L. Jonathan. 1975. "Spoken and Unspoken Meanings." *The Tell-Tale Sign: A Survey of Semiotics*, ed. by Thomas A. Sebeok, 19-25. Lisse: The Peter de Ridder Press.

Fillmore, Charles J. 1977. In *On the Other Hand: New Perspectives on American Sign Language*, ed by L. Friedman. New York: Academic Press.

Greenberg, Joseph H. 1973. "Linguistics as a Pilot Science." *Themes in Linguistics: The 1970's*, ed. by Eric P. Hamp, 45-60. (Janua Linguarum, Series Minor, 172.) The Hague: Mouton.

Hall, Edward T. 1972. "A System for the Notation of Proxemic Behavior." *Communication in Face to Face Interaction*, ed. by John Laver and Sandy Hutcherson, 247-273. (*American Anthropologist*, vol. 65, 1963, 1003-26.) Harmondsworth, Middlesex, England: Penguin Books, Inc.

Kess, Joseph F. 1976. *Psycholinguistics: Introductory Perspectives*. New York: Academic Press.

Lange-Seidl, Annemarie. 1977. *Approaches to Theories for Non-verbal Signs. (Studies in Semiotics*, vol. 17.) Lisse: The Peter de Ridder Press.

Marshall, J.C. 1970. "The Biology of Communication in Man and Animals," *New Horizons in Linguistics*, ed. by John Lyons, 229-241. Harmondsworth, Middlesex, England: Penguin Books, Inc.

Moravcsik, J.M.E. 1975. *Understanding Language: A Study of Theories of Language in Linguistics and Philosophy*. (Janua Linguarum, Series Minor, 169.) The Hague: Mouton.

Peirce, Charles S. 1931, 1960. *Collected Papers of Charles Sanders Peirce*, ed. by C. Hartshorne and P. Weiss, vols. 1, 5. Cambridge Mass.: Harvard University Press.

Pike, Kenneth L. 1954. *Language in Relation to a Unified Theory of the Structure of Human Behavior*. Preliminary edition, part 1. Glendale, California: Summer Institute of Linguistics.

Quirk, Randolph. 1970. "Aspect and Variant Inflection in English Verbs." *Language* 46: 300-311.

Ramat, Paolo. 1975. "Semiotics and Linguistics." *Versus* 10: 1-16.

Rauch, Irmengard. forthcoming. "The Language-Inlay in Semiotic Modalities." *Semiotica*.

Ruwet, Nicolas. 1972. *Langage, Musique, Poésie*. Paris: Editions du Seuil.

Saussure, Ferdinand de. 1959. *Course in General Linguistics*, ed. by C. Bally et al., transl. by W. Baskin. New York: Philosophical Library.

Shapiro, Michael. 1969. *Aspects of Russian Morphology: A Semiotic Investigation*. Cambridge, Mass.: Slavica Publishers, Inc.

Uspensky, Boris. 1976. *The Semiotics of the Russian Icon*, ed. by Stephen Rudy. Lisse: The Peter de Ridder Press.

Wardhaugh, Ronald. 1977. *Introduction to Linguistics*. New York: McGraw-Hill.

Weinreich, Uriel. 1963. "On the Semantic Structure of Language." *Universals of Language*, ed. by J.H. Greenberg, 114-171. Cambridge, Mass.: The M.I.T. Press.

Wells, Rulon S. 1947. "'De Saussure's System of Linguistics." *Word* 3: 1-31.

Worth, Sol. 1969. "The Development of a Semiotic of Film." *Semiotica* 1: 282-321.

CULTURAL SEMIOTICS AND ANTHROPOLOGY

Irene Portis Winner

INTRODUCTION

The growth of concern both in the East and in the West with problems of meaning and change in cultural context as inseparable from cultural structures or systems, as well as the renewed interest in the search for a common perspective that can unite all human behavior within a general framework, is everywhere in evidence, in spite of varied interpretations and considerable disagreements about ways to solve the new problems implied. For example, within the last five to six years there has been a veritable explosion of anthropological publications in the West under the various labels of semantic, cognitive, structural, symbolic and semiotic studies that have manifested such concerns, while studies specifically utilizing the term cultural semiotics have been extremely important in East Europe during the last decade, particularly in the so-called Moscow-Tartu School. If, as Peirce held, the whole universe is "perfused with signs, if not composed entirely of signs" (Peirce 1965-66: 5:448, n. 1), if, as Saussure said, "we need a science that studies the life of signs in society," and if, as Jakobson has held, the sign is a "renvoi" (1975) which Bär has said signals to us the polyvalence of the whole notion of semiotics (Bär 1976:380), then it follows that the broad approach called here cultural semiotics must be interdisciplinary in scope, using all data available from all cultures in time and space, in its attempt to elucidate and interrelate the many levels of culture within a semiotic framework.

In this sense cultural semiotics encompasses a broad domain within the still wider domain of general semiotics which is a part of the general theory of communications, and all of these areas share certain structural properties. In the most inclusive framework, Boulding's view of the universe as a general system assumes that all sciences, physical and social, share a common pattern of relationships, although each in differing degrees, and furthermore that the greatest task for the scientific community has been to transcend the mechanical and materialistic orientation which dominated its early history (Boulding 1977 in Singell 1978:289).

It appears that general semiotics and its subdivisions fall within this grand design. Accordingly, I propose that we may view cultural semiotics as a new paradigm or world view in Kuhn's term, unified by broad themes and

yet divided by wide differences and interpretations, and possibly encompassing several closely related, contiguous but differing, subparadigms. Kuhn has
described revolutions as shifts of vision, or transitions between incompatible
paradigms or world views. While paradigms exist in relation of tension to
each other, common values may unite separate world views, which facilitates
communication between them. However, communication goes on by translation, comparable to the process of translating into separate languages. As
Kuhn has noted, translation is a very threatening process (Kuhn 1970:203).
However, it is unavoidable since groups that have systematically different
sensations on receipt of the same stimuli, do—in a sense—live in different
worlds. "Our world is populated in the first instance not by stimuli but by
the objects of our sensations and thus need not be the same . . . group to
group" (Kuhn 1970:193).

To Kuhn, paradigms are very broad constellations affecting the way a
community perceives reality, covering on the one hand, beliefs, values, and
techniques shared by a given community, and on the other hand, concrete
puzzle solutions or "exemplars" which are used as models for solving problems (ibid.:170). However, according to Kuhn, rules, a kind of interpretation
and rationalization of the prior paradigm, may be absent, or merely implicit
or highly divergent (ibid.:42-44). Thus research projects within a paradigm
may not share a common and full set of rules and assumptions that characterize a tradition. Rather they "may relate by resemblance and by modeling
to one or another part of the scientific corpus . . ." (ibid.:44-46). Clearly a
translation between subparadigms and paradigms is the more difficult when
rules and assumptions are merely implicit.

As Kuhn has written, probably the most prevalent claim advanced by
the proponents of a new paradigm is that they can solve problems that led the
old ones to a crisis, and that the new theory is neater, more suitable, and has
an aesthetic appeal (ibid.:155). If cultural semiotics suggests to us one of
Kuhn's revolutions (which simply means a crisis of an old paradigm and a
move to a new one whether perceived or not as a revolution), then among the
unsolved problems that cultural semiotics attacks are the reconciliation of the
static and synchronic with the dynamic and diachronic within cultural systems, the relation of meaning and content to form and structure, and the
question of how cultural systems are internally organized, how such systems
change, how they are related to each other, and finally what is the significant
unit of culture. Some of these problems were already significantly advanced
in the thirties, before cultural semiotics became a recognized domain, by the
earlier work of the Prague Linguistic Circle and by Mukařovský's extension
of his semiotic and aesthetic concepts to culture in general (1970) as well as
by Bogatyrev's early semiotic study of folk costumes (1971). But only in the
last decades has cultural semiotics become a recognized term signifying a

whole new kind of anthropology that has been most specifically advanced by the so-called Moscow-Tartu school. But the outlook implied is worldwide. Anthropologists, from Japan to Eastern and Western Europe to the United States, Canada and Latin America, are now working in this broad direction.

Considering cultural semiotics as a broad paradigm, encompassing contiguous subparadigms which share underlying values and traditions that provide a general framework for the varying interpretations, assumptions and rules adopted, we note that all versions partake, to a greater or lesser extent, in the values and concepts of the sign as developed from the Stoics through medieval and enlightenment views to Peirce's and Saussure's extension of the concept of sign to all culture. Furthermore, all share, though in some cases only indirectly, in the later syntheses emanating from the structural linguistics and aesthetics of the Prague Linguistic Circle. However, while in a broad sense a paradigm of cultural semiotics is generating considerable research both in the East and in the West, it is nevertheless clear that there is lacking what Kuhn called "a full interpenetration or rationalization of it. . . ." Also lacking is "a standard interpretation or an agreed reduction to rules" (Kuhn 1970: 44).

It is the task of this discussion to isolate a few of the tensions within the general paradigm of cultural semiotics. My thesis here is that the greatest divergence is between the developments in cultural semiotics most directly influenced by the work of the early Prague Linguistic Circle, namely Moscow-Tartu semiotics and other East European groups and some Western scholars on the one hand, and several other Western semiotic traditions stemming from diverse other influences on the other hand. I do not suggest, however, that either Western or Eastern approaches are homogenous. There are significant differences here also. All approaches are to some extent influenced by Lévi-Strauss whose work has been effected by various influences from the Prague scholars and who is, in this sense, a mediator of a kind, conscious or not, between traditions. In this discussion I consider some American and English anthropological semiotic approaches, and comparisons are made to Lévi-Strauss and to Moscow-Tartu semiotics. All those scholars, working within this new paradigm, share a dominating interest in the problem of meaning and culture ruled out by the positivists, and in the mediating role of cultural world views in effecting perception. All, or nearly all, have departed from the assumption that there are many systems of signs of which language is only one, although probably the privileged one, and have concerned themselves, to some degree at least, with the interrelation of *langue* and *parole*. However, what the modeling role of language is, whether it is *the* model, what the significant unit of study in a culture is, and how open and dynamic structures are, these are some of the fundamentally unsettled issues, as well as others to be noted.

1. CONCEPTS AND TRENDS LEADING TO, AND A PART OF, SEMIOTICS OF CULTURE

1.1 COMMON HERITAGE

The roots of contemporary semiotics reach back to the writings of the Stoics, to St. Augustine, to Kant's emphasis on the thinking and perceiving mind, to Locke's concept of the sign and to Vico's hypothesis that man knows the world only imperfectly, since he knows only what he can do or make. Thus natural language is simply an adequate medium of communication, not a precise instrument, and is, in fact, a reflection of a whole cultural way of life. Vico's anticartesianism and his view that understanding culture is like understanding a language, since ways of life are embedded in ways of speaking, makes him a most important forerunner of semiotic anthropology and of semiotics of culture.

The immediate developments which made modern semiotics possible can be traced to the late nineteenth and early twentieth centuries, specifically to two mutually isolated sources: the writings of the American philosopher, Charles Sanders Peirce (1839-1914) and the Swiss linguist, Ferdinand de Saussure (1857-1915), both of whom independently laid the basis for the formal study of semiotics. For Peirce, semiotics became the focus of a general logic where the sign is seen as something that stands to somebody for something to which it points and with which it is never identical. While Peirce was essentially concerned with language as the most important sign system, he anticipated in important ways the extension of semiotics to other cultural systems. The positions that a sign is only a sign when it is perceived and interpreted, that every sign has an interpretant (another sign), and that signs must be typologized by the varying and interpenetrating and changing relations of expression to content, all anticipate semiotics of culture, since Peirce's signs are inherently dynamic and contextual.

For Saussure, semiotics was implied by the development of structural linguistic theory and methodology. Of fundamental importance for cultural semiotics is Saussure's distinction between *langue* and *parole,* his position that the verbal sign is arbitrary, the relational approach to sound and meaning and the foresighted advocacy of the extension of the field of semiotics to nonlinguistic and all cultural behavior. As Saussure wrote:

> Language is a system of signs that express ideas and is therefore comparable to the system of writing, the alphabet of deaf mutes, symbolic rites, polite formulas, military signals, etc. But it is the most important of all these systems.

A science that studies the life of signs within society is conceivable. . . . I shall call it semiology (Saussure 1966:16).

Furthermore, Saussure concluded:

By studying rites, customs, etc., as signs, I believe that we shall throw new light on the facts and point up the need for including them in a science of semiology and explaining them by its laws (*ibid.:*17).

1.2 THE PRAGUE LINGUISTIC CIRCLE

The groundwork for modern theories of semiotics of culture, which were called for by Saussure, must be attributed to the pioneering work of the Prague Linguistic Circle which was formed in 1926, the multiform roots of which were Russian Formalism, Husserlian phenomenology, *Gestalt* psychology and the Czech formalism of the so-called Herbartian School as well as Hegelian dialectics, and the writings of Saussure. (Peirce's writings were integrated into this tradition only later by Jakobson, beginning in the 1950s.)

The Prague structuralist movement arose partially as a rebellion against notions of static and closed systems, and against the idea that there are any areas that exist outside of system. Rather, the scholars of the Prague Linguistic Circle held that system is everywhere and that all systems are to a greater or lesser extent, interrelated, and thus they insisted on resolving the Saussurian dichotomy of *langue/parole*. In early statements, the basis was laid for a broad theory of structure encompassing both synchrony and diachrony, and harmony and conflict. The concept of immanence of structures was replaced by that of autonomy, since intrinsic and extrinsic elements were held to be dynamically interrelated by the process of change. Thus while intrinsic relations accounted for the specific characteristics of particular changes, extrinsic forms accounted for the particular direction and the speed of evolution. Furthermore, all structures were held to be in mutual relations forming a structure of structures (see Jakobson and Tynjanov 1928:37 and the *Theses* of the Prague Linguistic Circle 1929).

By the 1930s this group began to interest itself directly in theories of the sign and, by extension, in the semiotics of culture. Mukařovský, the leading aesthetician of the Prague Linguistic Circle who quickly extended his perspective to culture in general, discussed the evolution of structures (referring to verbal art) as an uninterrupted self-motion (using the Hegelian concept of *Selbstbewegung*) which, while directed by its own immanent laws, does not occur in isolation from other cultural phenomena. For all cultural phenomena are held to be mutually independent and in active interrelation-ship (Mukařovský 1934b). Furthermore Mukařovský considered art from a semiotic point of view and soon applied a semiotic approach, particularly his concept of polyfunctionality of human behavior and the dynamic aesthetic function, to all cultural behavior (1934a, 1970) (see I.P. Winner 1978a for a discussion of the cultural implications of the aesthetic function).

As Mukařovský stated, the aesthetic function is universally present, whether dominant or subsidiary, its norm-breaking characteristics funda-mentally affecting cultural behavior.

> This sphere is related to the sum of human activity, as well as to the whole world of things; every activity and everything can be-come—due to social convention or individual will—vehicles—per-manent or transitory—of the aesthetic function (1937:54).

Mukařovský emphasized the social and cultural role of the aesthetic function in his very original and far-reaching essay of 1936. Furthermore, Mukařovský's interpretation of the sign foresaw the importance of the many-leveled approach of modern semiotics. As he stated it:

> All psychic content exceeding the limits of individual conscious-ness acquires the character of a sign by the very fact of its com-municability. The science of the sign . . . must be elaborated in its entire scope; just as contemporary linguistics enlarges the field of semantics in treating from this point of view all the elements of the linguistic system, indeed even sounds, the results of linguistic semantics should be applied to all other series of signs and should be differentiated according to their special characteristics (1934a: 85).

Most importantly, Mukařovský also pointed out that sign systems are to be understood not only in terms of function, which he saw as a teleological concept relating to the goal of the sign, but also in relation to value (how well the sign fulfills, in view of the sign's cultural agents, its function) and norms (the rules that govern the production and perception of sign messages). While norms are similar to Saussure's *langue,* the "grammar" of sign systems, Mukařovský did not fully accept Saussure's position of arbitrariness, although Saussure also qualified this position. Suggesting Peircean concepts with which Mukařovský was not familiar at that time, Mukařovsky posited a multiform, ambiguous relation of art works, understood as signs, to reality. Thus he im-plied some kind of iconicity, although he did not use this term. In the same vein, Mukařovský's "semantic gesture" has been traced to the concept of "sound gesture" developed by the Russian linguist Polivanov (Cf. Steiner 1976:373), which assumes a nonarbitrary relation between some features of sound and emotional states. Thus the relation between signifier and signified may be motivated and nonarbitrary, as well as arbitrary, an extremely important concept for the later cultural semiotics.

It was Jakobson, however, who first formally synthesized the Peircean and Saussurian views of signs. Jakobson's synthesis of sign types works out the complex problem of what signs are arbitrary or conventional, as opposed to iconic and indexical, and demonstrates the interpenetration of these levels in all signs, a problem that had been foreseen by Mukařovský. His extension of the Peircean taxonomy of signs by the addition of imputed similarity (Jakobson 1970:12-13) has important implications for cultural semiotics, since it implies, as does Kuhn in the earlier quoted statement, that what is similar to reality in one world view may be different from reality in another, depending on underlying cultural values and categories.

One of the first practical investigations of the extensions of semiotics beyond the verbal behavior and beyond the arts in general was carried out by a member of the Prague Linguistic Circle, Petr Bogatyrev, who in a pioneering work, *The Functions of Folk Costumes in Moravian Slovakia*, published over thirty years ago, investigated the semiotics of the folk costume in all its functions. Bogatyrev, who was originally an ethnographer at the University of Moscow where he worked extensively on folklore, demonstrated in this essay (1971) and in other important essays (1936a, 1936b, 1939) the transition of Slovak folk costumes from everyday to holiday to ceremonial and, finally, to ritual stages, in respect to their changing hierarchy of functions, marked by the weakening of the practical function and the strengthening of the aesthetic and other functions. While the problem of the relation between sign and object is not completely resolved by Bogatyrev, the semiotic role of costumes seems to have been his primary point of departure. Thus he states that "in order to grasp the social function of costumes, we must learn to read them as signs in the same way that we learn to read and understand different languages" (1971:83). However several decades elapsed before others took up the challenge laid down by Bogatyrev and began to investigate the various sign systems that compose culture.

1.3 MOSCOW-TARTU SEMIOTICS OF CULTURE

The specific approach called "semiotics of culture" was first advanced by the Moscow-Tartu group which by now has produced a considerable body of publications expanding this point of view. Starting from the semiotics of various art systems, this group has devoted increasing attention to the semiotics of other cultural systems and to their mutual translatability. It was under the leadership of Jurij M. Lotman of the University of Tartu, that summer schools on sign systems were initiated in Kääriku in Soviet Estonia from 1964 to 1972, and by the 1970s the first attempts were made to integrate the various areas with which semiotics had begun to be preoccupied under one over-arching concept, namely that of culture seen as a system of information and communication. In an important essay of 1970, Lotman described culture as a "semiotic mechanism for the output and storage of information" (1970:2) and "a historically evolved bundle of semiotic systems (languages) which can be composed into a single hierarchy (supralanguages) which can also be a symbiosis of independent systems (*ibid.:* 8). The underlying concept in this approach is an analogy to memory of mankind or to some segment of mankind, memory implying here the capacity of systems for storage and accumulation of information.

It was not until 1973 that the Soviet scholars published an over-all statement advancing the semiotics of culture, the so-called "Theses on Semiotic Study of Culture" (*Theses* 1973. For a discussion of the *Theses* see Winner & Winner: 1976). The five signers of the *Theses,* B.A. Uspenskij, V.V. Ivanov, V.N. Toporov, A.M. Pjatigorskij, and Ju. M. Lotman, all are engaged in extensive research on the subject of semiotics of culture as are other Russian scholars.

The *Theses* opens with the following definition of culture:[1]

> In the study of culture the initial premise is that all human activity concerned with the processing, exchange, and storage of information possesses a certain unity. Individual sign systems, though they presuppose immanently organized structures, function only in unity, supported by one another. None of the sign systems possess a mechanism which would enable it to function culturally in isolation. Hence it follows that, together with an approach which permits us to construct a series of relatively autonomous sciences of the semiotic cycle, we shall admit another approach, according to which all of them examine particular aspects of the *semiotics of culture,* of the study of the functional correlation of different sign systems (*Theses* 1973:1.0.0).

This view of culture encompasses various far-reaching assumptions, among the most important of which are the following: 1) the understanding of culture as composing three inseparable realms: syntactics (the internal organization of structures and the relation of structures to each other), semantics (meaning

---

[1] References to the *Theses* will be made to paragraph numbers rather than pages.

at all levels from the most abstract basic oppositions to more and more specific contextual cultural symbols), and pragmatics (the perception of reality, the creation of sign systems, their encoding and decoding, how sign systems change, the dynamics of context and point of view); 2) the position that natural language is the primary and universal model, in relation to which all other semiotic systems are perceived as "secondary modeling systems," the arrangement being hierarchical. (However, as is discussed subsequently, this position has been increasingly modified even within the *Theses* since, even though natural language is the necessary sign system for culture, no culture exists with only one type of sign system, and it is possible that natural language does not provide the primary model for all other cultural sign systems.) 3) Finally, the last assumption appears to be the crucial one, that is the notion that texts are the primary element or basic significant unit of culture. (The concept of text is discussed in the final section of this paper.)

2. DIVERGENT INTERPRETATIONS OF PHILOSOPHICAL BASES OF STRUCTURAL AND CULTURAL SEMIOTICS

Various philosophical currents underscoring the dynamics of the subject and the receiver as well as of perception in general, and departing strongly from positivistic and formalistic traditions, had a marked effect upon Prague theories, although these are often not considered as part of structuralism or of cultural semiotics by Western scholars. Among them we note the following two areas:

2.1 THE ROLE OF PHENOMENOLOGY

Western scholars frequently dismiss the influence of phenomenology upon structuralism in general, and overlook its influence upon the Prague scholars, holding that structuralism is purely formal. For example, according to the British philosopher Pettit, Lévi-Strauss completely rejects subjective consciousness, intuition and empathy, and other phenomenological views. And according to the editors of the *First Reader in Symbolic Anthropology*, the structuralist approach (attributed primarily to Lévi-Strauss and other French scholars) radically separates problems of the form of thought (and therefore its expression) from the problem of its contents. In this respect, it is claimed, structuralism differs from a phenomenological perspective "which attempts to transcend Kant's extreme differentiation of form and content through the study of the *workings* of form." The editors assert that the structuralist's task is limited to demonstrating that all mental phenomena make use of basic structures (Dolgin, Kemnitzer and Schneider, eds. 1977: 30).

However, it is not clear that such critiques are justified insofar as they apply to East European traditions, or even to Lévi-Strauss. In fact, Husserl's differentiation of *Gegenstand* and *Bedeutung,* his refusal to separate the act and its object, as well as his theory of intention, were extremely important stimuli for the Prague group, effecting Jakobson's functional approach to language. Thus Holenstein documents his claim that Jakobson is a "phenomenological structuralist," holding that it was in Husserl's work that Jakobson found the first systematic formulation of general laws operative for a structural unit (Holenstein 1976:2). According to Holenstein, there are three specific themes where Husserl's influence can be directly observed, namely: the relation of linguistics to psychology, the program for universal grammar, and the defense of semantics as an integral part of linguistics. Indeed, Holenstein holds:

> There is hardly a basic theoretical methodological concept of structural linguistics and poetics that does not undergo an explicit or implicit phenomenological determination and elaboration by Jakobson (Holenstein 1976:3).

Affinity to phenomenology exists, according to Holenstein, in Husserl's division of phenomenology into four overlapping areas: 1) static phenomenology, the delineation of structural types, including the relation of the object to the subject by which it is intended (here we might add, Mukařovský particularly inquired into the role of the subject, emphasizing its dynamic aspects); 2) genetic phenomenology, related to Jakobson's teleological orientation; 3) eidetic phenomenology, related to the semiotic search for universals; and 4) transcendental phenomenology, i.e. all data are elucidated according to how their structure and signification appear to a subject, which would correlate with the semiotic of pragmatics (Holenstein 1976:4-5). Furthermore, Holenstein has also held that Jakobson's theory of binary oppositions and the marked/unmarked relationship have affinities to phenomenological principles of fundamental relations (Holenstein 1975:35).

2.2 INFLUENCE OF *GESTALT*

Similarly, Western scholars have frequently dismissed the influence of *Gestalt* psychology on structuralism in general and on Jakobson's linguistics and semiotic theories of culture. For example Pettit, who believes structuralism owes much to Jakobson, nevertheless holds that in the area beyond the sentence, structuralism has failed to establish an intuitively felt structure, and thus a unit like a text in culture is simply not intuitively felt (1975:47). Others imply that structuralism is still an additive concept, apparently having advanced little, if at all, beyond Russian formalism. For example, the editors of *Symbolic Anthropology* call structuralism "static formalism" (Dolgin et al. eds.: 1977:30). Such critiques are again countered by Holenstein. As he points out, the Prague School shares the anti-atomistic and holistic attitudes of *Gestalt* psychology, from which it follows that networks of relations are a part of the simplest data of perception and that "the natural parts into which perception can be dissected are already structured and have also a holistic character." Thus, for example, the *"Gestalt"* position that all perception is structured into partial wholes influenced Jakobson's concept of phonology (Holenstein 1976:16). We may add that it also underlies the Prague school investigation of larger units (up to the level of the text), and the interest in the relation of linguistic to aesthetic and cultural realms in general.

Still, Holenstein points out, Prague structuralism and semiotics also diverged from *Gestalt* theory in its emphasis on hierarchically organized systems rather than on fields, in the greater stress on the dynamic, and not static, aspect of systems, and on the dominant role of binary oppositions and conflicts, as well as in the emphasis on interrelations of systems that are not closed (Cf. Holenstein 1978:18). Thus the important role of context and the effect of culture upon perception are emphases of cultural semiotics which are not necessarily implied by *Gestalt* theory.

3. RECENT DIVERGENCES: MOSCOW-TARTU AND WESTERN APPROACHES TO SEMIOTICS OF CULTURE

Turning to more specifically contemporary issues, differently interpreted by scholars working in cultural semiotics in the East and the West, we note four areas which represent a relatively arbitrary number of the many possibilities, but which, nevertheless, signal focal tension points: They are the theory of the sign, the status of the linguistic model, the relation of cultural codes to nature, and reduction and meaning.

3.1 THE THEORY AND DYNAMICS OF THE SIGN

Some Western schools, in the broad tradition expressed by Cassirer, utilize the term "symbol" for the entire signifying function, or as the only, or primary, sign as does Geertz (who, following Langer, uses symbol "for any object, act, event, quantity or relation which serves as a vehicle or a conception.

The conception is the symbol's meaning" (Geertz 1973:91)). Others consider symbol to cover multivalent iconic, but not arbitrary, signs (Ricoeur 1970:11-12; Turner 1975:152). However, many scholars in Eastern Europe and in the Soviet Union, as well as Lévi-Strauss and Leach and others in the West, distinguish different sign types, following more closely the Peircean typology of signs and Jakobson's extension of such typologies, although some use symbol in both senses, in the broad sense of Ricoeur as well as in the more technical and restricted Peircean one. Furthermore, various interpretations of Peircean traditions, East and West (Ecco, Kristeva, Damisch, Jakobson, Lotman, etc.) have recently shown that the sign category and types of signs are not rigidly demarked areas. Thus Damisch sees art which is only a semi-sign (1975:35), and Lotman (1975) sees texts that are prior to signs. Furthermore, such analytical approaches attempt to overcome naïve views of the signifier/signified relationship. For example, in the effort to surmount rigid structural dichotomies, the *Tel Quel* group has, as Bär has remarked, gone so far as to reverse the Saussurian model for the sign. Thus the intelligible, *signifié*, becomes instrumental for the sensory, *signifiant*. "They dispense temporarily with the conceptual level of semiotic performances in order to reappropriate the sensory infrastructure" (Bär 1976:379). This re-emphasis on the iconic quality of the sign also preoccupies Jakobson in his forthcoming study on *Sounds of Language*.

As Kuhn noted, when people see the same situation differently, and use the same words, they are speaking from different viewpoints and translations are needed (Kuhn 1970:200). It seems that underlying problems contributing to this terminological and theoretical confusion are not only lack of agreements concerning ways to distinguish between iconicity and arbitrariness, but also between freedom and constraints, and between rigid and dynamic sign concepts.

3.2 THE STATUS OF THE LINGUISTIC MODEL IN RELATION TO OTHER MODELS OF COMMUNICATION

A second issue where confusion reigns, and which has many complex theoretical implications, concerns the question: Is natural language the material for the primary model for all perception and for all communicative systems making up culture? And if so, in what sense do we extend this model from the natural languages to the verbal arts, to the visual and auditory arts, and then to all customary behavior from gestures, to use of space, to economic transactions and to basic values and beliefs? Is the relationship between the linguistic and other communicative models one of determinacy, of automatic transference, or of metaphor, or is the relationship a polar one, of mutual influences of diverse and possibly radically different communicative structures? Given that cultures are composed of interrelated semiotic systems, one of which must be language, how similar are their basic structures?

Some Western critiques of cultural semiotics uphold the position that this approach can offer only the linguistic model and therefore must fail. For example Pettit holds that the linguistic model (which he believes is limited to the structure of the sentence) fails to be explanatory outside of the realm of natural language and consequently the whole area of cultural semiotics should be dismissed. Indeed, Pettit concludes that semiotic acts, except for those based on natural language, are in fact not communication at all (Pettit 1975:36). Finally Pettit opts for what he calls "differential semantics" to be applied to all levels except that of natural language, an approach which seems to be closer to the more traditional hermeneutic exegesis. Only in the area of linguistic behavior, according to Pettit, does the semiotic approach have a role (*ibid.:* 114).

Another critique, which at least implicitly assumes that for semiotics to be valid the linguistic model must explain all semiotic systems, is that of the anthropologist Dan Sperber, who holds that the Peircean view that the universe is perfused with messages, that is with meaning, may be a Western ethnocentric belief. Thus he faults Lévi-Strauss, Turner and others. Sperber's fieldwork in Ethiopia tells him, for example, that the Dorze apply meaning only to verbal statements (1974:83). This kind of example reveals Sperber's highly cognitive approach to meaning which dismisses the role of aesthetics, subliminal levels and connotations and ambiguities, highly important in Eastern European and Moscow-Tartu semiotics.

3.2.1 *The Position of Prague Linguistic Circle and Lévi-Strauss.* It appears that views which insist on the efficacy of the linguistic model as a test of cultural semiotics are not necessarily a justified interpretation. For example, in the early twenties of this century the Prague School linguist, Vilém Mathesius (1924), asserted that linguistics must be concerned with units larger than the sentence, already implying the concept of the culture text. Furthermore, Mukařovský did not uphold the linguistic model as prior and as determining others. In fact the impact of his ideas was to the contrary. Moreover, I believe that we can establish that both Jakobson and Lévi-Strauss provide considerable leeway in the interpretation of the role of the linguistic model in cultural semiotics. As Jakobson and Tynjanov stated in 1928 "the immanent laws of literary or linguistic evolution give us only an *indeterminate* equation which admits of the *possibility of several*—although a limited number—of solutions, and not necessarily only one" (1928:81-82) (underlining supplied). And as Jakobson wrote in 1970, the various functions of language, their different hierarchies and different kinds of messages, "must lead, *mutatis mutandis,* to an analogous study of other semiotic systems: with which of these, *or other* functions are they endowed, in what combination, in what hierarchical order"? (1970:11) (underlining supplied) And Jakobson's recent comments upon the complementary, but different, functions of the hemispheres of the brain in interpreting semiotic systems also lead in this direction.

In his article, "Social Structure," Lévi-Strauss held that culture does not exist exclusively of linguistic communication based on the system of the natural language, but also on "rules stating how the 'games of communication' should be played both on the natural and on the cultural levels" including kinship and marriage rules and rules of economics; and furthermore he suggested a fourth type of communication, relating to kinship, based on genes and phenotypes. While women and men are communicated in marriage, goods and services are communicated (or exchanged) in economics. The implication is that these objects are similar to verbal messages, since they are exchangeable (and thus must have value), and since they require signs in order to be exchanged (Lévi-Strauss 1963:296-297). But it is not implied that systems are necessarily equivalent to linguistic units.

It should be noted that Mukařovský's concept of value, most fully explicated in his 1936 essay, also suggests that economic exchange reflects values and that in this sense exchangeable material goods are signs (1970:71). Clearly Lévi-Strauss's concept of value, which he extends to nonlinguistic cultural units, as well as Mukařovský's concept of value, owe much to Saussure's concept of the relativism of linguistic value which Saussure also suggested should be applied beyond linguistic systems. As Saussure wrote, "The community is necessary if values that owe their existence solely to usage and general acceptance are to be set up: by himself the individual is incapable of fixing a single value" (1966:113). According to Saussure a value is not to be identified with signification which is merely the property of the word standing for a concept because "a language is a system of interdependent terms in which the value of each term results solely from the simultaneous presence of the others" (*ibid.:*114). Saussure concluded that "even outside language, all values are apparently governed by the same paradoxical principles." They are always composed of a dissimilar thing that can be exchanged for a thing of which the value is to be determined, and of similar things that can be compared to the thing of which the value is to be determined. Saussure gives the example of five francs. To determine its value we must know that it can be exchanged for a fixed quantity of different things, and it can be compared with similar values of the same system. In the same sense the value of a word is fixed only by the concurrence of everything outside it. Being a part of the system, it is endowed not only with signification but also with value (1966: 115).

Saussure emphasized that not only is the conceptual side of value made up solely of relations of differences with respect to other terms and language, the same is true of the material side. "The important thing in the word is not the sound alone but the phonic differences" (*ibid.:*118). Turning again to the example of money, Saussure pointed out that the value of a coin will vary according to the amount stamped upon it and according to its use inside or outside a political boundary, and is not necessarily determined by the metal in the piece of money (*ibid.:*118). Thus Saussure concluded that the value of the signifier and the signified, and the sign as a whole, accounts for the fact that "in language there are only differences." This is proved because the value of a term can be modified without changing its sound or meaning "solely because a neighboring term is modified" (*ibid.:*120).

It seems clear that the Saussurian concept of value influenced not only Lévi-Strauss's view of communication on three levels but also his later extension of this methodological strategy to cooking arts, to mythology and to all the arts in general. Here again the priority of language in Lévi-Strauss's system is an open question. While in his treatment of myth, Lévi-Strauss holds that primary codes are drawn from language, as opposed to secondary codes on which myth is based, there does not seem to be a direct dependence upon language codes. Thus the whole treatment of myth is also cast into a "code" derived from music. As Lévi-Strauss wrote:

> Myth and music share of both being languages which in different ways transcend articulate expression, while at the same time, like articulate speech, but unlike painting, requiring a temporal dimension in which to unfold (1969:15).

However, Lévi-Strauss continued, unlike language, myth and music are also instruments for the obliteration of linear time. Music goes beyond myth by appealing not only to psychological but also to visceral time. While music may be similar to language by utilizing a scale of musical sounds, it differs by its necessary exploitation of organic rhythms (*ibid.:*16).

I conclude that Lévi-Strauss's use of the linguistic model appears to have become primarily metaphorical, the comparison being based not only on similarity but also on opposition between the principles of language and other sign systems. If anything, the common invariants that unite sign systems stem from deeper levels rooted in the human brain in Lévi-Strauss's system, which brings up the whole question of the relation of cultural codes to nature which is considered subsequently.

3.2.2 *The Position of the Moscow-Tartu Group.* The position of the Moscow-Tartu school on the status of the linguistic model is also open to interpretation. As was stated in the *Theses,* a necessary condition for any culture is a pair of correlated semiotic systems, and the text in a natural language and the picture constitute the most usual combination of two languages making up culture. However, "the pursuit of heterogeneity of languages is a characteristic feature of culture" (*Theses* 1973:6.1.0). Culture is typically composed of numerous correlated pairs of semiotic systems hierarchically organized "the correlation between them being *to a considerable extent* realized through correlation with a system of the natural language (underlining supplied) (*ibid.:* 6.1.3).

Furthermore, there are the following statements in the *Theses* concerning the role of the natural language:

> Under secondary modeling systems we understand such semiotic systems, with the aid of which models of the world or its fragments are constructed. These systems are secondary in relation to the primary system of natural language, over which they are built—directly (the supralinguistic system of literature), or in a shape parallel to it (music, painting) (*ibid.:* 6.1.0 original Russian version in Mayenowa editor, 1973).

Furthermore it is also stated that

> The proposition concerning the insufficiency of natural language for the construction of culture can be connected with the fact that even natural language is not a strictly logical realization of a single structural principle (*ibid.:* 6.1.4).

Moreover, in the *Theses* and in various of Lotman's writings there are posited various oppositions between semiotic systems that may imply even more radical divergences which may override the verbal/nonverbal opposition. For example, it is stated in the *Theses* that the tension between discrete (usually verbal) texts and nondiscrete (usually visual or iconic) texts "constitutes one of the most permanent mechanisms of culture as a whole" (*ibid.:* 3.2.1). And such oppositions are described as playing a special role in the system of culture generating semiotic oppositions, since each type of text needs the other "in order to form the mechanism of culture." But each type also needs to be different "according to the principle of semiosis, that is to say, on the one hand equivalent, and on the other hand not entirely mutually convertible" (*ibid.:* 6.2.0). Furthermore, Ivanov (1975: 218-219) has held that one of the basic tasks for contemporary semiotics "remains the development of a general semiotic set of concepts and correspondences suited to the description of various sign systems, including those

structured quite differently from the natural language" (1975:218-19). We
may conclude, therefore, that according to the Moscow-Tartu group, while
the linguistic system is the priviledged one, the present orientation seems to
be toward the investigation of other radically different models as well, and
the fixed hierarchical relations between linguistic and other models of communication is no longer a dominant emphasis.

3.3 CULTURAL COMMUNICATION AND NATURE

The relation of all cultural codes to nature is a third fundamental issue
about which there is little agreement. Do natural and cultural systems share
some significant invariants with animal communication and with the genetic
code, as well as with the basic structure of the mind? If we follow Lévi-
Strauss (1973:20-21) and Ivanov (1973:143-44), all outside reality, because
it is encoded by the mind, has a common character which is discrete. It is
psychobiological factors, or nature, then, that account for the perception of
discrete distinctive features in time and space, and which encode rather than
photograph the outside world. These features then are selected, classified and
endowed with meaning in culture. But whether such views necessarily assume
a kind of mentalism and dualism, an *a priori* and fixed deep structure, which
some anthropologists have applied to Lévi-Strauss and to structuralism in
general, is open to question. According to Bär, it does not

> Description, in this view, has an irretrievable 'in-between' state
> reflecting both the order, forces, et cetera of the organism *and*
> the order, forces of the environment. Self imposes on world and
> world imposes upon self. The result is an ever-dynamic com-
> promise, a kind of pact or alliance which validates and corrects
> the symbolic map and behavior of each organism, including the
> human organism (Bär, 1978:2).

Lévi-Strauss has clearly rejected any dualism as an outmoded form of
conceptualization.

> For nature appears more and more made up of structural proper-
> ties undoubtedly richer although not different in kind from the
> structural codes into which the nervous system translates them,
> and from the structural properties elaborated by the understand-
> ing in order to go back, as much as it can do so, to the original
> structures of reality. It is not being mentalist or idealist to
> acknowledge that the mind is only able to understand the world

around us because the mind is itself part and product of this same world. Therefore the mind, when trying to understand it, only applies operations which do not differ in kind from those going on in the natural world itself (1973:22).

Thus the whole issue of the existence and characterization of deep structures of the Chomskian variety is widely disputed. For example, according to Boon (1977:179), Leach continues to invoke deep structures and isolated human brains as opposed to Lévi-Strauss's rejection of this. And clearly dualism is not meant to be implied by Moscow-Tartu semiotics.

3.4 REDUCTION AND MEANING

A fourth issue related to all the ones above, and complexly dividing Western scholars from each other and from East Europeans as well as from Lévi-Strauss, is the issue of reductionism. As the question is frequently put, if we decode, do we necessarily reduce and lose the level of meaning? According to Ricoeur and Geertz, the answer is "yes." (See Winner & Winner 1976: 122-127 on the hermeneutic critique.) Clearly, this is not the position of East European and Soviet semioticians, nor of Lévi-Strauss who wrote in 1960 "structuralism refuses to set the concrete against the abstract . . . structure . . . is content itself apprehended in a logical organization conceived as property of the real" (Lévi-Strauss 1976:115).

Positivist, materialist and dualist currents, implicit or explicit, continue to underlie many of these arguments, particularly that of reduction, dividing Western scholars from each other and from Eastern scholars. For example, Turner argues, it would seem, for the priority of the concrete where he locates symbols, a level which is to all intents and purposes separated from the abstract. He sees symbolic anthropology as a study of symbolic action where "symbols are seen as instrumentalities of various forces—physical, moral, economic, political and so on—operating in isolatable changing fields of social relationships" (Turner 1975:145). As Turner notes, other Western anthropologists see symbols similarly, as for example Firth (1973) and Cohen (1974), who stress the instrumental value of symbols. Thus to Firth symbols are not organized into coherent and logical systems, since they are highly manipulatable aspects of social action. On these grounds Firth rejects both the anthropologists' imposed systems and the belief that emic systems of native thought can be uncovered (Turner 1974:146 discussing Firth 1973). The implicit assumption is that symbol systems are necessarily consistent and unchanging and therefore cannot express multivocal, complex, ambiguous and conflicting reality. Therefore, faulted are the whole group of Western ethnoscientists and cognitive anthropologists who subscribe to the logical approach to symbols, and thus, it is held, neglect concrete social situations in their attention to reified "crystalline structures" following Chomsky's separation of competence and performance. Also criticized from this point of view are the studies of "core symbols" led by David Schneider and the many scholars he has influenced, since the concept of core symbol implies that the whole system is characterized in some general and static way according to underlying symbols around which the system is organized (Turner 1975:147). Here Turner agrees with Geertz that these approaches to symbols are "hermetical" since they seal off "cultural analysis 'from its proper object, the informal logic of actual life' " (*ibid.*:147 quoting Geertz 1973:17). Such a stance, Turner believes, overlooks the dynamics of symbolic change. While the implication is that a structural approach can not by its nature account for such factors, undoubtedly Schneider does not consider his system to be static, and joins with the other editors of *Symbolic Anthropology* in distinguishing it from what the editors term "static structuralism" (Dolgin, Kemnitzer and Schneider 1977:30). As these editors write, implicit in the structuralist method is the danger of *reductionism*, "the lack of concern with all of the many forces which go into the occurrence of a social fact or the production of a text or an act." (*ibid.*:30). Thus they claim that structuralists consider the discovery of an elementary structure as an explanation and interpretation of the phenomenon itself. However:

> In point of fact, of course, it does not: in the process of the kind of abstraction this procedure entails, the phenomenon itself is *lost,* and ceases to be the object of inquiry, being replaced by the elusive 'element.' (*Ibid.*:30).

A similar line of argument is that of Schwimmer, who holds that semiotic structures necessarily must remain without inner contradiction and therefore cannot account for external and contradictory data. As a result, they misrepresent complex reality. Thus Schwimmer (1977:157) sees a dichotomy between "semiotic facts" and "objective facts" which is interpreted as a conflict between culture "as a system of signs, intelligible in its conceptual coherence, and at the same time as a viable economic, political and social system, with contradictions which are managed by an appropriate superstructure" (*ibid.*:158). Thus Schwimmer holds that semiotics implies a reduction of anthropology and praises those in the West like Greimas and Bremond who, he believes, analyze their texts primarily from evidence internal to the closed corpora, which he calls "semiotic intelligibility." This approach is contrasted by Schwimmer to that of Lévi-Strauss (and by implication we could say to the whole East European and Moscow-Tartu tradition) which introduces issues outside of the system such as culture, history, ecology, social relations, thereby establishing contradictions such as those an ethnologist would find in. cultures. Such contradictions would then enter into the interpretation of the texts and the result is, according to Schwimmer, anthropological intelligibility which he distinguishes from semiotic intelligibility. Thus Schwimmer advises us to abandon Lévi-Strauss's demand for a semiotics of culture since, in fact, what Lévi-Strauss is achieving is anthropological intelligibility.

Opposed to the traditional view that structures are necessarily reductive, is the position developed by the Prague School, which is also that of the Moscow-Tartu school of cultural semiotics and to a large extent the position of Lévi-Strauss and some others in the West, as for example Boon and to a certain extent Leach, namely that structures are internally organized by both conflict and harmony, not closed, and in a constant process of change characterized by the inseparable processes of incorporating new, even antithetical, elements and by transformation. Structures are never to be understood as separate from context and are not purely cognitive, but unite emotive, aesthetic and cognitive functions in ever-changing hierarchies. Thus such structures encompass in an inseparable whole the concrete and the abstract, *langue* and *parole* or competence and performance.

Lotman has expanded upon this general problem in his article "The Dynamic Model of a Semiotic System" (1977), where he has pointed out that the distinction between the synchronic and the diachronic, while methodologically valuable, is of a relative and heuristic, rather than existential, nature. He calls attention to various antinomies that must be taken into account in a dynamic model of a semiotic system and which a static model ignores. The most important one is the contrast between the systematic, "those system elements and their relationships that remain invariant throughout any homomorphous transformations," and the extrasystematic (those elements characterized by instability and irregularity) (*ibid.:* 195). However the description of the extrasystematic is elusive, since in static models this realm may be held to be nonexistent, or may be held to belong to another system, and since the metalanguage of self-description of an object cannot itself be used to describe the dynamic models (which encompass the extrasystematic) because self-descriptions are, in fact, a part of the object to be described.

Rather, a dynamic model, according to Lotman, must not neutralize polar binary relationships, must depict ambivalences within the system, must distinguish between the more organized nucleus and the less organized periphery of a structure, must account for the fact that a description itself tends to heighten organization of a system, must distinguish between the necessary and the superfluous, noting that redundancy may be more dynamic than superfluous. All the above antinomies "are features of the dynamic state of a semiotic system, its immanent semiotic mechanisms which allow it, while changing with the changing social context, to preserve homeostasis, i.e. to remain itself" (*ibid.:* 208). Lotman concludes that most semiotic systems are found on a structural spectrum between static and dynamic models. The extremes are characterized by two kinds of semiotic systems: in one the function is primary communication, that is communication of a fact such as exemplified by artificial languages; and in the second the function is secondary communication, that is communication of all the realms that are not facts such as opinions and points of view. Only the first type, that is primary communication, has no need for extrasystematic surroundings to serve as dynamic reserves. For the second type, the extrasystematic is essential. However, Lotman rejects an absolute antithesis between the two types of semiotic systems. Rather they suggest two ideal poles "that are in complex, interacting relationship. And it is within the structural tension between these poles that the single complex semiotic whole that is culture unfolds" (*ibid.:* 209).

The kinds of fundamental divergences and conceptions of structure from the most static, and therefore reductionist, to the clearly dynamic and nonreductive which have been suggested in this discussion suggest tensions between subparadigms which require extensive translation.

4. THE MOSCOW-TARTU THEORY OF CULTURE TEXTS

The various concepts and divergent interpretations discussed in this essay all pertain, directly or indirectly, to the problem of the priority of the linguistic model and to the related issues of closed and static, versus open and dynamic, systems and to the underlying philosophical issues such as positivism, materialism, dualism and reductionism. I suggest that it does not follow, as some analysts hold, that cultural semiotics can offer only linguistic models, automatically and uncreatively applied to other systems, and that structures need be conceptualized as closed and static, ontologically separated from meaningful creativity and action and the concrete, or that cultural semiotics need imply a dualist stance.

It appears that the concept of culture text worked out in Moscow-Tartu cultural semiotics, based as it is on principles of dynamic models such as Lotman has explicated, advances the resolution of the various dichotomies discussed. In this view, texts are the primary elements, or basic significant units, of culture and, in fact, a culture itself is a macrotext composed of subtexts. Indeed, universal culture is the largest text, opposed then to some extraterrestrial unit. While a review of the complex theory of culture texts cannot be undertaken here (see Winner 1978b for a detailed discussion of typologies and culture texts), a few main points may be briefly summarized.

The use of text in its broad sense by the Moscow-Tartu group owes much to the position of Pjatigorskij who, in 1962, defined a text as a variety of signals composing a delimited autonomous whole. Such a communication is characterized in three spheres: a) in the syntactic sphere it must be spatially (optically, acoustically, or in some other fashion) fixed so that it is *intuitively* felt as distinct from a nontext. b) In the pragmatic sphere its spatial fixation is not accidental but the necessary means of conscious transmission of communication by its author or other individuals. Thus the text has an inner structure. c) In the sphere of semantics a text must be understandable, i.e., it must not contain unsurmountable difficulties hindering its comprehension (Pjatigorskij 1962:79).

The expansion of the term "text" to culture in general, including non-verbal systems, followed from the assumption that the system of natural language is the most fundamental of all systems and other semiotic systems are necessarily secondary modeling systems. However, as we have noted, this concept has received various modifications in the semiotics of the Moscow-Tartu school, and consequently the notion of texts may also be interpreted as serving to free semiotics from the dominance of the linguistic model over all others. In this view, a culture text is a very broad type including various subtypes with radically different structures in spite of certain very general invariants.

In the *Theses*, the concept of culture text is related to the concept of culture in the following ways. From the point of view of texts, culture is understood on three levels, namely "as a hierarchy of semiotic systems composed of texts, as the sum of the texts and the set of functions correlated with them, or as a certain mechanism which generates these texts" (*Theses* 1973:6.0.0).

Furthermore, culture texts are understood to be those messages that have the following characteristics: integral meaning; the fulfillment of a common function; the ascription of value accounting for the preservation of the text, a type of internal organization that places the text in a more inclusive group or genre; and construction of the text according to definite rules.

Finally, while texts, like culture, are ultimately based upon psycho-biological universals, they are interpreted contextually. Thus texts are relativistic concepts depending on context and point of view. For example, a message may be a text in one culture but not necessarily in another; and the character of a text depends upon how it is perceived. Thus from an inner point of view the text has integral meaning, while from an outer point of view, from that of an investigator of a culture, it is the carrier of integral function. Boundaries of texts are also interpreted within a relativistic framework. Thus the same message may appear as part of a text, a whole text or a set of texts, depending upon the context and the framework utilized. In the ultimate opposition, text is opposed to nontext or antitext as culture is opposed to nonculture or anticulture. As the *Theses* state, while those texts which the culture does not preserve are nontexts, those texts which the culture destroys are antitexts.

Over and above these distinctions between types of texts found in the *Theses*, are numerous other more complex ones which we cannot examine in this essay. For example, the relation of the linguistic model to other models pertaining to the various arts (verbal as well as nonverbal from architecture to painting, to film which is, of course, visual and verbal and auditory, to music and dance) as well as to all types of rites and all cultural behavior, are also being investigated in the context of varying oppositions such as discrete and nondiscrete, and transformation versus change by addition of new elements from outside the system, etc. Furthermore all textual structures are interpreted within the context of basic cultural values and related organizing perceptions of time and space, which require further dimensions of more complex typologies.

While Western theoreticians have also applied and extended the literary concept of text to culture in general, notably Ricoeur, Boon, Geertz, and certainly Lévi-Strauss, only the Moscow-Tartu scholars have submitted the concept of culture text to such rigorous and extensive analysis, demonstrating its significance and potentialities for further expansion and making explicit its synthesizing qualities that advance the resolution of the various dichotomies we have considered.

5. CONCLUSION: THE SEARCH FOR AN OBJECT

As we have seen, the first step toward semiotics of culture was based upon insights into the semiotics of natural language and the extension of these insights to other verbal and nonverbal systems. I suggest that the richness of this approach lies in its creative application to all cultural systems and their interrelationships. The holistic approach to culture seen as a communicative system, can, in fact, be traced to Tyler's famous definition of culture in 1871 where culture is, implicitly at least, unified by the human ability to speak and thus to acquire, preserve, accumulate, and hand down a cultural tradition (or memory and information in Lotman's system). However, the systematic implications of such insights are only now being realized in the new attempts to understand the structural dynamics and communicative characteristics of cultural traditions.

Here I wish to quote a few remarks about this subject by the American anthropologist, Marshall Sahlins. In a long overdue reappraisal of Western anthropology of this century and in a critique of the dominance of materialism and dualism that it implies, Sahlins has recently written that the urgent task of anthropology is "the conciliation of the diachronic with the synchronic and the meaningful with the material" (1977:14). Referring to the confines of Western ideology, he reminds us that

> For over a century, anthropology has struggled to escape from the prison house of utilitarianism. . . . (in order) to develop some science of the social fact in the midst of a society that denies the existence of any totality beyond the sum of its autonomous and enterprising individuals. . . . The problem amounts to the search for the properties of culture, for an *object* that would free the anthropological project from all traditional forms of natural science.

Sahlins continues,

> The specific difference of the anthropological object of culture is that it is *meaningfully constituted.* And I seek ways to extend that symbolic constitution to social action, to suggest that history itself is culture and structure (Sahlins 1976:14) (*italics* supplied).

Arguing against the division of the symbolic and the pragmatic, or structuralism and materialism, Sahlins holds that the final logic of culture forms bears some relation to material reality because of the very necessity of survival. Thus total relativism and complete arbitrariness in the Saussurian sense is rejected (*ibid.:*15).

We pause here to note that Saussure already foresaw limitations of his view of the arbitrary nature of the sign which seemed to interfere with integration of some patterns of behavior into the new science of semiotics for which he called.

For example, while Saussure was particularly impressed with the importance for semiotic systems of wholly arbitrary signs, he did not rule out other types. Thus he asked how semiotics could include such modes of expression as pantomime based on natural signs? In answer, Saussure noted that at least the organizing rules of such expressive behavior were arbitrary, being based on convention and being enforced by the collective, even though the signs themselves were not arbitrary, but in fact natural. Other examples are certain polite gestures which also seem to be natural (Saussure 1966:68). Furthermore, Saussure suggested that signs in general may be absolutely or only relatively arbitrary (*ibid.:*131-134). Thus Saussure qualified arbitrariness by iconic relations to nature and also, by implication at least, by the internal point of view of the culture bearer which perceives systems as motivated even if they are ultimately arbitrary. The latter point has been made explicit by Jakobson (1966:1133) and Lévi-Strauss (1963:91).

While, according to Sahlins, a human action is not purely arbitrary, it is nevertheless cast within a symbolic (arbitrary) design that gives order to practical experience:

> For action depends on a system of meaningful valuations. . . . The code thus governs the functionality of material forces, but as relative, and historic and semiotic, its own logic cannot be specified by the abstract and internal requirements of 'survival.' On the contrary, the specific terms of survival are predicated in the cultural order (Sahlins 1977:15).

Sahlins quotes with approval Lévi-Strauss's remark that a conceptual scheme that creates intelligible and empirical structures from the matter and form (neither of which exists independently) of outside reality always mediates between praxis and practices (Sahlins 1977:15 quoting Lévi-Strauss 1966:130).

A most important emphasis in Sahlins's call for a reassessment, is on the incorporation of the Saussurian concept of semantic value (discussed earlier in this essay) into cultural theory. Thus the Saussurian concept of the word, which is not directly linked to a referent, but rather to its own environment, its meaning depending on its situation and the system of language and culture, is stressed for its implication for culture in general. As Sahlins says, the cultural value of an object is based on differences of the object from others in its environment "and in the system of such differences is a cultural construction of 'reality' " (Sahlins 1977:16).

Finally, Sahlins decries the return to anthropological dualism, which was earlier rejected by Boas (who attempted to dissolve the dichotomy between subject and object by interposing an intervening cultural order which did not merely mediate but constituted by its logic "the relevant subjective and objective terms of the relationship"). Thus Sahlins states,

> Anthropological theory is still beset by a residual dualism: an idea of culture as generated on the one hand out of real material interests and of consisting, on the other hand, of symbolic representations. The object of study is a heterogeneous composite of manipulative action and symbolic means, or outcomes, of instrumental practices and ideological schemes. (1977:17)

In this most timely call for reassessment, Sahlins does not cite the scholars of the Moscow-Tartu group or Jakobson, nor is the theory of culture texts considered. However, his position is germane to the Moscow-Tartu approach to cultural semiotics since it unites meaning and structure, synchrony and diachrony, and searches for what he calls an object which must be characterized by criteria similar to those that define culture texts.

It is the position of this paper that the theory of culture texts advanced by the Moscow-Tartu school is a most interesting and pioneering "search for an object" so felicitously called for by Sahlins. I have noted that important theoretical bases for the new outlook were Saussurian concepts which inspired the Prague School development of structural linguistics and aesthetics, Peircean concepts and the later cultural semiotics of the Moscow-Tartu school. In Jakobson's scheme, the Saussurian concept of arbitrariness was modified in the light of Peircean theories, and the concept of selection and combination largely replaces Saussure's terms "syntagmatic" and "associative" (or "paradigmatic"). The latter form the basis for Jakobson's interpretations of metonomy and metaphor which have contributed to Moscow-Tartu textual typologies. However, the Saussurian basis was, in addition to being a fundamental inspiration, also one of the greatest hinderances since it implied irresolvable dichotomies and problems. But, as we have shown, such issues as *langue/parole* and arbitrary/nonarbitrary as well as the glottocentric implications of Saussure's systems are being superceded in the new directions being taken in cultural semiotics.

The overwhelming problem for modern cultural semiotics has been not only the resolution of some of these dichotomies, but also the pinning down of a definition of culture as an overarching system broadly conceived as emotive, aesthetic and cognitive, as well as the isolation of a significant and open-ended unit for the study of culture, namely the culture text. But we need to know many more characteristics of such units, particularly their specific inner structures, in order to construct more complex typologies of texts, and to discover means of segmenting them, and in order to define how texts are bounded and how they change. All of these problems and many other related ones are being investigated today and require the combined efforts of those interested in the cultural semiotic paradigm.

REFERENCES

Bär,Eugen.1976.Psychoanalysis and Semiotics. *Semiotica* 16.4: 369-388.

————. 1978. (forthcoming) Semiotics and Genetics: The Life of Language and the Language of Life. *Semiotica*. Cited from manuscript.

Bogatyrev, Petr. 1936a. Costume as Sign. *Slovo a slovesnost* 2:43-47. English version in Matejka and Titunik 1976:13-19.

_____ . 1936b. Folksong from a functional Point of View. In Matejka and Titunik 1976. Original: La chanson populaire de point de vue fonctionel. *Travaux du Cercle linguistique de Prague* 6.

_____ . 1939. Le folklore de la construction rurale en Slovaquie orientale et en Russie Subcarpathique. *Revue de Synthèse* XVIII. Paris: 105-08.

_____ . 1971. *The Functions of Folk Costume in Moravian Slovakia*. The Hague (Mouton). Original in 1937 in Czech.

Boon, James. 1977. Anthropology's *Devata. Semiotica* 21: 1/2. (on the works of Edmund Leach).

Boulding, Kenneth. 1977. The Universe as a General System. Paper at American Association for the Advancement of Science, as reported by Singell 1978.

Bühler, K. 1933. *Die Axiomatik der Sprachwissenschaft*. Berlin:(Kant Studien 38).

Cohen, A. 1974. *Two-Dimensional Man: An Essay on the Anthropology of Power and Symbolism in Complex Society*. London. Routledge & Kegan Paul.

Damisch, Hubert. 1975. Semiotics and Iconography. *In The Tell-Tale Sign*, ed. by T.A. Sebeok. Lisse: Peter de Ridder Press: 27-36.

Dolgin, Janet L., David S. Kemnitzer, and David Schneider, eds. 1977. *Symbolic Anthropology. A Reader in the Study of Symbols and Meanings*. New York: Columbia University Press.

Firth, R. 1973. *Symbols: Public and Private*. Ithaca: Cornell University Press.

Geertz, C. 1973. *The Interpretation of Culture*. New York: Basic Books.

Holenstein, Elmar. 1975. Jakobson phénomenologue. *L'Arc* (Paris). 60:29-39.

_____ . 1976. *Roman Jakobson's Approach to Language. Phenomenological Structuralism*. Bloomington: Indiana University Press.

Ivanov, V.V. 1973. The Category of Time in Twentieth Century Art and Culture. *Semiotica*. 8/1:1-45.

Jakobson, Roman. 1960. Closing Statement: Linguistics and Poetics, in T.A. Sebeok, ed. 1960.

_____ . 1966. Franz Boas' Approach to Language. In *Portraits of Linguists*, II. edited by T.A. Sebeok. Bloomington: Indiana University Press. 127-37.

_____ . 1970. Language in Relation to Other Communication Systems. In *Linguaggi nella società e nella tecnica*. Milano: Edizione di Communità. 1-16.

_____ . 1975. *Coup d'oeuil sur le dévélopement de la sémiotique*. Bloomington, Indiana (=Studies in Semiotics No. 3).

_____ and Jurij Tynjanov. 1972. (1928) Problems in the Study of Language and Literature in *Structuralists from Marx to Levi-Strauss*. New York: (Anchor). Translation of Problemy izucenija literatury i jazyka. *Novyj* LEF: 12 (1928). 36-37.

Kuhn, Thomas. 1970. *The Structure of Scientific Revolution*. Chicago: University of Chicago Press.

Levi-Strauss, Claude. 1963. *Structural Anthropology*. New York : Basic Books.

_____ . 1969. *The Raw and the Cooked*. New York: Harper.

_____ . 1973. Structuralism and Ecology. *Social Science Information*. 7:32.

Lotman, Jurij M. 1970. *Materialy k kursu teorii literatury*. Vyp.1. *Tipologija kul'tury*. Tartu.

_____ . 1977. The Dynamic Model of a Semiotic System. *Semiotica* 21 3/4:193-210.

_____ and B.A. Uspenskij. 1975. Myth-Name-Culture. *Soviet Studies in Literature* (IASP) X, 2-3:17-47. Originally published as Mif-imja-kul'tura. *Trudy po znakovym sistemam* No. 6. Tartu.

Matejka, L. and I. Titunik, eds. 1976. *Semiotics of Art. Prague School Contributions*. Cambridge: MIT.

Mayenowa, M.R., ed. 1973. *Semiotyka i struktura tekstu*. Warsaw:PAN.

Mukařovsky, Jan. 1934a. L'Art comme fait sémiologique. *Actes du huitième Congrès international de Philosophie à Prague*. 1936.

_____ . 1934b. Polákova "Vznešenost přírody". Pokus o rozbor a vývojové zařadění básnické struktury. *Sborník filologický*, X:1-68.

_____ 1937. La norme esthétique. *Travaux du IXe Congrès International de Philosophie*. vol.12, pt.3. Paris. Cited from Jan Mukařovský, *Structure, Sign and Function. Selected Essays*. Translated by Peter Steiner and John Burbank. New Haven: Yale University Press. 1978.

_____ . 1970. *Aesthetic Function, Norm and Value as Social Facts*. Ann Arbor (Michigan Slavic Contributions). Originally published as *Esteticka funkce, norma a hodnota jako socialni fakty*. Praha. Borovy. 1936.

Peirce, Charles Sanders. 1965-66 *Collected Papers of Charles Sanders Peirce*, edited by Charles Hartshorne, Paul Weiss and Arthur W. Burks. Cambridge: Harvard University Press.

Pettit, Phillip. 1975. *The Concept of Structuralism: A Critical Analysis*. Berkeley: University of California Press.

Pjatigorskij, A. 1962. Nekotorye obščie zamečanija otnositel'no rassmotrenija teksta kak raznovidnost signala. In *Strukturno-tipologiceskie issledovanija*. pod. red. T.N. Mološinoj. Moscow.

Prague Linguistic Circle. 1929. Téze předložené prvému sjezdu slovanskách filologů v Praze 1929. In *U základů pražské jazykovědne školy*. Edited by Josef Vachek. Prague. Academia. 35-65.

Ricoeur, P. 1970. *Freud and Philosophy*. New Haven: Yale University Press.

Sahlins, M. 1977. The State of the Art in Social/Cultural Anthropology: Search for an Object. In *Perspectives on Anthropology*. Edited by Anthony F.C. Wallace. (=American Anthropological Association).

Saussure, Ferdinand de. 1966. *Course in General Linguistics*. New York:McGraw Hill. Originally published 1915.

Schwimmer, Eric. 1977. Semiotics and Culture. In T.A. Sebeok, ed. 1977:153-79.

Sebeok, T.A. 1960. (Ed.)*Style in Language.* Cambridge:MIT Press.

_____ . 1977. (Ed.) *A Perfusion of Signs*. Bloomington:Indiana University Press (=Advances in Semiotics).

Singell, Larry D. 1978. Kenneth E. Boulding. President-Elect of the AAAS.*Science* 21. April 1978. vol. 200, No. 4339:289.

Sperber, Dan. 1974. *Rethinking Symbolism*. Cambridge Studies in Social Anthropology. Cambridge: Cambridge University Press.

Steiner, Peter. 1976. The Conceptual Base of Prague Structuralism. In *Sound, Sign and Meaning. Quinqvageneri of the Prague Linguistic Circle*. Ann Arbor (=Michigan Slavic Contributions): 351-385.

Theses. 1973. Theses on the Semiotic Study of Culture (as Applied to Slavic Texts). In *Structure of Texts and Semiotics of Culture*. Paris-The Hague:Mouton. (Cited by paragraph, rather than by page).

Turner, Victor. 1975. Symbolic Studies. *Annual Review of Anthropology*. IV: 145-161.

Winner, Irene Portis. 1978a. The Semiotic Character of the Aesthetic Function as Defined by the Prague Linguistic Circle. *Language and Thought*. Edited by W.C. McCormack and S.A. Wurm. Paris-The Hague:Mouton: 407-440.

_____ . 1978b. Ethnicity, Modernity and the Theory of Culture Texts. In *Semiotica*. (in press).

_____ and Thomas G. Winner. 1976. The Semiotics of Cultural Texts. *Semiotica* 18/2: 101-156.